COMPUTER GRAPHICS

Donald Hearn

Department of Computer Science, University of Illinois

M. Pauline Baker

Department of Computer Science, Western Illinois University

PRENTICE-HALL International

632

Printed in the United States of America

10 9 8 7 6 5 4 3

ISBN 0-13-165598-1

PRENTICE-HALL INTERNATIONAL (UK) LIMITED, *London*
PRENTICE-HALL OF AUSTRALIA PTY. LIMITED, *Sydney*
PRENTICE-HALL CANADA INC., *Toronto*
PRENTICE-HALL HISPANOAMERICANA, S.A., *Mexico*
PRENTICE-HALL OF INDIA PRIVATE LIMITED, *New Delhi*
PRENTICE-HALL OF JAPAN, INC., *Tokyo*
PRENTICE-HALL OF SOUTHEAST ASIA PTE. LTD., *Singapore*
EDITORA PRENTICE-HALL DO BRASIL, LTDA., *Rio de Janeiro*
WHITEHALL BOOKS LIMITED, *Wellington, New Zealand*
PRENTICE-HALL, *Englewood Cliffs, New Jersey*

TO OUR FOLKS

Rose, John, Millie, and J. Osborne

CONTENTS

PREFACE

Computer graphics is one of the most exciting and rapidly growing fields in computer science. Some of the most sophisticated computer systems in use today are designed for the generation of graphics displays. We all know the value of a picture as an effective means for communication, and the ability to converse pictorially with a computer is revolutionizing the way computers are being used in all areas.

This book presents the basic principles for the design, use, and understanding of graphics systems. We assume that the reader has no prior background in computer graphics but is familiar with fundamental computer science concepts and methods. The hardware and software components of graphics systems are examined, with a major emphasis throughout on methods for the design of graphics packages. We discuss the algorithms for creating and manipulating graphics displays, techniques for implementing the algorithms, and their use in diverse applications. Programming examples are given in Pascal to demonstrate the implementation and application of graphics algorithms. We also introduce the reader to the Graphical Kernel System (GKS), which is now both the United States and the international graphics-programming language standard. GKS formats for graphics-routine calls are used in the Pascal programs illustrating graphics applications.

The material presented in this text was developed from notes used in graduate and undergraduate graphics courses over the past several years. All of this material could be covered in a one-semester course, but this requires a very hasty treatment of many topics. A better approach is to select a subset of topics, depending on the level of the course. For the self-study reader, early chapters can be used to provide an understanding of graphics concepts, with individual topics selected from the later chapters according to the interests of the reader.

Chapter 1 is a survey of computer graphics, illustrating the diversity of applications areas. Following an introduction to the hardware and software components of graphics systems in Chapter 2, fundamental algorithms for the generation of two-dimensional graphics displays are presented in Chapters 3 and 4. These two chapters examine methods for producing basic picture components and techniques for handling color, shading, and other attributes. This introduces students to the programming techniques necessary for implementing graphics routines. Chapters 5 and 6 treat transformations and viewing algorithms. Methods for organizing picture components in segments and for interactive input are given in Chapters 7 and 8.

Three-dimensional techniques are introduced in Chapter 9. We then discuss the different ways that solid objects can be represented (Chapter 10) and manipulated (Chapter 11). Methods for forming three-dimensional views on a graphics display device are detailed in Chapter 12. The various algorithms for removing hidden surfaces of objects are discussed in Chapter 13, and models for shading and color are taken up in Chapter 14. These five chapters treat both the standard graphics methods and newer techniques, such as fractals, octrees, and ray tracing.

In Chapter 15, we explore techniques for modeling different systems. Modeling packages provide the structure for simulating systems, which is then passed to the graphics routines for display. Finally, methods for interfacing a graphics package to the user are examined in Chapter 16.

At the undergraduate level, an introductory course can be organized with a detailed treatment of fundamental topics from Chapters 2 through 8 plus an introduction to three-dimensional concepts and methods. Selected topics from the later chapters can be used as supplemental material. For a graduate course, the material on two-dimensional methods can be covered at a faster pace, with greater emphasis on the later chapters. In particular, methods for three-dimensional representations, three-dimensional viewing, hidden-surface removal, and shading and color models, can be covered in greater depth.

A great many people have contributed to this project in a variety of ways. To the many organizations and individuals who furnished photographs and other materials, we again express our appreciation. We are also grateful to our graphics students for their comments on the presentation of this material in the classroom. We thank the many people who provided comments on the manuscript, and we are especially indebted to Norman Badler, Brian Barsky, and Steve Cunningham for their helpful suggestions for improving the presentation of material. And a very special thanks goes to our editor, Jim Fegen, for his patience and encouragement during the preparation of this book, and to our production editors, Tracey Orbine and Kathy Marshak. Thanks also to our designer, Lee Cohen, and the Prentice-Hall staff for an outstanding production job.

Donald Hearn
M. Pauline Baker

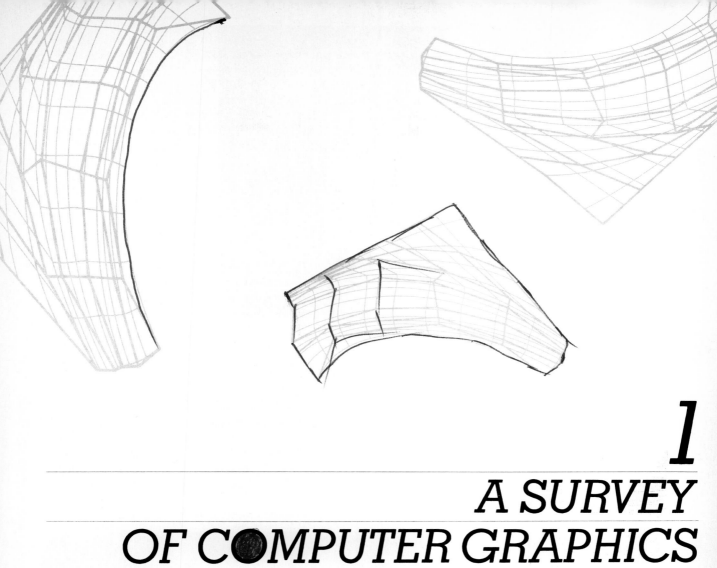

1

A SURVEY
OF COMPUTER GRAPHICS

Computers have become a powerful tool for the rapid and economical production of pictures. There is virtually no area in which graphical displays cannot be used to some advantage, and so it is not surprising to find the use of computer graphics so widespread. Although early applications in engineering and science had to rely on expensive and cumbersome equipment, advances in computer technology have made interactive computer graphics a practical tool. Today, we find computer graphics used routinely in such diverse areas as business, industry, government, art, entertainment, advertising, education, research, training, and medicine. Figure 1–1 shows a few of the many ways that graphics is put to use. Our introduction to the field of computer graphics begins with a tour through a gallery of graphics applications.

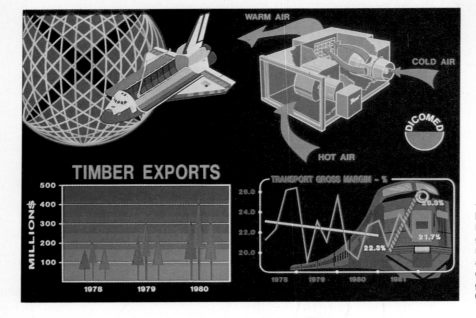

FIGURE 1–1
Examples of computer-
generated displays used in
modeling and simulation
applications, training
demonstrations, and the
graphing of information.
Courtesy DICOMED Corp.

1–1 Computer-Aided Design

For a number of years, the biggest use of computer graphics has been as an aid to design. Generally referred to as **CAD, computer-aided design** methods provide powerful tools. Parts design and drafting are done interactively, producing outlines (Fig. 1–2) or more realistic renderings (Fig. 1–3). When an object's dimensions have been specified to the computer system, designers can view any side of the object to see how it will look after construction. Experimental changes can be made

FIGURE 1–2
Drafting layout produced with a
CAD system. Courtesy Evans &
Sutherland.

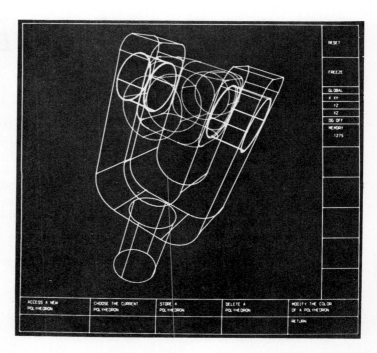

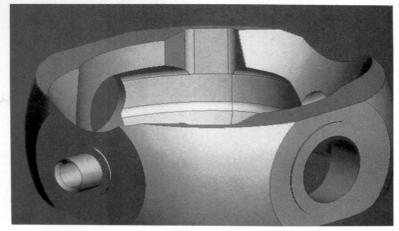

(a)

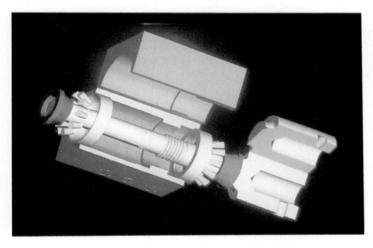

FIGURE 1–3
Three-dimensional rendering of machine parts using CAD systems. (a) Courtesy Lexidata Corp. (b) Bearing housing assembly, Courtesy Intergraph Corp.

(b)

freely since, unlike hand drafting, the CAD system quickly incorporates modifications into the display of the object. The manufacturing process also benefits in that layouts show precisely how the object is to be constructed. Figure 1–4 shows the path to be taken by machine tools over the surfaces of an object during its construc-

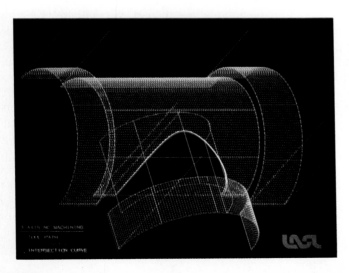

FIGURE 1–4
CAD layout for three-dimensional numerically controlled machining of a part. The part surface is displayed in one color and the tool path in another color. Courtesy Los Alamos National Laboratory.

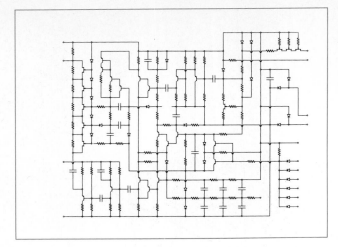

FIGURE 1–5
Circuit layout generated using CAD methods. Courtesy Precision Visuals, Inc., Boulder, Colorado.

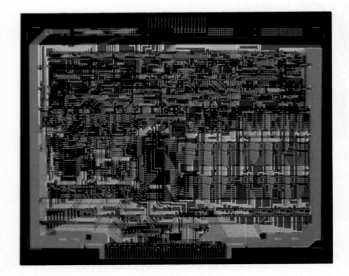

FIGURE 1–6
Computer board produced with a CAD system. Courtesy Lexidata Corp.

tion. Numerically controlled machine tools are then set up to manufacture the part according to these construction layouts.

Electrical and electronics engineers rely heavily on CAD methods. Electronic circuits, for instance, are typically designed with interactive computer graphics systems. Using pictorial symbols to represent various components, a designer can build up a circuit on a video monitor (Fig. 1–5) by successively adding components to the circuit layout. The graphics display can be used to try out alternate circuit schematics as the designer tries to minimize the number of components or the space required for the circuit. Figure 1–6 displays a completed circuit board generated on a video monitor. Similar techniques are used to design communications networks and water and electricity supply systems.

Automobile, aircraft, aerospace, and ship designers use CAD techniques in the design of various types of vehicles. Wire-frame drawings, such as those shown in Fig. 1–7, are used to model individual components and plan surface contours for automobiles, airplanes, spacecraft, and ships. Individual surface sections and vehicle components (Fig. 1–8) can be designed separately and fitted together to display the total object. Simulations of the operation of a vehicle are often run to test the

FIGURE 1–7

CAD systems are used by engineers to generate wire-frame layouts for overall body designs. (a) Courtesy Megatek Corp. (b) Courtesy Evans & Sutherland.

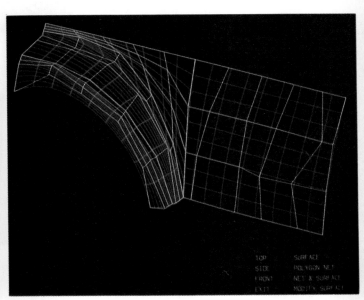

(a)

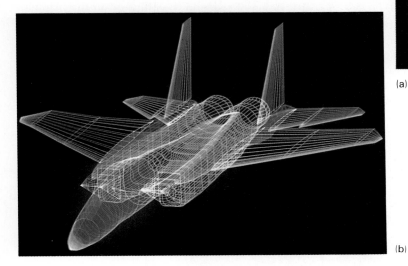

(b)

FIGURE 1–8

Surface sections and vehicle components are typically designed with CAD systems. Courtesy Evans & Sutherland.

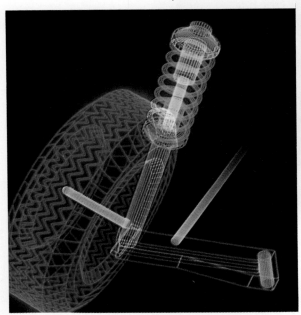

(a)

(b)

vehicle performance, as in the example of Fig. 1–9. Realistic renderings, such as those shown in Fig. 1–10, allow the designer to see how the finished product will appear.

Building designs are also created with computer graphics systems. Architects interactively design floor plans (Fig. 1–11), arrangements of doors and windows, and the overall appearance of a building. Working from the display of a building layout, the electrical designer can try out arrangements for wiring, electrical outlets, and fire warning systems. Utilization of space in the office or on the manufacturing floor is worked out using specially designed graphics packages.

Three-dimensional building models (Fig. 1–12) permit architects to study the appearance of a single building or a group of buildings, such as a campus or industrial complex. Using sophisticated graphics packages, designers can go for a simulated "walk" through the rooms or around the outsides of buildings to better appreciate the overall effect of a particular design.

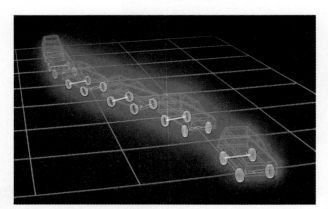

FIGURE 1–9
Simulation of Ford Bronco II performance during lane changes using a graphics display system. Courtesy Evans & Sutherland and Mechanical Dynamics, Inc.

(a)

FIGURE 1–10
Solid modeling of an automobile and ship hull using graphics design systems. (a) Courtesy DICOMED Corp. (b) Courtesy Intergraph Corp.

(b)

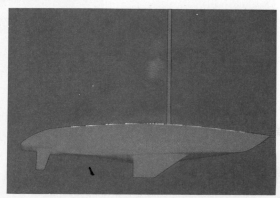

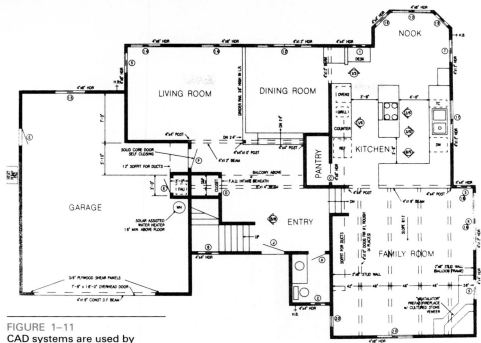

FIGURE 1–11
CAD systems are used by
architects in the design of
building layouts. Courtesy
Precision Visuals, Inc., Boulder,
Colorado.

(a)

FIGURE 1–12
Solid models generated with a
CAD system for the design of
the Filene Center II, the
summer festival theater at Wolf
Trap Farm Park for the
Performing Arts: (a) wire-frame
model; (b) shaded three-
dimensional model. Courtesy
Intergraph Corp.

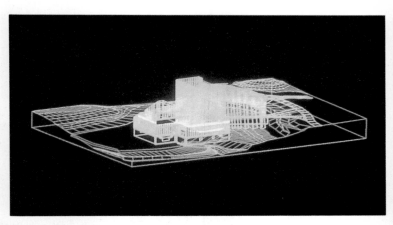

(b)

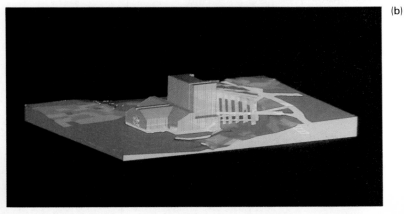

A number of commercially available graphics programs are designed specifically for the generation of graphs and charts. Often a graph-plotting program will have the capability of generating a variety of graph types, such as bar charts, line graphs, surface graphs, or pie charts. Many programs are capable of summarizing data in either two-dimensional or three-dimensional form. Three-dimensional plots are typically used to illustrate multiple relationships, as in the graphs of Figs. 1–13 and 1–14. In some cases (Fig. 1–15), three-dimensional graphs are used to provide a more dramatic or more attractive presentation of data.

Business graphics, one of the most rapidly growing areas of application, makes extensive use of visual displays as a means for rapidly communicating the vast amounts of information that are compiled for managers and other individuals in an organization. Graphs and charts are typically used to summarize financial, statisti-

FIGURE 1–13
Three-dimensional bar chart used to illustrate several relationships within one graph. Reprinted with permission from ISSCO Graphics, San Diego, California.

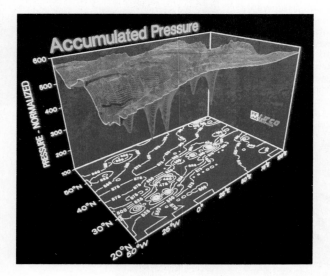

FIGURE 1–14
Three-dimensional pressure chart. Reprinted with permission from ISSCO Graphics, San Diego, California.

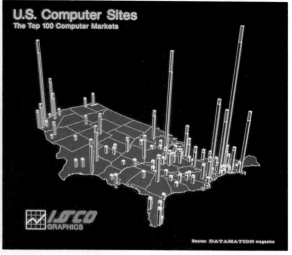

(a)

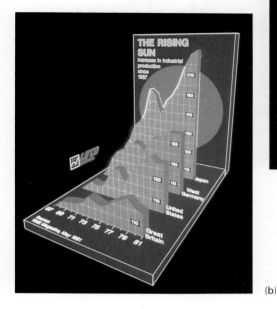

(b)

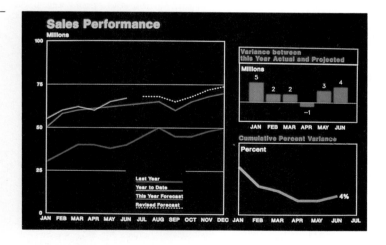

cal, mathematical, scientific, or economic data, and several graphs are often combined in one presentation (Fig. 1–16). These graphs are generated for research
reports, managerial reports, consumer information bulletins, and visual aids used
during presentations. Figure 1–17 illustrates a time chart used in task planning.
Project management techniques make use of time charts and task network layouts
to schedule and monitor projects. Some graphics systems include the capability of
generating 35mm slides or overhead transparencies from the graphs displayed on a
video monitor.

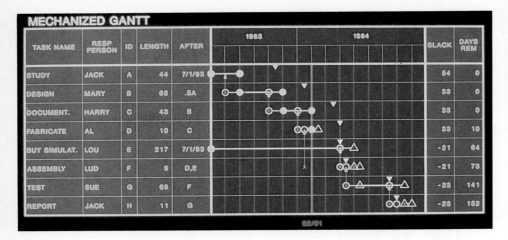

The behavior of physical systems is often studied by constructing graphs and models. When large amounts of data are to be analyzed, a color-coded graph, such as that in Fig. 1–18, can help researchers understand the structure of a system. Without the aid of such plots, it would be difficult for a researcher to interpret data tables containing millions of entries. In a similar way, computer-generated models (Fig. 1–19) are used to study the behavior of systems.

Computer-generated models of physical, financial, and economic systems are often used as educational aids. Models of physiological systems, population trends, or physical equipment, such as the color-coded diagram in Fig. 1–20, can help trainees to understand the operation of a system.

Many data-plotting applications are concerned with graphing some type of geographical information. Often such plots are used to display different types of regional or global statistics, such as plotting sales data in different districts. Programs designed to produce weather maps can take data from individual observation stations to produce plots such as those in Fig. 1–21. Cartographic programs are available for generating maps for selected geographic areas or the entire world.

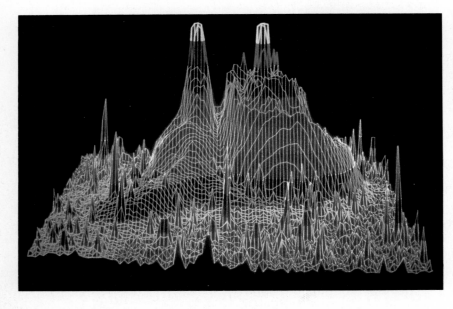

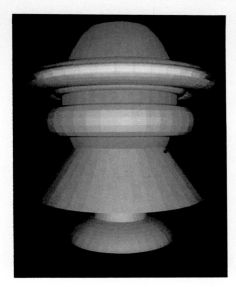

FIGURE 1-19
Graphics model of a test surface used in the study of atomic and nuclear collisions. Courtesy Los Alamos National Laboratory.

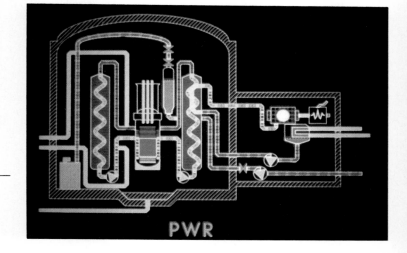

PWR

(a)

FIGURE 1-20
Color-coded diagram used to explain the operation of a nuclear reactor. Courtesy Los Alamos National Laboratory.

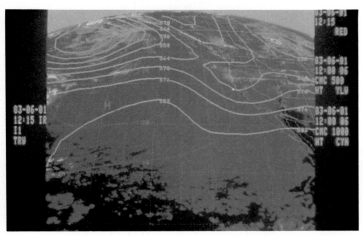

FIGURE 1-21
Weather charts generated with the aid of computer graphics for display on a newscast. Courtesy Gould Inc., Imaging & Graphics Division and GOES-WEST.

(b)

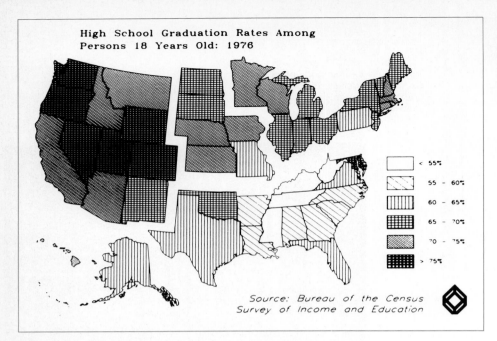

High School Graduation Rates Among
Persons 18 Years Old: 1976

< 55%
55 - 60%
60 - 65%
65 - 70%
70 - 75%
> 75%

Source: Bureau of the Census
Survey of Income and Education

FIGURE 1-22
Exploded map produced with a
cartographic program.
Courtesy Precision Visuals, Inc.,
Boulder, Colorado.

Some of these programs allow shading or color for the various geographic areas to be chosen by the user, and some allow sections to be separated (or "exploded") for emphasis (Fig. 1–22).

1–3 Computer Art

Both creative and commercial art applications make extensive use of computer graphics. The abstract display in Fig. 1–23 is created by plotting a series of mathematical functions in varying colors. Figure 1–24 illustrates another type of art design drawn with a pen plotter.

"Paintbrush" programs allow artists to create pictures on the screen of a video monitor, somewhat like the character in Fig. 1–25. Actually, the artist might draw the picture on a "graphics tablet" using a stylus as input. A paintbrush program was also used to create the characters in Fig. 1–26, who seem now to be busy on

FIGURE 1-23
Abstract design can be created
by plotting mathematical
functions in various colors.
Courtesy Melvin L. Prueitt, Los
Alamos National Laboratory.

FIGURE 1–24
Computer "art" produced on a pen plotter. Courtesy Computer Services, Western Illinois University.

FIGURE 1–25
Cartoon drawing produced with a paintbrush program, symbolically illustrating a creative artist at work on a video monitor. Courtesy Gould Inc., Imaging & Graphics Division and Aurora Imaging.

FIGURE 1–26
Cartoon demonstrations of an "artist" creating a picture with a paintbrush program. The picture, drawn on a graphics tablet, is displayed on the video monitor as the elves look on. In (b), the cartoon is superimposed on the famous Thomas Nast drawing of Saint Nicholas, which was input to the system with a video camera, then scaled and positioned. Courtesy Gould Inc., Imaging & Graphics Division and Aurora Imaging.

(a)

(b)

(a)

FIGURE 1–27
Examples of creative art
generated with an Aycon 16
series computer using a
paintbrush program. Courtesy
Aydin Controls, a division of
Aydin Corp.

(b)

(c)

(d)

a creation of their own. Paintbrush programs are not limited to cartoon characters; they are also used to produce the sort of art seen in Figs. 1–27 and 1–28.

Computer-generated art is widely used in commercial applications. Figure 1–29 illustrates a rug pattern that was designed with a computer graphics system. Logos and advertising designs for TV messages are now commonly produced with graphics systems. Figure 1–30 shows two examples of computer-generated art for use in TV advertising spots. In addition, graphics programs have been developed for applications in publishing and word processing, which allow graphics and text-editing operations to be combined. Figure 1–31 is an example of the type of output that can be generated with such systems.

FIGURE 1–28
This piece of art took a Japanese artist 15 minutes to create on an Aurora 100 paintbrush system. Courtesy Gould Inc., Imaging & Graphics Division.

FIGURE 1–29
Oriental rug pattern produced with computer graphics design methods. Courtesy Lexidata Corp.

(a)

(b)

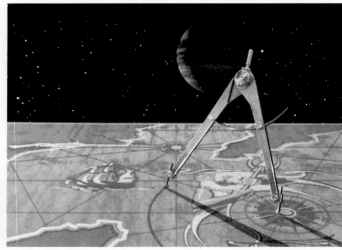

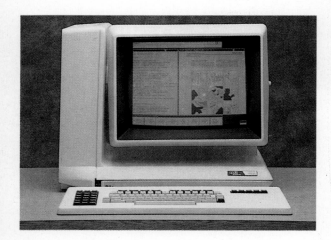

1–4 Computer Animation

Each of the photos in Fig. 1–30 represents one frame of an animation sequence. The glider in Fig. 1–30 (a) is moved slightly from one frame to the next to simulate motion about the room. Similarly, the compass in Fig. 1–30 (b) is displayed at a different position in each frame to simulate drawing of the curved line. Such frame techniques are used also in creating cartoons and science-fiction movies. Each frame is drawn with a graphics system and recorded on film, with only slight changes in the positions of objects from one frame to the next. When the frames are displayed in rapid succession, we have an animated movie sequence. Figure 1–32 shows artists creating a cartoon frame, and Fig. 1–33 shows some scenes that were generated for the movie *Star Trek—The Wrath of Khan*.

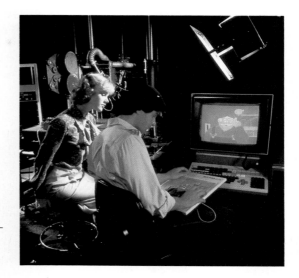

FIGURE 1–32
Artists designing a cartoon frame. Courtesy Lexidata Corp.

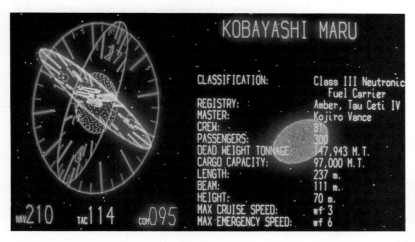

(a)

FIGURE 1–33
Graphics developed for the Paramount Pictures movie *Star Trek: The Wrath of Khan.* Courtesy Evans & Sutherland.

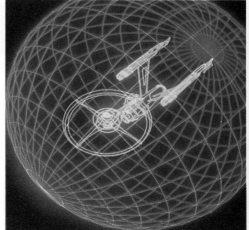

(b)

Animation methods are also used in education, training, and research applications. Figure 1–34, for example, is an animated simulation for the *Voyager* space probe. Such simulations can be used to study the behavior of physical systems or as an aid to instruction.

For some training applications, special systems are designed. Examples of such specialized systems are the simulators for training ship captains and aircraft pilots. One type of aircraft simulator is shown in Fig. 1–35. Figures 1–36 through 1–38 show some scenes that can be presented to a pilot operating a flight simulator. An output from an automobile-driving simulator is given in Fig. 1–39. This simulator is used to investigate the behavior of drivers in critical situations. The drivers' reactions are then used as a basis for optimizing vehicle design to maximize traffic safety.

(a)

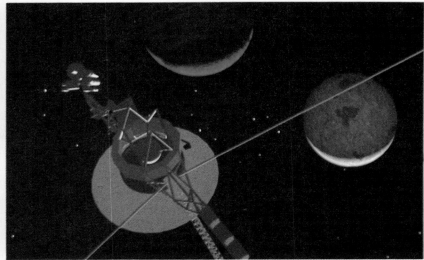

(b)

FIGURE 1–34

Graphics simulation of the trek of the *Voyager 2* space probe. (a) *Voyager 2* approaching Neptune's moon Triton, August 1989. (b) *Voyager 2* leaving Neptune and Triton in August 1989. (c) The closest encounter with Uranus, January 24, 1986. Courtesy Gould Inc., Imaging & Graphics Division and Computer Graphics Lab of the Jet Propulsion Laboratory.

(c)

FIGURE 1–35
The GE F-5 flight simulator
allows the instructor (in the
rear) to enter test conditions for
the pilot at the controls in front.
Courtesy General Electric.

FIGURE 1–36
A computer-generated scene
for the GE F-5 flight simulator
shown in Fig. 1–34. Courtesy
General Electric.

FIGURE 1–37
Computer-generated view of a
runway used by pilots
operating a flight simulator to
practice landings. Courtesy
Evans & Sutherland and
Rediffusion Simulation.

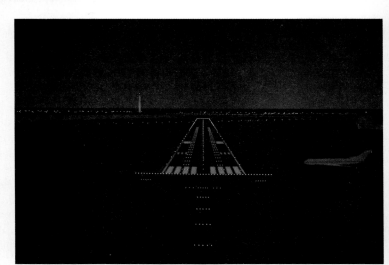

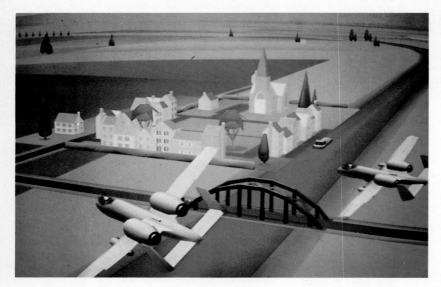

1–5 Graphical User Interfaces

Input options to many computer programs are designed as a set of **icons,** which are graphic symbols that look like the processing option they are meant to represent. Users of such programs select processing options by pointing to the appropriate icon. The advantage of such systems is that the icons can take up less screen space than the corresponding textual description of the functions, and they can be understood more quickly if well designed.

Figure 1–40 illustrates typical icons used in word processing programs. In these programs, the process for adding an item to a file is represented by a picture of a filing cabinet, a file drawer, or a file folder. Deleting a file can be represented by a wastebasket icon. A stop sign can stand for an exit operation, and a picture of a ruler can be used to adjust text margins. Icons can be useful in many applications.

FIGURE 1–40
Some icons that are useful in
word-processing applications.

1–6 Graphics for Home Use

A major use of computer graphics in home applications is in video games. All of these games employ graphics methods in one form or another. Some systems display graphics on built-in screens, but many are designed to be attached to a TV set.

With the increasing popularity of personal computers and the ever-increasing graphics capabilities of these systems, graphics applications in the home have been steadily expanding. Personal computers allow the home user to generate financial or calorie-counting graphs or to create designs, such as those in Fig. 1–41, for customized greeting cards or stationery.

FIGURE 1–41
Graphics designs can be
created on personal computers
for a variety of uses.

1–7 Image Processing

The graphics technique used for producing visual displays from photographs or TV scans is called **image processing**. Although computers are used with these displays, image processing methods differ from conventional computer graphics methods. In traditional computer graphics, a computer is used to create the picture. Image processing techniques, on the other hand, use a computer to digitize the shading and color patterns from an already existing picture. This digitized information is then transferred to the screen of a video monitor. Such methods are useful for viewing many systems or objects that we cannot see directly, such as TV scans from spacecraft or views from the eye of an industrial robot. Figure 1–42 displays an image-processed picture of one of the moons of the planet Jupiter.

Once a picture has been digitized, additional processing techniques can be applied to rearrange picture parts, to enhance color separations, or to improve the quality of shading. An example of the application of image processing methods to the enhancement of picture quality is shown in Fig. 1–43.

FIGURE 1–42
An enhanced display of Jupiter's moon Io. Courtesy Gould Inc., Imaging & Graphics Division.

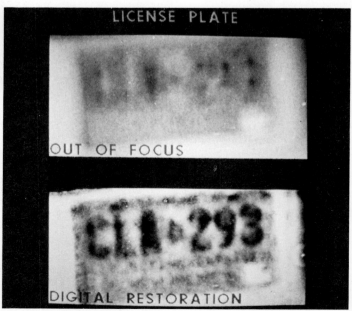

FIGURE 1–43
A blurred photograph of a license plate becomes legible after the application of image processing methods. Courtesy Los Alamos National Laboratory.

Image processing is used extensively in commercial art applications involving the retouching and rearranging of sections of photographs and other artwork. An image processing workstation for setting up advertising layouts is shown in Fig. 1–44.

Medical applications make use of image processing techniques both for picture enhancements and in tomography. Figure 1–45 shows a cancer cell enhanced through image processing. Tomography is a technique of X-ray photography that allows cross-sectional views of physiological systems to be displayed. Both computed X-ray tomography (CT) and position emission tomography (PET) use projec-

FIGURE 1–44
Image processing workstation used by commercial artists to produce advertising layouts. Courtesy COMTAL/3M Corp.

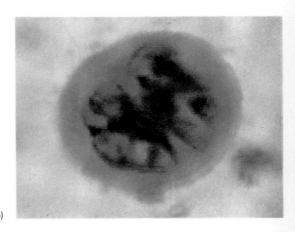

FIGURE 1–45
Image processing techniques applied to a picture of a cancerous cell, marked within a cell culture (a), produce the enlarged and enhanced picture (b). Courtesy Gould Inc., Imaging & Graphics Division and Johns Hopkins University.

(a)

(b)

tion methods to reconstruct cross sections from digital data. An example of a CT scan is given in Fig. 1–46, while Figs. 1–47 and 1–48 show PET scans. These techniques are also used to monitor internal functions and show cross sections during surgery. Other medical imaging techniques include ultrasonics and nuclear medicine scanners. With ultrasonics, high-frequency sound waves, instead of X-rays, are used to generate digital data. Nuclear medicine scanners collect digital data from radiation emitted from ingested radionuclides and plot color-coded images. Conventional graphics methods are also used in medical applications to model and study physical functions and in the design of artificial limbs.

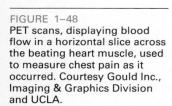

FIGURE 1–46
CT scan used to view
physiological functions.
Courtesy Gould Inc., Imaging &
Graphics Division.

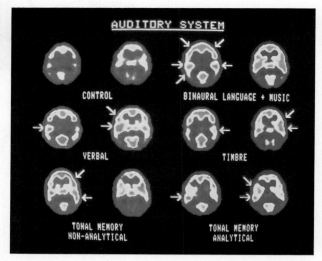

FIGURE 1–48
PET scans, displaying blood
flow in a horizontal slice across
the beating heart muscle, used
to measure chest pain as it
occurred. Courtesy Gould Inc.,
Imaging & Graphics Division
and UCLA.

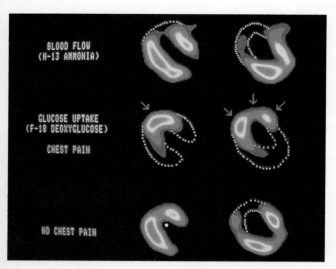

FIGURE 1–47
PET scans showing brain
activation from sound stimulus.
The scans show that verbal
stimulus produces left-brain
activation and music produces
right-brain activation. Scans on
the lower right came from a
musician who created mental
"histograms" of note
frequencies, producing left-
brain activation because his
perceptions were analytical.
Courtesy Gould Inc., Imaging &
Graphics Division and UCLA.

Numerous other fields make use of imaging techniques to generate pictures and analyze collected data. Figure 1–49 shows satellite photos used to analyze terrain features. The display of Fig. 1–50 was used to discover an oil field in the North Sea. Data from solar flares is plotted in Fig. 1–51, and galaxies are reconstructed in Fig. 1–52 from astronomical observations collected and arranged in large databases.

FIGURE 1–49
Landsat photos: (a) Kentucky mountain range color-coded to show areas destroyed by strip mining; (b) caldera on the border between Argentina and Chili. Courtesy Gould Inc., Imaging & Graphics Division.

(b)

(a)

FIGURE 1–50
Image showing oil deposits on either side of a salt plug (vertical red column) in the North Sea. Courtesy Gould Inc., Imaging & Graphics Division.

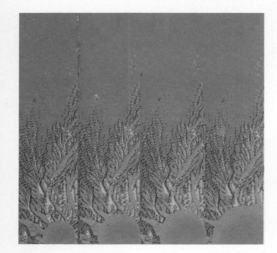

FIGURE 1–51
Display plotted from solar flare
data. Courtesy Gould Inc.,
Imaging & Graphics Division
and Science Applications, Inc.

(a)

(b)

FIGURE 1–52
Galaxies plotted from
astronomical observation data.
Courtesy Gould Inc., Imaging &
Graphics Division and
European Southern
Observatory.

REFERENCES   A detailed discussion of computer-aided design and manufacturing (CAD/CAM) is
given in Pao (1984). This book discusses applications in different industries and various design methods. Other sources for CAD applications include Bouquet (1978) and
Yessios (1979).

Graphics techniques for flight simulators are presented in Schachter (1983). Fu
and Rosenfeld (1984) discuss simulation of vision, and Weinberg (1978) gives an account of space shuttle simulation.

Sources for graphics applications in mathematics, science, and technology include Gardner and Nelson (1983), Grotch (1983), and Wolfram (1984).

A discussion of graphics methods for visualizing music is given in Mitroo, Herman, and Badler (1979). Graphics icon and symbol concepts are presented in Lodding
(1983) and in Loomas (1983).

For additional information on medical applications see Hawrylyshyn, Tasker,
and Organ (1977); Preston, et. al. (1984); and Rhodes (1983).

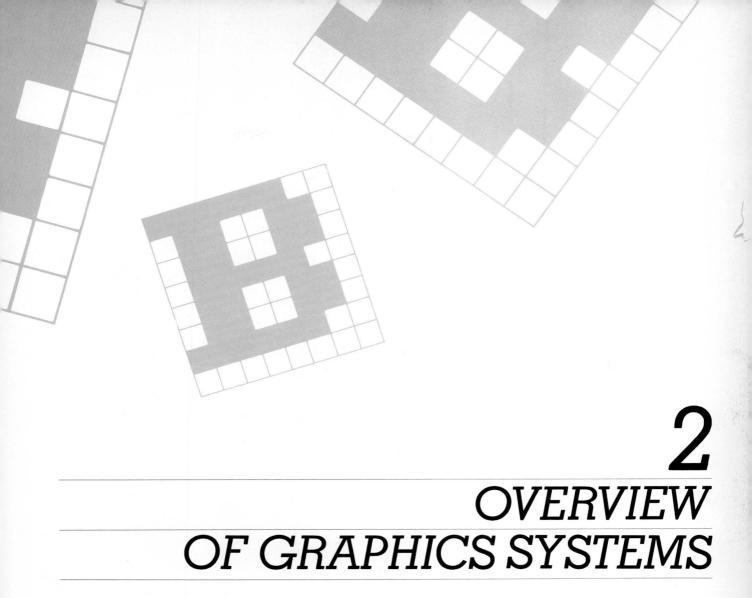

2

OVERVIEW
OF GRAPHICS SYSTEMS

Computer systems can be adapted to graphics applications in various ways, depending on the hardware and software capabilities. Any general-purpose computer can be used to do character graphics by using elements of the system's character set to form patterns. Output statements, such as PRINT and WRITE, are used to produce the appropriate character string across each print line of a printer or video monitor. Though simple in technique, character graphics can produce intricate designs (Fig. 2–1). With the addition of a plotter, line drawings such as those in Fig. 2–2 can be obtained. If a video monitor and line-drawing commands are part of our system, we can interactively create and manipulate these drawings on the monitor screen. For more sophisticated applications, a variety of software packages and hardware devices are available.

FIGURE 2–1
Pictures can be produced with
printers using various
combinations of characters and
overprinting to produce
shading patterns. Courtesy
Computer Services, Western
Illinois University.

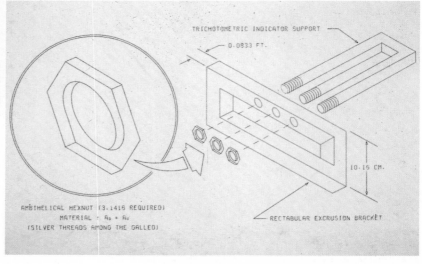

(a)

FIGURE 2–2
Examples of pen plotter output.
Courtesy Computer Services,
Western Illinois University and
CalComp Group; Sanders
Associates, Inc.

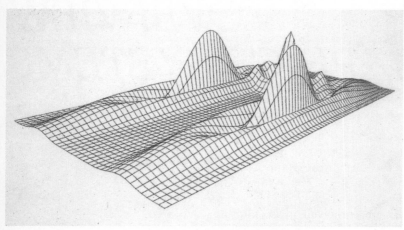

(b)

2–1 Display Devices

Interactive systems use some type of video monitor as the primary output device
(Fig. 2–3). The operation of most video monitors is based on the standard **cathode-
ray tube** (**CRT**) design, but several other technologies exist.

FIGURE 2–3
An interactive graphics system.
Courtesy CalComp Group;
Sanders Associates, Inc.

Refresh Cathode-Ray Tubes

Figure 2–4 illustrates the basic operation of a CRT. A beam of electrons (cathode rays), emitted by an electron gun, passes through focusing and deflection systems that direct the beam toward specified points on the phosphor-coated screen. The phosphor then emits a small spot of light at each point contacted by the electron beam. Since the light emitted by the phosphor fades very rapidly, some method is needed for maintaining the screen picture. One way to keep the phosphor glowing is to redraw the picture repeatedly by quickly directing the electron beam back over the same points. This type of display is called a **refresh CRT.**

Different types of phosphors are available for use in a CRT. Besides color, a major difference between phosphors is their persistence: how long they continue to emit light after the electron beam is removed. Persistence is defined as the time it takes emitted light to decay to one-tenth of its original intensity. Lower-persis-

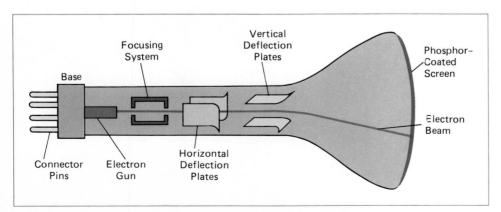

FIGURE 2–4
Basic design of a CRT, using
electrostatic deflection fields.

tence phosphors require higher refresh rates to maintain a picture on the screen without flicker. A phosphor with low persistence is useful for animation, while high-persistence phosphors are better suited for displaying highly complex, static pictures.

Deflection of the electron beam is done either with electric fields or with magnetic fields. The electrostatic method is illustrated in Fig. 2–4. Here the beam passes between two pairs of metal plates: one pair vertical, the other pair horizontal. A voltage difference is applied to each pair of plates according to the amount that the beam is to be deflected in each direction. As the electron beam passes between each pair of plates, it is bent toward the plate with the higher positive voltage. In Fig. 2–4, the beam is first deflected toward one side of the screen. Then, as the beam passes through the horizontal plates, it is deflected toward the top or bottom of the screen. Magnetic fields provide another method for deflecting the electron beam. The proper deflections can be attained by adjusting the current through coils placed around the outside of the CRT envelope.

The basic components of an electron gun in a CRT are the heated metal cathode and a control grid (Fig. 2–5). Heat is supplied to the cathode by directing a current through a coil of wire, called the filament, inside the cylindrical cathode structure. This causes electrons to be "boiled off" the hot cathode surface. In the vacuum inside the CRT envelope, the free, negatively charged electrons are then accelerated toward the phosphor coating by a high positive voltage. The accelerating voltage can be generated with a positively charged metal coating on the inside of the CRT envelope near the phosphor screen, or an accelerating anode can be used, as in Fig. 2–5. Sometimes the electron gun is built to contain the accelerating anode and focusing system within the same unit.

Intensity of the electron beam is controlled by setting voltage levels on the control grid, which is a metal cylinder that fits over the cathode. A high negative voltage applied to the control grid will shut off the beam by repelling electrons and stopping them from passing through the small hole at the end of the control grid structure. A smaller negative voltage on the control grid simply decreases the number of electrons passing through. Since the amount of light emitted by the phosphor coating depends on the number of electrons striking the screen, we control the brightness of a display by varying the voltage on the control grid. A control knob is available on video monitors to set the brightness for the entire screen. We also can set the intensity level of individual positions on the screen using program commands.

FIGURE 2–5
Operation of an electron gun
with an accelerating anode.

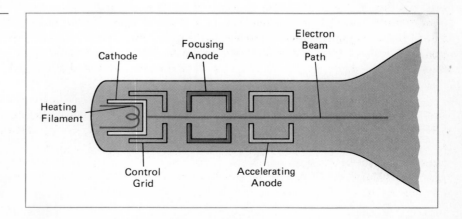

The focusing system in a CRT is needed to force the electron beam to converge into a small spot as it strikes the phosphor. Otherwise, the electrons would repel each other, and the beam would spread out as it approaches the screen. Focusing is accomplished with either electric or magnetic fields. For electrostatic focusing, the electron beam passes through a metal cylinder with a positive voltage, as shown in Fig. 2–5. The positive voltage forces the electrons to stay along the axis of the beam. Similar focusing forces can be applied to the electron beam with electromagnetic fields set up by coils mounted around the outside of the CRT envelope.

Another type of focusing is used in high-precision systems to keep the beam in focus at all screen points. The distance that the electron beam must travel to different points on the screen varies because the radius of curvature for most CRTs is greater than the distance from the focusing system to the screen center. Therefore, the electron beam will be focused properly only at the center of the screen. As the beam moves to the outer edges of the screen, displayed images become blurred. To compensate for this, the system can adjust the focusing according to the screen position of the beam.

The maximum number of points that can be displayed without overlap on a CRT is referred to as the **resolution.** A more precise definition of resolution is the number of points per centimeter that can be plotted horizontally and vertically, although it is often simply stated as the total number of points in each direction. Resolution of a CRT is dependent on the type of phosphor used and the focusing and deflection systems. High-precision systems can display a maximum of about 4000 points in each direction, for a total of 16 million addressable screen points. Since a CRT monitor can be attached to different computer systems, the number of screen points that are utilized depends on the capabilities of the system to which it is attached.

An important property of video monitors is their **aspect ratio.** This number gives the ratio of vertical points to horizontal points necessary to produce equal-length lines in both directions on the screen. (Sometimes aspect ratio is stated in terms of the ratio of horizontal to vertical points.) An aspect ratio of 3/4 means that a vertical line plotted with three points has the same length as a horizontal line plotted with four points.

Random-Scan and Raster-Scan Monitors

Refresh CRTs can be operated either as random-scan or as raster-scan monitors. When operated as a **random-scan** display unit, a CRT has the electron beam directed only to the parts of the screen where a picture is to be drawn. Random-scan monitors draw a picture one line at a time and, for this reason, are also referred to as **vector** displays (or **stroke-writing** or **calligraphic** displays). The component lines of a picture can be drawn and refreshed by a random-scan system in any order specified (Fig. 2–6). A pen plotter operates in a similar way and is an example of a random-scan, hard-copy device.

Raster-scan video monitors shoot the electron beam over all parts of the screen, turning the beam intensity on and off to coincide with the picture definition. The picture is created on the screen as a set of points (Fig. 2–7), starting from the top of the screen. Definition for a picture is now stored as a set of intensity values for all the screen points, and these stored values are "painted" on the screen one row (scan line) at a time. The capability of a raster-scan system to store intensity information for each screen point makes it well suited for displaying shading

FIGURE 2–6
A random-scan system draws
the component lines of a figure
in any order specified.

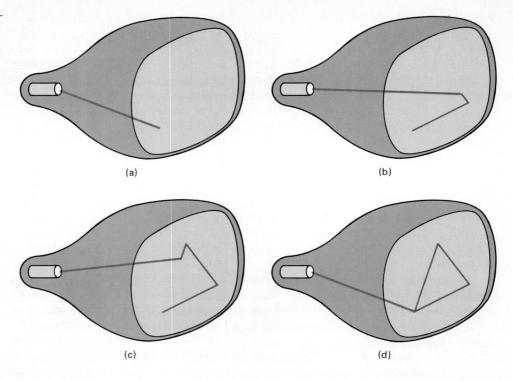

(a)

(b)

(c)

(d)

FIGURE 2–7
A raster-scan system displays
the object of Fig. 2–6 as a set of
points across each screen scan
line.

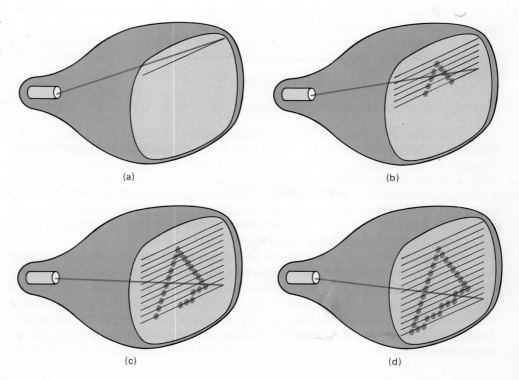

(a)

(b)

(c)

(d)

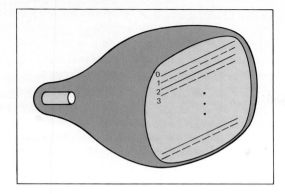

FIGURE 2–8
A raster-scan monitor can be set up to interlace scan lines: First, all points on the even-numbered (solid) lines are displayed; then all points along the odd-numbered (dashed) lines are displayed.

and color areas, whereas vector systems are restricted to line-drawing applications. Employing highly developed television technology, raster-scan monitors are now commonly used in the design of efficient and inexpensive computer graphics systems. Home television sets and printers are examples of other systems using raster-scan methods.

Often the refresh cycle in a raster-scan monitor (and in TV sets) is carried out by sweeping the beam across every other line on one pass from top to bottom, then returning (**vertical retrace**) to sweep across the remaining screen lines on the next pass down the screen (Fig. 2–8). This interlacing of the scan lines helps to reduce flicker at slower refresh rates. We essentially see the entire screen display in one-half the time it would have taken to sweep across all the lines at once from top to bottom.

Refreshing on raster-scan systems is done at rates of 30 to 60 frames per second. At the rate of 30 frames per second, the electron beam traces over all screen lines from top to bottom 30 times each second. A refresh rate below about 25 frames per second causes the picture to flicker. For systems with a large number of scan lines (1000 or more), higher refresh rates are usually needed. This is often accomplished by interlacing. In a 30-frames-per-second interlaced system (Fig. 2–8), each half of the set of screen lines is displayed in 1/60 second. This puts the overall refresh rate closer to 60 frames per second. This same refresh rate is accomplished with a 60-frames-per-second noninterlaced system employing faster processors.

Random-scan monitors are also often designed to draw the component lines of a picture 30 to 60 times each second, although some are designed to begin the refresh cycle immediately after all lines are drawn. Since random-scan systems are designed for line-drawing applications and do not store intensity values for all screen points, they generally have higher resolutions than raster systems.

Color CRT Monitors

A CRT monitor displays color pictures by using a combination of phosphors that emit different-colored light. By combining the emitted light from the different phosphors, a range of colors can be generated. The two basic techniques for producing color displays with a CRT are the beam-penetration method and the shadow-mask method.

The **beam-penetration** method for displaying color pictures has been used with random-scan monitors. Two layers of phosphor, usually red and green, are coated onto the screen, and the displayed color depends on how far the electron beam penetrates into the phosphor layers. A beam of slow electrons excites only the outer red layer. A beam of very fast electrons penetrates through the red layer and excites the inner green layer. At intermediate beam speeds, combinations of red and green light are emitted to show two additional colors, orange and yellow. The speed of the electrons, and hence the screen color at any point, is controlled by the beam acceleration voltage. Beam penetration has been an inexpensive way to produce color in random-scan monitors, but only four colors are possible, and the quality of pictures is not as good as with other methods.

Shadow-mask methods are commonly used in raster-scan systems (including color TV) since they produce a much wider range of colors than the beam-penetration method. A shadow-mask CRT has the screen coated with tiny triangular patterns, each containing three different closely spaced phosphor dots. One phosphor dot of each triangle emits a red light, another emits a green light, and the third emits a blue light. This type of CRT has three electron guns, one for each color dot, and a shadow-mask grid just behind the phosphor-coated screen (Fig. 2–9). The three electron beams are deflected and focused as a group onto the shadow mask, which contains a series of holes aligned with the phosphor-dot patterns. When the three beams pass through a hole in the shadow mask, they activate a dot triangle, which appears as a small color spot on the screen. The phosphor dots in the triangles are arranged so that each electron beam can activate only its corresponding color dot when it passes through the shadow mask.

Color variations in a shadow-mask CRT are obtained by combining different intensity levels of the three electron beams. By turning off the red and green guns, we get only the color coming from the blue phosphor. Other combinations of beam intensities produce a small light spot for each triangle, whose color depends on the amount of excitation of the red, green, and blue phosphors in the triangle. A white (or gray) area is the result of activating all three dots with equal intensity. Yellow is produced with the green and red dots only, magenta is produced with the blue and red dots, and cyan shows up when blue and green are activated equally. In low-cost systems, the electron beam can only be set to on or off, limiting displays to eight colors. More sophisticated systems can set intermediate intensity levels for the electron beams, allowing as many as several million different colors to be generated.

Personal computer systems with color graphics capabilities are often designed

FIGURE 2–9
Operation of a shadow-mask CRT. Three electron guns, arranged to coincide with the color dot patterns on the screen, are directed to each dot triangle by a shadow mask.

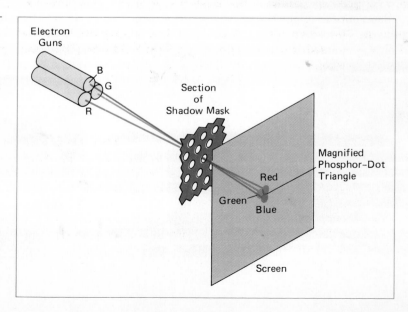

to be used with several types of CRT display devices. These devices include TV sets, composite monitors, and RGB (red-green-blue) monitors. An inexpensive system typically makes use of a color TV and an RF (radio-frequency) modulator. The purpose of the RF modulator is to simulate the signal from a broadcast TV station. This means that the color and intensity information of the picture must be combined and superimposed on the broadcast-frequency carrier signal that the TV needs to have as input. Then the circuitry in the TV takes this signal from the RF modulator, extracts the picture information, and paints it on the screen. As we might expect, this extra handling of the picture information by the RF modulator and TV circuitry decreases the quality of displayed images.

Composite monitors are adaptations of TV sets that allow bypass of the broadcast circuitry. These display devices still require that the picture information be combined, but no carrier signal is needed. Since picture information is combined into a composite signal and then separated by the monitor, the resulting picture quality is still not the best attainable.

High-quality color CRTs are designed as **RGB monitors.** These monitors take the intensity level for each electron gun (red, green, and blue) directly from the computer system without any intermediate processing. In this way, fewer signal distortions are generated.

Direct-View Storage Tubes

An alternative method for maintaining a screen image is to store the picture information inside the CRT instead of refreshing the screen. A **direct-view storage tube (DVST)** stores the picture information as a charge distribution just behind the phosphor-coated screen. Two electron guns are used in a DVST. One, the primary gun, is used to store the picture pattern; the second, the flood gun, maintains the picture display.

A simplified cross section of a DVST is shown in Fig. 2–10. In this device, the primary electron gun is used to draw the picture definition on the storage grid, a nonconducting material. High-speed electrons from the primary gun strike the storage grid, knocking out electrons, which are attracted to the collector grid. Since the storage grid is nonconducting, the areas where electrons have been removed will keep a net positive charge. This stored positive charge pattern on the storage grid is the picture definition. The flood gun produces a continuous stream of low-speed electrons that pass through the control grid and are attracted to the positive areas of the storage grid. These low-speed electrons penetrate through the storage grid to the phosphor coating, without appreciably affecting the charge pattern on the storage surface.

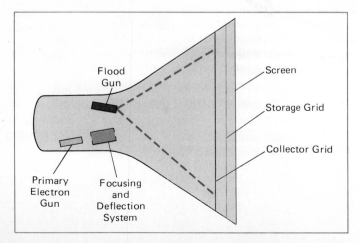

FIGURE 2–10
Operation of a DVST.

A DVST monitor has both disadvantages and advantages compared to the refresh CRT. Since no refreshing is needed, very complex pictures can be displayed clearly without flicker. As illustrated by the system in Fig. 2–11, very high resolution is possible, and the cost of DVST systems has been lower than many random-scan systems. Disadvantages of DVST systems are that they ordinarily do not display color and that selected parts of a picture cannot be erased. To eliminate a picture section, the entire screen must be erased by storing a positive charge over all parts of the storage grid. Then the flood gun electrons strike the phosphor coating at all points on the screen, erasing the picture in a flash of light. The entire picture is then redrawn, minus the parts to be omitted.

Plasma-Panel Displays

Although most graphics monitors contain CRTs, other technologies are used in some systems. **Plasma-panel displays** (Fig. 2–12) are constructed by filling the region between two glass plates with neon gas. A series of vertical and horizontal electrodes, placed on the front and rear glass panels, respectively, are used to light up individual points in the neon. One way to provide the individual points is to separate the gas into small "bulbs" with a center glass plate containing a number of closely spaced holes, as shown in Fig. 2–12.

An individual neon point in a plasma panel is turned on by applying a "firing voltage" of about 120 volts to the appropriate pair of horizontal and vertical electrodes. Once the point is turned on, the voltage on these electrodes is then lowered to a "sustaining voltage" level (about 90 volts) that keeps the neon cell glowing. A constant 90 volts can be applied across all electrode pairs, and those points that are to be lit have their electrode potentials momentarily raised to the firing voltage. This ensures that the points to be displayed continue to glow while all other points remain off. Thus the plasma panel is an inherent memory device that requires no refreshing. Erasing the screen is accomplished by lowering the voltage on each electrode below the sustaining voltage level.

The number of points that can be displayed by a plasma panel is limited, and its cost is somewhat higher than that of a refresh CRT. Advantages of plasma panels are that they are very rugged devices that require no refreshing. They also have flat screens and are transparent, so displayed images can be superimposed with pictures from slides or other media projected through the rear panel. Examples of plasma-panel systems are shown in Fig. 2–13.

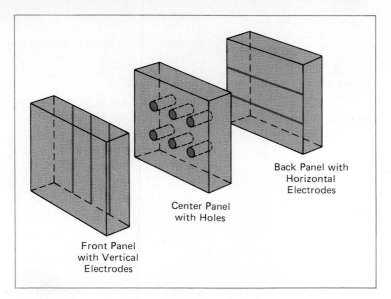

Front Panel
with Vertical
Electrodes

Center Panel
with Holes

Back Panel with
Horizontal
Electrodes

FIGURE 2–12
Plate construction in a plasma-panel display device.

FIGURE 2–13
Plasma-panel display systems: (a) large flat panel display with a resolution of about 1200 by 1600; (b) smaller 1024 by 768 portable terminal, showing graphics output superimposed on a map inserted behind the panels. Courtesy Magnavox Electronic Systems Co.

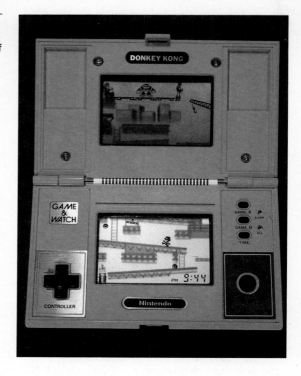

FIGURE 2–14
Liquid crystal display screens
used with a "pocket" version of
the Donkey Kong game. Each
of the two small screens
measures 5.5 cm by 3.5 cm.

LED and LCD Monitors

Two other technologies used in the design of graphics monitors are light-emitting diodes (LEDs) and liquid-crystal displays (LCDs). These devices use light emitted from diodes or crystals instead of phosphors or neon gas to display a picture. LEDs and LCDs are particularly useful in the design of the miniscreens used with some graphics games. A "pocket" video game with two 1 1/4-inch by 2-inch screens is shown in Fig. 2–14. Screens for some wristwatch games are even smaller.

An auxiliary memory, similar to a frame buffer, is used to store the screen patterns for a display. The system repeatedly cycles through the memory area, turning on the appropriate LED or LCD positions in succession by applying a firing voltage to appropriate horizontal and vertical wire pairs. Each LED or LCD fired produces a very short pulse of light. However, the firing rate is rapid enough so that the picture is perceived as a set of steadily glowing points.

Laser Devices

An additional non-CRT technique for generating graphics output is to trace patterns on photochromic film, which is temporarily darkened by exposure to light. The patterns are formed with a laser beam, deflected by electromechanically controlled mirrors. Another light source is then used to project the images on a screen. A change in screen displays is obtained by winding the roll of film to the next blank frame and repeating the process. Highly complex patterns can be displayed in a very short time with these systems, but no selective erasure is possible. Changes to a picture can be made only by completely redrawing the patterns on the next film frame.

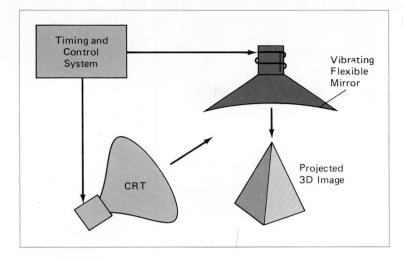

FIGURE 2–15
Basic operation of a three-dimensional display system using a vibrating mirror that changes focal length to match the depth of points in a scene.

Three-Dimensional Monitors

Graphics monitors for the display of three-dimensional scenes have been devised using a technique that reflects a CRT image from a vibrating, flexible mirror. The operation of such a system is demonstrated in Fig. 2–15. As the mirror (called a varifocal mirror) vibrates, it changes focal length. These vibrations are synchronized with the display of an object on a CRT so that each point on the object is reflected from the mirror at a position corresponding to the depth of that point. A viewer can see under, around, or over the top of the object. Figure 2–16 shows the Genisco SpaceGraph system, which uses a vibrating mirror to project three-

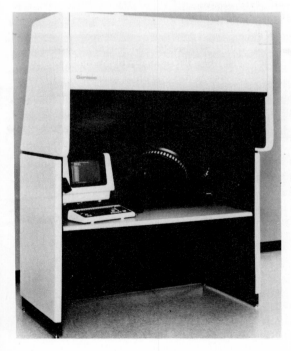

FIGURE 2–16
The SpaceGraph interactive graphics system displays objects in three dimensions using a vibrating, flexible mirror. Courtesy Genisco Computers Corp.

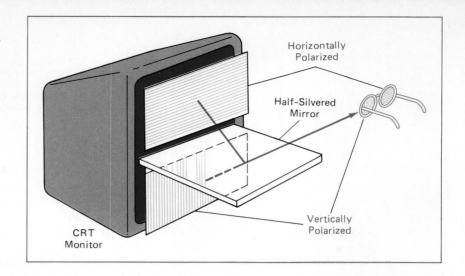

FIGURE 2–17
Stereoscopic viewing system,
employing polarizing viewing
filters and a half-silvered mirror
to combine the images from
two halves of a display screen.

Horizontally
Polarized

Half–Silvered
Mirror

Vertically
Polarized

CRT
Monitor

dimensional objects into a 25cm by 25cm by 25cm volume. This system is also capable of displaying two-dimensional cross-sectional "slices" of objects selected at different depths. Such systems are used in medical applications to analyze data from ultrasonography and CAT scan devices, in geological applications to analyze topological and seismic data, in design applications involving three-dimensional objects, and in three-dimensional simulations of systems, such as molecules and terrain.

Another technique for representing three-dimensional objects is displaying stereoscopic views. This method does not produce true three-dimensional images, but it does provide a three-dimensional effect by presenting a different view to each eye of an observer. One way to do this is to display the two views of a scene on different halves of a CRT screen. Each view is projected onto the screen from a viewing direction that the corresponding eye (left or right) would normally see. A polarizing filter is placed over each half of the screen, and the user views the screen through a pair of polarized glasses (Fig. 2–17). Each lens of the glasses is polarized to admit the light from only one half of the screen, so the user sees a stereoscopic view of the three-dimensional scene. A stereoscopic effect can also be achieved by displaying each of the two views across the entire screen on alternate refresh cycles. The screen is again viewed through glasses, but now each lens is designed to act as a rapidly alternating shutter that is synchronized to block out one of the views. Electric fields can be used to cause the material in each lens to alternate between opaque and clear. Other types of shutter devices could also be used to alternate the two views.

Stereoscopic views have also been generated using a headset arrangement that contains two small video monitors and an optical system. One of the video monitors displays a view for the left eye, and the other displays a view for the right eye. A sensing system in the headset keeps track of the viewer's position, so that the front and back of objects can be seen as the viewer "walks through" the display.

2–2 Hard-Copy Devices

Many graphics systems are equipped to produce hard-copy output directly from a video monitor in the form of 35mm slides or overhead transparencies. Hard-copy pictures can also be obtained by directing graphics output to a printer or plotter.

Although originally designed for producing text pages, standard printers are acceptable graphics devices for applications not requiring high-quality output. They are generally accessible, so that even systems without special graphics capabilities can be used to generate graphics output on an attached printer. Some printers may be specifically adapted for graphics applications. Also, printers provide one of the least expensive devices for producing hard-copy pictures.

Printers produce output by either impact or nonimpact methods. **Impact printers** press formed character faces against an inked ribbon onto the paper. The familiar line printer is an example of an impact device, with the typefaces mounted on bands, chains, drums, or wheels. The daisy-wheel printer uses the impact method to print characters one at a time. A dot-matrix print head, containing a rectangular array of tiny pins, is often used in impact character printers to form individual characters by activating selected pin patterns. **Nonimpact printers** are faster and quieter and often use a dot-matrix method to print characters or draw lines. Ink-jet sprays, laser techniques, xerographic processes (as used in photocopying machines), electrostatic methods, and electrothermal methods are all used in the design of nonimpact printers.

Dot-matrix methods offer extended possibilities for graphics output. Besides printing preset character patterns, these printers can be adapted to print any dot combination selected by a graphics program. A printed page can now be thought of as a grid of closely spaced points, rather than simply as an array of character positions. Figure 2–18 is an example of the type of output that can be produced with a dot-matrix impact printer.

Ink-jet methods produce output by squirting ink in horizontal rows across a roll of paper wrapped on a drum. The ink stream, which is electrically charged, is deflected by an electric field to produce dot-matrix patterns. Electrostatic methods place a negative charge on a flat sheet of paper, one complete row at a time along the length of the paper. Then the paper is exposed to a black toner. The toner is positively charged and so is attracted to the negatively charged areas, where it adheres to produce the specified output. Electrothermal methods use heat in the dot-matrix print head to output patterns on heat-sensitive paper. A laser printer

FIGURE 2–18
A picture generated on a dot-matrix impact printer, which permits shading control by varying the density of the dot patterns. Courtesy Apple Computer, Inc.

FIGURE 2–19
Color patterns displayed on an
ink-jet printer. Courtesy
PrintaColor Corp.

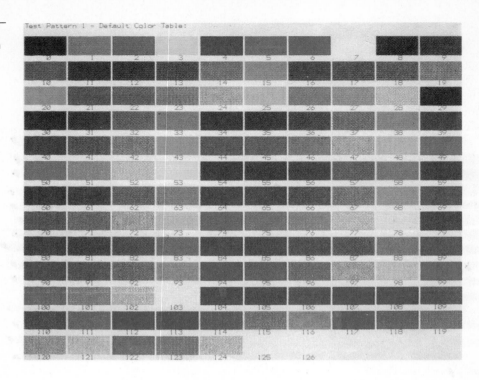

operates similarly to a Xerox copier. The laser beam creates a charge distribution on a drum coated with a photoelectric material, such as selenium. Toner is applied to the drum and then transferred to paper.

Both black-and-white and color printers are available. Different-colored ribbons have been used in impact printers to get color variations, but the nonimpact printers are better suited for color output. The nonimpact devices use various techniques to combine three color pigments (cyan, magenta, and yellow) to produce a range of color patterns. Laser and xerographic printers deposit the three pigments on separate passes; ink-jet printers shoot the three colors simultaneously on a single pass along each print line on the paper. Examples of color patterns produced with an ink-jet printer are given in Fig. 2–19.

Plotters

These devices produce hard-copy line drawings. The most commonly encountered plotters use ink pens to generate the drawings, but many plotting devices now employ laser beams, ink-jet sprays, and electrostatic methods. Unlike standard printers, plotters require additional software commands to direct the plotter output from an applications program.

Pen plotters normally use one or more ink pens mounted on a carriage, or crossbar, to draw lines on a sheet of paper. Wet ink, ball-point, and felt-tip pens are all possible choices for use with a pen plotter. The plotter paper is usually either stretched flat or rolled onto a drum or belt. Examples of **flatbed plotters** are shown in Fig. 2–20. The crossbar can move from one end of the plotter to the other, while the pen moves back and forth along the bar. Either clamps, a vacuum,

(a)

FIGURE 2–20
Flatbed plotters with ink pens mounted on a movable crossbar are available in a variety of sizes. (a) Courtesy CalComp Group; Sanders Associates, Inc. (b) Courtesy Tektronix, Inc.

(b)

or an electrostatic charge hold the paper flat as the carriage and pen move across the paper. These plotters can vary in size from about 12 by 18 inches to over 6 by 10 feet. Figure 2–21 shows one type of **drum plotter.** Here the carriage is stationary, and the paper is made to move forward and backward on the drum as the pen slides across the carriage. Drum plotters are available in sizes that vary from about 1 foot to 3 feet in width. A cross between a flatbed and a drum is the **beltbed plotter** (Fig. 2–22). This plotter moves the paper on a wide, continuous belt over a flat surface as the pen carriage moves across the paper to produce the drawing.

Typical commands to a pen plotter from an application program include those for raising and lowering the pen and for moving the pen to a specified position. An electromagnet is used to raise and lower the pen, and servomotors move the pens and either the carriage or the drum. Some plotters allow pen movement in unit steps only, while others are capable of accepting commands for moves of more than one unit in various directions. Depending on the capabilities of a plotter, from 4 to 16 different directions can be chosen for the pen movement. Microprocessors are

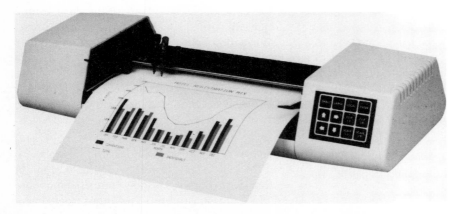

FIGURE 2–21
A small drum plotter, with ink pens mounted in a pen cartridge that can move laterally. The paper is attached to a rotating drum. Courtesy Houston Instrument.

often placed in plotters to allow automatic generation of common figures, such as lines, circles, and ellipses, and to output automatically different character patterns. Plotters with microprocessors are sometimes referred to as "vector" plotters.

Color drawings are produced with pen plotters by mounting different-colored pens on the carriage. Some plotters are designed to hold more than one pen on the carriage so that the different colors can be selected with program commands.

Plotters can also use pens of different widths to produce a variety of shadings and line styles. Sometimes plotters are equipped with a "pen stylus" to cut lines into a soft material or with a "pen light" to get the graphics output onto a photographic negative.

Line drawings can be produced by devices other than pen plotters. Printers employing ink-jet, laser, electrostatic, and other dot-matrix methods can be used interchangeably as either printers or plotters. These printer-plotter devices typically operate much faster than pen plotters, although the quality of the electrostatic devices is somewhat lower since the toner will spread slightly into uncharged areas. All of these methods require that the information for a drawing be stored in a buffer and delivered to the output device so that the drawing can be produced one row at a time from the top of the page to the bottom.

2–3 Interactive Input Devices

Graphics workstations, such as those shown in Figs. 2–23 and 2–24, typically include several types of input and output devices. Many systems, such as the one in Fig. 2–24, provide two monitors so that both high-resolution line drawings and raster color pictures can be displayed. In addition, a number of input devices are

FIGURE 2–23
A menu-driven artist's workstation, the Dicomed Imaginator, featuring a color raster monitor, a recessed keyboard, and a graphics tablet with hand cursor. Additional features are a light table for transparency analysis, disk drives, and a telephone with modem for voice and data communication. Courtesy DICOMED Corp.

FIGURE 2–24
A graphics workstation featuring both a vector and a raster display. Input devices include light pen and graphics tablet. Magnetic tape and hard disk units are also included. Courtesy Information Displays, Inc.

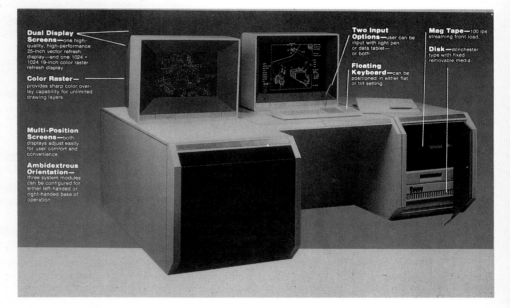

made available for interaction with the displays. A complete discussion of the operational features of input devices and the various interactive input methods appears in Chapter 8. Here, we briefly mention a few of the commonly used input devices and their primary function.

Keyboards are included on most graphics systems for the input of character strings and data values. Various types of keys, dials, and switches can be included on a keyboard to handle different applications. Some special-purpose keyboards contain only a set of dials or switches.

Coordinate values specifying screen positions are most often input with a graphics tablet, light pen, mouse, or a joystick. These devices typically are used to sketch pictures or make menu selections. A tablet inputs coordinate positions by activating a hand cursor or a stylus at selected positions on the tablet surface. A light pen pointed at a video monitor records coordinate positions by responding to the light emitted from phosphors on the screen. And a mouse or joystick is used to position the screen cursor at the coordinate locations to be selected.

Several other types of input devices are useful in graphics applications. They include touch panels, voice systems, and devices for entering three-dimensional coordinate information.

2–4 Display Processors

Interactive graphics systems typically employ two or more processing units. In addition to the central processing unit, or CPU, a special-purpose **display processor** is used to interact with the CPU and control the operation of the display device (Fig. 2–25). Stand-alone systems, such as microcomputers with graphics capabilities, contain both processors, while graphics terminals connecting to a host computer might only contain the display processor. Basically, the display processor is used to convert digital information from the CPU into corresponding voltage values needed by the display device. The manner in which this digital-to-analog conversion takes place depends on the type of display device used and the particular graphics functions that are to be hardware-implemented. In some systems, more than one processor is used to implement the graphics display functions.

Application programs for interactive graphics systems provide picture information to the display processor in terms of light-intensity levels for coordinate points on the screen. For many graphics monitors, the coordinate origin is defined at the lower left screen corner (Fig. 2–26). The screen surface is then represented as the first quadrant of a two-dimensional coordinate system, with positive x values increasing to the right and positive y values increasing from bottom to top. On some microcomputers, the coordinate origin is referenced at the upper left corner of the screen, so the y values are inverted. Graphics systems often allow applications programs to define picture points using any coordinate reference that is convenient for the user. A transformation is then performed by the system to convert user coordinates to screen values.

A fundamental task for the display processor is the display of line segments. Intensity levels (or color values) to be used in plotting coordinate positions along a line are supplied by the application program and converted to voltage levels, which

FIGURE 2–25
Simplified hardware diagram of an interactive graphics system.

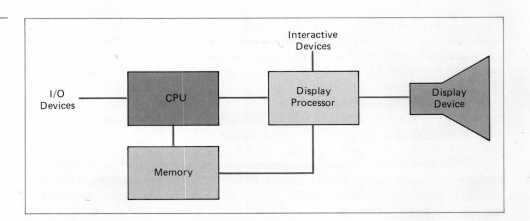

are then applied to the display device. For simple black-and-white systems, no intensity information need be specified in the program, since any point is either on or off. Higher-quality systems allow the intensity of screen points to be varied so that shades of gray can be displayed.

Another typical function of a display processor is character generation. A standard character set is available on all systems, but some systems also allow user-generated character patterns to be stored and reproduced by the display processor.

Advanced display processors are designed to perform a number of additional operations. These functions include generating various line styles (dashed, dotted, or solid), displaying color areas, producing curved lines, and performing certain transformations and manipulations on displayed objects. Also, display processors are typically designed to interface with interactive input devices, such as a light pen.

With refresh CRT systems, the display processor may also be required to cycle through the picture definition, refreshing the screen often enough to eliminate flicker. The picture definition is kept in a refresh storage area. On many systems, this screen-refreshing task can be assigned to an additional processor, called the **display controller.** This allows the display processor to devote full time to the other functions.

Random-Scan Systems

Figure 2–27 is a simplified diagram of the logical operations performed by a random-scan system. Graphics commands in an application program are translated into a **display file program,** which is accessed by the display processor to refresh the screen. The display processor cycles through each command in the display file program once during every refresh cycle.

When a display controller is included in a random-scan system, two files can be used. The translated graphics commands are first stored in a display file, as shown in Fig. 2–28. Then the display processor copies commands into a **refresh display file** for access by the display controller. This refresh display file is created by applying the viewing operations that select the particular view to be displayed on the screen. During the refresh process, which is now carried out by the display controller, the display processor may be updating the refresh file as interactive commands are input. These updates must be synchronized with the refreshing process so as not to distort the picture while it is in the process of being refreshed.

Graphics patterns are drawn on a random-scan system by directing the electron beam along the component lines of the picture. Lines are defined by the values for their coordinate endpoints, and these input coordinate values are converted to x and y deflection voltages. A scene is then drawn one line at a time by positioning the beam to fill in the line between specified endpoints.

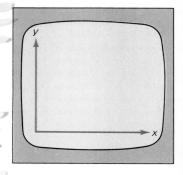

FIGURE 2–26
The origin of the coordinate system for identifying screen positions is usually specified in the lower left corner.

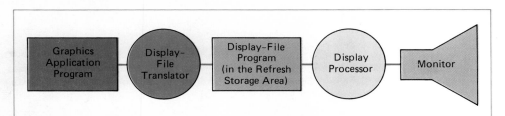

| Graphics Application Program | Display-File Translator | Display-File Program (in the Refresh Storage Area) | Display Processor | Monitor |

FIGURE 2–27
Simplified block diagram of the functions performed by a random-scan system.

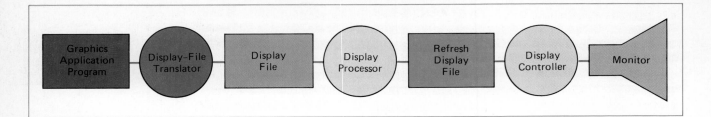

FIGURE 2–28
Block diagram of the functions performed by a random-scan system with a display controller.

FIGURE 2–29
Rectangular grids can be used to define characters as a set of points.

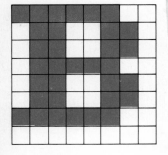

Straight lines are drawn in a random-scan system with a **vector generator,** the hardware component of the display processor (or display controller), which produces deflection voltages for the electron beam. These deflection voltages can be generated in one of two ways. An **analog vector generator** sends the electron beam directly from one line endpoint to the other by linearly varying the deflection voltages. This produces a smooth straight line between the two points. A **digital vector generator** calculates successive points along the line, starting at one end, and converts these coordinate values to voltages. In this way, a straight line is constructed as a set of points. Although the digital method does not produce as smooth a line as the analog method, it is generally faster and less expensive. Line styles, such as a dashed line, are handled by turning the electron beam alternately on and off as the line is drawn.

Curved lines can be generated by methods similar to those for drawing straight lines. Given the functional representation of the curve, hardware implementations can be devised to display the curve as a series of short, straight line segments or as a set of points.

Character generators also use either the point method or the line method to display letters, numbers, and other symbols. A common method is to define each character as a rectangular point grid (Fig. 2–29). The array of points used to define each character can vary from about 5 by 7 up to about 9 by 14, for higher-quality displays. A character is displayed by superimposing the rectangular grid pattern onto the screen at a specified coordinate position. A line-generation method for displaying characters can also employ a rectangular grid. In this case, each character is defined as a set of line segments within the grid rather than a point pattern.

DVST Systems

Display processors for a DVST can be designed to operate with or without a refresh storage area. A processor would employ a refresh area whenever a "write-through" capability is desired. This feature allows images to be superimposed on the stored picture as a refresh process. Without refresh storage, the display processor can generate lines and characters for direct storage with the same methods used in a random-scan system. Additional functions needed for a DVST display processor include commands for storing the picture information and for erasing the screen.

Raster-Scan Systems

The operation of a raster-scan system differs from that of a random-scan system in that the refresh storage area is used to store intensity information for each screen position, instead of graphics commands. For raster-scan systems, the refresh

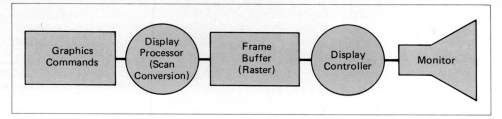

FIGURE 2–30
Simplified block diagram of a raster-scan system.

storage is usually referred to as the **frame buffer** or **refresh buffer** (Fig. 2–30). Other names for the frame buffer are **raster** and **bit map.** Each position in the frame buffer is called a **picture element, or pixel.** Pictures are painted on the screen from the frame buffer, one row at a time, from top to bottom. Each horizontal line of pixels is referred to as a **scan line,** and the process of generating pixel information into the frame buffer from the application program is called **scan conversion.** Intensity values are entered into the raster during the vertical-retrace time.

Pixel positions in the frame buffer are organized as a two-dimensional array of intensity values, corresponding to coordinate screen positions. The number of pixel positions in the raster is called the **resolution** of the display processor (or resolution of the frame buffer). Good-quality raster systems have a resolution of about 1024 by 1024, although higher-resolution systems are available. Since the resolution of a CRT monitor depends on the size of the phosphor dot that can be produced, a graphics system may have two resolutions, one for the monitor used with the system and one for the frame buffer. To generate the best-quality pictures, the resolution for the video monitor should be equal to or higher than the resolution of the frame buffer.

Graphics commands are translated by the scan-conversion process into intensity values for storage in the frame buffer. In a simple black-and-white system, each screen point is either on or off, so only one bit per pixel is needed to control the intensity of screen positions. A bit value of 1, for example, would mean that the electron beam is to be turned on at that position, while a value of 0 indicates that the beam intensity is to be off. Additional bits are needed when color and intensity variations can be displayed. Up to 24 or more bits per pixel are included in high-quality systems, although storage requirements for the frame buffer then get quite high. A system employing 24 bits per pixel with a screen resolution of 1024 by 1024 would require a frame buffer with 3 megabytes of storage.

Straight lines, curves, and characters are represented by the digital techniques discussed for random-scan systems. Each line is stored as a set of points, and characters are stored as dot-matrix patterns. A major advantage of the storage of intensity values in frame buffers is in the representation of areas that are to be filled with color or shading patterns. Once an area has been scan-converted, intensity values for all points within this area are stored in the raster for immediate use by the display controller.

In an effort to reduce memory requirements in random-scan systems, methods have been devised for organizing the raster as a linked list and encoding the intensity information. One way to do this is to store each scan line as a set of integer pairs. One number of each pair indicates an intensity value, and the second number specifies the number of adjacent pixels on the scan line that are to have that intensity. This technique, called **run-length encoding,** can result in a considerable saving in storage space if a picture is to be constructed mostly with long runs of a single color each. A similar approach can be taken when pixel intensities change linearly. Another approach is to encode the raster as a set of rectangular areas (**cell encoding**). The disadvantages of encoding runs are that intensity changes are difficult to make and storage requirements actually increase as the length of the runs decreases. In addition, it is difficult for the display controller to process the raster when many short runs are involved.

2–5 Graphics Software

Programming commands for displaying and manipulating graphics output are designed as extensions to existing languages. An example of such a graphics package is the PLOT 10 system developed by Tektronix, Inc., for use with FORTRAN on their graphics terminals. Basic functions available in a package designed for the graphics programmer include those for generating picture components (straight lines, polygons, circles, and other figures), setting color and intensity values, selecting views, and applying transformations. By contrast, application graphics packages designed for nonprogrammers are set up so that users can produce graphics without worrying about how they do it. The interface to the graphics routines in such packages allows users to communicate with the programs in their own terms. Examples of such applications packages are the artist's painting programs and various business, medical, and CAD systems.

Coordinate Representations

Most graphics packages are designed to use Cartesian coordinate systems. More than one Cartesian system may be referenced by a package, since different output devices can require different coordinate systems. In addition, packages usually allow picture definitions to be set up in any Cartesian reference system convenient to the application at hand. The coordinates referenced by a user are called **world coordinates,** and the coordinates used by a particular output device are called **device coordinates,** or **screen coordinates** in the case of a video monitor. World coordinate definitions allow a user to set any convenient dimensions without being hampered by the constraints of a particular output device. Architectural layouts might be specified in fractions of a foot, while other applications might define coordinate scales in terms of millimeters, kilometers, or light-years. Once the world coordinate definitions are given, the graphics system converts these coordinates to the appropriate device coordinates for display.

A typical procedure used in graphics packages is first to convert world coordinate definitions to **normalized device coordinates** before final conversion to specific device coordinates. This makes the system flexible enough to accommodate a number of output devices (Fig. 2–31). Normalized x and y coordinates are each assigned values in the interval from 0 to 1. These normalized coordinates are then transformed to device coordinates (integers) within the range (0, 0) to (x_{max}, y_{max}) for a particular device. To accommodate differences in scales and aspect ratios, normalized coordinates can be mapped into a square area of the output device so that proper proportions are maintained. On a video monitor, the remaining area of the screen is often used to display messages or list interactive program options.

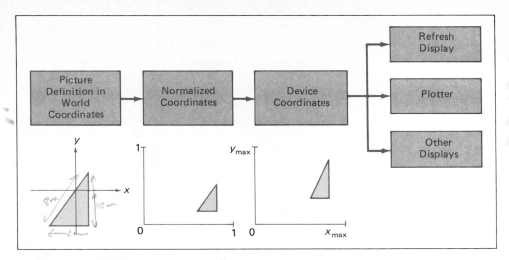

FIGURE 2–31
A transformation from a user's picture definition (world coordinates) to normalized coordinates is often performed by a graphics system in order to provide an interface to different types of output devices.

Graphics Functions

A general-purpose graphics package provides users with a variety of functions for creating and manipulating pictures. These routines can be categorized according to whether they deal with output, input, attributes, segment transformations, viewing, or general control.

The basic building blocks for pictures are referred to as **output primitives**. They include character strings and geometric entities, such as points, straight lines, polygons, and circles. Routines for generating output primitives provide the basic tools for constructing pictures.

Attributes are the properties of the output primitives. They include intensity and color specifications, line styles, text styles, and area-filling patterns. Functions within this category can be used to set attributes for groups of output primitives.

Given the primitive and attribute definition of a picture in world coordinates, a graphics package projects a selected view of the picture on an output device. **Viewing transformations** are used to specify the view that is to be presented and the portion of the output display area that is to be used.

Pictures can be subdivided into component parts, or **segments.** Each segment defines one logical unit of the picture. A scene with several objects could define the construction of each object in a separate named segment. Routines for processing segments carry out operations such as the creation, deletion, and transformation of segments.

Interactive graphics applications make use of various types of input devices, such as light pens, tablets, and joysticks. **Input operations** are used to control and process the data flow from these interactive devices.

Finally, a graphics package typically contains a number of housekeeping tasks, such as clearing a display screen or initializing parameters. We can lump the functions for carrying out these chores under the heading **control operations**.

Software Standards

The main goal of standardized graphics software is portability. When packages are designed with standard graphics functions, software can be moved easily to different types of hardware systems and used in different implementations and applications. Without standards, programs designed for one hardware system often cannot be transferred to another system without rewriting the software.

International and national standards-planning organizations in many countries have cooperated in an effort to develop a generally accepted standard for computer graphics. After considerable effort, this work on standards led to the development of the **Graphical Kernel System (GKS)**. This system has been adopted as the graphics software standard by the International Standards Organization (ISO) and by various national standards organizations, such as the American National Standards Institute (ANSI). Although GKS was originally designed as a two-dimensional graphics package, a three-dimensional GKS extension was subsequently developed.

The final GKS functions, adopted as standards, were influenced by several earlier proposed graphics standards. Particularly important among these earlier proposals is the **Core Graphics System** (or simply **Core**), developed by the Graphics Standards Planning Committee of SIGGRAPH, the Special Interest Group on Computer Graphics of the Association for Computing Machinery (ACM).

Standard graphics functions are defined as a set of abstract specifications, independent of any programming language. To implement a graphics standard in a particular programming language, a **language binding** must be defined. This binding defines the syntax for accessing the various graphics functions specified within the standard. For example, GKS specifies a function to generate a sequence of connected straight line segments with the descriptive title

```
polyline (n, x, y)
```

In FORTRAN 77, this procedure is implemented as a subroutine with the name GPL. A graphics programmer, using FORTRAN, would invoke this procedure with the subroutine call statement

```
CALL GPL (N, X, Y)
```

GKS language bindings have been defined for FORTRAN, Pascal, Ada, C, PL/I, and COBOL. Each language binding is defined to make best use of the corresponding language capabilities and to handle various syntax issues, such as data types, parameter passing, and errors.

In the following chapters, we use the standard functions defined in GKS as a framework for discussing basic graphics concepts and the design and application of graphics packages. Example programs are presented in Pascal to illustrate the algorithms for implementation of the graphics functions and to illustrate also some applications of the functions. Descriptive names for functions, based on the GKS definitions, are used whenever a graphics function is referenced in a program.

Although GKS presents a specification for basic graphics functions, it does not provide a standard methodology for a graphics interface to output devices. Nor does it specify methods for real-time modeling or for storing and transmitting pictures. Separate standards have been developed for each of these three areas. Standardization for device interface methods is given in the **Computer Graphics Interface (CGI)** system. The **Computer Graphics Metafile (CGM)** system specifies standards for archiving and transporting pictures. And the **Programmer's Hierarchical Interactive Graphics Standard (PHIGS)** defines standard methods for real-time modeling and other higher-level programming capabilities not considered by GKS.

REFERENCES   A general treatment of display devices is available in Sherr (1979). The conceptual design of display devices is discussed in Haber and Wilkinson (1982) and in Myers (1984). Storage tubes are surveyed in Preiss (1978), and flat panel devices are discussed in Margolin (1985), Slottow (1976), and Tannas (1978). Woodsford (1976) describes the operation of a laser system.

Three-dimensional terminals are discussed in Ikedo (1984) and in Vickers (1970). Stereoscopic methods are presented in Roese and McCleary (1979).

Further information on graphics processors and system architecture is available in Carson (1983), Clark (1982), Foley and van Dam (1982), Levy (1984), Matherat (1978), and Niimi (1984).

For additional discussions of software standards see Graphics Standards Planning Committee (1977 and 1979), Hatfield and Herzog (1982), and Warner (1981).

Hopgood, et al. (1983) present an excellent introduction to the two-dimensional GKS graphics standard. A comparison of GKS and CORE concepts is given in Encarnaçao (1980). Other sources of information on GKS include Bono, et al. (1982), Enderle, Kansy, and Pfaff (1984), and Mehl and Noll (1984).

EXERCISES

2–1. List the relative advantages and disadvantages of the major display technologies for video monitors: vector refresh systems, raster refresh systems, DVST systems, and plasma panels.

2–2. For each of the various display technologies used in video monitors, list some applications in which that type of monitor might be appropriate.

2–3. Compare the advantages and disadvantages of a three-dimensional monitor using a varifocal mirror with conventional "flat" monitors. What techniques could be used by a two-dimensional monitor to provide three-dimensional views of objects?

2–4. Determine the resolution (pixels per centimeter) in the x and y directions for the video monitor in use on your system. Calculate the aspect ratio for this monitor, and explain how relative proportions of objects can be maintained on this system.

2–5. Consider a raster system with a resolution of 1024 by 1024. What is the size of the raster (in bytes) needed to store 4 bits per pixel? How much storage is required if 8 bits per pixel are to be stored?

2–6. For each of the rasters in Ex. 2–5, how long would it take to load the raster if 10^5 bytes can be transferred per second?

2–7. For each raster size in Ex. 2–5, how many pixels are accessed per second by a display controller that refreshes the screen at a rate of 30 frames per second? What is the access time per pixel?

2–8. Video monitor screen size is often specified by the length of the screen diagonal. A 19-inch screen is one with a diagonal length of 19 inches. What is the diameter of each point on a 19-inch screen that displays 1024 by 1024 pixels with equal resolution in each direction?

2–9. Refresh rates for video monitors are sometimes expressed as scan rates in units of Hertz (Hz), which specify the number of scan lines that can be displayed per second. (A television scan rate of 15.75 kHz means that a screen with 525 scan lines can be refreshed 30 times per second.) If the vertical retrace time of a system is eight percent of the total refresh cycle time, what scan rate in kHz would be required to refresh a 1024 by 1024 monitor 60 times each second?

2–10. Compare the functions performed by display processors in random-scan and in raster-scan systems. How is the erasure of a selected section of a screen accomplished in each of these systems?

2-11. Define the world coordinate system that would be appropriate for each of several application areas. For each type of application, state the units to be used for the coordinate axes and the range of coordinate values appropriate for describing an object or scene (group of objects).

2-12. Outline the procedures that would be necessary to convert normalized device coordinates to the device coordinates used by various types of output devices.

2-13. Illustrate the distinction between a graphics package designed for a programmer and one intended for a nonprogrammer by describing the structure of ''commands'' available to a user of each package.

2-14. What are some of the important considerations in designing a standard graphics package?

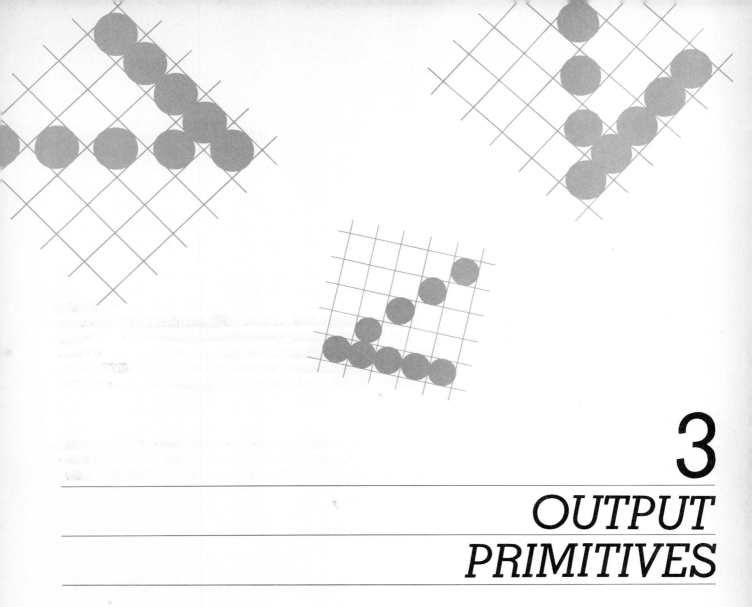

3

OUTPUT
PRIMITIVES

Procedures that display output primitives direct an output device to produce specified geometric structures at designated locations. Such procedures take coordinate input and invoke display algorithms to construct a geometric shape on a selected output device. The simplest geometric components of a picture are points and lines. Other types of output primitives are polygon areas, curved figures, and character strings. For each type of output primitive, we consider the basic techniques and algorithms for displaying the primitive on different types of graphics systems, such as raster and vector systems. The major emphasis, however, is on methods appropriate to interactive graphics systems. Output primitive functions in GKS are examined, following the discussion of the display-generation algorithms.

3–1 Points and Lines

Point plotting is implemented in a graphics package by converting the coordinate information from an application program into appropriate instructions for the output device in use. With a CRT monitor, for example, the electron beam is turned on to illuminate a phosphor dot at the screen location specified. This is accomplished with a black-and-white raster display by setting the bit value at the specified coordinate position within the frame buffer to 1. Then, as the electron beam sweeps across each horizontal scan line, it emits a burst of electrons (plots a point) whenever a value of 1 is encountered in the frame buffer. For random-scan monitors, the point-plotting instruction is stored in the display file, and coordinates are converted to voltage deflections that move the electron beam to that position during each refresh cycle.

Line-drawing instructions in an application program define component lines of a picture by specifying endpoint coordinates for each line. The output device is directed to fill in the straight-line path between each pair of endpoints. For analog devices, such as a pen plotter or a random-scan display with an analog vector generator, a straight line is drawn smoothly from one endpoint to the other. Linearly varying horizontal and vertical deflection voltages are generated that are proportional to the required changes in the x and y directions to produce the smooth line.

Digital devices, such as a raster-scan display, produce a line by plotting pixels between the two endpoints. Pixel positions are computed from the equation of the line, and the appropriate bits are set in the frame buffer. Reading from the frame buffer, the display controller then activates corresponding positions on the screen. Since pixels are plotted at integer positions, the plotted line may only approximate actual line positions between the specified endpoints. For example, if position $(10.33, 20.72)$ is calculated to be on the line, the pixel position $(10, 21)$ is plotted. This rounding of coordinate values to integers causes lines to be displayed with a stairstep appearance ("the jaggies"), which can be quite noticeable on lower-resolution systems (Fig. 3–1). The appearance of raster lines can be improved by using high-resolution systems and also by applying techniques that have been specially developed for smoothing point-generated lines.

FIGURE 3–1
Stairstep effect ("jaggies") produced when a line is generated as a series of pixel positions.

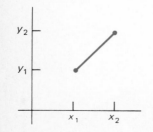

3–2 Line-Drawing Algorithms

The equation for a straight line can be stated in the form

$$y = m \cdot x + b \tag{3–1}$$

with m as the slope of the line and b as the y intercept. Given that the two endpoints of a line segment are specified as (x_1, y_1) and (x_2, y_2), as shown in Fig. 3–2, we can determine values for the slope m and y intercept b with the following calculations:

$$m = \frac{y_2 - y_1}{x_2 - x_1} \tag{3–2}$$

$$b = y_1 - m \cdot x_1 \tag{3–3}$$

Algorithms for displaying straight lines are based on the line equation 3–1 and the calculations given in Eqs. 3–2 and 3–3.

FIGURE 3–2
Line segment, specified by coordinate endpoints (x_1, y_1) and (x_2, y_2).

For any given x interval Δx along a line, we can compute the corresponding y interval Δy from Eq. 3–2 as

$$\Delta y = m \cdot \Delta x \qquad (3\text{–}4)$$

This equation forms the basis for determining deflection voltages in analog devices. The change in the horizontal deflection voltage is set proportional to Δx, and the change in the vertical deflection voltage is set proportional to the value of Δy calculated from Eq. 3–4. These deflections are then used to generate a line with slope m between the specified endpoints.

DDA Algorithm

The digital differential analyzer (DDA) is an algorithm for calculating pixel positions along a line, using Eq. 3–4. This is accomplished by taking unit steps with one coordinate and calculating corresponding values for the other coordinate.

We first consider a line with positive slope, as shown in Fig. 3–2. If the slope is less than or equal to 1, we take the change in the x-coordinate values to be 1 and compute each succeeding y-coordinate value as

$$y_{i+1} = y_i + m \qquad (3\text{–}5)$$

Subscript i takes integer values starting from 1, for the first point, and increases by 1 until the final endpoint is reached. Since m can be any real number, the calculated y values must be rounded to the nearest integer.

For lines with a positive slope greater than 1, we reverse the roles of x and y. That is, we move in unit y steps and calculate each succeeding x value as

$$x_{i+1} = x_i + \frac{1}{m} \qquad (3\text{–}6)$$

Equations 3–5 and 3–6 assume that we are proceeding along the line from the left endpoint to the right endpoint (Fig. 3–2). If these endpoints are reversed, so that the starting endpoint is at the right, then either we have $\Delta x = -1$ and

$$y_{i+1} = y_i - m \qquad (3\text{–}7)$$

or (when the slope is greater than 1) we have $\Delta y = -1$ with

$$x_{i+1} = x_i - \frac{1}{m} \qquad (3\text{–}8)$$

Equations 3–5 through 3–8 can also be used to calculate points along a line with a negative slope. If the absolute value of the slope is less than 1 and the start endpoint is at the left, we set $\Delta x = 1$ and calculate y values with Eq. 3–5. When the start endpoint is at the right (for the same slope), we set $\Delta x = -1$ and obtain y positions from Eq. 3–7. Similarly, when the absolute value of a negative slope is greater than 1, we use $\Delta y = -1$ and Eq. 3–8 or we use $\Delta y = 1$ and Eq. 3–6.

This algorithm is summarized in the following procedure, which accepts as input the line endpoints $(x1, y1)$ and $(x2, y2)$. Differences in the input coordinate values in each direction are calculated as parameters dx and dy. The difference with the greater magnitude determines the value of parameter *steps*, which specifies the number of points to be plotted along the line. Starting at position $(x1, y1)$, an amount is added to each coordinate to generate the next coordinate position. This is repeated *steps* times. If the magnitude of *dx* is greater than the magnitude of *dy* and *x1* is less than *x2*, the values of the increments in the *x* and *y* direction are 1 and *m*, respectively. If the greater change is in the *x* direction, but *x1* is greater than *x2*, then the values -1 and $-m$ are added to generate each new point on the line. Otherwise, we use a unit increment (or decrement) in the *y* direction and an *x* increment (or decrement) of $1/m$. We assume that points are to be plotted on a single-intensity system so that the command *set_pixel* is a call to the procedure for storing a pixel value of 1 ("on") in the frame buffer at the position specified by coordinate parameters *x* and *y*.

```
procedure dda (x1, y1, x2, y2 : integer);
  var
    dx, dy, steps, k : integer;
    x_increment, y_increment, x, y : real;
  begin
    dx := x2 - x1;
    dy := y2 - y1;
    if abs(dx) > abs(dy) then steps := abs(dx)
      else steps := abs(dy);
    x_increment := dx / steps;
    y_increment := dy / steps;
    x := x1; y := y1;
    set_pixel (round(x), round(y));
    for k := 1 to steps do begin
      x := x + x_increment;
      y := y + y_increment;
      set_pixel (round(x), round(y))
    end {for k}
  end; {dda}
```

The DDA algorithm is a faster method for calculating pixel positions than the direct use of Eq. 3–1. It eliminates the multiplication in Eq. 3–1 by taking advantage of raster characteristics, so that unit steps are taken in either the *x* or *y* direction to the next pixel location along the line. However, the calculations are slowed by the divisions needed to set increment values, the use of floating-point arithmetic, and the rounding operations.

Bresenham's Line Algorithm

A more efficient line algorithm to determine pixel positions, developed by Bresenham, finds the closest integer coordinates to the actual line path using only integer arithmetic. Figures 3–3 and 3–4 illustrate sections of a display screen where straight line segments are to be drawn. Pixel positions on the screen are represented by the rectangular areas between grid lines. In each of these examples, we need to decide between two pixel choices at each *x* position. Starting from the left endpoint of the line in Fig. 3–3, we need to determine whether the next point along the line is to be plotted at position (11, 10) or at (11, 11). Similarly, Fig. 3–4 shows a line path with a negative slope. Here, we need to decide between the points (51, 50) and (51, 49) as the next pixel position to be turned on. The next pixel to be plotted in each of these two examples is the one whose *y* value is closer to the actual *y* position on the line.

Again, we start with a line whose slope is positive and less than 1. Pixel positions along the line path can then be plotted by taking unit steps in the *x*

FIGURE 3–3
Section of a display screen where a straight line segment is to be displayed, starting from position (10, 10). Pixel positions are represented by the numbered rectangular areas.

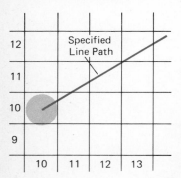

direction and determining the y-coordinate value of the nearest pixel to the line at each step. To establish the calculations needed in the algorithm, we consider the situation shown in Fig. 3–5. In this figure, we assume that pixel position (x_i, y_i) has been plotted and we now need to decide which is the next pixel to plot. The two choices for the next pixel position are at coordinates $(x_i + 1, y_i)$ and $(x_i + 1, y_i + 1)$.

In Fig. 3–6, the coordinate differences between the center of the two pixels and the line coordinate y are labeled d_1 and d_2. Position y can be calculated as

$$y = m(x_i + 1) + b$$

Then

$$d_1 = y - y_i$$
$$= m(x_i + 1) + b - y_i$$

and

$$d_2 = (y_i + 1) - y$$
$$= y_i + 1 - m(x_i + 1) - b$$

The difference between these two distances is

$$d_1 - d_2 = 2m(x_i + 1) - 2y_i + 2b - 1 \qquad (3\text{–}9)$$

We now define a parameter that provides a measure of the relative distances of two pixels from the actual position on a given line. Substituting $m = \Delta y/\Delta x$, we can rewrite Eq. 3–9 so that it involves only integer arithmetic:

$$p_i = \Delta x(d_1 - d_2)$$
$$= 2\Delta y \cdot x_i - 2\Delta x \cdot y_i + c \qquad (3\text{–}10)$$

The constant c has the value $2\Delta y + \Delta x(2b - 1)$ and could be calculated once for all points, but we will see that Eq. 3–10 can be revised to eliminate this constant. The parameter p_i has a negative value if the pixel at position y_i is closer to the line than the upper pixel. In that case, we select the lower pixel; otherwise the upper pixel is chosen.

Equation 3–10 is simplified by relating parameters for successive x intervals. Then the value for each succeeding parameter is obtained from the previously calculated parameter. We can rewrite Eq. 3–10 in the form

$$p_{i+1} = 2\Delta y \cdot x_{i+1} - 2\Delta x \cdot y_{i+1} + c$$

Subtracting Eq. 3–10 from this expression, we have

$$p_{i+1} - p_i = 2\Delta y(x_{i+1} - x_i) - 2\Delta x(y_{i+1} - y_i)$$

But $x_{i+1} = x_i + 1$, so that

$$p_{i+1} = p_i + 2\Delta y - 2\Delta x(y_{i+1} - y_i) \qquad (3\text{–}11)$$

This equation gives us a way to calculate the value of each successive parameter from the previous one. The first parameter, p_1, is obtained by evaluating Eq. 3–10 with (x_1, y_1) as the starting endpoint and $m = \Delta y/\Delta x$:

$$p_1 = 2\Delta y - \Delta x \qquad (3\text{–}12)$$

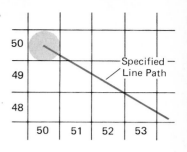

FIGURE 3–4
Section of a display screen where a line segment with negative slope is to be drawn. The left endpoint of the line is at position (50, 50).

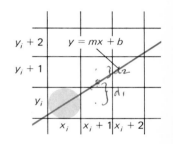

FIGURE 3–5
Section of the screen grid where a line passing through (x_i, y_i) is to be displayed.

FIGURE 3–6
Coordinate differences between pixel centers and the y position on the line path at $x_i + 1$.

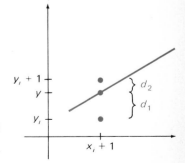

FIGURE 3–7
Bresenham's line algorithm.

1. Input line endpoints. Store left endpoint in (x_1, y_1). Store right endpoint in (x_2, y_2).
2. The first point to be selected for display is the left endpoint (x_1, y_1).
3. Calculate $\Delta x = x_2 - x_1$, $\Delta y = y_2 - y_1$, and $p_1 = 2\Delta y - \Delta x$. If $p_1 < 0$, the next point to be set is $(x_1 + 1, y_1)$. Otherwise, the next point is $(x_1 + 1, y_1 + 1)$.
4. Continue to increment the x coordinate by unit steps. At position $x_i + 1$, the coordinate to be selected, y_{i+1}, is either y_i or $y_i + 1$, depending on whether $p_i < 0$ or $p_i \geq 0$. The calculations for each parameter p depend on the last one. If $p_i < 0$, the form for the next parameter is

$$p_{i+1} = p_i + 2\Delta y$$

But if $p_i \geq 0$, the next parameter is

$$p_{i+1} = p_i + 2(\Delta y - \Delta x)$$

Then, if $p_{i+1} < 0$, the next y coordinate to be selected is y_{i+1}. Otherwise, select $y_{i+1} + 1$. (Coordinate y_{i+1} was determined to be either y_i or y_{i+1} by the parameter p_i in step 3.)
5. Repeat the procedures in step 4 until the x coordinate reaches x_2.

We summarize the steps for Bresenham's algorithm in Fig. 3–7, for a line with a positive slope less than 1. Since the constants $2\Delta y$, Δx, and $2(\Delta y - \Delta x)$ need be evaluated and stored only once, the arithmetic involves only integer addition and subtraction.

A procedure for implementing the algorithm of Fig. 3–7 is given in the following program. Endpoint coordinates for the line are input to this procedure through parameters $x1$, $y1$, $x2$, and $y2$. The call to *set_pixel* sets the position in the frame buffer for the point selected.

```
procedure bres_line (x1, y1, x2, y2 : integer);
  var
    dx, dy, x, y, x_end, p, const1, const2 : integer;
  begin
    dx := abs(x1 - x2);
    dy := abs(y1 - y2);
    p := 2 * dy - dx;
    const1 := 2 * dy;
    const2 := 2 * (dy - dx);
    {determine which point to use as start, which as end}
    if x1 > x2 then begin
        x := x2; y := y2;
        x_end := x1
      end {if x1 > x2}
    else begin
        x := x1; y := y1;
        x_end := x2
      end; {if x1 <= x2}
    set_pixel (x, y);
    while x < x_end do begin
        x := x + 1;
        if p < 0 then p := p + const1
```

```
        else begin
            y := y + 1;
            p := p + const2
          end; {else begin}
        set_pixel (x, y)
      end {while x < x_end}
   end; {bres_line}
```

So far we have limited the discussion to lines with a positive slope between 0 and 1. We can extend the algorithm to positive slopes greater than 1 by interchanging the roles of the x and y coordinates. That is, we step along the y direction in unit steps and calculate successive x positions. For negative slopes, the procedures are similar, except that now one coordinate decreases as the other increases.

Loading the Frame Buffer

Whenever points and lines are to be displayed with a raster system, the frame buffer contents must be modified to contain appropriate intensity values for the specified coordinate positions. We have assumed that this is accomplished with the *set_pixel* procedure. This procedure converts coordinate values to corresponding addresses within the raster and stores intensity values at these positions in the frame buffer array.

As a specific example, suppose that the frame buffer array is addressed in row-major order for a display monitor with coordinate locations varying from $(0, 0)$ at the lower left corner to (x_{max}, y_{max}) at the top right corner (Fig. 3–8). For a bilevel monitor (requiring one bit of storage per pixel), the bit address within the raster for a screen coordinate position (x, y) is calculated as

$$\text{ADDR}(x, y) = \text{ADDR}(0, 0) + y(x_{max} + 1) + x \qquad (3\text{–}13)$$

This calculation is implemented in the *set_pixel* procedure when a single point is to be plotted and when the intensity value for the starting endpoint of a line is to be set.

For a line-drawing algorithm, we can simplify the calculations in Eq. 3–13 for intermediate points along the line by taking advantage of the fact that we are making unit steps in the x and y directions. The calculation of addresses within the frame buffer for these points can be carried out by incrementing previously calcu-

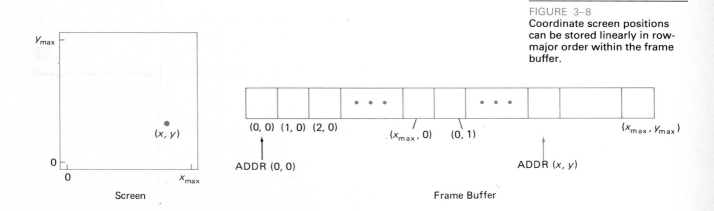

FIGURE 3–8
Coordinate screen positions can be stored linearly in row-major order within the frame buffer.

lated addresses. For example, from any position (x, y), the next address to be loaded in the raster (for a line with positive slope less than 1) can be calculated as one of the following two possibilities:

$$ADDR(x + 1, y) = ADDR(x, y) + 1 \qquad (3\text{–}14)$$

$$ADDR(x + 1, y + 1) = ADDR(x, y) + x_{\max} + 2 \qquad (3\text{–}15)$$

Similar recursive calculations for other coordinate changes can be obtained from Eq. 3–13. These relations provide an efficient method for addressing since the calculations involve only integer addition.

Methods for storing the frame buffer and implementing the *set_pixel* procedure depend on the capabilities of a particular system and the design requirements of the software package. With systems that make use of color or a range of intensity values, an additional input parameter for *set_pixel* would specify the intensity value to be stored in the frame buffer.

3–3 Antialiasing Lines

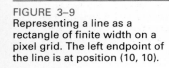

FIGURE 3–9
Representing a line as a rectangle of finite width on a pixel grid. The left endpoint of the line is at position (10, 10).

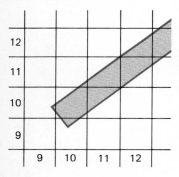

FIGURE 3–10
Unequal length lines displayed with the same number of pixels in each line.

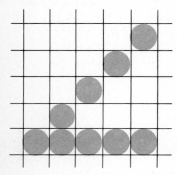

The raster algorithms we have discussed so far generate lines that have a jagged, or stairstep, appearance. Higher resolutions can be used to improve the appearance of lines, but this requires increased refresh buffer sizes, and this approach does not completely remove the stairstep effect. Object representations mapped onto a raster are subject to distortions because of **aliasing.** The digitization process rounds coordinate points on the object to discrete integer pixel positions in the raster. We can modify line-drawing algorithms to compensate for this raster effect by adding **antialiasing** routines that smooth out the display of a line on a video monitor. Antialiasing techniques remove the stairstep appearance by adjusting pixel intensities along the line path.

One method for developing an antialiasing routine is based on **sampling theory.** The idea behind this method is that natural geometric entities, such as points and lines plotted on a display screen, have finite dimensions. A pixel is not an infinitesimal mathematical point but a spot of light covering a small area of the screen. And lines have a width approximately equal to that of a pixel. When natural objects are digitized onto a rectangular grid (raster), the grid areas are "sampled" to determine appropriate light-intensity values. Raster systems that can display more than two intensity levels can use this method to adjust pixels so that each grid area is assigned the proper intensity.

Figure 3–9 shows a line represented with finite width on a pixel grid. Pixel areas are assumed to be square, and the width of the line is set equal to the width of a pixel. Instead of plotting the line with a single pixel at each x position, all pixels that are overlapped by the line area are displayed with an intensity proportional to the area of overlap. In the example shown, pixels at positions (11, 10) and (11, 11) are about half covered by the line. So each of these pixels is set to an intensity level of approximately 50 percent of the maximum. Similarly, the pixel at location (9, 10) is set to an intensity of about 10 percent of maximum. Although this method for antialiasing can improve the appearance of lines, the calculations are time-consuming.

Adjusting pixel intensities along the length of a line also compensates for another raster effect, illustrated in Fig. 3–10. Both lines are plotted with the same number of pixels, yet the diagonal line is longer than the horizontal line by a factor

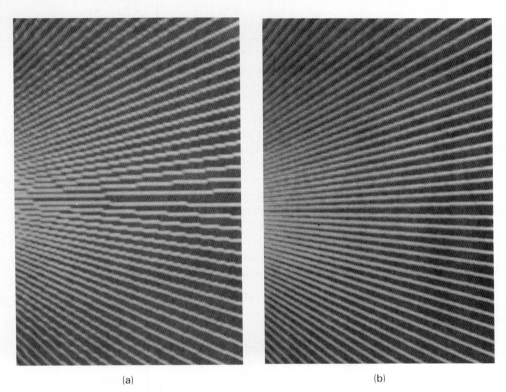

(a)   (b)

FIGURE 3–11
Jagged lines (a), plotted on the Merlin 9200 system, are smoothed (b) with an antialiasing technique called pixel phasing. This technique increases the number of addressable points on the system from 768 × 576 to 3072 × 2304. Courtesy Megatek Corp.

of $\sqrt{2}$. The visual effect of this is that the diagonal line appears less bright than the horizontal line, since the diagonal line is displayed with a lower intensity per unit length. A line-drawing algorithm could be adapted to compensate for this effect by adjusting the intensity of each line according to its slope. Horizontal and vertical lines would be displayed with the lowest intensity, while 45° lines would be given the highest intensity. However, if antialiasing techniques are applied to a display, intensities are automatically compensated. When the finite width of lines is taken into account, pixel intensities are adjusted so that lines display a total intensity proportional to their length.

Another technique for antialiasing lines is the **pixel phasing** approach developed by the Megatek Corporation. Intensities of line edges are adjusted by "micro-positioning" of the electron beam. The systems incorporating this technique are designed so that individual pixel positions can be shifted by a fraction of a pixel diameter. By allowing shifts of 1/4, 1/2, and 3/4 of a pixel diameter, a line can be displayed by plotting points closer to the true path of the line. These systems also allow the size of individual pixels to be altered. Figure 3–11 illustrates antialiasing of lines using the pixel phasing technique.

3–4 Line Command

Graphics packages can be designed to include one command for basic line drawing and another for plotting individual points. However, the usefulness of a separate command to plot a single point is limited. Most graphics applications involve the construction of figures with straight line segments. Moreover, a single command can serve both purposes, since a point can be considered as a very short line segment.

A command for plotting both points and lines can be defined in the form:

```
polyline (n, x, y)
```

For our purposes, we will assume that the *polyline* function is to be provided as the basic output primitive command in a graphics package. This command is used to specify a single point, a single straight line segment, or a series of connected line segments, depending on the value assigned to parameter *n*. Coordinate values for the line endpoints (or single point) are stored in arrays *x* and *y*.

Implementation of the *polyline* function is through the *set_pixel* and line-drawing procedures, such as the Bresenham algorithm. When a single point is to be plotted, the *set_pixel* routine is invoked. When a line, or series of lines, is to be drawn, *polyline* causes the line-drawing procedure to be executed.

For point generation, a user would set the value of *n* at 1 and give the (x, y) coordinate values in $x[1]$ and $y[1]$. As an example, the statements

```
x[1] := 150;
y[1] := 100;
polyline (1, x, y);
```

specify that a single point is to be plotted at coordinate position (150, 100). We assume that coordinate references in the *polyline* command are stated as **absolute coordinate** values. This means that the values specified are the actual point positions in the coordinate system in use.

Some graphics systems employ line (and point) commands with **relative coordinate** specifications. In this case, coordinate values are stated as offsets from the last position referenced (called the **current position**). For example, if location (3, 2) is the last position that has been referenced in an application program, a relative coordinate specification of $(2, -1)$ corresponds to an absolute position of (5, 1).

A straight line segment is obtained with a command such as *polyline* by setting *n* to 2 and assigning values for the two coordinate endpoints of the line to the *x* and *y* arrays. The following example program segment specifies a line with endpoints at (50, 100) and (250, 25).

```
x[1] := 50;
y[1] := 100;
x[2] := 250;
y[2] := 25;
polyline (2, x, y);
```

With graphics packages employing the concept of current position, a user need only give one coordinate point in a line-drawing statement. This signals the system to display a line from the current position to the given coordinates. The current position is then updated to the coordinate location stated in the line command. A series of connected lines is produced with such packages by a sequence of line commands, one for each line to be drawn.

Since any number of points can be specified with the *polyline* function, a user has the capability to generate a sequence of connected line segments with one statement. This is done by setting *n* equal to the number of line endpoints and storing the endpoint coordinates in arrays *x* and *y*. The graphics package then displays a series of $n - 1$ line segments that connect the n adjacent coordinates from position $(x[1], y[1])$ to position $(x[n], y[n])$.

We can implement the *polyline* command for $n > 2$ with a procedure that makes repeated calls to the line-drawing algorithm. Each successive call to the line-drawing algorithm passes the coordinate pair needed to plot the next line segment. The line-drawing algorithm is accessed by this procedure a total of $n - 1$ times.

3–5 Fill Areas

When shading or color patterns are to be applied to areas of a scene or graph, it is convenient for a user to be able to specify the area that is to be filled. Although fill patterns could be applied to the interiors of polygon borders defined with a line command, processing is simplified if a separate procedure is used to define a fill area. This approach allows a designated area to be immediately flagged as one that is to be displayed with a specified interior.

We introduce the following command to define a polygon fill area:

    fill_area (n, x, y)

The area to be filled is inside the boundary defined by the series of n connected line segments from $(x[1], y[1])$ to $(x[n], y[n])$ and back to $(x[1], y[1])$.

Implementation of the *fill_area* command in a graphics package depends on the type of fill that is to be used to display the area. A user might want the area left blank or filled with a solid color or some pattern. When the interior of the area is left blank, *fill_area* simply produces the boundary outline. This is analogous to using the *polyline* procedure with the starting and ending coordinates set to the same values.

3–6 Circle-Generating Algorithms

Since the circle is a common component in many types of pictures and graphs, procedures for generating circles (and ellipses) are often included in graphics packages. The basic parameters that define a circle are the center coordinates (xc, yc) and the radius r (Fig. 3–12). We can express the equation of a circle in several forms, using either Cartesian or polar coordinate parameters. Figure 3–13 shows the relationship between Cartesian and polar parameters.

Circle Equations

A standard form for the circle equation is the Pythagorean theorem:

$$(x - xc)^2 + (y - yc)^2 = r^2 \qquad (3–16)$$

This equation could be used to draw a circle by stepping along the x axis in unit steps from $xc - r$ to $xc + r$ and calculating the corresponding y values at each position as

$$y = yc \pm \sqrt{r^2 - (x - xc)^2} \qquad (3–17)$$

Obviously, this approach involves considerable computation at each step, and the

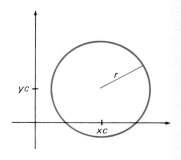

FIGURE 3–12
Circle with center coordinates *(xc, yc)* and radius *r*.

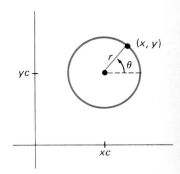

FIGURE 3–13
Relationship between Cartesian and polar coordinates.

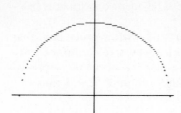

FIGURE 3–14
Positive half of a circle plotted
with Eq. 3–17 and *(xc, yc)* =
(0, 0).

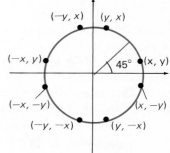

FIGURE 3–15
Symmetry of a circle.
Calculation of a point *(x, y)* on
the first one-eighth circle
segment also yields the seven
additional points shown on the
circle.

spacing between plotted pixel positions is not uniform, as demonstrated in Fig. 3–14. We could adjust the spacing by interchanging x and y (stepping through y values and calculating x values) whenever the absolute value of the slope of the circle became greater than 1. But this adds computations and checking to the algorithm.

One way to eliminate the unequal spacing associated with Eq. 3–17 is to calculate points along the circular boundary using polar coordinates. Expressing the circle equation in parametric polar form yields the pair of equations

$$x = xc + r \cdot \cos\theta$$
$$y = yc + r \cdot \sin\theta \qquad (3\text{–}18)$$

When a display is generated with these equations using a fixed angular value for θ, a circle is plotted with equally spaced points along the circumference. The step size chosen for θ depends on the application. For circle generation with a raster-scan system, we can set the step size at $1/r$ and calculate closely spaced pixel positions. This step size gives us pixels that are approximately one unit apart.

An improvement in these methods can be made by taking advantage of the symmetry of circles. A given point on the circumference can be mapped into several other circle points by interchanging coordinates and alternating the sign of the coordinate values. As illustrated in Fig. 3–15, a point at position (x, y) on a one-eighth circle sector can be used to plot the other seven points shown. Using this approach, we could generate all pixel positions around a circle for a raster display by calculating only the points within the sector from $x = 0$ to $x = y$.

Determining pixel positions along a circle circumference using either Eq. 3–17 or Eq. 3–18 requires a good deal of computation time. The Pythagorean theorem approach involves multiplications and square root calculations, while the parametric equations contain multiplications and trigonometric calculations. We can improve the efficiency of circle generation by using a method that reduces the computations as much as possible to integer arithmetic.

Bresenham's Circle Algorithm

As in the line-generating algorithm, integer positions along a circular path can be obtained by determining which of two pixels is nearer the circle at each step. To simplify the algorithm statements, we first consider a circle centered at the coordinate origin ($xc = 0$ and $yc = 0$). We also calculate the points for a one-eighth circle segment, assuming that we are going to get the remaining points by symmetry for storage in a raster. (A random-scan system with a vector generator could extend the calculations through one complete cycle.) Unit steps are taken in the x direction, starting from $x = 0$ and ending when $x = y$. The starting coordinate in our algorithm is then $(0, r)$.

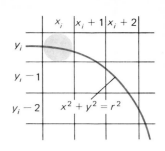

The situation at some arbitrary step in the algorithm is shown in Fig. 3–16. We assume that position (x_i, y_i) has been determined to be closer to the circle path. The next position is then either $(x_i + 1, y_i)$ or $(x_i + 1, y_i - 1)$.

From Eq. 3–16, the actual y value on the circle path is determined as

$$y^2 = r^2 - (x_i + 1)^2$$

Figure 3–17 illustrates the relationship between y and the integer coordinate values, y_i and $y_i - 1$. A measure of the difference in coordinate positions can be defined in terms of the square of the y values as

$$\begin{aligned} d_1 &= y_i^2 - y^2 \\ &= y_i^2 - r^2 + (x_i + 1)^2 \end{aligned} \tag{3–19}$$

and

$$\begin{aligned} d_2 &= y^2 - (y_i - 1)^2 \\ &= r^2 - (x_i + 1)^2 - (y_i - 1)^2 \end{aligned} \tag{3–20}$$

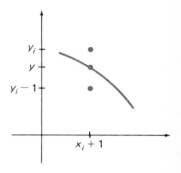

FIGURE 3–17
Coordinate differences between pixel centers and the y position on a circle at $x_i + 1$.

We now set up a parameter for determining the next coordinate position as the difference between d_1 and d_2:

$$\begin{aligned} p_i &= d_1 - d_2 \\ &= 2(x_i + 1)^2 + y_i^2 + (y_i - 1)^2 - 2r^2 \end{aligned} \tag{3–21}$$

If p_i is negative, we select the pixel at position y_i. Otherwise, we select the pixel at location $y_i - 1$.

The test for selecting the next pixel holds whether the actual path passes above y_i or below $y_i - 1$, as shown in Fig. 3–18. For the first case, Fig. 3–18 (a),

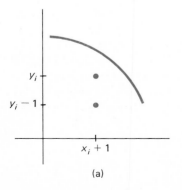

(a)

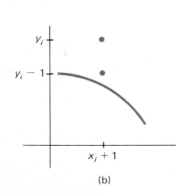

(b)

FIGURE 3–18
Possible pixel positions: (a) Both pixel centers are below the circle path, and (b) both pixel centers are above the circle path.

we have $d_1 < 0$, $d_2 > 0$, and $p_i < 0$, so that the point at y_i would be selected. In the second case, Fig. 3–18 (b), $d_1 > 0$ and $d_2 < 0$. Now $p_i > 0$, and the point at $y_i - 1$ is selected.

A recursive form for the parameter p is obtained by evaluating p_{i+1} in terms of p_i:

$$p_{i+1} = 2[(x_i + 1) + 1]^2 + y_{i+1}^2 + (y_{i+1} - 1)^2 - 2r^2$$

This expression can be written in terms of Eq. 3–21 as

$$p_{i+1} = p_i + 4x_i + 6 + 2(y_{i+1}^2 - y_i^2) - 2(y_{i+1} - y_i) \tag{3–22}$$

The y position y_{i+1} is either the same as y_i or the same as $y_i - 1$, depending on the value of p_i. Starting from p_1, the algorithm determines each successive p parameter from the preceding one. We obtain p_1 by setting $(x_1, y_1) = (0, r)$ in Eq. 3–21:

$$p_1 = 3 - 2r \tag{3–23}$$

Figure 3–19 summarizes the steps for calculating integer coordinates closest to the defined circle. To generalize the algorithm so that a circle with an arbitrary center position can be plotted, we simply add xc to each successive x value and add yc to each calculated y value.

FIGURE 3–19
Bresenham's circle algorithm.

1. Select the first position for display as
$$(x_1, y_1) = (0, r)$$
2. Calculate the first parameter as
$$p_1 = 3 - 2r$$
   If $p_1 < 0$, the next position is $(x_1 + 1, y_1)$. Otherwise, the next position is $(x_1 + 1, y_1 - 1)$.
3. Continue to increment the x coordinate by unit steps, and calculate each succeeding parameter p from the preceding one. If for the previous parameter we found that $p_i < 0$, then
$$p_{i+1} = p_i + 4x_i + 6.$$
   Otherwise (for $p_i \geq 0$),
$$p_{i+1} = p_i + 4(x_i - y_i) + 10$$
   Then, if $p_{i+1} < 0$, the next point selected is $(x_i + 2, y_{i+1})$. Otherwise, the next point is $(x_i + 2, y_{i+1} - 1)$. The y coordinate is $y_{i+1} = y_i$, if $p_i < 0$ or $y_{i+1} = y_i - 1$, if $p_i \geq 0$.
4. Repeat the procedures in step 3 until the x and y coordinates are equal.

Although a multiplication is required in the calculation of each parameter, the multiplier is a power of 2, so the multiplication can be implemented as a logical shift operation. All other operations are simply integer additions or subtractions. The following procedure is a coding for this circle algorithm. Input to the procedure are the coordinates for the circle center and the radius. The procedure loads the frame buffer array with points along the circle circumference by calls to the *set_pixel* operation.

```
procedure bres_circle (x_center, y_center, radius : integer);
   var
      p, x, y : integer;
```

```
procedure plot_circle_points;
  begin
    set_pixel (x_center + x, y_center + y);
    set_pixel (x_center - x, y_center + y);
    set_pixel (x_center + x, y_center - y);
    set_pixel (x_center - x, y_center - y);
    set_pixel (x_center + y, y_center + x);
    set_pixel (x_center - y, y_center + x);
    set_pixel (x_center + y, y_center - x);
    set_pixel (x_center - y, y_center - x)
  end;   {plot_circle_points}

begin   {bres_circle}
  x := 0;
  y := radius;
  p := 3 - 2 * radius;
  while x < y do begin
      plot_circle_points;
      if p < 0 then p := p + 4 * x + 6
      else begin
          p := p + 4 * (x - y) + 10;
          y := y - 1
        end;   {if p not < 0}
      x := x + 1
    end;   {while x < y}
    if x = y then plot_circle_points
  end;   {bres_circle}
```

Ellipses

A circle-drawing algorithm can be extended to plot either circles or ellipses. In Fig. 3–20 we show one orientation for an ellipse, with r_1 labeling the semimajor axis and r_2 as the semiminor axis. The standard form for the elliptical equation is

$$\left(\frac{x - xc}{r_1}\right)^2 + \left(\frac{y - yc}{r_2}\right)^2 = 1 \qquad (3\text{–}24)$$

Using polar coordinates r and θ, we can also write the elliptical equations in parametric form:

$$x = xc + r_1 \cdot \cos\theta$$
$$y = yc + r_2 \cdot \sin\theta \qquad (3\text{–}25)$$

Bresenham's algorithm can be modified to generate elliptical shapes by using Eq. 3–24, instead of the circle equation, in the evaluation of parameter p_i. That is, for an ellipse centered at the origin, we can express y values in the form

$$y^2 = r_2^2 \left(1 - \frac{x^2}{r_1^2}\right) \qquad (3\text{–}26)$$

The only difference in the algorithm is in the form of the p parameters. An ellipse is plotted at an arbitrary position by adding offsets to the output x and y values, as in the generation of circle positions.

To provide users with the capability for generating ellipses (and circles), a graphics package could include a command of the form

```
ellipse (xc, yc, r1, r2)
```

FIGURE 3–20
Ellipse centered at *(xc, yc)* with semimajor axis r_1 and semiminor axis r_2.

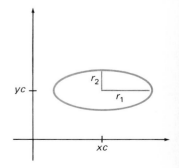

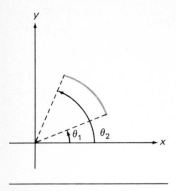

Coordinates for the ellipse center are assigned to parameters xc and yc, and the semimajor and semiminor axes are specified in $r1$ and $r2$. If the values assigned to $r1$ and $r2$ are equal, the system displays a circle. These parameters are passed to the ellipse-generating algorithm, which plots the specified figure.

Commands to generate circles and ellipses often include the capability of drawing curve sections by specifying parameters for the line endpoints. Expanding the parameter list allows specification of the beginning and ending angular values for an arc, as illustrated in Fig. 3–21.

3–7 Other Curves

Procedures to display various curves use methods similar to those that generate circles and ellipses. Commonly encountered curves include sine functions, exponential functions, polynomials, probability distributions, and spline functions.

If we can express a curve in functional form, $y = f(x)$, values for y can be calculated and plotted over a specified interval for x. The coordinate values must be rounded to the nearest integer, and the curve path can be filled in with either individual points or straight line segments. For most applications, curves approximated with line segments are more convenient. A point-plotting method leaves gaps in the curve in areas where the magnitude of the slope is greater than 1. To avoid the gaps with a point-plotting method means that we must obtain the inverse function, $x = f^{-1}(y)$, and calculate values of x for given y values whenever the magnitude of the slope becomes large.

Symmetry considerations improve the efficiency of some curve-generating algorithms. Many curves have repeated patterns, so it may be possible to obtain more than one point on the curve with a single calculation. Parabolas and the normal probability distribution are symmetric about a center point, while all points within one cycle of a sine curve can be generated from the points in a 90° interval.

For a curve defined by a data set of discrete coordinate points, we must graph the curve in other ways. One method is simply to plot the individual data points and connect them with straight line segments. Another approach is to use curve-fitting techniques to obtain a curve approximation to the data points. Special curve-fitting methods have been devised for design applications, and we return to this topic in Chapter 10.

1	1	1	1	1	1	0	0
0	1	1	0	0	1	1	0
0	1	1	0	0	1	1	0
0	1	1	1	1	1	0	0
0	1	1	0	0	1	1	0
0	1	1	0	0	1	1	0
1	1	1	1	1	1	0	0
0	0	0	0	0	0	0	0

3–8 Character Generation

Rectangular-grid patterns are typically used to define and plot characters. Figure 3–22 illustrates a bit pattern for the letter B, defined on an 8 by 8 dot matrix for use with a bilevel raster system. When this pattern is copied to some area of the frame buffer, the 1 bits designate which pixel positions are to be displayed on the monitor. Rectangular grids for character definitions vary from about 5 by 7 to 9 by 14 or more and are used with both raster and vector systems, although some vector systems generate characters with line segments. Standard character patterns for letters, numbers, and other symbols are predefined and stored in read-only memory. With some systems, additional user-defined character patterns can be accommodated, allowing specialized fonts.

In addition to allowing users to define special characters, graphics packages can provide options for various types of character manipulation. Characters can be shifted relative to each other to provide special effects or spacing, and character patterns can be rotated or scaled to vary their size.

User commands to output character strings are provided with all graphics packages. A basic character-string command can be defined as

```
text (x, y, string)
```

Parameter *string* is assigned any character sequence, which is displayed starting at **text position** (x, y). For example, the statement

```
text (100, 450, "population distribution")
```

could be used as a label on a distribution graph.

Text position (x, y) sets the coordinate location for the lower left corner of the first character of the horizontal string to be displayed. This provides the reference for copying the character grid definitions onto the frame buffer. The *text* command is implemented by a routine that places the character bit patterns into the raster array, one at a time from left to right starting at the text position. Graphics packages often allow for other string orientations, such as vertical lettering. For these options, the text position (x, y) may be interpreted differently by the *text* routine.

Another convenient character command is one that places a designated character (marker symbol) at one or more selected positions. This command can be defined similarly to the line command:

```
polymarker (n, x, y)
```

Parameters n, x, and y in *polymarker* are given the same meaning as in the *polyline* command. The difference is that *polymarker* causes a predefined character to be placed at each of the n coordinate positions specified in arrays x and y. The type of symbol used in *polymarker* depends on the particular implementation, but we assume for now that an asterisk is to be used. Figure 3–23 illustrates plotting of a data set with the statement

```
polymarker (6, x, y)
```

The implementation of *polymarker* is carried out by a routine that repeatedly copies the marker grid definition into the frame buffer at the designated coordinate position. In this function, the coordinate specifications set the position for the center of the character grid.

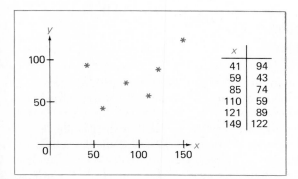

x	
41	94
59	43
85	74
110	59
121	89
149	122

FIGURE 3–23
Sequence of data points specified with the polymarker command.

3-9 Instruction Sets for Display Processors

Output primitive functions stated in an application program are converted by the graphics system into a form suitable for the display processor to generate the picture on an output device. The specific instruction set used by the display processor to generate output depends on the type of device in use.

Raster-Scan Systems

A number of registers are made available to the processors in a raster system to store coordinate positions and various instructions. Four registers can be used to hold coordinate values for line endpoints, circle and ellipse parameters, and positions for character strings or markers. The size of these registers is determined by the resolution of the system. If the raster is designed to display 1024 by 1024 pixels, coordinate registers need 10 bits to store the coordinate values from 0 to 1023. Additional registers are used to store output operations and the instructions for processing the output primitive commands. Typical size of the instruction registers is from 12 to 24 bits.

Instruction formats for the display processor are organized into opcode and address fields. The opcode field determines the type of operation to be performed, such as loading a register, drawing a line, or displaying a character. Address fields are used to specify register or memory locations.

Each output primitive command in an application program is compiled into a corresponding instruction format. The scan-conversion routine then loads the instruction into a register and processes it using an appropriate hardware-implemented procedure, such as the Bresenham line-drawing algorithm or retrieval of a character pattern. Pixel intensity values generated by the scan-conversion procedure are then loaded into the frame buffer at the specified positions.

Intensity values in the raster are used by a refresh procedure to display the picture on the video monitor. Two registers are used to store the coordinates of a pixel. Initially, the x register is set to 0 and the y register is set to the coordinate value for the top of the screen (say 1023). The value stored in the raster for this pixel position is then used to adjust the intensity of the electron beam of a refresh CRT. Then the x register is incremented by 1, and the process repeated for the next pixel on the top scan line. This procedure is repeated for each pixel along the scan line. After the last pixel on the top scan line has been processed, the x register is reset to 0 and the y register is decremented by 1. Pixels along this scan line are processed in turn, and the procedure is repeated for each scan line. When the pixels along the bottom scan line ($y = 0$) have been displayed, the y register is reset to the top value and the refresh process starts over. This refresh process is carried out at a rate of 30 to 60 frames per second.

Random-Scan Systems

Instruction formats for vector systems are similar to those for raster systems. The major difference is that a display file of instructions is created for the refresh process instead of loading a frame buffer.

To carry out the refresh process, the first instruction in the display file is loaded into a register. Appropriate subroutines are then referenced to display a line or character string on the output device, using either analog or digital vector-generation techniques. Next, an instruction counter is incremented, and the next instruction is retrieved from the display file and processed. After all instructions in the display file have been processed, the instruction counter is reset, and the refresh procedure is repeated from the beginning of the file. Depending on the type of vector generator used, a line can be refreshed by a random-scan system at rates varying from a few microseconds to a tenth of a microsecond.

3–10 Summary

Table 3–1 lists the output primitives discussed in this chapter and the command formats for displaying them from an application program. These primitives provide the basic tools for constructing displays with straight lines, areas, curves, and text.

TABLE 3–1.
Summary of Output Primitives

Output Primitive Function	Description
polyline (n, x, y)	Defines a connected sequence of n − 1 line segments. The n endpoints of the lines are specified in the arrays x and y. If n = 1, a point is specified.
fill_area (n, x, y)	Defines a polygon fill area with the coordinates for the n polygon vertices specified in arrays x and y.
text (x, y, string)	Displays a character string starting at coordinate position (x, y). The string to be displayed is specified in parameter string.
polymarker (n, x, y)	Displays a series of predefined characters at each of the n coordinate positions specified in arrays x and y.
ellipse (xc, yc, r1, r2)	Defines an ellipse centered at position (xc, yc) with axes r1 and r2. A circle is displayed if r1 = r2.

3–11 Applications

Following are some example programs illustrating the use of output primitives. The first program produces a line graph of a household's natural gas consumption for a year. Output of this procedure is drawn in Fig. 3–24.

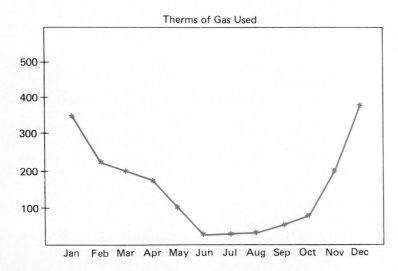

Therms of Gas Used

FIGURE 3–24
A plot of data points output by procedure line_graph.

{*The following are already defined as constants—
max_points, grid_left, grid_right, grid_top, grid_bottom,
grid_height, grid_center, first_mark, and interval.
Convert_to_string is a predefined function that returns
string equivalent of an integer; Max returns the maximum
value found in the array of data values*}

```
type
  data = array [1..12] of integer;
  points = array [1..max_points] of integer;

procedure line_graph (therms : data);
  var   x, y : points;

  procedure axes_and_labels;
    var   k : integer;
    begin
      x[1] := grid_left;      y[1] := grid_bottom;
      x[2] := grid_right;     y[2] := grid_bottom;
      x[3] := grid_right;     y[3] := grid_top;
      x[4] := grid_left;      y[4] := grid_top;
      fill_area (4, x, y);   {make outer box}
      {put title and bottom labels}
      text (grid_center − 72, grid_top + 6, 'Therms of Gas Used');
      text (grid_left, 0,
            'Jan Feb Mar Apr May Jun Jul Aug Sep Oct Nov Dec');
      {make tic marks and labels on left}
      x[1] := grid_left − 3;
      x[2] := grid_left + 3;
      for k := 1 to 5 do begin
        y[1] := grid_bottom + k * 32;
        y[2] := y[1];
        polyline (2, x, y);
        text (1, y[1] − 4, convert_to_string(k*100))
      end
    end; {axes_and_labels}

  procedure graph_data;
    var
      marker_placement : real;
      k, data_range : integer;

    begin
      data_range := max(therms)
      for k := 1 to 12 do begin
        marker_placement := grid_height * (therms[k]/data_range);
        y[k] := grid_bottom + round(marker_placement);
        x[k] := first_mark + interval * (k − 1)
      end;
      polymarker (12, x, y);
      polyline (12, x, y)
    end; {graph_data}

  begin {line_graph}
    axes_and_labels;
    graph_data
  end; {line_graph}
```

Pie charts are used to show the percentage contribution of individual parts to the whole. The next procedure constructs a pie chart, with the number and relative size of the slices determined by input. A sample output from this procedure appears in Fig. 3–25.

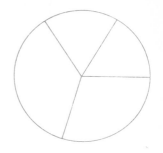

FIGURE 3–25
Output generated from procedure pie_chart.

```
const
   max_slice = 8;
type
   data = array [1..max_slice] of integer;

procedure pie_chart (xc, yc, radius, slices : integer; data_values : data);
   var
      total, k, : integer;
      last_slice, new_slice : real;
   begin
      ellipse (xc, yc, radius, radius);
      total := 0;
      for k := 1 to slices do total := total + data_values[k];
      x[1] := xc;        {every slice line will start at pie center}
      y[1] := yc;
      last_slice := 0;
      for k := 1 to slices do begin
         new_slice := 6.28 * data_values[k] / total + last_slice;
         x[2] := round(xc + radius * cos(new_slice));
         y[2] := round(yc + radius * sin(new_slice));
         polyline (2, x, y);
         last_slice := new_slice    {update last slice}
      end
   end;   {pie_chart}
```

Some variations on the circle equations are output by this next procedure. The shapes shown in Fig. 3–26 are generated by varying the radius r of a circle. Depending on how we vary r, we can produce a spiral, cardioid, limacon, or other similar figure.

FIGURE 3–26
Curved figures produced with procedure draw_shape.

```
type
   shape = (cardioid, three_leaf, spiral, four_leaf, limacon);

procedure draw_shape (figure : shape; xc, yc, a, b : integer);
   {xc, yc is figure center. a and b are used to compute radius}
   var
      theta, dtheta, r : real;
   begin
      theta := 0;
      dtheta := 1 / a;   {angle increment}
      {set first point for figure}
      y[1] := yc;
      case figure of
         cardioid   : x[1] := round(xc + a * 2);
```

```
three_leaf : x[1] := round(xc + a);
spiral     : x[1] := xc;
four_leaf  : x[1] := round(xc + a);
limacon    : x[1] := round(xc + b + a)

end;
{compute other points}
while theta < 6.28 do begin
    case figure of
        cardioid   : r := a * (1 + cos(theta));
        three_leaf : r := a * cos(3 * theta);
        spiral     : r := a * theta;
        four_leaf  : r := a * cos(2 * theta);
        limacon    : r := b + a * cos(theta)

    end;   {case}
    x[2] := round(xc + r * cos(theta));
    y[2] := round(yc + r * sin(theta));
    polyline (2, x, y);
    x[1] := x[2];              {save the current point}
    y[1] := y[2];
    theta := theta + dtheta    {update the angle}
    end   {while theta}
end;   {draw_shape}
```

REFERENCES   Sources of information on algorithms for generating output primitives include Bresenham (1965 and 1977), McIlroy (1983), and Pavlidis (1982).

Antialiasing techniques are discussed in Crow (1981), Fujimoto and Iwata (1983), Korein and Badler (1983), Pitteway and Watkinson (1980), and Turkowski (1982).

For additional information on output primitive functions in GKS see Enderle, Kansy, and Pfaff (1984) and Hopgood, et al. (1983).

EXERCISES   3–1. Implement the *polyline* command using the DDA algorithm, given any number (*n*) of input points. A single point is to be plotted when $n = 1$.

3–2. Extend Bresenham's line algorithm to generate lines with any slope. Implement the *polyline* command using this algorithm as a routine that displays the set of straight lines between the *n* input points. For $n = 1$, the routine displays a single point.

3–3. Implement the *set_pixel* routine in Bresenham's line algorithm of Ex. 3–2 so that the frame buffer is loaded using efficient address-calculation methods, such as those in Eqs. 3–14 and 3–15.

3–4. Modify a line-drawing algorithm so that the intensity of the output line is set according to its slope. That is, by adjusting pixel intensities according to the value of the slope, all lines are displayed with the same intensity per unit length.

3–5. Implement an antialiasing procedure by extending Bresenham's line algorithm to adjust pixel intensities in the vicinity of a line path.

3–6. Modify Bresenham's circle algorithm to display any ellipse, as specified by input values for the ellipse center and the major and minor axes. Write a program to implement this algorithm on your system.

3–7. Implement the *set_pixel* operation in the program of Ex. 3–6 using efficient methods for loading the frame buffer, such as those in Eqs. 3–14 and 3–15.

3–8. Outline a method for antialiasing a circle boundary. How would this method be modified to antialias elliptical boundaries?

3–9. Write a routine to implement the *text* function.

3–10. Write a routine to implement the *polymarker* function.

3–11. Devise an efficient algorithm that takes advantage of symmetry properties to display a sine function.

3–12. Extend the algorithm of Ex. 3–11 to display the function describing damped harmonic motion:

$$y = A e^{-kx} \sin (\omega x + \theta)$$

where ω is the angular frequency and θ is the phase of the sine function. Plot y as a function of x for several cycles of the sine function or until the maximum amplitude is reduced to $A/10$.

3–13. Choose any three functions that possess some form of symmetry, and explain how efficient methods could be devised to minimize the calculations needed to plot each function.

3–14. Write a program to display a bar graph using the *polyline* command. Input to the program is to include the data points and the labeling required for the x and y axes. The data points are to be scaled by the program so that the graph is displayed across the full screen area.

3–15. Extend the program of Ex. 3–14 to allow the graph to be displayed in any selected screen area.

3–16. Write a procedure to display a line graph for any input set of data points in any selected area of the screen. The input data set is then to be scaled to fit the selected screen area. Data points are to be displayed as asterisks joined with straight line segments, and the x and y axes are to be labeled according to input specifications.

3–17. Modify the procedure in Ex. 3–16 to display the data points as small circles.

3–18. Using the *ellipse* function, write a routine to display any specified pie chart with appropriate labeling. Input to the routine is to include the relative percentage of each section, the name of the piechart, and the section names. Each section label is to be displayed outside the boundary of the pie chart near the corresponding pie section.

3–19. Design an instruction set for a raster-scan system using 16-bit words.

3–20. Design an instruction set for a random-scan display processor using 16-bit word lengths.

4

ATTRIBUTES
OF OUTPUT PRIMITIVES

We can display output primitives with a variety of attributes. Lines can be dotted or dashed, fat or thin. Areas might be filled with a particular color or with a combination of colors used in a pattern. Text can appear reading from left to right, slanted diagonally across the screen, or in vertical columns. And individual characters can be displayed in different colors and sizes.

One way to incorporate attribute options into a graphics package is to extend the parameter list associated with each output primitive command to include the appropriate attributes. A point-plotting command, for example, could contain a color parameter in addition to coordinate parameters. This attribute parameter is passed directly to the output primitive routine.

Another approach is to maintain a system list of attributes and their current values. Separate commands are then included in the graphics package for setting the attribute values in the system attribute list. To display an output primitive, the system checks the relevant attributes and draws the primitive according to the current attribute settings. Some packages provide users with both attribute functions and attribute parameters in the output primitive commands. Our approach is to consider a package designed with functions that modify a system attribute list, and we discuss how a standard set of attributes can be defined and implemented in this fashion.

4–1 Line Styles

Attributes for line style determine how a line is to be displayed by a line-drawing routine. Typical attributes of a line are its type, its width, and its color. Routines for line drawing must be structured to produce lines with the specified characteristics.

Line Type

The line type attributes include solid lines, dashed lines, and dotted lines. They are implemented in a graphics package through modifications to the line-drawing algorithms to accommodate the type of line requested by a user. When a dashed line is to be displayed, the line-drawing algorithm outputs short solid sections along the line while leaving intervening sections blank. A dotted line could be generated by plotting every other point, or every third point, along the line path. Any number of line type variations can be built into the basic line-generating algorithms.

To set line type attributes in an applications graphics package, we introduce the function

```
set_linetype (lt)
```

We assume here that the line type parameter *lt* is assigned values such as *solid*, *dashed*, and *dotted*. Other values for *lt* could be used to provide a combination of dots and dashes or for variations in the dot-dash patterns.

With the *linetype* command, a user sets the current value of the line type attribute. All subsequent line-drawing commands produce lines with this line type. The following program segment illustrates use of a *linetype* command to display the data plots in Fig. 4–1.

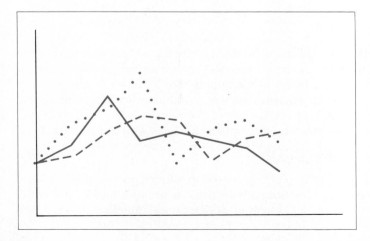

FIGURE 4–1
Plotting three data sets with three different line styles, as output by procedure line_type_chart.

{*Draw_axes and get_data are predefined procedures.
Get_data returns arrays x and y, specifying
12 coordinate positions to be plotted.*}

```
type
  points = array [1..8] of integer;

procedure line_type_chart;
  var k : integer; x, y : points;
  begin
    draw_axes;
    for k := 1 to 3 do begin
      get_data (x, y);
      case k of
        1 : set_linetype (solid);      {set line type}
        2 : set_linetype (dashed);
        3 : set_linetype (dotted)
      end; {case}
      polyline (8, x, y)               {draw line}
    end {for k}
  end; {line_type_chart}
```

Line Width

Implementation of line width options depends on the type of output device used. A heavy line on a video monitor could be drawn as adjacent parallel lines, while a pen plotter might require pen changes. As with other attributes, a line width command can be used to set a current line width value in the attribute list. This value is used by the line-drawing algorithms to control the width of lines generated with subsequent output primitive commands.

A command for setting the line width attribute is defined as

```
set_linewidth_scale_factor (lw)
```

Line width parameter *lw* is assigned a positive number to indicate the relative width of the line to be displayed. Assuming that a value of 1 specifies a standard-width line, a user could set *lw* to a value of 0.5 to generate a line whose width is one-half that of the standard line. Values greater than 1 would be used to produce lines thicker than the standard.

Line Color

When a system provides color (or intensity) options, a parameter giving the current color index is included in the list of system attribute values. This color index is then stored in the frame buffer at the appropriate locations by the *set_pixel* procedure. The number of color choices depends on the number of bits of storage available per pixel in the raster.

A graphics package can provide color options for lines with the command

```
set_line_color_index (lc)
```

Nonnegative integer values, corresponding to various color choices, can be assigned to the line color parameter *lc*. This parameter is used as an index into a color table, which lists the available colors for the output device in use. Any line drawn in the background color is invisible, and a user can erase previously displayed lines on a video monitor by respecifying them in the background color.

An example of the use of the various line attribute commands in an applications program is given by the following sequence of statements:

```
set_linetype (dashed);
set_linewidth_scale_factor (2);
set_line_color_index (5);
polyline (n1, x1, y1);

set_line_color_index (6);
polyline (n2, x2, y2);
```

This program segment would display two figures, drawn with double-wide, dashed lines. The first is displayed in a color corresponding to code 5, and the second in color 6.

In a color raster system, the number of bits of storage needed per pixel depends on the number of color choices available and the method used for storing color values. Color tables can be structured to provide extended color capabilities to a user without requiring huge frame buffers.

4–2 Color and Intensity

Various color and intensity-level options can be made available to a user, depending on the capabilities and design objectives of a particular system. Some systems provide for a wide choice of colors; others have only a few options. Raster-scan systems, for example, are often designed to display a great many colors, while random-scan monitors typically offer only a few color choices, if any. The color codes are usually assigned numeric values ranging from 0 through the positive integers. For a CRT, these color codes are converted to intensity-level settings for the electron beams in either shadow-mask or beam-penetration monitors. With a color plotter, the codes could control ink-jet deposits or pen changes.

Color Tables

A simple scheme for storing color code selections in the frame buffer of a raster system is shown in Fig. 4–2. When a particular color code is specified in an application program, the corresponding binary value is stored in the frame buffer

COLOR CODE	STORED COLOR VALUES IN FRAME BUFFER			DISPLAYED COLOR
	RED	GREEN	BLUE	
0	0	0	0	Black
1	0	0	1	Blue
2	0	1	0	Green
3	0	1	1	Cyan
4	1	0	0	Red
5	1	0	1	Magenta
6	1	1	0	Yellow
7	1	1	1	White

FIGURE 4–2
Color codes stored in a frame buffer with three bits per pixel.

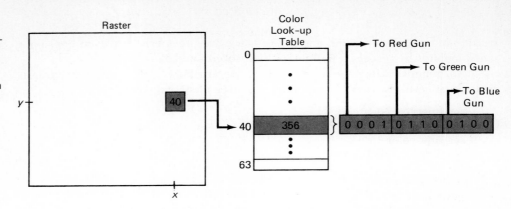

FIGURE 4–3
A color lookup table, providing 12 bits per entry, used with a raster containing 6 bits for each pixel position. A value of 40 stored in raster position *(x, y)* references the location in this lookup table containing the value 356. Each 4-bit segment of this entry controls the intensity level of one of the three electron guns in an RGB monitor, as shown.

for each component pixel in the output primitives to be displayed in that color. The scheme given in Fig. 4–2 allows eight color choices with 3 bits per pixel of storage. Each of the three bit positions is used to control the intensity level (either on or off) of the corresponding electron gun in an RGB monitor. The leftmost bit controls the red gun, the middle bit controls the green gun, and the rightmost bit controls the blue gun. Adding more bits per pixel to the frame buffer increases the number of color choices. In a raster with 6 bits per pixel, 2 bits can be used for each gun. This provides four intensity levels for each color gun (red, green, and blue), and 64 different color codes could be stored.

Another method for storing color codes is diagrammed in Fig. 4–3. In this scheme, the electron gun intensities are controlled by values stored in a **color lookup table** instead of by the values stored in the raster. The raster values are used as indices into the lookup table. For the example shown in this figure, a raster with 6 bits per pixel can reference any one of the 64 positions in the lookup table. Each entry in the table uses 12 bits to specify a color, so that a total of 4096 different colors is now available. Four bits of intensity information is provided for each electron gun. Systems employing this lookup table would permit a user to select any combination of 64 colors from a 4096-color palette. Also, the lookup table entries could be changed at any time, allowing designs, scenes, or graphs displayed on the screen to take on new color combinations.

Color table entries could be set by a user with the command

```
set_color_table (ct, c)
```

Parameter *ct* is used as a color table position number (0 to 64 for the example in Fig. 4–3), and parameter *c* is the code for one of the possible color choices.

Use of a color lookup table can dramatically increase the color options without corresponding increases in raster size. Some high-quality color systems use as many as 24 bits for each position in the color lookup table and 9 bits per pixel in the frame buffer. This allows 512 colors to be used in each display, with over 16 million color choices for the lookup table entries.

Gray Scale

With monitors that have no color capability, the *line_color* command can be used in an application program to set the intensity level, or **gray scale,** for points along displayed lines. Many packages use numeric values within the range of 0 to 1 to set gray scale levels. This allows the package to be adapted to hardware with differing gray scale capabilities.

INTENSITY CODES	STORED INTENSITY VALUES IN THE FRAME BUFFER (Binary Code)		DISPLAYED GRAY SCALE
0.0	0	(00)	Black
0.33	1	(01)	Dark Gray
0.67	2	(10)	Light Gray
1.0	3	(11)	White

FIGURE 4–4
Conversion of intensity values to integer codes for storage in a frame buffer accommodating a gray scale with four levels. Two bits of storage for each pixel position are needed in the frame buffer.

Storing intensity levels in a raster is similar to storing color codes. If only one bit per pixel is provided in the raster, on (white) and off (black) are the only possibilities for the gray scale. Three bits per pixel can accommodate eight different intensity levels. Higher-quality systems might provide 8 or more bits per pixel in the frame buffer for the intensity levels.

Intensity values specified in an application program are converted to appropriate binary codes for storage in the raster. Figure 4–4 illustrates conversion of user specifications to codes for a four-level gray scale. In this example, any intensity input value near 0.33 would store the binary code 01 in the frame buffer and result in a dark gray shading for these pixels. In an alternative scheme, the user specification might be converted directly to the voltage value that produces this gray scale level on the output device in use.

4–3 Area Filling

An advantage of raster systems is their ability to easily store and display areas filled with a color or shading pattern. Fill patterns for such areas are stored as color or intensity values in a frame buffer. Displaying shaded areas on a vector system is considerably more difficult, since area fill requires drawing line segments within the area boundary during each refresh cycle. Various algorithms have been developed for displaying filled areas on raster systems. One method uses the boundary definition to identify which pixels belong to the interior of an area. Other methods start from a position within the area and paint outward from this point.

Scan-Line Algorithm

A scan-line algorithm uses the intersections between area boundaries and scan lines to identify pixels that are inside the area. Figure 4–5 illustrates an area outline and an individual scan line passing through a polygon. Pixel positions along the

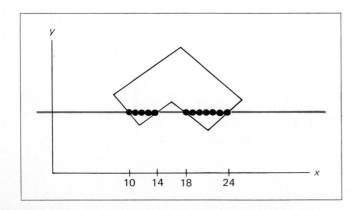

FIGURE 4–5
Interior pixels along a scan line passing through an area to be filled.

scan line that are within the polygon definition are set to the intensity or color values specified in the application program. We first consider how a scan-conversion algorithm can be set up for polygons. The algorithm can then be adapted to other figures, such as circles, by replacing the straight-line equations with the equations defining the figure boundary to be filled.

Taking each scan line in turn, a scan-conversion algorithm locates the intersection points of the scan line with each edge of the area to be filled. Proceeding from left to right, intersections are paired, and the intervening pixels are set to the specified fill intensity or color. In the example of Fig. 4–5, the four intersection points with the polygon boundaries define two stretches of interior pixels.

When a scan line intersects a polygon vertex, it may require special handling. A scan line passing through a vertex intersects two polygon edges at that position, adding two points to the list of intersections for the scan line. In Fig. 4–6, scan line 1 intersects a polygon boundary four times. Two interior stretches are defined: one from the left boundary to the vertex, and a second from the vertex to the right edge of the polygon. But scan line 2 generates five intersections with polygon edges, and resultant pairs do not correspond to the polygon interior.

To fill a polygon correctly, its overall topology must be considered. If the vertices of the polygon are specified in clockwise order, scan line 2 in Fig. 4–6 intersects a vertex whose connecting edges are monotonically decreasing in the y direction. When successive edges of the polygon are monotonically increasing or decreasing, a correct determination of interior points along a scan line is obtained by recording only one intersection point for the vertex. The vertex intersection on scan line 1 in this figure connects two lines with opposite y directions. One line has decreasing y-coordinate values, and the other has increasing y-coordinate values. When such a local minimum (or a local maximum) is encountered by a scan line, two intersection points should be generated to correctly identify interior pixels along the scan line.

Scan-conversion algorithms typically process a polygon from the top of the screen to the bottom and from left to right across each scan line. Calculations performed in such algorithms can be dramatically reduced by making use of various **coherence** properties of the objects being processed. Very often, we can expect properties of pixels along a scan line to be related, so that the properties of one pixel can be determined from those of the preceding pixel. Similarly, we can expect the properties of each scan line to be quite like those of the preceding scan line.

We can take advantage of coherence in calculating scan-line intersections with a polygon by noting that each successive scan line has a y value that is only one

FIGURE 4–6
Intersection points along scan lines that pass through polygon vertices. Scan line 1 generates an even number of intersections that can be paired to correctly identify interior pixels. Scan line 2, however, generates an odd number of intersections.

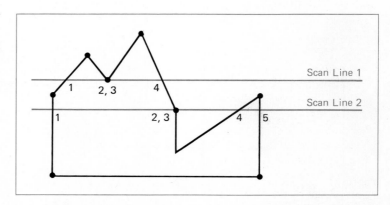

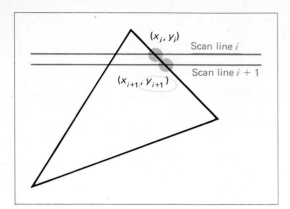

FIGURE 4–7
Two successive scan lines
intersecting a polygon
boundary.

85
Sec. 4-3   Area Filling

unit smaller than the previous line. Figure 4–7 shows two successive scan lines
crossing a side of a polygon. The slope of this polygon boundary line is

$$m = \frac{y_{i+1} - y_i}{x_{i+1} - x_i}$$

Since the changes in y coordinates is simply

$$y_{i+1} - y_i = -1$$

the x-intersection value x_{i+1} on the lower scan line can be determined from the
x-intersection value x_i on the preceding scan line as

$$x_{i+1} = x_i - \frac{1}{m} \qquad (4\text{-}1)$$

Once the first x-coordinate intersection value x_1 for a polygon side is found for one
scan line, we can obtain the x-coordinate values for intersection points on each
successive scan line by subtracting the inverse of the slope.

In many cases, we can expect an individual scan line to intersect only some
of the total number of sides defining a fill area. To avoid unnecessary checking for
intersection points, we can maintain a list of the polygon sides that are crossed by
the current scan line. To do this, we create a list of all the polygon sides, sorted on
the larger y coordinate of each side. Pointers into this list define the active list of
sides for each scan line. Figure 4–8 illustrates the specification of an active list with
pointers into the total list of sorted sides. As we move to the next scan line, the
pointers are updated to define a new active list.

Procedure *fill_area_solid* incorporates these ideas to fill a defined polygon
with a solid color. It accepts parameters specifying the number of vertices in the
polygon and the coordinates of the vertices, given in clockwise order. The array of
records *sides* stores information about each edge in the polygon. An entry in the
array includes the larger y coordinate (*y_top*) of the edge, the length of the edge in
the y direction (*delta_y*), and the inverse slope (*x_change_per_scan*). Initially, *x_int*
contains the x coordinate of the vertex with the larger y value. When the edge is
on the active list, this entry is updated to contain the x coordinate of the edge
intersection with the current scan line.

A number of routines are defined within the scope of *fill_area_solid*. Routine
sort_on_bigger_y creates the edge table and also returns, as parameter *bottomscan*,

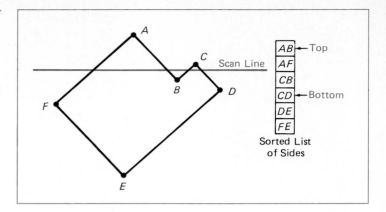

FIGURE 4–8
The active list of sides for a scan line passing through a polygon can be set up as pointers into the sorted list of all polygon sides. Pointers for the scan line shown are labeled Top and Bottom.

the *y* coordinate of the lowermost vertex. The polygon is filled from the top scan line to *bottomscan*. Routine *update_first_&_last* modifies the pointers *first_s* and *last_s* that define the active list for the current scan line. The number of intersection points for this scan line is determined by *process_x_intersections*, and *draw_lines* pairs the intersections and sets the interior pixels to the fill color. Array *sides* is then updated and made ready for the next scan line.

```
type
    points  =  array [1..max_points] of integer;

procedure fill_area_solid (count : integer; x, y : points);
  type
    each_entry = record
      y_top : integer;                     {larger y coordinate for line}
      x_int : real;                        {x that goes with larger y}
      delta_y : integer;                   {difference in y coordinates}
      x_change_per_scan : real             {x change per unit change in y}
      end;   {each_entry}
    list = array [0..max_points] of each_entry;
  var
    sides : list;
    side_count, first_s, last_s, scan, bottomscan, x_int_count, r :
        integer;

  begin {fill_area_solid}
    sort_on_bigger_y (count, x, y, sides, side_count, bottomscan);
    first_s := 1; last_s := 1; {initialize pointers into sorted list}
    for scan := sides[1].y_top downto bottomscan do begin
      update_first_&_last (sides, count, scan, first_s, last_s);
      process_x_intersections (sides, scan, first_s, last_s,
          x_int_count);
      draw_lines (sides, scan, x_int_count, first_s);
      update_sides_list (sides)
    end   {for scan}
  end;   {fill_area_solid}
```

The first of the second-level routines, *sort_on_bigger_y*, enters edge information in *sides*. Endpoints of each edge are passed to *put_in_sides_list*. In this routine,

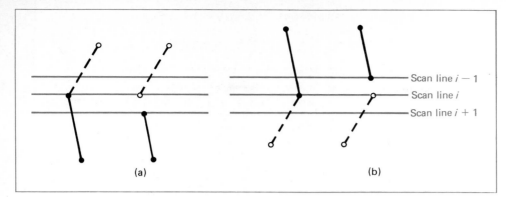

FIGURE 4–9
Adjusting endpoint y values for a polygon edge (solid line). In (a), vertex y coordinates are increasing, so the edge is lowered one unit. In (b), vertex y coordinates are decreasing, so the edge is raised one unit.

a check is made to determine if this edge and the next nonhorizontal edge are monotonically increasing or decreasing. If so, the edge being processed is shortened, to ensure that only one intersection point is generated for the scan line going through the vertex joining the edges. Figure 4–9 illustrates shortening the edge. When the y coordinates of the edges are increasing, the y value of the endpoint is decreased by 1, as in Fig. 4–9 (a). The y value is increased, as in Fig. 4–9 (b), if the y coordinates of the edges are monotonically decreasing. In both cases, the x value of the edge at the adjusted y coordinate is found.

Only nonhorizontal edges are entered into *sides*. An insertion sort based on the larger y coordinate of the edge's endpoints determines placement of the edge in the table. Information stored for the edge are the larger y coordinate and its corresponding x value, the difference between y coordinates of the edge endpoints, and the inverse slope.

```
procedure sort_on_bigger_y (n : integer; x, y : points;
           var sides : list; var side_count, bottomscan : integer);
  var   k, x1, y1, : integer;

  function next_y (k : integer) : integer;
    begin
      {returns y value of the next vertex whose
       y coordinate is not equal to y[k]}
    end;   {next_y}

  procedure put_in_sides_list (var sides : list;
            entry, x1, y1, x2, y2, next_y : integer);
    var
      maxy : integer;
      x2_temp, x_change_temp : real;

    begin
      {make adjustments for problem vertices}
      x_change_temp := (x2 − x1) / (y2 − y1);
      x2_temp := x2;
      if (y2 > y1) and (y2 < next_y) then begin
          y2 := y2 − 1;
          x2_temp := x2_temp − x_change_temp
        end
      else
```

```
      if (y2 < y1) and (y2 > next_y) then begin
          y2 := y2 + 1;
          x2_temp := x2_temp + x_change_temp
      end;
   {insert into sides list}
   if y1 > y2 then maxy := y1 else maxy := y2;
   while (entry > 1) and (maxy > sides[entry - 1].y_top) do begin
       sides[entry] := sides[entry - 1];
       entry := entry - 1
   end;   {while}
   with sides[entry] do begin
       y_top := maxy;
       delta_y := abs(y2 - y1) + 1;
       if y1 > y2 then x_int := x1 else x_int := x2_temp;
       x_change_per_scan := x_change_temp
   end   {with}
end;   {put_in_sides_list}


begin   {sort_on_bigger_y}
   side_count := 0;
   y1 := y[n]; x1 := x[n];            {initialize}
   bottomscan := y[n];
   for k := 1 to n do begin
       if y1 <> y[k] then begin   {put nonhorizontal edges in table}
           side_count := side_count + 1;
           {pass old point, current point, and}
           {y of next nonhorizontal point}
           put_in_sides_list (sides, side_count, x1, y1, x[k], y[k],
               next_y[k])
       end   {if}
       else   {horizontal}
           {draw x1,y1 to x[k],y1 with fill_color}
       if y[k] < bottomscan then bottomscan := y[k];
       y1 := y[k]; x1 := x[k]   {save for next side}
   end   {for k}
end;   {sort_on_bigger_y}
```

Procedure *update_first_&_last* is called once for each scan line, and it updates the pointers defining the beginning and end of the active list. Figure 4–10 shows a polygon and its list of sorted edges. The pointers *first_s* and *last_s* remain positioned as shown for processing of all lines between the polygon's top scan line and scan line *i*. When processing of scan line *i* is completed, the active list is redefined for the next scan line ($i + 1$). Pointer *last_s* is moved to the table's fifth entry (GA), but *first_s* stays where it is since edge AB intersects scan line $i + 1$. Edge FG is now no longer an active side, but it is embedded within the range of the active-list pointers.

One way to eliminate edge FG from further processing is to shift the entries for edges AB, BC, and EF down one spot in *sides* to maintain a contiguous active list. To avoid shifting edges around in the table, we use the *delta_y* parameter of each edge to indicate the status of that edge in the active list. When this entry has the value 0, the edge is no longer considered active even though it is included within the range of the pointers. This entry is originally set to the difference in *y* values of the two endpoints, and its value is equal to the number of times this edge will intersect

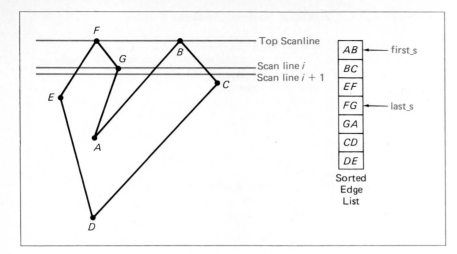

FIGURE 4–10
Processing of pointers for the active list within the sorted edge list for a specified fill area. The sorted edge list is obtained from the input vertices, specified here in the order A through G. Positions of the pointers first_s and last_s show the active list for all scan lines from the top of the polygon through scan line i.

with subsequent scan lines. Each time we process a scan line, *delta_y* is decremented by 1. Active edges, then, are those that have a *delta_y* value greater than 0 and that reside between the *first_s* and *last_s* pointers. The pointer *first_s* is updated only when the *delta_s* value of the entry it points to has become 0.

```
procedure update_first_&_last (sides : list; count, scan : integer;
          var first_s, last_s : integer);
  begin
    while (sides[last_s + 1].y_top >= scan) and
          (last_s < count) do
      last_s := last_s + 1;
    while sides[first_s].delta_y = 0 do
      first_s := first_s + 1
  end;  {update_first_&_last}
```

Taking note of the *delta_y* value for each edge, *process_x_intersections* identifies elements of the active list that intersect the current scan line. These edges are shuffled within the active list to facilitate pairing the intersections that define the polygon interior. The list is reordered on increasing *x_int* values. For example, the active list shown in Fig. 4–10 would assume the new ordering EF, FG, AB, BC. Movement needed within the active list is minimized by the fact that an established ordering will remain constant across a number of scan lines.

The task of identifying pairs of intersections is left to the routine *draw_lines*. This routine takes two successive *x_int* values and sets the intervening pixels on this scan line to the specified fill color.

```
procedure process_x_intersections (var sides : list;
                                   scan, first_s, last_s : integer;
                                   var x_int_count : integer);

  var k : integer;

    {swap is predefined and reverses placement
    of two entries within the table sides}
```

```
procedure sort_on_x (entry, first_s : integer);
  begin
    while (entry > first_s) and
          (sides[entry].x_int < sides[entry-1].x_int) do begin
        swap (sides[entry], sides[entry - 1]);
        entry := entry - 1
      end   {while}
  end;   {sort_on_x}


begin   {process_x_intersections}
  x_int_count := 0;
  for k := first_s to last_s do
    if sides[k].delta_y > 0 then begin
        x_int_count := x_int_count + 1;
        sort_on_x (k, first_s)
      end
end;   {process_x_intersections}


procedure draw_lines (sides : list; scan, x_int_count, index : integer);
  var k, x, x1, x2 : integer;
  begin
    for k := 1 to round(x_int_count / 2) do begin
        while sides[index].delta_y = 0 do index := index + 1;
        x1 := round(sides[index].x_int);
        index := index + 1;
        while sides[index].delta_y = 0 do index := index + 1;
        x2 := round(sides[index].x_int);
        for x := x1 to x2 do
          set_pixel (x, scan, fill_color);
        index := index + 1
      end   {for k}
  end;   {draw_lines}
```

Procedure *update_sides_list* is the last of the second-level routines. Its job is to ready the entries in *sides* for processing of the next scan line. For each edge on the active list, *delta_y* is decremented, and *x_change_per_scan* is subtracted from *x_int*.

```
procedure update_sides_list (var sides : list);
  var k : integer;
  begin
    for k := first_s to last_s do with sides[k] do
      if delta_y > 0 then begin
          {determine next x_int, decrease delta_y}
          delta_y := delta_y - 1;
          x_int := x_int - x_change_per_scan
        end   {if delta_y > 0}
  end;   {update_sides_list}
```

To produce a patterned fill, we modify these scan-line procedures so that a selected pattern is superimposed onto the scan lines. Beginning from a specified start position for a pattern fill, the rectangular patterns would be positioned horizontally across corresponding scan lines and vertically across groups of scan lines. Figure 4–11 illustrates the method for positioning a pattern across a defined area.

FIGURE 4–11
From the start position shown, patterns are laid out so as to cover all scan lines passing through the interior of the specified fill area.

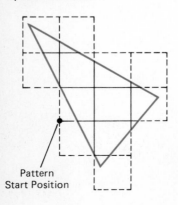

Pattern
Start Position

Antialiasing Area Boundaries

The antialiasing concepts we have discussed for lines can be applied to the boundaries of areas to remove the jagged appearance generated on raster systems. We can implement these procedures into a scan-line algorithm to smooth the area outline as the area is generated.

If system capabilities permit the repositioning of pixels, area boundaries can be smoothed by adjusting boundary pixel positions so that they are along the line defining an area boundary. Other methods adjust each pixel intensity at a boundary position according to the percent of pixel area that is inside the boundary. This situation is depicted in Fig. 4–12, where each pixel area is represented as a small rectangle.

In this example, the pixel at position (x, y) has about half its area inside the polygon boundary. Therefore, the intensity at that position would be adjusted to one-half its assigned value. At the next position $(x + 1, y + 1)$ along the boundary, the intensity is adjusted to about one-third the assigned value for that point. Similar adjustments, based on the percent of pixel area coverage, are applied to the other intensity values around the boundary.

Various techniques can be used to estimate the amount of each pixel inside the boundary of an area. One way to estimate this interior area is to subdivide the total area and determine how many subdivisions are inside the boundary. In Fig. 4–13, each pixel area is partitioned into four parts so that the original 5 by 5 grid of pixels is subdivided into a 10 by 10 grid. This turns the original five scan lines covering these pixels into ten scan lines for the subdivisions. A scan-line method can then be used to determine which subdivisions are on or inside the boundary line, as shown in Fig. 4–14. In this example, the two scan lines are processed to determine that three subdivisions are inside the boundary. The pixel intensity, therefore, is adjusted to 75 percent of its assigned value. With this method, the accuracy of intensity setting depends on the number of pixel subdivisions used.

Another method for determining the percent of pixel area within a boundary, developed by Pitteway and Watkinson, is based on Bresenham's line algorithm. This algorithm selects the next pixel along a line by determining which of two pixels is closer to the line, as determined by the sign of a parameter p that measures relative distances of the two pixels from the line. By slightly modifying the form of p, we obtain a quantity that gives the percent of pixel area that is covered by a surface.

We consider the method for a line with slope m in the range from 0 to 1. In Fig. 4–15, a line with equation $y = mx + b$ is shown on a pixel grid. Assuming that the pixel at position (x_i, y_i) has been plotted, the next pixel nearest the line at $x = x_i + 1$ is either the pixel at y_i or the one at $y_i + 1$. We can determine which pixel is nearer with the calculation

$$y - y_{\text{mid}} = [m(x_i + 1) + b] - (y_i + 0.5) \qquad (4\text{-}2)$$

This gives the distance from the y coordinate on the line to the halfway point between pixels at positions y_i and $y_i + 1$. If this difference calculation is negative, the pixel at y_i is closer to the line. If the difference is positive, the pixel at $y_i + 1$ is closer. We can adjust this calculation so that it produces a positive number in the range from 0 to 1 by adding the quantity $1 - m$:

$$p = [m(x_i + 1) + b] - (y_i + 0.5) + (1 - m) \qquad (4\text{-}3)$$

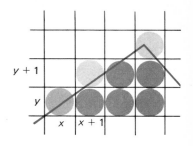

FIGURE 4–12
Adjusting pixel intensities along an area boundary.

FIGURE 4–13
A 5 by 5 pixel section of a raster display subdivided into a 10 by 10 grid.

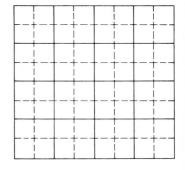

FIGURE 4–14
A subdivided pixel area with three subdivisions inside the boundary line.

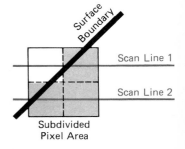

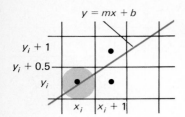

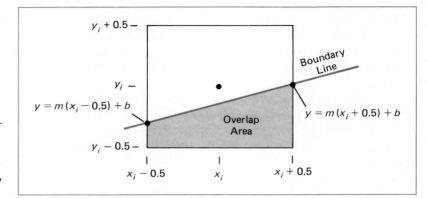

FIGURE 4–15
Boundary line of an area
passing through a pixel grid
section.

FIGURE 4–16
A pixel represented as a
rectangular area with center at
(x_i, y_i) has an overlap with a
bounded region as indicated by
the shaded area.

Now the pixel at y_i is nearer if $p < 1 - m$, and the pixel at $y_i + 1$ is nearer if $p > 1 - m$.

Parameter p also measures the amount of a pixel that is overlapped by an area. For the rectangular pixel in Fig. 4–16, the part of the pixel that is inside the boundary line has an area that can be calculated as

$$area = mx_i + b - y_i + 0.5 \qquad (4-4)$$

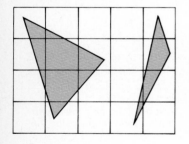

FIGURE 4–17
Areas on a pixel grid that have
more than one boundary line
passing through a pixel region.

This expression for the overlap area of the pixel at (x_i, y_i) is the same as that for parameter p in Eq. 4–3. Therefore, by evaluating p at each successive pixel position, we can determine the percent of area coverage for the preceding pixel. This value then sets the intensity level for the pixel.

We can incorporate this method into a scan-line algorithm by adjusting the pixel intensities at the points on each scan line that intersect the area boundaries. Also, the parameters in p can be adjusted to accommodate lines with negative slopes and slopes greater than 1. This provides an efficient method for antialiasing boundaries when only one edge of an area passes through a pixel. More than one side of a boundary can cross a single pixel at polygon vertices and when very skinny areas are to be displayed (Fig. 4–17). For these cases, we can apply other methods, such as pixel subdivision.

The various antialiasing methods can be applied to polygon areas or to regions with curved boundaries. In either case, boundary equations are used to determine the position of the boundaries relative to pixel positions. Using a scan-line method, coherence techniques are used to simplify the calculations from one scan line to the next.

Boundary-Fill Algorithm

As an alternative to the scan-line method, an area can be filled by starting at a point inside the figure and painting the interior in a specified color or intensity. Painting proceeds until the figure's boundary is encountered. This method, called the **boundary-fill algorithm,** is useful in interactive sketching and painting packages. Using a graphics tablet or other interactive device, a user sketches a figure outline, picks an interior point, and selects a color or pattern from a color palette. The system then paints the figure interior.

A boundary-fill algorithm accepts as input the coordinates of the interior point (x, y), a fill color, and a boundary color. Starting from (x, y), neighboring points are tested to determine whether they are of the boundary color. If not, they are painted with the fill color. In this way, all points are tested up to the area boundary.

Figure 4–18 shows two methods for proceeding to neighboring points from the interior start point (x, y). In Fig. 4–18 (a), four neighboring points are tested. These are the points that are above, below, to the right, and to the left of the starting point. Areas filled by this method are called **4-connected.** Another approach, shown in Fig. 4–18 (b), is used to fill more complex figures. Here the set of neighboring points also includes the four diagonal pixels. Fill methods using this approach are called **8-connected.** An 8-connected boundary-fill algorithm would correctly fill the interiors of the areas defined in Fig. 4–19, but a 4-connected boundary-fill algorithm produces the partial fill shown.

The following procedure illustrates a recursive method for filling a 4-connected area with an intensity specified in parameter *fill_color* up to a border color specified by *boundary.*

```
{inquire_color is predefined function that
 returns the current color of point (x, y)}

procedure boundary_fill (x, y, fill_color, boundary : integer);
  var present_color : integer;
  begin
    present_color := inquire_color (x, y);
    if (present_color <> boundary) and
       (present_color <> fill_color) then begin
       set_pixel (x, y, fill_color);
       boundary_fill (x + 1, y    , fill_color, boundary);
       boundary_fill (x − 1, y    , fill_color, boundary);
       boundary_fill (x    , y + 1, fill_color, boundary);
       boundary_fill (x    , y − 1, fill_color, boundary);
    end {if present color}
  end; {boundary_fill}
```

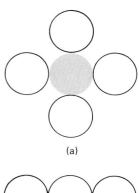

(a)

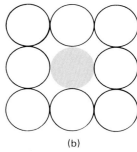

(b)

FIGURE 4–18
Boundary-fill methods applied to (a) a 4-connected area and (b) an 8-connected area. Hollow circles represent pixels to be tested from the interior start point (solid).

FIGURE 4–19
The defined areas (a) are only partially filled (b) by a 4-connected boundary-fill algorithm.

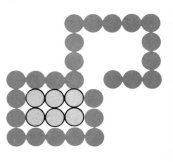

Start Position

(a)

(b)

Since this procedure requires considerable stacking of neighboring points, more efficient methods are generally employed. These methods fill in all points along each horizontal line, one at a time, instead of testing 4-connected or 8-connected neighboring points. The general approach is first to completely fill in the scan line containing the starting point. Then process all lines below the start line, down to the bottom boundaries. Finally, all lines above the start line are processed, up to the top boundaries.

Flood-Fill Algorithm

Another way to fill an area from some start point (x, y) is to specify an interior color value that is to be replaced by the fill color. Instead of looking for a specified boundary color, this **flood-fill algorithm** looks for the interior color that is to be replaced. Using either the 4-connected or 8-connected approach, this procedure stops when no neighboring points have the specified interior color. In a scan-line approach, adjacent pixels with the specified interior color would be set to the fill color until a different color is encountered.

Area-Filling Commands

Several attribute options for fill areas can be provided to a user of a graphics package. These attributes include fill style, fill color, and fill pattern. Fill style refers to the general type of interior, such as hollow or patterned, and fill pattern references the particular pattern code to be used. Parameters specifying these options can be added to the system attribute list and used by the scan-line algorithm to generate fill areas.

A user might select a particular type of interior fill with a command such as

```
set_fill_area_interior_style (fs)
```

Possible types of fill that could be chosen for the fillstyle parameter *fs* are *hollow, solid,* and *patterned* (Fig. 4–20). As with line attributes, the fill style parameter would be recorded in the list of system attributes so that areas defined by subsequent commands (such as *fill_area* and *ellipse* would be displayed with this fill style.

Hollow areas are displayed with only a boundary outline. The color for an area outline, or for a solid interior, is chosen with an area color command:

```
set_fill_area_color_index (fc)
```

where fill color *fc* is set to the desired color code.

Patterns can be specified with the command

```
set_fill_area_pattern_index (pi)
```

where the pattern index parameter *pi* is assigned a pattern code. If integer codes are used to select patterns, the following set of statements would fill the area defined in the *fill_area* command with the second pattern type stored in the pattern table:

```
set_fill_area_interior_style (patterned);
set_fill_area_pattern_index (2);
fill_area (n, x, y);
```

FIGURE 4–20
Interior polygon fill styles.

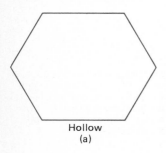

Hollow
(a)

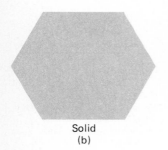

Solid
(b)

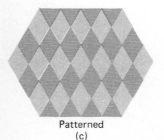

Patterned
(c)

A set of standard patterns can be predefined for a user, or a pattern table could be created with user-defined patterns. Commands to create patterns can be made available to a user in the form

```
set_pattern_representation (pi, nx, ny, cp)
```

Parameter *pi* sets the pattern index number, *nx* and *ny* specify the number of points in the *x* and *y* directions to be defined in the pattern, and *cp* is a two-dimensional color pattern array of size *nx* by *ny*. The program segment

```
cp[1,1] := 4; cp[2,2] := 4;
cp[1,2] := 0; cp[2,1] := 0;
set_pattern_representation (1, 2, 2, cp);
```

could be used to set the first entry in the pattern table of Fig. 4–21. This pattern, when applied to a defined area, produces alternate red and black diagonal lines.

Positioning patterns on the interior of a fill area is specified with the statement

```
set_pattern_reference_point (xp, yp)
```

The scan-line algorithm uses the coordinates (*xp, yp*) to fix the lower left corner of the rectangular pattern. From this starting position, the pattern is then mapped onto all scan lines covering the area to be filled. To illustrate the use of the pattern commands, the following program example creates a black-and-white pattern on the interior of the area in Fig. 4–22.

```
type
   points = array [1..max_points] of integer;

procedure fill_triangle;
   var
      pattern : array [1..3,1..3] of integer;
      x, y : points;
```

FIGURE 4–21
A pattern table with two entries, using the color codes of Fig. 4–2.

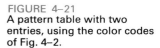

INDEX (PI)	PATTERN (CP)
1	$\begin{pmatrix} 4 & 0 \\ 0 & 4 \end{pmatrix}$
2	$\begin{pmatrix} 2 & 1 & 2 \\ 1 & 2 & 1 \\ 2 & 1 & 2 \end{pmatrix}$

FIGURE 4–22
A defined fill pattern (a) is superimposed on a triangular fill area to produce the patterned display (b).

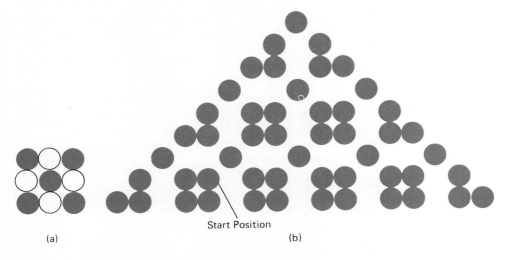

Start Position

(a)   (b)

```
begin
  pattern[1,1] := 1;  pattern[1,2] := 0;  pattern[1,3] := 1;
  pattern[2,1] := 0;  pattern[2,2] := 1;  pattern[2,3] := 0;
  pattern[3,1] := 1;  pattern[3,2] := 0;  pattern[3,3] := 1;
  set_pattern_representation (8, 2, 2, pattern);
  x[1] := 10;  y[1] := 10;
  x[2] := 26;  y[2] := 10;
  x[3] := 18;  y[3] := 18;
  set_fill_area_interior_style (patterned);
  set_fill_area_pattern_index (8);   {use pattern from above}
  set_pattern_reference_point (14, 11);
  fill_area (3, x, y);
end;   {fill_triangle}
```

Another option that can be made available for patterned fill is modification of the pattern size. Graphics packages providing this option include a command to change the dimensions of previously defined pattern arrays. Pattern size can be changed relative to the lower left corner of the array. If a pattern is to be reduced, an appropriate portion of the lower left corner of the array is maintained. For enlargement, the pattern is expanded out from the lower left corner.

4–4 Character Attributes

The appearance of displayed characters is controlled by attributes such as color, style, and orientation. Procedures for displaying character attributes operate on the grid definitions of characters and their placement in the raster. Attributes can be set both for character strings (text) and for additional characters defined as marker symbols.

Text Attributes

Some packages provide a number of choices for text style. The different styles can be made available to the package as predefined sets of grid patterns. Each style can be assigned a text font code, and the character style chosen for display is determined by the current text font setting in the system attribute list. An applications programmer could select a particular code with the text font parameter *tf* in the command

```
set_text_font (tf)
```

Color settings for displayed text are stored in the system attribute list and used by the procedures that load character definitions into the raster array. When a character string is to be displayed, the character grid patterns are entered into the raster with the current color values. Control of text color (or intensity) can be managed from an application program with

```
set_text_color_index (tc)
```

where text color parameter *tc* specifies an allowable color code.

Text size can be adjusted by scaling the height and width of characters. This scaling is applied to the character grid definitions in the horizontal and vertical directions before storage in the frame buffer. Graphics packages can provide separate size adjustment for height and width, or a single attribute parameter can be

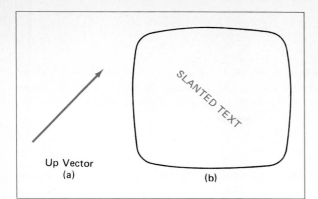

used. When a single parameter is used, a standard ratio of width to height is maintained. A command for specifying text size is

> set_character_height (ch)

This command determines both the height and width of characters. A value of 1 for the character height parameter *ch* displays characters in the standard size. Values greater than 1 enlarge text, and values smaller than 1 scale down the character sizes.

The orientation for a displayed character string can be set according to the direction of a **character up vector.** Two parameters can be used to specify the slope of this vector, and text is then aligned so that the tops of characters are in the direction of the up vector. A procedure for orienting text would rotate each character string so that the string is stored in the raster in a direction that is perpendicular to the direction of the up vector. Figure 4–23 illustrates the appearance of text oriented by an up vector at 45°. The direction of the up vector is set with the command

> set_character_up_vector (dx, dy)

where the slope of the vector is equal to the ratio *dy/dx*.

It is useful in many applications to be able to arrange character strings vertically or horizontally (Fig. 4–24). An attribute parameter for this option could be used to direct a routine to load character patterns into the raster horizontally from the start position or vertically down from the start position. These options could be set by a user with the statement

> set_text_path (tp)

where the text path parameter *tp* is assigned a value of *right* or *down*. Other possible options for text path are *left* and *up*.

Character strings can also be oriented by using a combination of up vector and text path specifications to produce slanted horizontal and vertical text. Figure 4–25 shows the directions of character strings generated by the various text path settings for a 45° up vector. Examples of text generated for *down* and *right* text path values with a 45° up vector are illustrated in Fig. 4–26.

Another handy attribute for character strings is alignment. Figure 4–27 shows various possibilities for text alignment with horizontal and vertical strings. The characters in a string can be aligned on the left, on the right, at the top or bottom, or they can be centered on some position. Once the alignment parameters have been given, procedures for displaying text load the characters into the frame buffer accordingly. A package can provide for alignment with the command

FIGURE 4–24
Text path attributes can be set to produce horizontal or vertical arrangements of character strings.

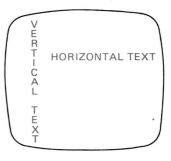

FIGURE 4–25
An up-vector direction (a) can be used to control directions for text path (b).

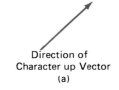

Direction of
Character up Vector
(a)

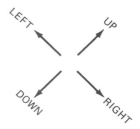

Text Path Direction
(b)

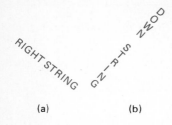

(a)   (b)

FIGURE 4–26
The 45° up vector in Fig. 4–25 produces the string (a) for a right path and the string (b) for a down path.

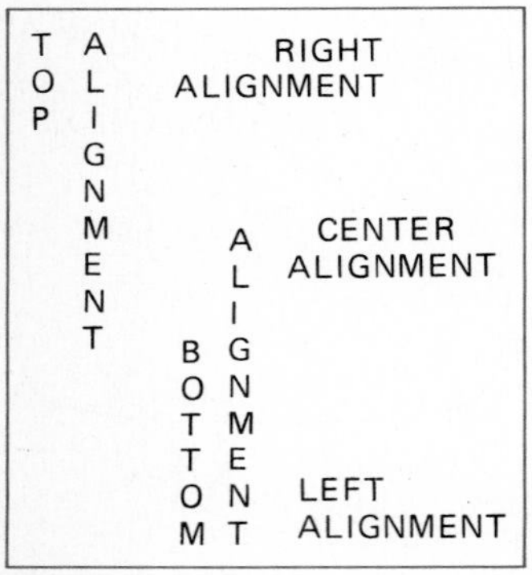

FIGURE 4–27
Possible character string alignments.

```
T  A              RIGHT
O  L           ALIGNMENT
P  I
   G
   N
   M       A     CENTER
   E       L   ALIGNMENT
   N       I
   T       G
       B   N
       O   M
       T   E
       T   N     LEFT
       O   T  ALIGNMENT
       M
```

set_text_alignment (h, v)

Parameters *h* and *v* control horizontal and vertical alignment, respectively. Value *right*, *left*, or *center* is assigned to *h*, and *v* can be assigned *top* or *bottom*. These values specify which part of the string is to be placed at the starting coordinates given in the *text* command.

Marker Attributes

Basic marker attributes are the same as those for text. Markers can be different colors or sizes, and different marker symbols can be chosen. These attributes are implemented by procedures that load a selected symbol into the raster at the defined positions with the specified color and size.

Packages can provide for user settings of these attributes with *set_marker* commands. A command to set the marker type parameter is

set_marker_type (mt)

Similarly, different colors can be chosen with

set_marker_color_index (mc)

and marker size is adjusted with

set_marker_size_scale_factor (ms)

where the marker scale parameter *ms* specifies character enlargement when assigned values greater than 1 and size reductions for values less than 1.

4–5 Inquiry Functions

When attributes are repeatedly changed in an application program, it can be helpful to a user to be able to check current settings of the attribute values. Inquiry functions are used for this purpose. They allow current attribute values to be copied into specified parameters. These attribute values can then be saved for later use, or they could be used to provide for program checks in case of errors.

Examples of inquiry functions that can be included in a graphics package are

inquire_linetype (ilt);

and

inquire_fill_area_color_index (ifc)

Current values for line type and fill color indices are then copied into parameters *ilt* and *ifc*. Similar functions would be used for the other attribute options.

An example of the use of inquiry functions to save an attribute value for later use is given in the following program segment. Here, the user saves the current line type value while drawing with some new line style.

```
inquire_linetype (old_style);
set_linetype (new_style);
        .
        .
        .
set_linetype (old_style);
```

98

4–6 Bundled Attributes

The attribute-setting commands we have described are designed to specify exactly how an output primitive is to be displayed. Each line type parameter value, for instance, is defined as one explicit line style. These attributes are called **unbundled attributes,** and they are meant to be used with an output device that is capable of displaying primitives with the specified attributes. If an application program, employing unbundled attributes, is interfaced to several types of output devices, some of the devices may not have the capability to reproduce the intended attributes. A program using unbundled color attributes may have to be modified to produce acceptable output on a monochromatic monitor.

Unbundled attribute commands provide a simple and direct method for specifying attributes when a single type of output device is to be used. When several types of output devices are available at a graphics installation, it is convenient for a user to be able to say how a particular attribute setting is to be interpreted on each of the different devices. In this case, an application program could specify an attribute index that maps into a table defining which attributes, corresponding to the input index, are to be generated on the different output devices. Attributes specified in this manner are called **bundled attributes.** The table defining specific attributes for each output device is called the **bundle table.** An application program can set up its own bundle table for the various attributes, or the bundle tables can be established by the installation. Graphics packages can be designed to accommodate both types of attribute specifications, with one type chosen as the default mode.

With bundle attributes, an application program must specify the type of output device to be used, as well as the attribute index for the output primitives. As a means for identifying various devices, a user **workstation** is defined to be the set of input/output devices available for a particular application. Figure 4–28 illustrates some categories of workstations that might be defined at an installation. Some of these categories include both input and output devices; others are output devices only. To use a particular workstation, a command such as

```
activate_workstation (ws)
```

is issued in the application program. All output is then directed to the devices defined by the workstation code *ws*. When the output devices are to be changed, a new workstation is activated. Attributes for each workstation type can be set by a user with separate commands for each of the attribute categories: line, area fill, text, and marker.

WORKSTATION TYPE CODE	WORKSTATION DESCRIPTION
1	Raster Color Monitor with Keyboard
2	Raster Color Monitor with Keyboard and Graphics Tablet
3	DVST with Keyboard and Thumb Wheels
4	Vector Refresh Monitor with Keyboard
5	Color Plotter

FIGURE 4–28
Possible categories of workstations used with bundled attribute specifications.

Line Attributes

To specify attributes for lines, a single command,

    set_line_index (li)

is used in place of the three separate commands for line type, line width, and line color. Line index parameter li points into the bundle table, which defines possible attribute combinations for the workstation specified.

The bundle table for line attributes is established for the various workstations with

    set_line_representation (ws, li, lt, lw, lc)

Parameter ws is the workstation code, and li is the line index. Attribute parameters lt, lw, and lc set the line type, line width, and line color specifications. For example, the following commands set line attributes for index number 3 on two different workstations:

    set_line_representation (1, 3, 2, 0.5, 1);
    set_line_representation (4, 3, 1, 1, 7);

These statements might be used to display dashed lines at half thickness in a blue color on workstation number 1, while on workstation 4, this same index generates solid, standard-sized white lines.

Each workstation code may have several line indices, defining a range of possible line attributes. For example, line indices 1 through 8 might define solid lines of standard width in eight different colors. Line indices 9 through 16 could be used to specify dashed lines, with standard widths, in the same eight colors. In this way, an extensive table of line indices can be defined for each workstation.

Color and Intensity Attributes

Color indices specified for line, fill area, and text primitives are pointers into color and intensity lookup tables. These lookup tables can be set up for each workstation independently with the command

    set_color_representation (ws, ci, r, g, b)

Again, ws identifies the workstation, and ci is the color index parameter. Floating-point values for parameters r, g, and b could be assigned in the range from 0 to 1, establishing the amount of red, green, and blue components in the color defined by index ci.

An illustration of how a table could be set up for a color monitor is given in Fig. 4–29. Figure 4–30 shows a possible intensity table specification.

Area-Filling Attributes

For a bundled attribute specification, the command

    set_fill_area_index (fi)

selects attributes on each workstation for a given fill index fi. This single statement replaces the three commands for setting fill style, fill color, and pattern index. Integer values are assigned to fi, which map into a bundle table for fill attributes.

COLOR INDEX CI	RED COMPONENT (R)	GREEN COMPONENT (G)	BLUE COMPONENT (B)	COLOR DESCRIPTION
0	0	0	0	Black
1	0.25	0	0	
2	0.50	0	0	Shades
3	0.75	0	0	of Red
4	1.0	0	0	
5	0	0.25	0	
6	0	0.50	0	Shades
7	0	0.75	0	of Green
8	0	1.0	0	
•	•	•	•	•
•	•	•	•	•
•	•	•	•	•

FIGURE 4–29
Color table defined for a particular workstation specification.

COLOR INDEX CI	RED COMPONENT (R)	GREEN COMPONENT (G)	BLUE COMPONENT (B)	GRAY-SCALE DESCRIPTION
0	0	0	0	Black
1	0.33	0.33	0.33	Dark Gray
2	0.67	0.67	0.67	Light Gray
3	1.0	1.0	1.0	White

FIGURE 4–30
A gray-scale intensity table defined for a particular workstation category.

Bundle tables for fill areas are set with

set_fill_area_representation (ws, fi, fs, fc, pi)

which defines the attribute list for fill index *fi* on workstation *ws*. Parameters *fs*, *fc*, and *pi* are assigned values for the fill style, color code, and pattern index, respectively.

Commands for setting pattern attributes are similar to those used in the unbundled mode. The difference is that a workstation must be named for each pattern defined. A user could set pattern representation, pattern reference point, and pattern size with

set_pattern_representation (ws, fsi, nx, ny, cp);
set_pattern_reference_point (xp, yp);
set_pattern_size (sx, sy);

Color codes are set in the *nx* by *ny* array *cp*. Position (*xp*, *yp*) establishes the starting point for the left corner of the rectangular area *cp*, and the size of the pattern to be used is defined by *sx* and *sy*.

Text Attributes

An index for text attributes is chosen with

set_text_index (ti)

and a user no longer employs individual commands for setting text font, color, or spacing. The text index *ti* maps into the text bundle table, which is established with

```
set_text_representation (ws, ti, tf, te, ts, tc)
```

Parameters *tf* and *tc* set the text font and text color for workstation *ws*. Additional parameters, *te* and *ts*, are used to adjust character size and spacing. The text expansion parameter *te* defines the ratio of width to height for characters, and *ts* specifies the spacing to be used between characters.

Other text attributes are set by the same commands used with unbundled attributes. They include setting the character up vector, text path, character height, and text alignment.

Marker Attributes

The marker index setting is accomplished with

```
set_marker_index (mi)
```

and the marker bundle table for this index is defined with the command

```
set_marker_representation (ws, mi, mt, ms, mc)
```

This defines the marker type *mt*, marker scale factor *ms*, and marker color *mc* for index *mi* on workstation *ws*. Values for the attributes parameters *mt*, *ms*, and *mc* can be set with the same commands used with unbundled attributes.

4–7 Summary

In this chapter, we have explored the various types of attributes that affect the appearance of output primitives. Procedures for displaying primitives use attribute settings to adjust the output of line-, area-, and character-generating algorithms.

The basic line attributes are those for line type, line color, and line width. These attributes are generated with a line-drawing algorithm modified to accommodate attribute choices by a user.

Area attributes include the type of interior fill, the area color, and the fill pattern. The basic area-filling procedure is the scan-line algorithm, which can be adapted to generate patterned fill. Two other methods for filling areas are the boundary-fill and flood-fill algorithms.

Characters can be displayed in different colors, sizes, and orientations. Procedures for controlling the display of character attributes use parameter settings to modify character grid definitions and store the altered grid patterns in the raster.

Graphics packages can be devised to handle both unbundled and bundled attribute specifications. Unbundled attributes are those that are defined for only one type of output device. Bundled attribute specifications allow different sets of attributes to be used on different devices, as defined in a bundle table. Bundle tables may be installation-defined, user-defined, or both. Commands to set the bundle table specify the type of workstation to be used and the attributes for a given attribute index.

Table 4–1 lists the attribute discussed in this chapter for the output primitive classifications: line, fill area, text, and marker. The attribute commands that can be used in graphics packages are listed for each category.

TABLE 4–1.

Summary of Attributes

Output Primitive Type	Associated Attributes	Attribute-Setting Commands	Bundled-Attribute Commands
Line	Type Color Width	set_linetype set_line_color_index set_linewidth_scale_factor	set_line_index set_line_representation

Fill Area	Interior Style
	Fill Color
	Pattern
		set_fill_area_interior_style
		set_fill_area_color_index
		set_fill_area_pattern_index
		    set_pattern_representation
		    set_pattern_reference_point
		    set_pattern_size
			set_fill_area_index
			set_fill_area_representation

Text	Font Color Size Orientation	set_text_font set_text_color_index set_character_height set_character_up_vector set_text_path set_text_alignment	set_text_index set_text_representation
Marker	Type Color Size	set_marker_type set_marker_color_index set_marker_size_scale_factor	set_marker_index set_marker_representation

REFERENCES

Algorithms for filling polygons are treated in Barrett and Jordan (1974), Dunlavey (1983), Jordan and Barrett (1973), and Pavlidis (1978 and 1982).

Color and gray scale considerations are discussed in Crow (1978) and in Heckbert (1982).

Additional information on GKS workstations and attribute operations can be found in Enderle, Kansy, and Pfaff (1984) and in Hopgood, et. al. (1983).

EXERCISES

4–1. Implement the *linetype* command by modifying Bresenham's line-drawing algorithm to display either solid, dashed, or dotted lines.

4–2. A line specified by two endpoints and a width can be converted to a rectangular polygon with four vertices and then displayed using a scan-line method. Develop an efficient algorithm for computing the four vertices needed to define such a rectangle using the line endpoints and line width.

4–3. Implement the *linewidth* command in a line-drawing program so that any one of three line widths can be displayed.

4–4. Write a program to output a line graph of three data sets defined over the same *x* coordinate range. Input to the program is to include the three sets of data values, labeling for the axes, and the coordinates for the display area on the screen. The data sets are to be scaled to fit the specified area, each plotted line is to be displayed in a different line type (solid, dashed, dotted), and labeled axes are to be provided.

4–5. Write the program of Ex. 4–4 so that the coordinate axes and each plotted line is in a different color. If possible, harmonious color combinations should be used.

4–6. Define and implement a function for controlling the line type (solid, dashed, dotted) of displayed ellipses.

4–7. Define and implement a function for setting the width of displayed ellipses.

4–8. Devise an algorithm for implementing a color lookup table and the *set_color_table* operation.

4–9. Write a routine to display a bar graph in any specified screen area. Input is to include the data set, labeling for the coordinate axes, and the coordinates for the screen area. The data set is to be scaled to fit the designated screen area, and the bars are to be displayed in a solid color.

4–10. Write the routine of Ex. 4–9 to display two data sets defined over the same *x* coordinate range. The bars for one of the data sets are to be displaced horizontally to produce an overlapping bar pattern for easy comparison of the two sets of data. Use a different color or a different fill pattern for the two sets of bars.

4–11. Modify the scan-line algorithm to apply any specified rectangular fill pattern to a polygon interior, starting from a designated pattern position.

4–12. Write a program to scan-convert the interior of an ellipse into a solid color.

4–13. Extend the program of Ex. 4–12 to generate either a solid or a patterned fill.

4–14. Develop an algorithm for antialiasing elliptical boundaries.

4–15. Extend the Pitteway-Watkinson algorithm for antialiasing an area so that the intensity for boundary lines with any slope can be adjusted.

4–16. Write a program to implement the algorithm of Ex. 4–15 as a scan-line procedure to fill a polygon interior, using the routine *set_pixel* (*x, y, p*) to load intensity level *p* into the frame buffer at location (*x, y*).

4–17. Modify the scan-line algorithm for area fill to incorporate antialiasing. Use coherence techniques to reduce calculations on successive scan lines.

4–18. Modify the boundary-fill algorithm for a 4-connected region to avoid excessive stacking by incorporating scan-line methods.

4–19. Write a boundary-fill procedure to fill an 8-connected region.

4–20. Develop and implement a flood-fill algorithm to fill the interior of any specified area.

4–21. Write a procedure to implement the *set_pattern_representation* function.

4–22. Define and implement a command for changing the size of an existing rectangular fill pattern.

4–23. Devise an algorithm for adjusting the height and width of characters defined as rectangular bit grids.

4–24. Implement routines for setting the character up vector and the text path for controlling the display of character strings.

4–25. Write a program to align text as specified by input values for the alignment parameters.

4–26. Develop procedures for implementing the marker attribute functions.

4–27. Compare attribute-implementation procedures needed by systems that employ bundled attributes to those needed by systems using unbundled attributes.

4–28. Develop procedures for storing and accessing attributes in unbundled system attribute tables. The procedures are to be designed to store designated attribute values in the system tables, to pass attributes to the appropriate output routines, and to pass attributes to memory locations specified in inquiry commands.

4–29. Set up the procedures in Ex. 4–28 to handle bundled system attribute tables.

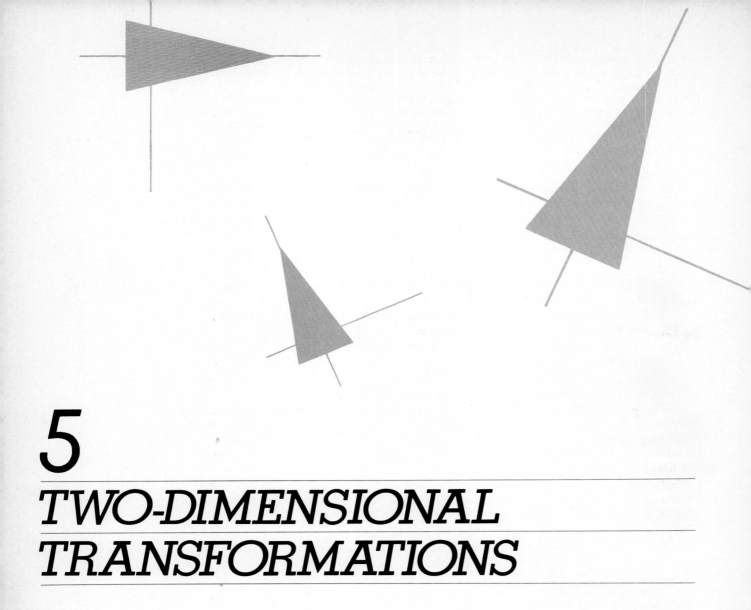

5

TWO-DIMENSIONAL TRANSFORMATIONS

With the procedures for displaying output primitives and their attributes, we can create a variety of picture and graph forms. In many applications, there is also a need for altering or manipulating displays. Sometimes we need to reduce the size of an object or graph to place it into a larger display. Or we might want to test the appearance of design patterns by rearranging the relative positions and sizes of the pattern parts. For animation applications, we need to produce continuous motion of displayed objects about the screen. These various manipulations are carried out by applying appropriate geometric transformations to the coordinate points in a display. The basic transformations are translation, scaling, and rotation. We first discuss methods for performing these transformations and then consider how transformation functions can be incorporated into a graphics package.

5–1 Basic Transformations

Displayed objects are defined by sets of coordinate points. Geometric transformations are procedures for calculating new coordinate positions for these points, as required by a specified change in size and orientation for the object.

Translation

A **translation** is a straight-line movement of an object from one position to another. We translate a point from coordinate position (x, y) to a new position (x', y') by adding **translation distances,** Tx and Ty, to the original coordinates:

$$x' = x + Tx, \qquad y' = y + Ty \qquad (5-1)$$

The translation distance pair (Tx, Ty) is also called a **translation vector** or **shift vector.**

Polygons are translated by adding the specified translation distances to the coordinates of each line endpoint in the object. Figure 5–1 illustrates movement of a polygon to a new position as determined by the translation vector $(-20, 50)$.

Objects drawn with curves are translated by changing the defining coordinates of the object. To change the position of a circle or ellipse, we translate the center coordinates and redraw the figure in the new location.

Translation distances can be specified as any real numbers (positive, negative, or zero). If an object is translated beyond the display limits in device coordinates, the system might return an error message, clip off the parts of the object beyond the display limits, or present a distorted picture. Systems that contain no provision for handling coordinates beyond the display limits will distort shapes because coordinate values overflow the memory locations. This produces an effect known as **wraparound,** where points beyond the coordinate limits in one direction will be displayed on the other side of the display device (Fig. 5–2).

Scaling

A transformation to alter the size of an object is called **scaling.** This operation can be carried out for polygons by multiplying the coordinate values (x, y) for each boundary vertex by **scaling factors** Sx and Sy to produce transformed coordinates (x', y'):

$$x' = x \cdot Sx, \qquad y' = y \cdot Sy \qquad (5-2)$$

Scaling factor Sx scales objects in the x direction, while Sy scales in the y direction.

Any positive numeric values can be assigned to the scaling factors Sx and Sy. Values less than 1 reduce the size of objects; values greater than 1 produce an enlargement. Specifying a value of 1 for both Sx and Sy leaves the size of objects unchanged. When Sx and Sy are assigned the same value, a **uniform scaling** is produced, which maintains relative proportions of the scaled object. Unequal values for Sx and Sy are often used in design applications, where pictures are constructed from a few basic shapes that can be modified by scaling transformations (Fig. 5–3).

When an object is redrawn with scaling equations 5–2, the length of each line

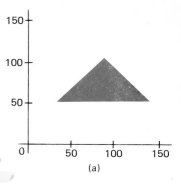

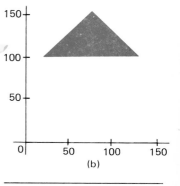

FIGURE 5–1
Translation of an object from position (a) to position (b) with translation distances (−20, 50).

FIGURE 5–2
Possible effects of wraparound on the display of a polygon with one vertex *(P)* specified beyond the display coordinate limits. Point *P* is wrapped around to position *P'*, with a corresponding distortion (solid lines) in the display of the figure.

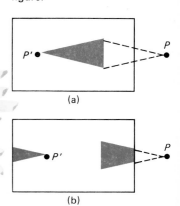

in the figure is scaled according to the values assigned to Sx and Sy. In addition, the distance from each vertex to the origin of the coordinate system is also scaled. Figure 5–4 illustrates scaling a line by setting Sx and Sy to 1/2 in Eqs. 5–2. Both the line length and the distance to the origin are reduced by a factor of 1/2. Enlarged objects are moved away from the coordinate origin.

We can control the location of a scaled object by choosing a position, called the **fixed point**, which is to remain unchanged after the scaling transformation. Coordinates for the fixed point, (x_F, y_F) can be chosen as one of the vertices, the center of the object, or any other position (Fig. 5–5). A polygon is then scaled relative to the fixed point by scaling the distance from each vertex to the fixed point. For a vertex with coordinates (x, y), the scaled coordinates (x', y') are calculated as

$$x' = x_F + (x - x_F)Sx, \qquad y' = y_F + (y - y_F)Sy \qquad (5-3)$$

We can rearrange the terms in these equations to obtain scaling transformations relative to a selected fixed point as

$$x' = x \cdot Sx + (1 - Sx)x_F \qquad (5-4)$$
$$y' = y \cdot Sy + (1 - Sy)y_F$$

where the terms $(1 - Sx)x_F$ and $(1 - Sy)y_F$ are constant for all points in the object.

As in translation, a scaling operation might extend objects beyond display coordinate limits. Transformed lines beyond these limits could be either clipped or distorted, depending on the system in use.

Scaling transformations 5–4 are applied to the vertices of a polygon. Other types of objects could be scaled with these equations by applying the calculations to each point along the defining boundary. For standard figures, such as circles and ellipses, these transformations can be carried out more efficiently by modifying distance parameters in the defining equations. We scale a circle by adjusting the radius and possibly repositioning the circle center.

Rotation

Transformation of object points along circular paths is called **rotation**. We specify this type of transformation with a **rotation angle**, which determines the amount of rotation for each vertex of a polygon.

Figure 5–6 illustrates displacement of a point from position (x, y) to position (x', y'), as determined by a specified rotation angle θ relative to the coordinate origin. In this figure, angle ϕ is the original angular position of the point from the horizontal. We can determine the transformation equations for rotation of the point from the relationships between the sides of the right triangles shown and the associated angles. Using these triangles and standard trigonometric identities, we can write

$$x' = r\cos(\phi + \theta) = r\cos\phi\cos\theta - r\sin\phi\sin\theta$$
$$y' = r\sin(\phi + \theta) = r\sin\phi\cos\theta + r\cos\phi\sin\theta \qquad (5-5)$$

where r is the distance of the point from the origin. We also have

$$x = r\cos\phi, \qquad y = r\sin\phi \qquad (5-6)$$

so that Eqs. 5–5 can be restated in terms of x and y as

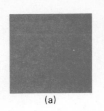

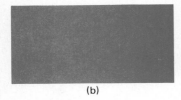
(a)

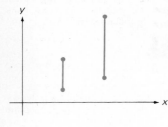
(b)

FIGURE 5–3
Turning a square (a) into a rectangle (b) by setting $S_x = 2$ and $S_y = 1$.

FIGURE 5–4
A line scaled with Eqs. (5–2) and $S_x = S_y = \dfrac{1}{2}$ is reduced in size and moved closer to the coordinate origin.

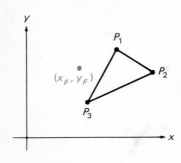

FIGURE 5–5
Scaling relative to a chosen fixed point (x_F, y_F). Distances from each polygon vertex to the fixed point are scaled by transformation equations (5–3).

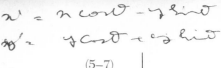
$$x' = x\cos\theta - y\sin\theta$$
$$y' = y\cos\theta + x\sin\theta$$
$$(5\text{--}7)$$

Positive values for θ in these equations indicate a counterclockwise rotation, and negative values for θ rotate objects in a clockwise direction.

Objects can be rotated about an arbitrary point by modifying Eqs. 5–7 to include the coordinates (x_R, y_R) for the selected **rotation point** (or **pivot point**). Rotation with respect to an arbitrary rotation point is shown in Fig. 5–7. The transformation equations for the rotated coordinates can be obtained from the trigonometric relationships in this figure as

$$x' = x_R + (x - x_R)\cos\theta - (y - y_R)\sin\theta$$
$$y' = y_R + (y - y_R)\cos\theta + (x - x_R)\sin\theta$$
$$(5\text{--}8)$$

The pivot point for the rotation transformation can be set anywhere inside or beyond the outer boundary of an object. When the pivot point is specified within the object boundary, the effect of the rotation is to spin the object about this internal point. With an external pivot point, all points of the object are displaced along circular paths about the pivot point.

Since the rotation calculations involve trigonometric functions and several arithmetic operations for each point, computation time can become excessive. This is of particular concern in applications that require transformation of a large number of points or many repeated rotations. For animation and other applications that may involve small rotation angles, we can make some improvements in the efficiency of the rotation calculations. When the rotation angle is small (less than 10°), the trigonometric functions can be replaced with approximation values. For small angles, $\cos\theta$ is approximately 1 and $\sin\theta$ has a value that is very close to the value of θ in radians. The error introduced by these approximations will decrease as the rotation angle decreases.

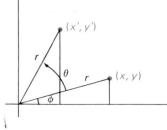

FIGURE 5–6
Rotation of a point from position *(x, y)* to position *(x', y')* through a rotation angle θ, specified relative to the coordinate origin. The original angular position of the point from the *x* axis is ϕ.

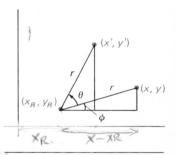

FIGURE 5–7
Rotation of a point from *(x, y)* to *(x', y')* through an angle θ, specified relative to a pivot point at (x_R, y_R).

5–2 Matrix Representations and Homogeneous Coordinates

There are many applications that make use of the basic transformations in various combinations. A picture, built up from a set of defined shapes, typically requires each shape to be scaled, rotated, and translated to fit into the proper picture position. This sequence of transformations could be carried out one step at a time. First, the coordinates defining the object could be scaled, then these scaled coordinates could be rotated, and finally the rotated coordinates could be translated to the required location. A more efficient approach is to calculate the final coordinates directly from the initial coordinates using matrix methods, with each of the basic transformations expressed in matrix form.

We can write transformation equations in a consistent matrix form by first expressing points as **homogeneous coordinates**. This means that we represent a two-dimensional coordinate position (x, y) as the triple $[x_h \; y_h \; w]$, where

$$x_h = x \cdot w, \qquad y_h = y \cdot w \qquad (5\text{--}9)$$

The parameter w is assigned a nonzero value in accordance with the class of transformations to be represented. For the two-dimensional transformations discussed in the last section, we can set $w = 1$. Each two-dimensional coordinate position then has the homogeneous coordinate form $[x\ y\ 1]$. Other values for w are useful with certain three-dimensional viewing transformations.

With coordinate positions expressed in homogeneous form, the basic transformation equations can be represented as matrix multiplications employing 3 by 3 **transformation matrices.** Equations 5–1, for translation, become

$$[x'\ y'\ 1] = [x\ y\ 1] \begin{bmatrix} 1 & 0 & 0 \\ 0 & 1 & 0 \\ Tx & Ty & 1 \end{bmatrix} \tag{5-10}$$

We also introduce the abbreviated notation $T(Tx, Ty)$ for the 3 by 3 transformation matrix with translation distances Tx and Ty

$$T(Tx, Ty) = \begin{bmatrix} 1 & 0 & 0 \\ 0 & 1 & 0 \\ Tx & Ty & 1 \end{bmatrix} \tag{5-11}$$

Using this notation, we can write the matrix form for the translation equations more compactly as

$$P' = P \cdot T(Tx, Ty) \tag{5-12}$$

where $P' = [x'\ y'\ 1]$ and $P = [x\ y\ 1]$ are 1 by 3 matrices (three-element row vectors) in the matrix calculations.

Similarly, the scaling equations 5–2 are now written as

$$[x'\ y'\ 1] = [x\ y\ 1] \begin{bmatrix} Sx & 0 & 0 \\ 0 & Sy & 0 \\ 0 & 0 & 1 \end{bmatrix} \tag{5-13}$$

or as

$$P' = P \cdot S(Sx, Sy) \tag{5-14}$$

with

$$S(Sx, Sy) = \begin{bmatrix} Sx & 0 & 0 \\ 0 & Sy & 0 \\ 0 & 0 & 1 \end{bmatrix} \tag{5-15}$$

as the 3 by 3 transformation matrix for scaling with parameters Sx and Sy.

Equations 5–7, for rotation, are written in matrix form as

$$[x'\ y'\ 1] = [x\ y\ 1] \begin{bmatrix} \cos\theta & \sin\theta & 0 \\ -\sin\theta & \cos\theta & 0 \\ 0 & 0 & 1 \end{bmatrix} \tag{5-16}$$

or as

$$P' = P \cdot R(\theta) \tag{5-17}$$

where

$$R(\theta) = \begin{bmatrix} \cos\theta & \sin\theta & 0 \\ -\sin\theta & \cos\theta & 0 \\ 0 & 0 & 1 \end{bmatrix} \tag{5-18}$$

is the 3 by 3 transformation matrix for rotation with parameter θ.

Matrix representations are standard methods for implementing the basic transformations in graphics systems. In many systems, the scaling and rotation transformations are always stated relative to the coordinate origin, as in Eqs. 5–13 and 5–16. Rotations and scalings relative to other points are handled as a sequence of transformations. An alternate approach is to state the transformation matrix for scaling in terms of the fixed-point coordinates and to specify the transformation matrix for rotation in terms of the pivot-point coordinates.

5–3 Composite Transformations

Any sequence of transformations can be represented as a **composite transformation matrix** by calculating the product of the individual transformation matrices. Forming products of transformation matrices is usually referred to as a **concatenation,** or **composition,** of matrices.

Translations

Two successive translations of an object can be carried out by first concatenating the translation matrices, then applying the composite matrix to the coordinate points. Specifying the two successive translation distances as (Tx_1, Ty_1) and (Tx_2, Ty_2), we calculate the composite matrix as

$$\begin{bmatrix} 1 & 0 & 0 \\ 0 & 1 & 0 \\ Tx_1 & Ty_1 & 1 \end{bmatrix} \cdot \begin{bmatrix} 1 & 0 & 0 \\ 0 & 1 & 0 \\ Tx_2 & Ty_2 & 1 \end{bmatrix} = \begin{bmatrix} 1 & 0 & 0 \\ 0 & 1 & 0 \\ Tx_1 + Tx_2 & Ty_1 + Ty_2 & 1 \end{bmatrix} \qquad (5\text{–}19)$$

which demonstrates that two successive translations are additive. Equation 5–19 can be written as

$$T(Tx_1, Ty_1) \cdot T(Tx_2, Ty_2) = T(Tx_1 + Tx_2, Ty_1 + Ty_2) \qquad (5\text{–}20)$$

The transformation of coordinate points for a composite translation is then expressed in matrix form as

$$P' = P \cdot T(Tx_1 + Tx_2, Ty_1 + Ty_2) \qquad (5\text{–}21)$$

Scalings

Concatenating transformation matrices for two successive scaling operations produces the following composite scaling matrix:

$$S(Sx_1, Sy_1) \cdot S(Sx_2, Sy_2) = S(Sx_1 \cdot Sx_2, Sy_1 \cdot Sy_2) \qquad (5\text{–}22)$$

The resulting matrix in this case indicates that successive scaling operations are multiplicative. That is, if we were to triple the size of an object twice in succession, the final size would be nine times that of the original.

Rotations

The composite matrix for two successive rotations is calculated as

$$R(\theta_1) \cdot R(\theta_2) = R(\theta_1 + \theta_2) \qquad (5\text{–}23)$$

As is the case with translations, successive rotations are additive.

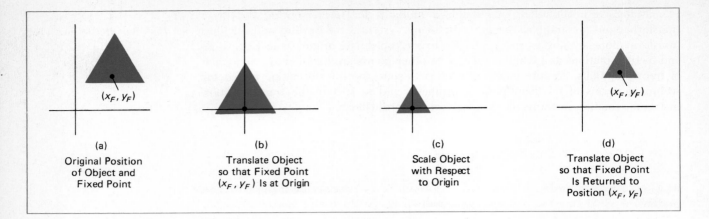

(a)	(b)	(c)	(d)
Original Position of Object and Fixed Point	Translate Object so that Fixed Point (x_F, y_F) Is at Origin	Scale Object with Respect to Origin	Translate Object so that Fixed Point Is Returned to Position (x_F, y_F)

FIGURE 5–8
Sequence of transformations necessary to scale an object with respect to a fixed point using transformation matrices (5–11) and (5–15).

Scaling Relative to a Fixed Point

Using the transformation matrices for translation (Eq. 5–11) and scaling (Eq. 5–15), we can obtain the composite matrix for scaling with respect to a fixed point (x_F, y_F) by considering a sequence of three transformations. This transformation sequence is illustrated in Fig. 5–8. First, all coordinates are translated so that the fixed point is moved to the coordinate origin. Second, coordinates are scaled with respect to the origin. Third, the coordinates are translated so that the fixed point is returned to its original position. The matrix multiplications for this sequence yield

$$
\begin{bmatrix} 1 & 0 & 0 \\ 0 & 1 & 0 \\ -x_F & -y_F & 1 \end{bmatrix} \cdot \begin{bmatrix} Sx & 0 & 0 \\ 0 & Sy & 0 \\ 0 & 0 & 1 \end{bmatrix} \cdot \begin{bmatrix} 1 & 0 & 0 \\ 0 & 1 & 0 \\ x_F & y_F & 1 \end{bmatrix} = \begin{bmatrix} Sx & 0 & 0 \\ 0 & Sy & 0 \\ (1 - Sx)x_F & (1 - Sy)y_F & 1 \end{bmatrix} \quad (5\text{–}24)
$$

Rotation About a Pivot Point

Figure 5–9 illustrates a transformation sequence for obtaining the composite matrix for rotation about a specified pivot point (x_R, y_R). First, the object is translated so that the pivot point coincides with the coordinated origin. Second, the object is rotated about the origin. Third, the object is translated so that the pivot point returns to its original position. This sequence is represented by the matrix product:

$$
\begin{bmatrix} 1 & 0 & 0 \\ 0 & 1 & 0 \\ -x_R & -y_R & 1 \end{bmatrix} \cdot \begin{bmatrix} \cos\theta & \sin\theta & 0 \\ -\sin\theta & \cos\theta & 0 \\ 0 & 0 & 1 \end{bmatrix} \cdot \begin{bmatrix} 1 & 0 & 0 \\ 0 & 1 & 0 \\ x_R & y_R & 1 \end{bmatrix}
$$

$$
= \begin{bmatrix} \cos\theta & \sin\theta & 0 \\ -\sin\theta & \cos\theta & 0 \\ (1 - \cos\theta)x_R + y_R \cdot \sin\theta & (1 - \cos\theta)y_R - x_R \cdot \sin\theta & 1 \end{bmatrix} \quad (5\text{–}25)
$$

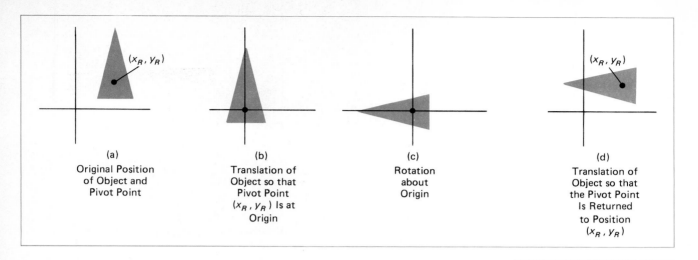

(a)	(b)	(c)	(d)
Original Position of Object and Pivot Point	Translation of Object so that Pivot Point (x_R, y_R) Is at Origin	Rotation about Origin	Translation of Object so that the Pivot Point Is Returned to Position (x_R, y_R)

FIGURE 5–9
Sequence of transformations necessary to rotate an object about a pivot point using transformation matrices (5–11) and (5–18).

Arbitrary Scaling Directions

Scaling parameters Sx and Sy affect only the x and y directions. We can scale objects in other directions by performing a combination of rotations and scaling transformations.

Suppose we wanted to apply scaling factors with values specified by S_1 and S_2 in the directions shown in Fig. 5–10. To accomplish this, we first perform a rotation so that the directions for S_1 and S_2 coincide with the x and y axes, respectively. Then the scaling transformation is applied, followed by an opposite rotation to return points to their original orientations. The composite matrix resulting from the product of these three transformations is

$$\begin{bmatrix} S_1 \cdot \cos^2\theta + S_2 \cdot \sin^2\theta & (-S_1 + S_2)\sin\theta\cos\theta & 0 \\ (-S_1 + S_2)\sin\theta\cos\theta & S_1 \cdot \sin^2\theta + S_2 \cdot \cos^2\theta & 0 \\ 0 & 0 & 1 \end{bmatrix} \quad (5\text{–}26)$$

As an example of the application of this scaling transformation, we turn a square into a parallelogram (Fig. 5–11) by stretching it along the diagonal from $(0, 0)$ to $(1, 1)$. Our transformation rotates this diagonal onto the y axis and applies a scaling factor to double its length. We do this by setting $\theta = 45°$, $S_1 = 1$, and $S_2 = 2$ in the matrix 5–26.

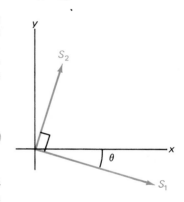

FIGURE 5–10
Scaling parameters S_1 and S_2 are applied in directions determined by an angular displacement θ from the x axis.

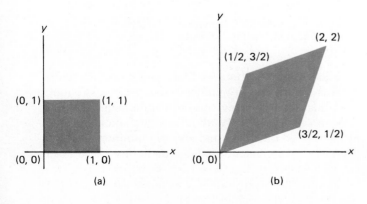

FIGURE 5–11
A square (a) is converted to a parallelogram (b) using the composite transformation matrix (5–26), with $S_1 = 1$, $S_2 = 2$, and $\theta = 45°$.

FIGURE 5–12
The order in which
transformations are performed
affect the final position of an
object. In (a), the object is first
translated, then rotated. In (b),
the object is rotated first, then
translated.

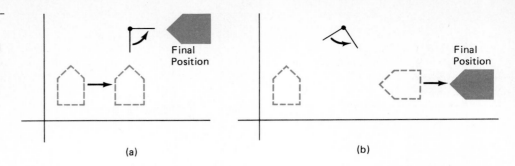

(a)

(b)

Concatenation Properties

Matrix multiplication is associative. That is, for any three matrices, A, B, and C, the matrix product $A \cdot B \cdot C$ can be performed by first multiplying A and B or by first multiplying B and C:

$$A \cdot B \cdot C = (A \cdot B) \cdot C = A \cdot (B \cdot C) \tag{5–27}$$

Therefore, we can evaluate composite matrices in either order.

On the other hand, composite transformations may not be commutative: The matrix product $A \cdot B$ is not equal to $B \cdot A$, in general. This means that if we want to translate and rotate an object, we must be careful about the order in which the composite matrix is evaluated (Fig. 5–12). For some special cases, the multiplication of transformation matrices is commutative. Two successive transformations of the same kind are commutative. For example, two successive rotations could be performed in either order and the final position would be the same. This commutative property holds also for two successive translations or two successive scalings. Another commutative pair of operations is a uniform scaling ($Sx = Sy$) and a rotation.

General Transformation Equations

Any general transformation, representing a combination of translations, scalings, and rotations, can be expressed as

$$[x' \ y' \ 1] = [x \ y \ 1] \begin{bmatrix} a & d & 0 \\ b & e & 0 \\ c & f & 1 \end{bmatrix} \tag{5–28}$$

Explicit equations for calculating the transformed coordinates are then

$$x' = ax + by + c, \qquad y' = dx + ey + f \tag{5–29}$$

These calculations involve four multiplications and four additions for each coordinate point in an object. This is the maximum number of computations required for the determination of a coordinate pair for any transformation sequence, once the individual matrices have been concatenated. Without concatenation, the individual transformations would be applied one at a time and the number of calculations could be significantly increased. An efficient implementation for the transformation operations, therefore, is to formulate transformation matrices, concatenate any transformation sequence, and calculate transformed coordinates by Eqs. 5–29.

The following procedure implements composite transformations. A transformation matrix T is initialized to the identity matrix. As each individual transformation is specified, it is concatenated with the total transformation matrix *T*. When all transformations have been specified, this composite transformation is applied to a given object. For this example, a polygon is scaled, rotated, and translated. Figure 5–13 shows the original and final positions of a polygon transformed by this sequence.

```
procedure transform_object;
  type
    matrix = array [1..3,1..3] of real;
    points = array [1..10] of real;
  var
    t : matrix;
    x, y : points;
    xc, yc : integer;

  procedure transform_points (n : integer; var x, y : points);
    var k : integer; tempx : real;
    begin
      for k := 1 to n do begin
        tempx := x[k] * t[1,1] + y[k] * t[2,1] + t[3,1];
        y[k] :=x[k] * t[1,2] + y[k] * t[2,2] + t[3,2];
        x[k] := tempx
      end
    end; {transform_points}

  procedure fill_area (n : integer; x, y : points);
    begin
      {remainder of fill_area steps}
    end;   {fill_area}

  procedure get_vertices_and_center (n : integer; var x, y: points;
                                     var xc, yc : integer);
    begin
      {get vertices and center point}
    end;

  procedure make_identity (var m : matrix);
    var   r, c : integer;
    begin
      for r := 1 to 3 do
        for c := 1 to 3 do
          if r = c then m[r,c] := 1 else m[r,c] :=0
    end; {make_identity}

  procedure combine_transformations (var t : matrix; m : matrix);
    var r, c : integer; temp : matrix;
    begin
      for r := 1 to 3 do
        for c:= 1 to 3 do
          temp[r,c] := t[r,1]*m[1,c] + t[r,2]*m[2,c] + t[r,3]*m[3,c];
      for r := 1 to 3 do
        for c := 1 to 3 do
          t[r,c] := temp[r,c]
    end; {combine_transformations}

  procedure scale (sx, sy : real; xf, yf : integer);
    var   m : matrix;
```

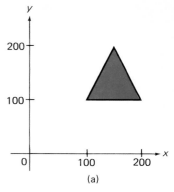

(a)

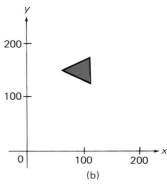

(b)

FIGURE 5–13
A polygon (a) is transformed into (b) by the composite operations in procedure transform_object.

```
   begin
      make_identity (m);
      m[1,1] := sx;   m[2,2] := sy;
      m[3,1] := (1 - sx) * xf;
      m[3,2] := (1 - sy) * yf;
      combine_transformations (t, m) {multiply m into t}
   end; {scale}

procedure rotate (a : real; xr, yr : integer);
   var   ca, sa : real;   m : matrix;
   function radian_equivalent (a : real) : real;
      begin
         radian_equivalent := a * 3.14159 / 180
      end;   {radian_equivalent}
   begin   {rotate}
      make_identity (m);
      a := radian_equivalent (a);
      ca := cos(a);   sa := sin(a);
      m[1,1] := ca; m[1,2] := sa;
      m[2,1] := -sa; m[2,2] := ca;
      m[3,1] := xr * (1 - ca) + yr * sa;
      m[3,2] := yr * (1 - ca) - xr * sa;
      combine_transformations (t, m) {multiply m into t}
   end; {rotate}

procedure translate (tx, ty : integer);
   var   m : matrix;
   begin
      make_identity (m);
      m[3,1] := tx;   m[3,2] := ty;
      combine_transformations (t, m) {multiply m into t}
   end; {translate}

begin   {transform_object}
   get_vertices_and_center (3, x, y, xc, yc);
   make_identity (t);
   set_fill_area_interior_style (hollow);
   set_fill_area_color_index (1);
   fill_area (3, x, y);
   scale (0.5, 0.5, xc, yc);
   rotate (90, xc, yc);
   translate(-60, 20);
   fill_area (3, x, y)
end;   {transform_object}
```

5–4 Other Transformations

Basic transformations such as translation, scaling, and rotation are included in most graphics packages. Some packages provide a few additional transformations that are useful in certain applications. Two such transformations are reflection and shear.

Reflection

A **reflection** is a transformation that produces a mirror image of an object. The mirror image is generated relative to an **axis of reflection**.

Objects can be reflected about the x axis using the following transformation matrix

$$\begin{bmatrix} 1 & 0 & 0 \\ 0 & -1 & 0 \\ 0 & 0 & 1 \end{bmatrix} \qquad (5\text{--}30)$$

This transformation keeps x values the same, but "flips" the y values. The resulting orientation of an object after it has been reflected about the x axis is shown in Fig. 5–14.

A reflection about the y axis flips the x coordinates while keeping y coordinates the same. We can perform this reflection with the transformation matrix

$$\begin{bmatrix} -1 & 0 & 0 \\ 0 & 1 & 0 \\ 0 & 0 & 1 \end{bmatrix} \qquad (5\text{--}31)$$

Figure 5–15 illustrates the change in position of an object that has been reflected about the y axis.

Another type of reflection is one that flips both the x and y coordinates by reflecting relative to the coordinate origin. (The axis of reflection in this case is the line perpendicular to the xy plane and passing through the origin.) We write the transformation matrix for this type of reflection as

$$\begin{bmatrix} -1 & 0 & 0 \\ 0 & -1 & 0 \\ 0 & 0 & 1 \end{bmatrix} \qquad (5\text{--}32)$$

An example of reflection about the origin is shown in Fig. 5–16.

The following matrix performs a reflection transformation about the line $y = x$ (Fig. 5–17).

$$\begin{bmatrix} 0 & 1 & 0 \\ 1 & 0 & 0 \\ 0 & 0 & 1 \end{bmatrix} \qquad (5\text{--}33)$$

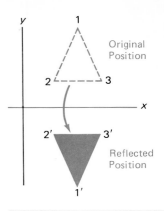

FIGURE 5–14
Reflection of an object about the x axis.

FIGURE 5–15
Reflection of an object about the y axis.

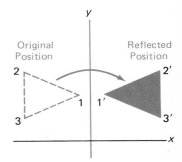

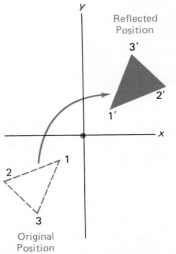

FIGURE 5–16
Reflection of an object relative to the coordinate origin.

FIGURE 5–17
Reflection of an object with respect to the line $y = x$.

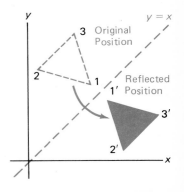

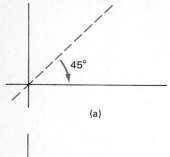

(a)

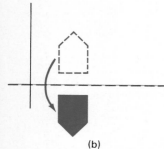

(b)

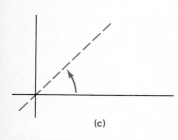

(c)

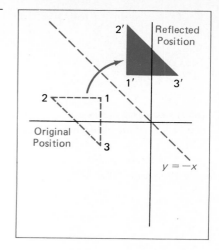

This transformation could be obtained from a sequence of rotations and coordinate-axis reflections. One possible sequence is shown in Fig. 5–18. Here, we first perform a clockwise rotation through a 45° angle, which rotates the line $y = x$ onto the x axis. The final step is to rotate the line $y = x$ back to its original position with a counterclockwise rotation through 45°. Concatenating this sequence of three transformations yields the matrix 5–33. An equivalent sequence of transformations is first to reflect the object about the x axis, then rotate counterclockwise 90°.

To obtain a reflection about the line $y = -x$, we perform the transformation sequence: (1) clockwise rotation by 45°, (2) reflection about the y axis, and (3) counterclockwise rotation by 45°. This sequence produces the transformation matrix

$$\begin{bmatrix} 0 & -1 & 0 \\ -1 & 0 & 0 \\ 0 & 0 & 1 \end{bmatrix} \qquad (5\text{--}34)$$

Figure 5–19 shows the original and final positions for an object reflected about the line $y = -x$.

Reflections about other lines can be accomplished with similar sequences of transformations. For a reflection line in the xy plane passing through the origin, we can rotate the line onto a coordinate axis, reflect about that axis, and rotate the line back to its original position. For reflection lines that do not pass through the origin, we first translate the line so that it does pass through the origin, then carry out the rotate, reflect, rotate sequence.

Shear

These transformations produce shape distortions that represent a twisting, or **shear,** effect, as if an object were composed of layers that are caused to slide over each other. Two common shearing transformations are those for x-direction shear and y-direction shear.

An x-direction shear is produced with the transformation matrix

$$\begin{bmatrix} 1 & 0 & 0 \\ SHx & 1 & 0 \\ 0 & 0 & 1 \end{bmatrix} \qquad (5\text{--}35)$$

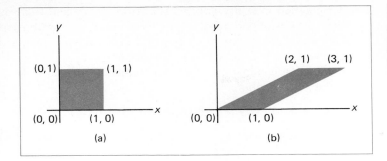

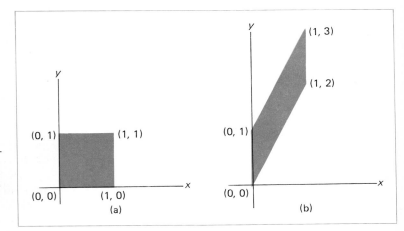

Any real number can be assigned to the parameter *SHx*. This transformation affects only the *x* coordinates; *y*-coordinate values remain unchanged. Each point in an object is displaced horizontally by a distance that is proportional to the *y* coordinate. Setting *SHx* to 2 changes the square in Fig. 5–20 into a parallelogram. Negative values for *SHx* would produce horizontal shifts to the left.

A similar shearing transformation matrix can be set up to generate *y*-direction shearing:

$$\begin{bmatrix} 1 & SHy & 0 \\ 0 & 1 & 0 \\ 0 & 0 & 1 \end{bmatrix} \qquad (5\text{--}36)$$

This transformation generates vertical shifts in coordinate positions. Parameter *SHy* can be set to any real number, which alters the *y* component of a coordinate position by an amount that is proportional to the *x* value. Figure 5–21 illustrates the conversion of a square into a parallelogram with *SHy* = 2.

5–5 Transformation Commands

Graphics packages can be structured so that separate commands are provided to a user for each of the transformation operations, as in *procedure transform_object*. A combination of transformations is then performed by referencing each individual function. An alternate formulation is to use one transformation command that can be used for a combination of transformations or a single operation. Since transformations are often performed in combination, a composite transformation command can provide a more convenient method for applying transformations.

We introduce the following command to perform composite transformations involving translation, scaling, and rotation:

```
create_transformation_matrix (xf,yf,sx,sy,xr,yr,a,tx,ty,matrix)
```

Parameters in this command are the scaling fixed point (*xf*, *yf*), scaling parameters *sx* and *sy*, rotation pivot point (*xr*, *yr*), rotation angle *a*, translation vector (*tx*, *ty*), and the output *matrix*. We assume that this command evaluates the transformation sequence in the fixed order: first scale, then rotate, then translate. The resulting composite transformation for this sequence is then stored in the parameter *matrix*. A procedure for implementing this command performs a concatenation of transformation matrices, using the values specified for the input parameters.

A single transformation, or a sequence of two or three transformations (in the order stated), can be carried out with this transformation command. To translate an object, a user sets $sx = sy = 1$, $a = 0$, and assigns translation values to *tx* and *ty*. The fixed-point and pivot-point coordinates could be set to any values, since they do not affect the transformation calculations when no scaling or rotation takes place. Similarly, rotations are specified by setting $sx = sy = 1$, $tx = ty = 0$, and giving appropriate rotation-angle and pivot-point values to parameters *a*, *xr*, and *yr*.

Since the transformation command can carry out only one fixed sequence of transformations, we can provide for alternative sequences by defining an additional command:

```
accumulate_transformation_matrix (matrix_in, xf, yf, sx, sy,
    xr, yr, a, tx, ty, matrix_out)
```

Parameters *xf*, *yf*, *sx*, *sy*, *xr*, *yr*, *a*, *tx*, and *ty* are the same as in the *create_transformation_matrix* command. This accumulate operation will take any previously defined transformation matrix *(matrix_in)* and concatenate it with the transformation operations defined by the parameter list, in the order *matrix_in*, scale, rotate, translate. The resulting transformation matrix is stored in *matrix_out*.

Using the *accumulate_transformation_matrix* command in conjunction with *create_transformation_matrix* allows a user to perform transformations in any order. For instance, a translation followed by a rotation cannot be carried out with the *create* command alone. But this transformation sequence could be accomplished with the following program statements:

```
create_transformation_matrix (0, 0, 1, 1, 0, 0, 0, tx, ty, m1);
accumulate_transformation_matrix (m1, 0, 0, 1, 1, xr, yr, a, 0, 0,
    m2);
```

The composite matrix *m2* is then applied to the points defining the object to be translated and rotated.

Several transformation matrices could be constructed in an application program. The particular matrix that is to be applied to subsequent output primitives could be selected with a function such as

```
set_transformation (matrix)
```

Parameter *matrix* stores the matrix elements that are to be applied to all subsequent output primitive commands until the transformation is reset. A method for turning off the transformation operations is to set *matrix* to the identity matrix.

Another implementation method for applying a particular matrix to a defined object is to group and label related output primitives (picture components). A transformation command could then be structured so that it is applied to a selected object by referencing the label assigned to the group of primitives defining the object. We return to this topic in Chapter 7.

5-6 Raster Methods for Transformations

The particular capabilities of raster systems suggest an alternate way to approach some transformations. Raster systems store picture information by setting bits in the frame buffer. Some simple transformations can be carried out by manipulating the frame buffer contents directly. Few arithmetic operations are needed, so the transformations are particularly efficient.

Figure 5–22 illustrates a translation performed as a block transfer of a raster area. All bit settings in the rectangular area shown are copied as a block into another part of the raster. This translation is accomplished by reading pixel intensities from a specified rectangular area of the raster into an array, then copying the array back into the raster at the new location. The original object could be erased by filling its rectangular area with the background intensity.

Two functions can be provided to a user for carrying out these translation operations. One function is used for reading a rectangular area of the raster into a specified array, and the other is used to copy the pixel values in the array back into the frame buffer. Parameters for a read function are the name of the array and the size and location of the raster area. Parameters for a copy function are the name of the array and the copy position within the raster.

Some implementations provide options for the copy function so that bit values in the array can be combined with the raster values in various ways. Depending on the mode selected, the copy function could simply replace bit settings in the frame buffer with those in the array, or a Boolean or binary arithmetic operation could be applied. For example, bit settings to be introduced into some area of the frame buffer might be combined with the existing contents of the buffer using an *and* or an *or* operation. The Boolean *exclusive-or* can be particularly useful. With the *exclusive-or* mode, two successive copies of a block to the same raster area restores the values that were originally present in that area. This technique can be used to move an object across a scene without destroying the background.

In addition to translation, rotations in 90° increments could be done using block transfers. A 90° rotation is accomplished by copying each row of the block into a column in the new frame buffer location. Reversing the order of bits within each row rotates the block 180°.

Block transfers of raster areas, sometimes referred to as bit-block transfers or bit-blt, are quick. These techniques form the basis for many animation implementations. Once an array of bit settings has been saved for an object, it can be repeatedly placed at different positions in the raster to simulate motion.

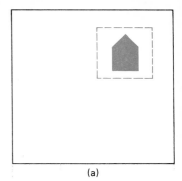
(a)

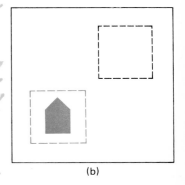
(b)

FIGURE 5–22
Block transfer of a raster area can be used to translate an object from one screen position to another.

Two-dimensional transformations are discussed in Pavlidis (1982). Additional information on transformation operations in GKS can be found in Enderle, Kansy, and Pfaff (1984) and in Hopgood, et. al. (1983).

REFERENCES

5–1. Write a program to continuously rotate an object about a pivot point. Small angles are to be used for each successive rotation, and approximations to the sine and cosine function are to be used to speed up the calculations. The rotation angle for each step is to be chosen so that the object makes one complete revolution in less then 30 seconds. Because of the accumulation of coordinate errors, the original coordinate values for the object are to be reused at the start of each new revolution.

5–2. Write a set of procedures to implement the *create_transformation_matrix* and the *accumulate_transformation_matrix* operations to produce a composite transformation matrix.

5–3. Write a program that utilizes the procedures of Ex. 5–2 to apply any specified sequence of transformations to a displayed object. The program is to be designed so that a user selects the transformation sequence and associated parameters from displayed menus, and the composite transformation is used to transform the object. Display the original object and the transformed object in different colors or different fill patterns.

5–4. Modify transformation matrix (5–26), for scaling in an arbitrary direction, to include coordinates for any specific scaling fixed point (x_F, y_F).

5–5. Prove that the multiplication of transformation matrices for the following sequence of operations is commutative:
   a. Two successive rotations
   b. Two successive translations
   c. Two successive scalings

5–6. Prove that a uniform scaling ($Sx = Sy$) and a rotation form a commutative pair of operations but that, in general, scaling and rotation are not commutative operations.

5–7. Show that transformation matrix (5–33), for a reflection about the line $y = x$, is equivalent to a reflection relative to the x axis followed by a counterclockwise rotation of 90°.

5–8. Show that transformation matrix (5–34), for a reflection about the line $y = -x$, is equivalent to a reflection relative to the y axis followed by a counterclockwise rotation of 90°.

5–9. Determine the form of the transformation matrix for a reflection about an arbitrary line with equation $y = mx + b$.

5–10. Determine a sequence of basic transformations that are equivalent to the x-direction shearing matrix (5–35).

5–11. Determine a sequence of basic transformations that are equivalent to the y-direction shearing matrix (5–36).

5–12. Set up procedures for implementing a block transfer of a rectangular area of a raster, using one function to read the area into an array and another function to copy the array into the designated transfer area.

5–13. Determine the results of performing two successive block transfers into the same area of a raster using the various Boolean operations.

5–14. What are the results of performing two successive block transfers into the same area of a raster using the binary arithmetic operations?

5–15. Implement a routine to perform block transfers in a raster using any specified Boolean operation or a replacement (copy) operation.

5–16. Write a routine to implement rotations in raster block transfers.

6

WINDOWING
AND CLIPPING

Applications programs define pictures in a world coordinate system. This can be any Cartesian coordinate system that a user finds convenient. Pictures defined in world coordinates are then mapped by the graphics system into device coordinates. Typically, a graphics package allows a user to specify which area of the picture definition is to be displayed and where it is to be placed on the display device. A single area could be chosen for display, or several areas could be selected. These areas can be placed in separate display locations, or one area can serve as a small insert into a larger area. This transformation process involves operations for translating and scaling selected areas and for deleting picture parts outside the areas. These operations are referred to as windowing and clipping.

FIGURE 6–1
A window-to-viewport
mapping.

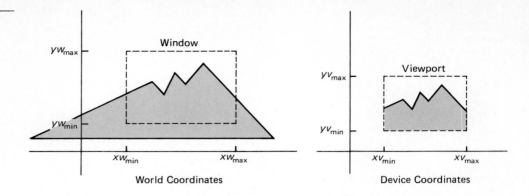

Window

yw_{max}

yw_{min}

xw_{min} xw_{max}

World Coordinates

Viewport

yv_{max}

yv_{min}

xv_{min} xv_{max}

Device Coordinates

6–1 Windowing Concepts

A rectangular area specified in world coordinates is called a **window.** The rectangular area on the display device to which a window is mapped is called a **viewport.** Figure 6–1 illustrates the mapping of a picture section that falls within the window area onto a designated viewport. This mapping is called a **viewing transformation,** **windowing transformation,** or **normalization transformation.**

Commands to set the window and viewport areas from an application program can be defined as

```
set_window (xw_min, xw_max, yw_min, yw_max)
set_viewport (xv_min, xv_max, yv_min, yv_max)
```

Parameters in each function are used to define the coordinate limits of the rectangular areas. The limits of the *window* are specified in world coordinates. Normalized device coordinates are most often used for the *viewport* specification, although device coordinates may be used if there is only one output device in the system. When normalized device coordinates are used, the programmer considers the output device to have coordinate values within the range 0 to 1. A viewport specification is given by values within this interval. The following specifications place a portion of a world coordinate definition into the upper right corner of a display area, as illustrated in Fig. 6–2.

```
set_window (−60.5, 41.25, −20.75, 82.5);
set_viewport (0.5, 0.8, 0.7, 1.0);
```

If a window is to be mapped onto the full display area, the viewport specification is given as

```
set_viewport (0, 1, 0, 1)
```

Coordinate positions expressed in normalized device coordinates must be converted to device coordinates before display by a specific output device. A device-specific routine is included in graphics packages for this purpose. The advantage of using normalized device coordinates is that the graphics package is largely device-independent. Different output devices can be used by providing the appropriate device drivers.

All coordinate points referenced in graphics packages must be specified relative to a Cartesian coordinate system. Any picture definitions that might originally

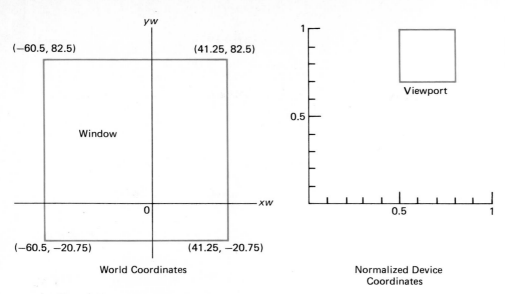

FIGURE 6–2
Mapping a window to a
viewport in normalized device
coordinates.

be defined in another system, such as polar coordinates, must first be converted by the user to a Cartesian world coordinate specification. These Cartesian coordinates are then used in window commands to identify the picture parts for display.

Window and viewport commands are stated before the procedures to specify a picture definition. Specifications for the window and viewport remain in effect for any subsequent output commands until new specifications are given.

By changing the position of the viewport, objects can be displayed at different positions on an output device. Also, by varying the size of viewports, the size and proportions of objects can be changed. When different-sized windows are successively mapped onto a viewport, **zooming** effects can be achieved. As the windows are made smaller, a user can zoom in on some part of a scene to view details that are not shown with the larger windows. Similarly, more overview is obtained by zooming out from a section of a scene with successively larger windows. **Panning** effects are produced by moving a fixed-size window across a large picture.

An example of the use of multiple window and viewpoint commands is given in the following procedure. Two graphs are displayed on different halves of a display device (Fig. 6–3).

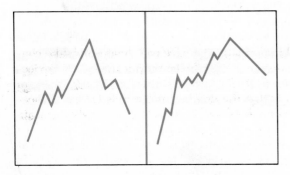

FIGURE 6–3
Simultaneous display of two
graphs, using multiple window
and viewport specifications.

```
type
   points = array [1..max_points] of real;
procedure two_graphs;
   var x, y. : points; k : integer;
   begin
      set_window (0, 1, 0, 1);              {draw center dividing line}
      set_viewport (0, 1, 0, 1);
      x[1] := 0.5; y[1] := 0; x[2] := 0.5; y[2] := 1;
      polyline (2, x, y);

      for k := 1 to 9 do begin              {read data for first graph}
         x[k] := k;
         readln (y[k])                      {data values between 300 and 700}
      end; {for k}
      set_window (1, 9, 300, 700);
      set_viewport (0.1, 0.4, 0.2, 0.8);      {put in left part of screen}
      polyline (9, x, y);

      for k := 1 to 13 do begin             {read data for second graph}
         x[k] := k;
         readln (y[k])                      {data values between 10 and 100}
      end; {for k}
      set_window (1, 13, 10, 100);
      set_viewport (0.6, 0.9, 0.2, 0.8);      {put in right part of screen}
      polyline (13, x, y)
   end; {two graphs}
```

FIGURE 6–4
Displaying viewports in priority
order. Lower-numbered
viewports are given higher
priority.

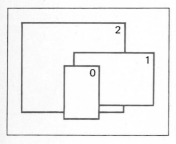

FIGURE 6–5
Rotated window, specified with
angle parameter *a*.

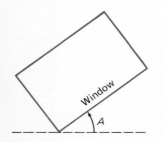

Another method for establishing multiple window and viewport areas in a graphics package is to assign a label to each specification. This could be done by including a fifth parameter in the window and viewport commands to identify each defined area. The parameter can be an integer index (0, 1, 2, . . .) that numbers the window or viewport definition. An additional command is then needed to indicate which window-to-viewport transformation number is to be applied to a set of output statements. This numbering scheme could also be used to associate a priority with each viewport, so that the visibility of overlapping viewports is decided on a priority basis. Viewports displayed according to priority are shown in Fig. 6–4.

For implementations that include multiple workstations, an additional set of window and viewport commands might be defined. These commands include a workstation number to establish different window and viewport areas on different workstations. This would allow a user to display various parts of the final image on different output devices. An architect, for example, might display the whole of a house plan on one monitor and just the second story on a second monitor.

The window and viewport commands we have introduced are used with rectangular areas, whose boundaries are parallel to the cordinate axes. Some graphics packages allow users to select other types of windows and viewports. A rotated window, as in Fig. 6–5, could be specified with an additional angle parameter *A* in a window command. Another possibility is to designate any type of polygon as the window by giving the sequence of vertices that define the polygon boundary. We begin by presenting algorithms for implementing rectangular windows and viewports whose boundaries are parallel to the *x* and *y* axes. The special handling required for arbitrarily shaped windows is then discussed as extensions to these algorithms.

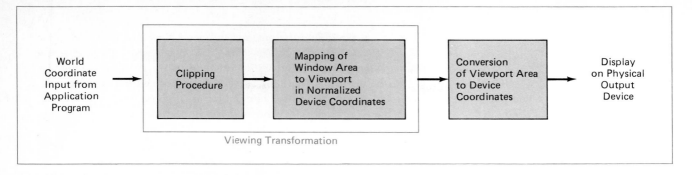

FIGURE 6–6
Processing input window
specifications into displayed
viewports.

6–2 Clipping Algorithms

Mapping a window area onto a viewport results in the display of only the picture
parts within the window. Everything outside the window is discarded. Procedures
for eliminating all parts of a defined picture outside of specified boundaries are
referred to as **clipping algorithms** or simply **clipping.**

Implementation of a windowing transformation is often performed by clipping
against the window, then mapping the window interior into the viewport (Fig.
6–6). Alternatively, some packages map the world coordinate definition into normalized device coordinates first and then clip against the viewport boundaries. In
the following discussion, we assume that clipping is to be performed relative to the
window boundaries in world coordinates. After clipping is completed, points within
the window are mapped to the viewport.

Point clipping against a window specification simply means that we test coordinate values to determine whether or not they are within the boundaries. A point
at position (x, y) is saved for transformation to a viewport if it satisfies the following
inequalities:

$$xw_{min} \leq x \leq xw_{max}, \quad yw_{min} \leq y \leq yw_{max} \tag{6–1}$$

If any one of these four inequalities is not satisfied, the point is clipped. In Fig.
6–7, point P_1 is saved, and point P_2 is clipped.

FIGURE 6–7
Point and line clipping against
a window boundary.

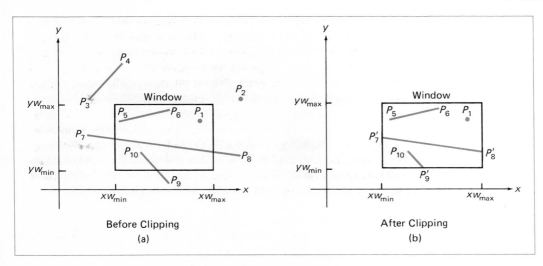

Before Clipping
(a)

After Clipping
(b)

Figure 6–7 illustrates possible relationships between line positions and window boundaries. We test a line for clipping by determining whether the endpoints are inside or outside the window. A line with both endpoints inside the window boundaries, such as the line from P_5 to P_6, is saved. A line with one endpoint outside (P_9) and one endpoint inside (P_{10}) is clipped off at the boundary intersection point (P'_9). Lines that have both endpoints beyond the boundaries are either totally outside the window or cross two window boundaries. The line from P_3 to P_4 is completely clipped. But the line from P_7 to P_8 extends beyond the window boundaries on both sides, and so the section of the line from P'_7 to P'_8 is saved.

A line-clipping algorithm determines which lines are wholly within the window boundaries and which lines are to be totally or partially clipped. For lines that are to be partially clipped, the intersection points with the window boundaries must be calculated. Since a picture definition can contain thousands of line segments, the clipping process should be performed as efficiently as possible. Before performing intersection calculations, an algorithm should identify all lines that are to be completely saved or completely clipped. With these lines eliminated from consideration, the determination of intersection points for the remaining lines should be carried out with a minimum of calculations.

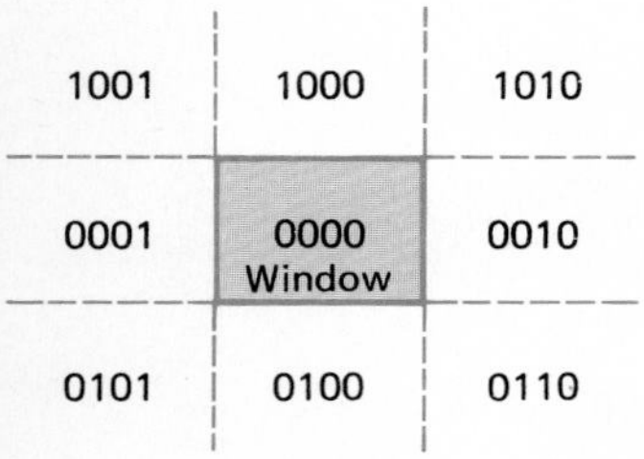

One approach to line clipping is based on a coding scheme developed by Cohen and Sutherland. Every line endpoint in a picture is assigned a four-digit binary code, called a **region code,** that identifies the coordinate region of the point. Regions are set up in reference to the window boundaries, as shown in Fig. 6–8. Each bit position in the region code is used to indicate one of the four relative coordinate positions of the point with respect to the window: to the left, right, top, or bottom. Numbering the bit positions in the region code as 1 through 4 from right to left, the coordinate regions can be correlated with the bit positions as

> bit 1 – left
> bit 2 – right
> bit 3 – below
> bit 4 – above

A value of 1 in any bit position indicates that the point is in that relative position; otherwise, the bit position is set to 0. If a point is within the window, the region code is 0000. A point that is below and to the left of the window has a region code of 0101.

Bit values in the region code are determined by comparing endpoint coordinate values (x, y) to the window boundaries. Bit 1 is set to 1 if $x < xw_{min}$. The other three bit values can be determined using similar comparisons. For languages in which bit manipulation is possible, region-code bit values can be determined by these steps: (1) Calculate differences between endpoint coordinates and window boundaries. (2) Use the resultant sign bit of each difference calculation to set the corresponding value in the region code. Bit 1 is the sign bit of $x - xw_{min}$; bit 2 is the sign bit of $xw_{max} - x$; bit 3 is the sign bit of $y - yw_{min}$; and bit 4 is the sign bit of $yw_{max} - y$.

Once we have established region codes for all line endpoints, we can quickly determine which lines are completely inside the window and which are clearly

---

FIGURE 6–8

Binary region codes for line endpoints, used to define coordinate areas relative to a window.

1001	1000	1010
0001	0000 Window	0010
0101	0100	0110

outside. Any lines that are completely contained within the window boundaries have a region code of 0000 for both endpoints, and we trivially accept these lines. Any lines that have a 1 in the same bit position in the region codes for each endpoint are completely outside the window, and we trivially reject these lines. We would discard the line that has a region code of 1001 for one endpoint and a code of 0101 for the other endpoint. Both endpoints of this line are left of the window, as indicated by the 1 in the first bit position of each region code. A method that can be used to test lines for total clipping is to perform the logical *and* operation with both region codes. If the result is not 0000, the line is outside the window.

Lines that cannot be identified as completely inside or completely outside a window by these tests are checked for intersection with the window boundaries. As shown in Fig. 6–9, such lines may or may not cross into the window interior. We can process these lines by comparing an endpoint that is outside the window to a window boundary to determine how much of the line can be discarded. Then the remaining part of the line is checked against the other boundaries, and we continue until either the line is totally discarded or a section is found inside the window. We set up our algorithm to check line endpoints against window boundaries in the order left, right, bottom, top.

To illustrate the specific steps in clipping lines against window boundaries using the Cohen-Sutherland algorithm, we show how the lines in Fig. 6–9 could be processed. Starting with the bottom endpoint of the line from P_1 to P_2, we check P_1 against the left, right, and bottom boundaries in turn and find that this point is below the window. We then find the intersection point P'_1 with the bottom boundary and discard the line section from P_1 to P'_1. The line now has been reduced to the section from P'_1 to P_2. Since P_2 is outside the window, we check this endpoint against the boundaries and find that it is above the window. Intersection point P'_2 is calculated, and the line section for P'_1 to P'_2 is saved. This completes processing for this line, so we save this part and go on to the next line. Point P_3 in the next line is to the left of the window, so we determine the intersection P'_3 and eliminate the line section from P_3 to P'_3. By checking region codes for the line section from P'_3 to P_4, we find that the remainder of the line is below the window and can be discarded also.

Intersection points with the window boundary are calculated using the line-equation parameters. For a line with endpoint coordinates (x_1, y_1) and (x_2, y_2), the y coordinate of the intersection point with a vertical window boundary can be obtained with the calculation

$$y = y_1 + m (x - x_1) \qquad (6\text{–}2)$$

where the x value is set either to xw_{min} or to xw_{max}, and the slope m is calculated as $m = (y_2 - y_1) / (x_2 - x_1)$. Similarly, if we are looking for the intersection with a horizontal boundary, the x coordinate can be calculated as

$$x = x_1 + \frac{y - y_1}{m} \qquad (6\text{–}3)$$

with y set either to yw_{min} or to yw_{max}.

The following procedure demonstrates the Cohen-Sutherland line-clipping algorithm. Codes for each endpoint are maintained as four-element arrays of Boolean values.

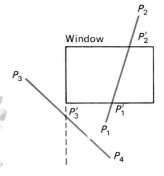

FIGURE 6–9
Lines extending from one coordinate region to another may pass through the window, or they may intersect window boundaries without entering the window.

```pascal
var
  xw_min, xw_max, yw_min, yw_max : real;

procedure clip_a_line (x1, y1, x2, y2 : real);
  type
    boundaries = (left, right, bottom, top);
    code = array [boundaries] of boolean;
  var
    code1, code2 : code;
    done, display : boolean;
    m : real;

  procedure encode (x, y : real; var c : code);
    begin
      if x < xw_min then c[left] := true
        else c[left] := false;
      if x > xw_max then c[right] := true
        else c[right] := false;
      if y < yw_min then c[bottom] := true
        else c[bottom] := false;
      if y > yw_max then c[top] := true
        else c[top] := false
      end; {encode}

  function accept (c1, c2 : code) : boolean;
    var k : boundaries;
    begin
      {if either point has 'true' in its code,
       a trivial accept is not possible}
      accept := true;
      for k := left to top do
        if c1[k] or c2[k] then accept := false
    end; {accept}

  function reject (c1, c2 : code) : boolean;
    var k : boundaries;
    begin
      {if endpoints have matching 'trues',
       line can be rejected}
      reject := false;
      for k := left to top do
        if c1[k] and c2[k] then reject := true
    end; {reject}

  procedure swap_if_needed (var x1, y1, x2, y2: real;
                            var c1, c2 : code);
    begin
      {insures that x1, y1 is a point outside
       of window and c1 contains its code}
    end; {swap_if_needed}

  begin {clip_a_line}
    done := false;
    display := false;
    while not done do begin
      encode (x1, y1, code1);
      encode (x2, y2, code2);
```

```
if accept (code1, code2) then begin
    done := true;
    display := true
  end {if accept}
else
  if reject (code1, code2) then done := true
  else begin {find intersection}
      {make sure that x1, y1 is outside window}
      swap_if_needed (x1, y1, x2, y2, code1, code2);
      m := (y2−y1) / (x2−x1);
      if code1[left] then begin
        y1 := y1 + (xw_min − x1) * m;
        x1 := xw_min
        end {crosses left}
      else
        if code1[right] then begin
          y1 := y1 + (xw_max − x1) * m;
          x1 := xw_max
          end {crosses right}
        else
          if code1[bottom] then begin
            x1 := x1 + (yw_min− y1) / m;
            y1 := yw_min
            end {crosses bottom}
          else
            if code1[top] then begin
              x1 := x1 + (yw_max − y1) / m;
              y1 := yw_max
              end {crosses top}
    end {else find intersection}
  end; {while not done}
  if display then {draw x1, y1, to x2, y2}
end; {clip_a_line}
```

A technique for locating window intersections without the line-equation calculations is a binary search procedure, called **midpoint subdivision.** Initial testing of lines is again carried out using region codes. Any lines that are not completely accepted or rejected with the region code checks are tested for window intersections by examining line midpoint coordinates.

This approach is illustrated in Fig. 6–10. For any line with endpoints (x_1, y_1) and (x_2, y_2), the midpoint of the line is calculated as

$$x_m = \frac{x_1 + x_2}{2}, \quad y_m = \frac{y_1 + y_2}{2} \tag{6–4}$$

Each calculation for a midpoint coordinate involves only an addition and a division by 2 (a shift operation). Once the midpoint coordinates have been determined, each half of the line can be tested for total acceptance or rejection. If half of the line can be accepted or rejected, then the other half is processed in the same way. This continues until an intersection point is found. If one half of the line cannot be trivially accepted or rejected, each half is processed until either the line is totally rejected or a visible section is found. Hardware implementation of this method can provide fast line clipping against the viewport boundaries after object descriptions have been transformed to device coordinates.

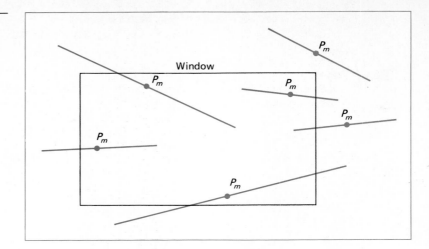

FIGURE 6–10
Line midpoints, P_m, used in a clipping algorithm.

Handwritten margin notes:

$xw_{min} \quad yw_{min}$

$xw_{max} \quad yw_{max}$

$x_1 + u \Delta x$

$xw_{min} \leq x_1 + \Delta x u \leq xw_{max}$

$yw_{min} \leq y_1 + \Delta y u \leq yw_{max}$

$p_k u \leq q_k$

$k = 1, 2, 3, 4$

$p_1 = -\Delta x$

$p_2 = \Delta x$

$p_3 = -\Delta y$

$p_4 = \Delta y$

$q_1 = x_1 - xw_{min}$

$q_2 = xw_{max} - x_1$

$q_3 = y_1 - yw_{min}$

$q_4 = yw_{max} - y_1$

parallel
line if $p_k = 0$

$q_k < 0$

Other techniques for line clipping have been devised that use a parametric form of the line equation. We can write the equation of a line segment defined between endpoints (x_1, y_1) and (x_2, y_2) in the parametric form

$$x = x_1 + (x_2 - x_1)u = x_1 + \Delta x\, u \qquad (6\text{–}5)$$
$$y = y_1 + (y_2 - y_1)u = y_1 + \Delta y\, u$$

where $\Delta x = x_2 - x_1$ and $\Delta y = y_2 - y_1$. Parameter u is assigned values between 0 and 1, and coordinates (x, y) represent a point on the line specified by a value of u in this range. When $u = 0$, $(x, y) = (x_1, y_1)$. At the other end of the line, $u = 1$ and $(x, y) = (x_2, y_2)$.

An efficient line-clipping algorithm using these parametric equations has been developed by Liang and Barsky. They note that if a point (x, y) along the line is inside a window defined by coordinates (xw_{min}, yw_{min}) and (xw_{max}, yw_{max}), the following conditions are satisfied:

$$xw_{min} \leq x_1 + \Delta x\, u \leq xw_{max} \qquad (6\text{–}6)$$
$$yw_{min} \leq y_1 + \Delta y\, u \leq yw_{max}$$

These four inequalities can be rewritten in the form

$$p_k u \leq q_k, \quad k = 1, 2, 3, 4 \qquad (6\text{–}7)$$

where p and q are defined as

$$
\begin{aligned}
p_1 &= -\Delta x, & q_1 &= x_1 - xw_{min} \\
p_2 &= \Delta x, & q_2 &= xw_{max} - x_1 \\
p_3 &= -\Delta y, & q_3 &= y_1 - yw_{min} \\
p_4 &= \Delta y, & q_4 &= yw_{max} - y_1
\end{aligned}
\qquad (6\text{–}8)
$$

Any line that is parallel to one of the window boundaries has $p_k = 0$ for the value of k corresponding to that boundary ($k = 1$, 2, 3, and 4 correspond to the left, right, bottom, and top boundaries, respectively). If, for that value of k, we also find $q_k < 0$, then the line is completely outside the boundary and can be eliminated from further consideration. If $q_k \geq 0$, the parallel line is inside the boundary.

When $p_k < 0$, the infinite extension of the line proceeds from the outside to the inside of the infinite extension of this particular window boundary. If $p_k > 0$, the line proceeds from the inside to the outside. For a nonzero p_k, we can calculate the value of u that corresponds to the point where the infinitely extended line intersects the extension of the window boundary k as

$$u = q_k/p_k \qquad (6\text{--}9)$$

For each line, we can calculate values for parameters u_1 and u_2 that define that part of the line that lies within the window. The value of u_1 is determined by looking at the window edges for which the line proceeds from the outside to the inside ($p < 0$). For these window edges, we calculate $r_k = q_k / p_k$. The value of u_1 is taken as the largest of the set consisting of 0 and the various values of r. Conversely, the value of u_2 is determined by examining the boundaries for which the line proceeds from inside to outside ($p > 0$). A value of r_k is calculated for each of these window boundaries, and the value of u_2 is the minimum of the set consisting of 1 and the calculated r values. If $u_1 > u_2$, the line is completely outside the window and it can be rejected. Otherwise, the endpoints of the clipped line are calculated from the two values of parameter u.

This algorithm is presented in the following procedure. Line intersection parameters are initialized to the values $u1 = 0$ and $u2 = 1$. For each window boundary, the appropriate values for p and q are calculated and used by the function *cliptest* to determine whether the line can be rejected or whether the intersection parameters are to be adjusted. When $p < 0$, the parameter r is used to update $u1$; when $p > 0$, parameter r is used to update $u2$. If updating $u1$ or $u2$ results in $u1 > u2$, we reject the line. Otherwise, we update the appropriate u parameter only if the new value results in a shortening of the line. When $p = 0$ and $q < 0$, we can discard the line since it is parallel to and on the outside of this boundary. If the line has not been rejected after all four values of p and q have been tested, the endpoints of the clipped line are determined from values of $u1$ and $u2$.

```
var
   xwmin, xwmax, ywmin, ywmax : real;

procedure clipper (var x1, y1, x2, y2 : real);
   var
      u1, u2, dx, dy : real;

   function cliptest (p, q : real; var u1, u2 : real);
      var
         r : real;
         result : boolean;
      begin {cliptest}
         result := true;
         if p < 0 then begin              {line from outside to inside
                                           of this boundary}

            r := q / p;
            if r > u2 then result := false  {reject line or}
            else if r > u1 then u1 := r     {update u1 if appropriate}
         end {if p < 0}
         else
            if p > 0 then begin           {line from inside to outside
                                           of this boundary}
```

```
              r := q / p;
            if r < ul then result := false        {reject line or}
            else if r < u2 then u2 := r           {update u2 if appropriate}
          end {if p > O}
        else                                      {p = O; line parallel to
                                                   boundary}
            if q < O then result := false;        {outside of boundary}
        cliptest := result
      end; {cliptest}


    begin {clipper}
      ul := O;
      u2 := l;
      dx := x2 - xl;
      if cliptest (-dx, xl - xwmin, ul, u2) then
        if cliptest (dx, xwmax - xl, ul, u2) then begin
            dy := y2 - yl;
            if cliptest (-dy, yl - ywmin, ul, u2) then
              if cliptest (dy, ywmax - yl, ul, u2) then begin
                {if ul and u2 are within range of O to 1,
                 use to calculate new line endpoints}
                if ul > O then begin
                    xl := xl + ul * dx;
                    yl := yl + ul * dy
                  end; {if ul > O}
                if u2 < 1 then begin
                    x2 := xl + u2 * dx;
                    y2 := yl + u2 * dy
                  end {if u2 < 1}
              end {if cliptest}
          end {if cliptest}
    end; {clipper}
```

The Liang and Barsky line-clipping algorithm reduces the computations that are needed to clip lines. Each update of u_1 and u_2 requires only one division, and window intersections of the line are computed only once, when values of u_1 and u_2 have been finalized. In contrast, the Cohen and Sutherland algorithm repeatedly calculates points of intersection between the line and window boundaries, and each intersection calculation requires both a division and a multiplication.

When rotated windows or arbitrarily shaped polygons are used for windows and viewports, the line-clipping algorithms discussed would require some modification. It is still possible to do preliminary screening of the lines. A rotated window, or any other polygon shape, can be enclosed within a larger rectangle whose sides are parallel to the coordinate axes (Fig. 6–11). Any lines outside the larger bounding rectangle are outside the window also. Inside tests are not so easily done, and intersection points must be calculated using line equations for the window boundaries as well as for the lines to be clipped.

Area Clipping

Hollow polygons used in line-drawing applications can be clipped by processing each component line through the line-clipping algorithms discussed. A polygon processed in this way is reduced to a series of clipped lines (Fig. 6–12).

FIGURE 6–11
Rotated window enclosed by a larger bounding rectangle whose boundaries are parallel to coordinate axes.

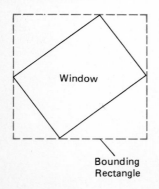

Window

Bounding
Rectangle

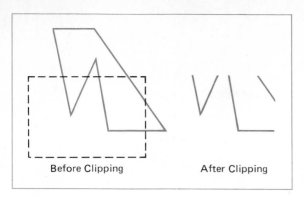

FIGURE 6–12
Polygon clipped by a line-clipping algorithm.

When a polygon boundary defines a fill area, as in Fig. 6–13, a modified version of the line-clipping algorithm is needed. In this case, one or more closed areas must be produced to define the boundaries for area fill.

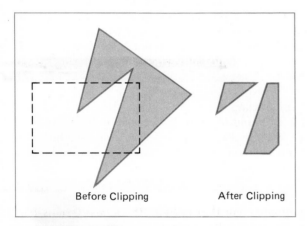

FIGURE 6–13
A shaded area, before and after clipping.

A technique for polygon clipping, developed by Sutherland and Hodgman, performs clipping by comparing a polygon to each window boundary in turn. The output of the algorithm is a set of vertices defining the clipped area that is to be filled with a color or shading pattern. The basic method is illustrated in Fig. 6–14.

Polygon areas are defined by specifying an ordered sequence of vertices. To clip a polygon, we compare each of the vertices in turn against a window boundary. Vertices inside this window edge are saved for clipping against the next boundary;

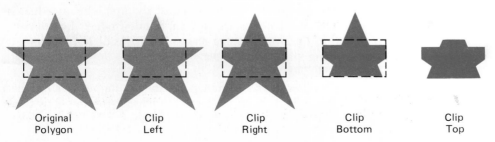

FIGURE 6–14
Clipping a polygon area against successive window boundaries.

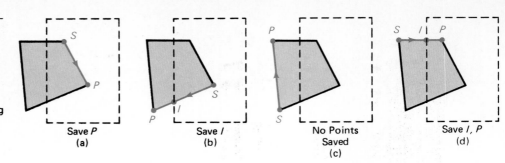

FIGURE 6–15

Processing vertices of a polygon boundary (dashed lines). From vertex *S*, the next vertex point processed *(P)* may generate one point, no points, or two points to be saved by a clipping algorithm.

Save *P*
(a)

Save *I*
(b)

No Points
Saved
(c)

Save *I*, *P*
(d)

vertices outside the window edge are discarded. If we proceed from a point inside the window edge to an outside point, we save the intersection of the line with the window boundary. Both the intersection and the vertex are saved if we cross from the outside of a window edge to the inside. The four possible situations that can occur as we process a point *(P)* and the previous point *(S)* against a window boundary are illustrated in Fig. 6–15. A point inside the window boundary is saved (case a), while an outside point is not (case c). If a point *P* and the previous point *S* are on opposite sides of a boundary, the intersection *I* is calculated and saved (cases b and d). In case d, the point *P* is inside and the previous point *S* is outside so both the intersection *I* and the point *P* are saved. Once all vertices have been processed for the left window boundary, the set of saved points is clipped against the next window boundary.

We illustrate this method by processing the area in Fig. 6–16 against the left window boundary. Vertices 1 and 2 are found to be on the outside of the boundary. Passing to vertex 3, which is inside, we calculate the intersection and save both the intersection point and vertex 3. Vertices 4 and 5 are determined to be inside, and they also are saved. The sixth and final vertex is outside, so we find and save the intersection point. Using the five saved points, we repeat the process for the next window boundary.

Implementing the algorithm as described necessitates the use of extra storage space for the saved points. This can be avoided if we take each point that would be saved and immediately pass it to the clipping routine, along with instructions to clip it against the next boundary. We save a point (either an original vertex or a calculated intersection) only after it has been processed against all boundaries. It is as if we have a pipeline of clipping routines, with each stage in the pipeline clipping against a different window boundary. A point that is inside or on the window boundary at one stage is passed along to the next stage. A point that is outside at some stage simply does not continue in the pipeline.

The following procedure demonstrates this approach. An array, *s*, records the most recent point that was clipped for each window edge. The main routine passes each vertex *p* to the *clip_this* routine for clipping against the first window edge. If the line defined by endpoints *p* and *s[edge]* crosses this window edge, the intersection is found and is passed to the next clipping stage. If *p* is inside the window, it is passed to the next clipping stage. Any point that survives clipping against all window edges is then entered into the output arrays *x_out* and *y_out*. The array *first_point* stores for each window edge the first point that is clipped against that edge. After all polygon vertices have been processed, a closing routine clips lines defined by the first and last points clipped against each edge.

FIGURE 6–16

Clipping a polygon against the left edge of a window, starting with vertex 1. Primed numbers are used to label the points saved by the clipping algorithm.

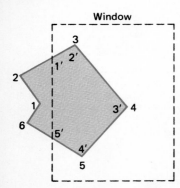

Window

```
type
   point = array [1..max_points] of real;

procedure polygon_clip (n : integer; x, y : points; var m : integer;
                           var x_out, y_out : points);
   const
      boundary_count = 4;
   type
      vertex = array [1..2] of real;
      boundary_range = 1..boundary_count;
   var
      k : integer;
      p : vertex;
      s, first_point : array [1..boundary_count] of vertex;
      new_edge : array [1..boundary_count] of boolean;

   function inside (p : vertex; edge : boundary_range) : boolean;
      begin
         {returns true if vertex p is inside of window edge}
      end;   {inside}

   function cross (p, s : vertex; edge : integer) : boolean;
      begin
         {returns true if polygon side ps intersects window edge}
      end; {cross}

   procedure output_vertex (p : vertex);
      begin
         m := m + 1;
         x_out[m] := p[1]; y_out[m] := p[2]
      end; {output_vertex}

   procedure find_intersection (p, s : vertex;
                                   edge : boundary_range; var i : vertex);
      begin
         {returns in parameter i the intersection of ps with window edge}
      end; {intersection}

   procedure clip_this (p : vertex; edge : boundary_range);
      var i : vertex;
      begin  {clip_this}
         {save the first point clipped against a window edge}
         if new_edge[edge] then begin
            first_point[edge] := p;
            new_edge[edge] := false
          end   {new_edge}
         else
           {if ps crosses window edge, find intersection,
            clip intersection against next window edge}
           if cross (p, s[edge], edge) then begin
               find_intersection (p, s[edge], edge, i);
               if edge < boundary_count then clip_this (i, edge + 1)
               else output_vertex (i)
               end; {if p & s cross edge}
         {update saved vertex}
```

```
        s[edge] := p;
        {if p is inside this window edge,
         clip it against next window edge}
        if inside (p, edge) then
          if edge < boundary_count then clip_this (p, edge + 1)
          else output_vertex (p)
      end; {clip_this}


  procedure clip_closer;
      {closing routine. For each window edge, clips the
       line connecting the last saved vertex and the first_point
       processed against the edge}
      var
        i : vertex;
        edge : integer;
      begin
        for edge := 1 to boundary_count do
            if cross (s[edge], first_point[edge], edge) then begin
                find_intersection (s[edge], first_point[edge], edge, i);
                if edge < boundary_count then clip_this (i, edge + 1)
                else output_vertex (i)
                end  {if s and first_point cross edge}
            end; {clip_closer}

begin   {polygon_clip}
  m := 0;                             {number of output vertices}
  for k := 1 to boundary_count do
    new_edge[k] := true;
  for k := 1 to n do begin            {puts each vertex into pipeline}
      p[1] := x[k]; p[2] := y[k];
      clip_this (p, 1)                {clip against first window edge}
    end;  {for k}
  clip_closer                         {close polygon}
end;   {polygon_clip}
```

When a concave polygon is clipped against a rectangular window, the final clipped area may actually represent two or more distinct polygons. Since this area-clipping algorithm produces only one list of vertices, these separate areas will be joined with connecting lines. An example of this effect is shown in Fig. 6–17. Special considerations can be given to such cases to remove the extra lines, or more general clipping algorithms can be employed.

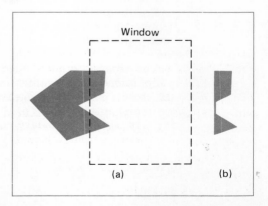

FIGURE 6–17
Clipping the concave polygon in (a) against the window generates the two connected areas in (b).

Although we have limited our discussion to rectangular windows aligned with the *x* and *y* axes, we could implement this algorithm to clip against a window of any polygon shape. We would need to store information about each of the window boundaries, and we would need to modify the routines *inside* and *find_intersection* to handle arbitrary boundaries.

Another approach to polygon-area clipping is to employ parametric-equation methods. Arbitrarily shaped windows would then be processed by using parametric line equations to describe both the window boundaries and the boundaries of the areas to be clipped.

Clipping areas other than polygons requires a little more work, since the area boundaries are not defined with straight-line equations. In Fig.6–18, for example, circle equations are needed to find the two intersection points on the window boundary.

Text Clipping

There are several techniques that can be used to provide text clipping in a graphics package. The particular implementation chosen will depend on the methods used to generate characters and the amount of sophistication needed by a user of the package in the processing of text.

The simplest method for processing character strings relative to a window boundary is to use the "all-or-none text-clipping" strategy shown in Fig. 6–19. If all of the string is inside a window, we keep it. Otherwise, the string is discarded. This procedure can be implemented by considering a bounding rectangle around the text pattern. The boundary positions of the rectangle are then compared to the window boundaries, and the string is rejected if there is any overlap. This method produces the fastest text clipping.

An alternative to rejecting an entire character string that overlaps a window boundary is to use the "all-or-none character-clipping" strategy. Here we discard only those characters that are not completely inside the window (Fig. 6–20). In this case, the boundary limits of individual characters are compared to the window. Any character that either overlaps or is outside a window boundary is clipped.

A final method for handling text clipping is to clip individual characters. We now treat characters in much the same way that we treated lines. If an individual character overlaps a window boundary, we clip off the parts outside the window (Fig. 6–21). Characters formed with line segments can be processed in this way using a line-clipping algorithm. Processing characters formed with bit maps requires clipping individual pixels by comparing the relative position of the grid patterns to the window boundaries.

Blanking

Instead of saving information inside a defined region, a window area can be used for **blanking** (erasing) anything within its boundaries. What is saved is outside.

Blanking all output primitives within a defined area is a convenient means for overlapping different pictures. This technique is often used for designing page layouts in advertising or publishing applications or for adding labels or design patterns to a picture. The technique can also be used for combining graphs, maps, or schematics. Figure 6–22 illustrates some applications of blanking.

When two displays are to be overlaid using blanking methods, one display can be thought of as the foreground and the other as the background. A blanking window, encompassing the foreground display area, is superimposed on the back-

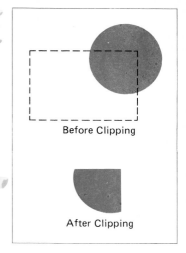

FIGURE 6–18
Clipping a circular area.

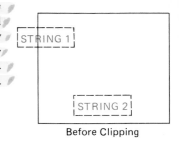

FIGURE 6–19
Text clipping using bounding rectangles. Any rectangles overlapping the boundary are entirely discarded.

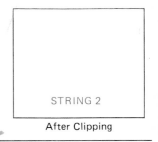

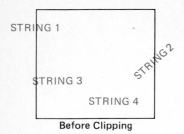

STRING 1

STRING 2

STRING 3

STRING 4

Before Clipping

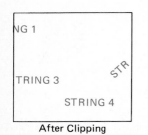

NG 1

STR

TRING 3

STRING 4

After Clipping

FIGURE 6–20
Character strings can be clipped so that only characters that are completely inside a window are retained.

FIGURE 6–21
Clipping individual characters.

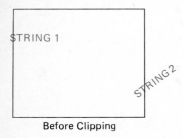

STRING 1

STRING 2

Before Clipping

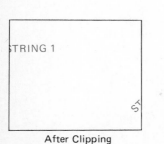

STRING 1

ST

After Clipping

ground picture, and the picture parts within the window area are blanked. The two displays are then combined, with the foreground information placed within the blanked window area.

6–3 Window-to-Viewport Transformation

Once all points, lines, polygons, and text have been clipped, they are mapped onto the viewport area for display. This transformation to the viewport is carried out so that relative coordinate positions are maintained.

In Fig. 6–23, a point at position (xw, yw) in a window is mapped into position (xv, yv) in a viewport. To maintain the same relative placement in the viewport as in the window, we require that

$$\frac{xw - xw_{min}}{xw_{max} - xw_{min}} = \frac{xv - xv_{min}}{xv_{max} - xv_{min}} \tag{6-10}$$

and

$$\frac{yw - yw_{min}}{yw_{max} - yw_{min}} = \frac{yv - yv_{min}}{yv_{max} - yv_{min}} \tag{6-11}$$

We can rewrite Eqs. 6–10 and 6–11 as explicit transformation calculations for the coordinates xv and yv:

$$xv = \frac{xv_{max} - xv_{min}}{xw_{max} - xw_{min}} (xw - xw_{min}) + xv_{min}$$

$$yv = \frac{yv_{max} - yv_{min}}{yw_{max} - yw_{max}} (yw - yw_{min}) + yv_{min} \tag{6-12}$$

These window-to-viewport transformation calculations can be written more compactly as

$$xv = sx(xw - xw_{min}) + xv_{min}$$

$$yv = sy(yw - yw_{min}) + yv_{min} \tag{6-13}$$

which include both scaling and translation factors. The ratios represented by sx and sy scale objects according to the relative sizes of the window and viewport. These ratios must be equal if objects are to maintain the same proportions when they are mapped into the viewport. When the window and viewport are the same size ($sx = sy = 1$), there is no change in the size of transformed objects. Values for xv_{min} and yv_{min} provide the translation factors for moving objects into the viewport area.

Character strings can be handled in two ways when they are mapped to a viewport. The simplest mapping maintains a constant character size, even though the viewport area may be enlarged or reduced relative to the window. This method would be employed when text is formed with standard character fonts that cannot be changed. In systems that allow for changes in character size, string definitions can be windowed the same as other primitives. For characters formed with line segments, the mapping to the viewport could be carried out as a sequence of line transformations.

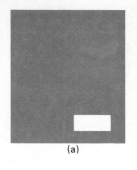 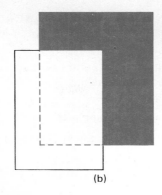

(a)

(b)

FIGURE 6–22
Examples of blanking: (a) An area is provided for labeling; (b) an area used to erase part of a previous display to provide a blank area for overlays.

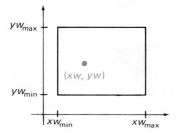 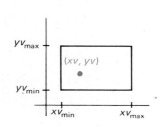

FIGURE 6–23
A point at position (xw, yw) in a window is mapped to the viewport point (xv, yv). The mapping is performed so that relative proportions in the two areas are the same.

REFERENCES

Line-clipping algorithms are discussed in Liang and Barsky (1984), Pavlidis (1982), and Sproull and Sutherland (1968). Cyrus and Beck (1978) describe an algorithm that is similar to the Liang-Barsky clipping procedures and that can be used to clip against an arbitrarily shaped window.

The reentrant polygon clipping procedure is presented in Sutherland and Hodgman (1974). A method for polygon clipping using parametric line equations is given in Liang and Barsky (1983). And Weiler and Atherton (1977) discuss general techniques for clipping arbitrarily shaped polygons against each other.

Sources of information on windowing and clipping functions in GKS are Enderle, Kansy, and Pfaff (1984) and Hopgood, et. al. (1983).

EXERCISES

6–1. Implement the Cohen-Sutherland clipping algorithm with Pascal sets used to represent region codes. That is, the region code for a line endpoint is represented as a subset of the set *code = set of (left, right, bottom, top)*.

6–2. Carefully discuss the rationale behind the various tests and methods for calculating the intersection parameters u_1 and u_2 in the Liang-Barsky line-clipping algorithm.

6–3. Compare the number of arithmetic operations performed in the Cohen-Sutherland and the Liang-Barsky line-clipping algorithms for several different line orientations relative to a clipping window.

6–4. Implement the Liang-Barsky line-clipping algorithm on your system.

6–5. Devise an algorithm to perform line clipping using the midpoint-subdivision method. Would a software implementation of this algorithm offer any benefits over the other two line-clipping algorithms discussed in this chapter?

6–6. Set up an algorithm to clip lines against a rotated window, defined with minimum and maximum coordinate values and a rotation angle as shown in Fig. 6–5.

6–7. Modify the polygon-clipping algorithm to clip concave polygon areas correctly. (One method for accomplishing this is to divide the concave polygon into a number of convex polygons.)

6–8. Adapt the Liang-Barsky line-clipping algorithm to polygon clipping.

6–9. Write a routine to clip an ellipse against a rectangular window.

6–10. Assuming that characters are defined in a pixel grid, develop a text-clipping algorithm that clips individual characters according to the "all-or-none" strategy.

6–11. Develop a text-clipping algorithm that clips individual characters, assuming that the characters are defined in a pixel grid.

6–12. Write a routine to perform blanking on any part of a defined picture using any specified blanking window size.

6–13. Set up procedures to implement the *window* and *viewport* commands. That is, the procedures are to take the coordinate parameters in these commands and perform the complete viewing transformation for a specified scene: clipping in world coordinates, transformation to normalized coordinates, then transformation to device coordinates.

6–14. Expand the procedures in Ex. 6–13 to allow multiple, numbered windows and viewports to be used in an application program. The parameter list in the *window* and *viewport* commands will now include a transformation number, specified as a nonnegative integer. In addition, the application program must state which window and viewport are to be used. This is accomplished with the command: *select_normalization_transformation (n),* where integer *n* identifies the window-viewport pair to be used with subsequent output primitive statements.

6–15. Compare the relative advantages and disadvantages of clipping in world coordinates to clipping in device coordinates (either normalized or physical device coordinates). Factors to be considered include hardware versus software implementations, application of geometric transformations (allowing possible composition of matrices), use of rotated windows or viewports, and the structure of a picture relative to the window boundaries.

7

SEGMENTS

For many applications, graphics displays are handled most efficiently by defining and modifying a picture as a set of subpictures. Graphics packages that are designed to store and manipulate pictures in terms of their component parts are more complicated, but they allow users greater flexibility. By defining each object in a picture as a separate module, a user can make modifications to the picture more easily. In design applications, different positions and orientations for a component of a picture can be tried out without disturbing other parts of the picture. Or a component can be taken out of a version of the picture, then later put back into the display. An animation program can apply transformations to an individual object definition so that the object is moved around while the other objects in the scene remain stationary.

A set of output primitives (and their associated attributes) that are arranged and labeled as a group is called a **segment.** To allow for segment operations, a graphics package must include capabilities for creating and deleting segments. When a segment is created by a user, the coordinate positions and attribute values specified in the segment are stored as a labeled group in a system segment list. As segments are deleted, they are removed from this list. Routines must then be provided in the package for allocating and reclaiming the segment storage areas.

Packages can provide for the creation of a segment with the command

```
create_segment (id)
```

The label for the segment is the positive integer assigned to parameter *id*. After all primitives and attributes have been listed, the end of the segment is signaled with a *close_segment* statement. For example, the following program statements define segment number 6 as the line sequence specified in *polyline:*

```
create_segment (6);
  polyline (n, x, y);
close_segment;
```

Any number of segments can be defined for a display using these commands. In most systems, only one segment can be open at a time. The open segment must be closed before a new segment can be created. This method eliminates the need for a segment identification number in the *close_segment* statement.

A user deletes a segment with the command

```
delete_segment (id)
```

Once a segment has been deleted, its name can be reused for another sequence of primitive statements.

In some situations, a user may want to modify a segment after it has been closed. Another command could be defined for reopening segments or for appending to segments, but the processing required to implement such functions is complex and costly. Generally, packages do not allow closed segments to be modified. The user can, of course, delete an existing segment and then re-create it with the desired changes. For example, a new segment 6 is created with the following statements:

```
delete_segment (6);
create_segment (6);
  polyline (n, x, y);
  text (xt, yt, "figure label");
close_segment;
```

Some systems do provide a function for copying the contents of an existing segment into a newly opened segment. While not strictly an append operation, this can be used to produce the same effect.

It is sometimes useful to rename a segment. For this purpose, we define

```
rename_segment (id_old, id_new)
```

One use for the rename operation is to consolidate the numbering of the segments after several segments have been deleted.

7–2 Segment Files

We will refer to any list of segments maintained by a graphics system with the generic term **segment file.** A segment file can take on a number of forms, depending on the type of graphics system. The display file program of a simple vector system can be structured according to a user's definition of segments. In this case, the display file program is a type of segment file, referred to as a **segmented display file.** On vector systems with both a display processor and a display controller, more than one segment file may be maintained by the system (Fig. 7–1).

Raster systems display a picture from the definition in a frame buffer, not from a display file program as in vector systems. However, graphics packages to be used on raster-scan equipment can be designed to maintain a **pseudo display file** as an internal data structure. The pseudo display file is a type of segment file that contains the segment definitions and other information regarding the structure of a picture. Scan-conversion routines work from this file and set appropriate bits in the frame buffer, as shown in Fig. 7–2. Maintaining such a segment file on a raster system requires extra memory, but it allows for greater compatibility with vector systems. Pseudo display files are also used because they provide a fast and efficient method for regeneration of a picture after modifications have been made.

Segment files can be physically stored in a number of ways. A linked-list structure, as in Fig. 7–3, offers the most flexible arrangement for handling segment creation, deletion, and manipulation. Segments are added to the linked list by setting appropriate pointer fields. If segments are assigned priorities, the linked list is organized in priority order, with each new segment inserted into the list at the proper position.

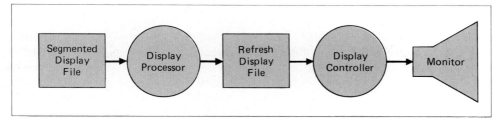

FIGURE 7–1
Segment file organizations for a random-scan system.

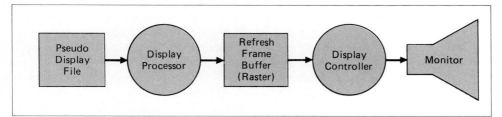

FIGURE 7–2
A segmented display file is used to update the frame buffer in a raster system.

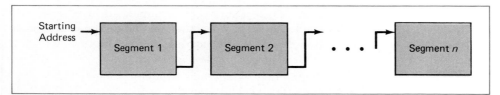

FIGURE 7–3
A segment file organized as a linked list.

145

FIGURE 7–4
A segment fragmented for
storage in three fixed-size
memory blocks.

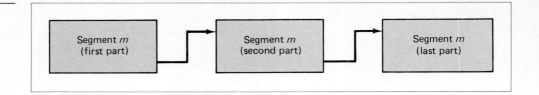

A memory management routine is used to handle segment storage assignments. Blocks of storage are assigned to segments as they are created, and storage blocks are returned to the storage pool when a segment is deleted. A procedure for deleting a segment sets pointer fields in the list to bypass the segment and then returns the segment block address to the storage pool. Different strategies adopted for assigning storage include fixed-size block assignments and variable-length block assignments to accommodate the different lengths of segments. Also, different memory compaction schemes are possible with variable-sized blocks to collect unused storage and minimize wasted space.

Fixed-size blocks are easy to manage, but they can result in fragmented segments (Fig. 7–4). If a segment is too big for the assigned block, it is overflowed into another block. The overflow process continues into successive blocks until all of the segment is stored. This approach requires some threading through pointer fields to locate all parts of large segments, and the refresh process is slowed if this method is used as the storage scheme for the refresh display file of a vector system.

Variable-sized blocks avoid fragmented segments, but they involve more processing by the memory management routines. Since the size of a segment is not known until it is closed, the correct-sized block cannot be assigned in advance. One way to accommodate the different-sized segments is simply to begin storing a segment in the first available storage block. If a segment overflows the assigned block, a larger block is requested immediately. In this way, a large segment is continually being transferred to larger blocks as it grows. Another possibility is to fragment a large segment over more than one block as it is being created and then compact it into a larger block after the segment is closed.

There often will be unused space at the end of a segment block. To simplify processing, this unused space could be left in the block rather than returned to the memory pool. If the memory pool should run out of blocks, a compaction method can be used to collect some of the unused space.

To insert and delete segments efficiently, we need a quick method for locating segments within the segment file. One method is to store segment names and related information in a separate segment directory. Alternatively, these data could be stored in segment headers at the beginning of each segment block.

Figure 7–5 shows one arrangement for a segment directory. When a segment is to be located, the directory is searched to find the address for the given segment name. A binary search procedure can be used to locate segments when entries are sorted on the name field. Using a directory to locate segments can be useful when a large number of segments are to be stored and manipulated. However, this method does require sorting and searching procedures for the directory and some method, such as an expandable directory size, for handling arbitrary numbers of segments.

A scheme for storing information in segment headers is illustrated in Fig. 7–6. Following the name field is the "visibility pointer field." Normally, this field

Name	Address	Length	Visibility	Other Parameters
N1	ADDR1	L1	V1	• • •
N2	ADDR2	L2	V2	• • •
• • •	• • •	• • •	• • •	• • •

FIGURE 7–5
Organization of a segment directory.

points to the beginning of the output primitive entries. Segments are made invisible by setting this field to the address of the next segment. The "next-segment pointer field" is provided at the beginning of the block to speed up searches through the linked list. Without this entry, a segment search would need to find the pointer field at the end of the block to proceed to the next segment. Finally, the "end-of-segment pointer field" can mark the segment end by pointing back to the "next-segment pointer field," as in Fig. 7–6. Such headers have advantages over storing the segment addresses in two places. The last field of each segment is always set to point back to the third field within each segment, and only one pointer field in a segment needs to be set during a deletion or insertion operation.

Another possible organization for a segment file is shown in Fig. 7–7. Here, segments are stored as adjacent blocks within a one-dimensional array. This scheme simplifies the setting of pointer fields, and it is particularly suitable as a simple

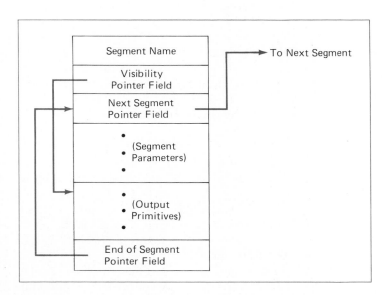

FIGURE 7–6
Organization of a segment block with a header. The visibility pointer field is used to set the visibility condition. A segment is invisible if this field points to the next segment.

Segment 1	Segment 2	• • •	Segment *n*

FIGURE 7–7
Organization of a segment file as a linear array.

organization for a vector display file program. As with linked lists, searches through this segment file can be done with a segment directory or with headers. Deletion is accomplished by removing segments from the array and compacting the blocks back into contiguous locations. Similarly, insertions are carried out by shifting blocks to make room for new segments. Visibility changes are again implemented by setting pointer fields. A segment is made invisible by setting the visibility pointer to the next segment address. It is made visible again by setting the pointer field to the starting address of the primitive entries.

On a vector system, the refresh display file is accessed by both the display processor running the graphics package and the display controller. The two processors operate concurrently and share the segment file data structure. Synchronization between the two processors is important. If the operations of the processors are not synchronized, updates to the file could cause the display controller to produce a distorted picture on the display device. Usually, the display processor locks the file while making an update, denying access to the display controller.

7–3 Segment Attributes

A number of parameters, or attributes, can be assigned to a created segment. Most graphics packages permit users to set the values for a segment's visibility, its priority, and whether or not it is to be highlighted. Some packages also allow a transformation matrix to be associated with a segment. With this transformation matrix attribute, a user can vary the size, position, and orientation of a segment.

Visibility of segments is established by a user with the command

```
set_visibility (id, v)
```

Parameter v is used to control the display of segments. If v is set to the value *invisible* for a specified segment *id*, that segment is maintained in the segment list but is not displayed on the output device in use. Setting v to *visible* causes the segment to be displayed.

The ability to turn segments on and off is useful in design applications where the effects of different segments are to be tested. It is also useful for setting up menu and message segments that can be displayed at certain times to direct interactive input to a program.

Priority can be set for segments with the command

```
set_segment_priority (id, p)
```

A numeric value between 0 and 1 is assigned to priority parameter p. These numbers determine the order for displaying segments, and they are mostly used on raster-scan systems. Lower-priority segments (values near 0) are displayed first up to the highest-priority segment, which is displayed last. Higher-priority segments "paint" over the lower-priority segments in areas of overlap. This gives the user a convenient way to set up background and foreground segments in applications such as animation, where objects move past each other.

In any implementation of the priority command, only a finite number of priority levels will be allowed. This number could be quite large on some systems, while other systems might restrict the priority levels to a very few values, such as 0, 0.5, and 1. Any other numbers assigned as priorities are rounded to the nearest level. When two segments are assigned the same priority number, the system must use another method to decide which to display first. A first-come, first-served scheme could be used, or some other property such as segment number could be used to break the priority tie.

Highlighting a segment is done with

```
set_highlighting (id, h)
```

where parameter *h* can take values *highlighted* and *normal.* By setting *h* to *highlighted*, a user specifies that some mechanism is to be applied to accent the designated segment. The type of highlighting displayed depends on the type of output device in use. With a video monitor, a highlighted segment could be displayed in a higher intensity, or it could be set to blink on and off.

When segment transformations are allowed in a graphics package, a user can specify the transformation matrices that are to be applied to individual segments. Typically, the identity matrix is linked to a segment when it is first created. Subsequently, the application program can change the associated matrix with the command

```
set_segment_transformation (id, matrix)
```

Parameter *matrix* contains the elements of the transformation matrix, as set by the methods discussed in Chapter 5. During the picture-generation process, all output primitives within the given segment are transformed according to the operations specified in *matrix.* The user can vary the appearance of the segment by associating a new transformation matrix with the segment.

Clipping and the window-to-viewport transformation must also be applied to output primitives making up a segment. Usually the window and viewport specifications that are current when the segment is opened are used to generate the display of that particular segment.

In our previous discussions, clipping was performed in world coordinates using the window boundaries. The interior of the window was then mapped to the viewport. This is not the most efficient arrangement for packages that allow transformations of segment definitions. Each time a transformation matrix is associated with a segment, the window-to-viewport mapping would be repeated. Since this mapping doesn't change, it is advantageous to omit it from the repeated reprocessing of the segment.

To do this, we can convert world coordinates to normalized device coordinates first, before the output primitives are even stored in the segment file. The current window and viewport specifications are used to supply the normalization transformation factors. All world coordinate values, regardless of their relationship to the window, are now normalized. As seen in Fig. 7–8, it is possible for some normalized points to extend beyond the normalized coordinate range from 0 to 1. Segment transformations are then applied to the normalized description of the object, and then clipping is performed against the viewport boundaries. This sequence of operations is demonstrated in Fig.7–9.

Since segment primitives are stored in normalized coordinates, segment transformation parameters must be applied in normalized coordinates. However, it is usually more convenient for the user to describe transformation matrices in world coordinates. In this case, the graphics package first applies the window-to-viewport normalization to the transformation parameters (fixed point, pivot point, and translation distances) before constructing the transformation matrix.

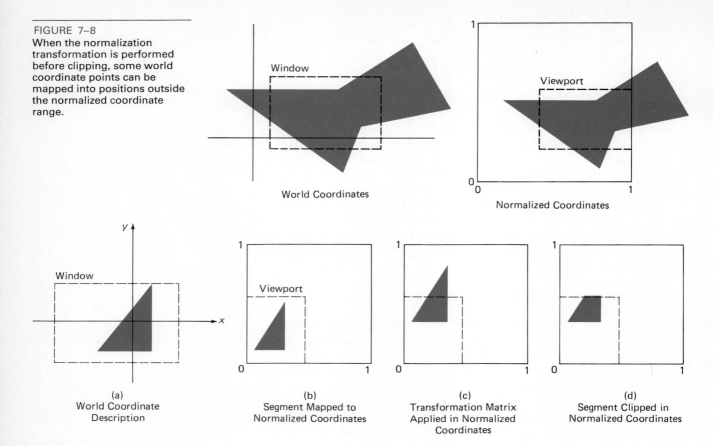

FIGURE 7–8
When the normalization transformation is performed before clipping, some world coordinate points can be mapped into positions outside the normalized coordinate range.

World Coordinates

Normalized Coordinates

Window

Viewport

y

Window

x

Viewport

(a)
World Coordinate
Description

(b)
Segment Mapped to
Normalized Coordinates

(c)
Transformation Matrix
Applied in Normalized
Coordinates

(d)
Segment Clipped in
Normalized Coordinates

FIGURE 7–9
Sequence of operations performed when a normalization transformation is applied to a segment before clipping.

7–4 Multiple Workstations

Graphics systems often utilize several output devices, each identified with a unique workstation number. When multiple output devices are available, a user may be provided with the means to control the display of segments on the various workstations. This can be accomplished by allowing the user to activate and deactivate workstations. When a segment is created, it is associated with only those workstations that are active. For example,

```
activate_workstation (5);
create_segment (12);
        .
        .
        .
```

```
close_segment;
activate_workstation (2);
create_segment (13);

        .
        .
        .

close_segment;
deactivate_workstation (5);
create_segment (14);

        .
        .
        .

close_segment;
deactivate_workstation (2);
```

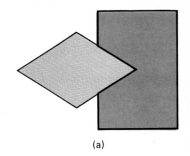

(a)

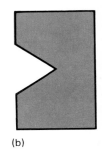

(b)

attaches segments 12 and 13 to workstation 5, while segments 13 and 14 are associated with workstation 2.

Additional commands are provided to manage segments on the individual workstations. All segments are deleted from workstation *ws* with *clear_workstation (ws)*, while the command *delete_segment_from_workstation (ws, id)* removes a single segment.

Deleting a segment from a specific workstation can be handled in various ways. With a vector system, segments are deleted simply by removing them from the refresh display file. A fast method for deleting a segment with a raster system is to reset all of the segment pixels in the frame buffer to the background color. This method for erasing a segment also erases any overlapping parts of other segments, leaving gaps in a displayed picture (Fig. 7–10). To redraw the picture so that such gaps are eliminated, a user could issue the command

```
redraw_segments_on_workstation (ws)
```

FIGURE 7–10
Erasing an object (segment) that overlaps another object (a) by redrawing the object in a background color also erases part of the background object (b).

Alternatively, a graphics package could be structured to redraw segments automatically after a deletion. Since many segments may be involved in a picture, it could be more efficient for a package to find and redraw only those objects that overlap a deleted segment. One way to locate these segments is to check each segment for overlap with the bounding rectangle of the deleted object, as shown in Fig. 7–11. The area within the bounding rectangle could be set to the background color, and all overlapping segments could be redrawn.

Greater flexibility in making segment assignments to workstations can be attained using a central, device-independent segment file. Segments are initially stored in the central file and later selectively assigned to various workstations, using some form of copy function. Construction and manipulation of segments could be monitored on a video display. When the user is satisfied with the appearance of all segments, the final picture could be directed to a plotter or other hard-copy device.

So far, we have discussed only files for the temporary storage of segments. These files exist only during the current session with a graphics package. A file used for long-term storage of graphical information is referred to as a **metafile.** Segment definitions in the metafile are retained and used during subsequent sessions with a graphics package. An important feature of metafiles is that they can be used by different graphics packages. Segments created in the metafile with one package can be read and used by other packages.

FIGURE 7–11
Locating overlapping objects using a bounding rectangle.

Bounding
Rectangle

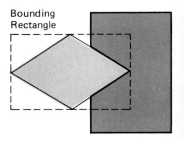

7–5 Summary

A segment defined in an application program is a group of output statements specifying a picture component. By creating pictures with individual segments, a user can easily add, delete, or manipulate picture components independently of one another. As segments are created by a user, they are entered by the graphics package into a segment file.

Segment files are usually organized as linked lists, to facilitate addition, deletion, and other operations on segments. One segment list may be maintained by a system and used by all output devices. Separate segments lists might also be maintained for each workstation available on the system.

Attribute parameters determine how segments are to be displayed. With the visibility parameter, a user can turn off the display of a segment while retaining it in the segment list. Priority specifies the display order among segments, so that foreground objects are displayed over background objects. A highlighting parameter is used to emphasize a displayed segment with blinking, color, or high-intensity patterns. And transformation matrices can be applied to each segment, allowing manipulation of individual picture components.

Table 7–1 lists the categories of segment operations. The various functions for manipulating segments are those for creating, deleting, and renaming segments and those for setting segment attributes.

TABLE 7–1.
Summary of Segment Functions

Function	Description
Creating and Deleting Segments	
create_segment (id)/close_segment	Creates segment with name specified in parameter *id*
delete_segment (id)	Deletes a segment from segment file
rename_segment (id_old, id_new)	Changes segment name
Workstation Operations	
delete_segment_from_workstation (ws, id)	Deletes segment *id* from workstation ws
clear_workstation (ws)	Deletes all segments from workstation *ws*
redraw_segments_on_workstation (ws)	Clears the device and redraws all segments
copy_segment_to_workstation (ws, id)	Copies segment *id* from a central, workstation-independent file to workstation *ws*
Segment Attributes	
set_segment_transformation (id, matrix)	Transformation elements in *matrix* applied to segment in normalized coordinates
set_visibility (id, v)	Parameter *v* set to *visible* or *invisible*
set_segment_priority (id, p)	Parameter *p* set to a real number in the range 0 to 1
set_highlighting (id, h)	Parameter *h* set to *highlighted* or *normal*

For additional information on segment operations within GKS see Enderle, Kansy, and Pfaff (1984) or Hopgood, et. al. (1983)

REFERENCES

EXERCISES

7-1. List the relative advantages and disadvantages of allowing more than one segment to be open at one time.

7-2. Consider how a graphics package could be designed to include a function to append information to a previously defined segment. For what types of applications would such an operation be preferable to deleting the segment and re-creating it with the new information? In general, what are the trade-offs in the two approaches?

7-3. Write a procedure to implement a segment directory table.

7-4. Write a procedure to manage a segment display file organized as a linked list with segment headers.

7-5. Consider the relative advantages and disadvantages of storing segments in doubly linked lists.

7-6. What are the relative advantages and disadvantages of using a binary tree structure or hash coding to store segment directories?

7-7. Discuss procedures for implementing the visibility attribute for the different segment file organizations.

7-8. Discuss various implementation procedures for the priority attribute, depending on the organization of the segment file.

7-9. Write a procedure to implement the highlighting function with a blinking operation.

7-10. Implement the segment-transformation command with a procedure for transforming all output primitives within the segment according to values in the transformation matrix.

7-11. Implement a viewing transformation for segments that first converts world coordinates to normalized coordinates. Any specified segment transformation matrix is also to be converted to normalized coordinates and applied to the segment. Finally, the segment is to be clipped against the viewport boundaries.

7-12. Develop an algorithm for locating any segments that overlap a segment that is to be deleted from a segment file. These overlapping segments are to be passed to a routine that redraws them after the unwanted segment has been removed from the segment file.

7-13. Discuss implementation details for maintaining separate workstation segment files and for maintaining a central segment file accessed by multiple workstations.

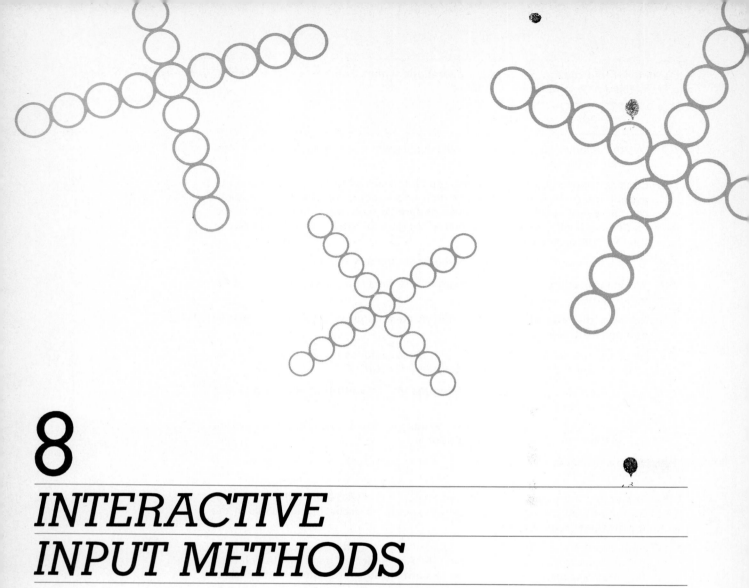

8
INTERACTIVE
INPUT METHODS

Our discussion of graphics methods has concentrated, until now, on generating output in its various forms. We have seen how output primitives can be defined, how attributes are set, how picture segments can be managed, and how to apply transformations. However, we have yet to consider how a graphics package can be made interactive. To handle interactive input, a system must allow the user dynamically to input coordinate positions, select functions, or specify transformation parameters. A variety of input devices exists, and we consider now how graphics packages can be designed to interface with the different types of input and to carry on a dialogue with users.

8-1 Physical Input Devices

Various devices are available for data input on a graphics workstation. Most interactive systems have a keyboard and one or more additional devices specially designed for interactive input. These include dials, touch panels, light pens, tablets, voice systems, joysticks, trackballs, and mice.

Keyboards

An alphanumeric keyboard on a graphics system is used primarily as a device for entering text. The keyboard is an efficient device for inputting such nongraphic data as picture labels associated with a graphics display. Keyboards can also be provided with features to facilitate entry of screen coordinates, menu selections, or graphics functions.

Cursor-control keys and function keys are typical features found on general-purpose keyboards. Function keys allow users to enter commonly used operations in a single keystroke, and cursor-control keys select coordinate positions by positioning the screen cursor on a video monitor. Additionally, a numeric keypad is often included on the keyboard for fast entry of numeric data. Figure 8–1 shows two types of general-purpose keyboard layouts providing alphanumeric keys, cursor-control keys, programmable function keys, and a numeric keypad. The "joydisk" in the upper left corner of the keyboard in Fig. 8–1(a) is used to position the screen cursor.

(a)

FIGURE 8–1
Examples of general-purpose display terminal keyboards. (a) Courtesy Tektronix, Inc. (b) Courtesy Information Displays, Inc.

(b)

(a)

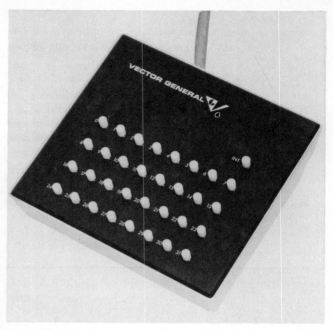

(b)

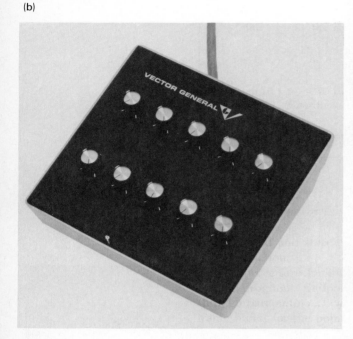

FIGURE 8–2
Special-purpose keyboards
using buttons (a) or dials (b)
can be used to select
predefined graphics functions.
Courtesy Vector General.

For specialized applications, a keyboard may contain only the set of buttons, dials, or switches that select the customized graphics operations needed in a particular application (Fig. 8–2). Buttons and switches are often used to input predefined functions, and dials are common devices for entering scalar values. Real numbers within some defined range are selected for input with dial rotations.

Dials can be used as fast input devices for moving the screen cursor. One dial can control horizontal movement of the cursor, and a second dial can control vertical movement. Potentiometers are used to measure dial rotations, which are then converted to deflection voltages for cursor movement. The two dials are sometimes arranged as "thumb wheels" on a keyboard, as shown in Fig. 8–3. The thumb wheels are placed at right angles to each other and have serrated edges so that they

FIGURE 8–3
A keyboard with thumbwheels.
Courtesy Tektronix, Inc.

can be easily rotated with the operator's thumb. Dials are convenient for horizontal and vertical movement of the cursor, but they are less effective than a joystick or trackball for cursor movement along diagonal lines or curves.

Touch Panels

As the name implies, these devices allow screen positions to be selected with the touch of a finger, as shown in Fig. 8–4. A **touch panel** is a transparent plate that fits over the CRT screen. When the plate is touched the contact position is recorded by an optical, electrical, or acoustical method.

Optical touch panels employ a line of light-emitting diodes (LEDs) along one vertical edge and along one horizontal edge of the frame. The opposite vertical and horizontal edges contain light detectors. These detectors are used to record which beams are interrupted when the panel is touched. The two crossing beams that are interrupted identify the horizontal and vertical coordinates of the screen position selected. Positions can be selected with an accuracy of about 1/4 inch. With closely spaced LEDs, it is possible to break two horizontal or two vertical beams simultaneously. In this case, an average position between the two interrupted beams is recorded. The LEDs operate at infrared frequencies so that the light is not visible to a user. Figure 8–5 illustrates the arrangement of LEDs in an optical touch panel.

FIGURE 8–4
A touch panel allows operators quickly and easily to select processing options by pointing to their graphical representations. Courtesy Carroll Touch Technology.

FIGURE 8–5
An optical touch panel, showing the arrangement of infrared LED units and detectors around the edges of the frame. Courtesy Carroll Touch Technology.

An electrical touch panel is constructed with two transparent plates separated by a small distance. One of the plates is coated with a conducting material, and the other plate is coated with a resistive material. When the outer plate is touched, it is forced into contact with the inner plate. This contact creates a voltage drop across the resistive plate that is converted to the coordinate values of the selected screen position.

In acoustical touch panels, high-frequency sound waves are generated in the horizontal and vertical directions across a glass plate. Touching the screen causes part of each wave to be reflected from the finger to the emitters. The screen position at the point of contact is calculated from a measurement of the time interval between the transmission of each wave and its reflection to the emitter.

Light Pens

Figure 8–6 shows two styles of **light pens.** These pencil-shaped devices are used to select screen positions by detecting the light coming from points on the CRT screen. They are sensitive to the short burst of light emitted from the phosphor coating at the instant the electron beam strikes a particular point. Other light sources, such as the background light in the room, are not detected by a light pen. An activated light pen, pointed at a spot on the screen as the electron beam lights up that spot, generates an electrical pulse that signals the computer to record the coordinate position of the electron beam. Since the electron beam sweeps across the screen 30 to 60 times every second, the detection of a lighted spot is essentially instantaneous. Coordinates entered with a light pen are often used by graphics programs for selecting or positioning objects on the screen.

Activating a light pen is accomplished with a mechanical or capacitive switch. Pens with a mechanical switch, such as those in Fig. 8–6, are activated either with a push tip or with a side button. Capacitive switches are formed with a metal band near the tip that must be touched with a finger to activate the pen.

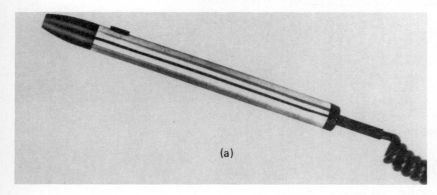

(a)

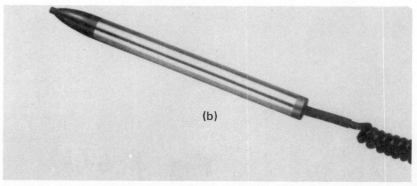

(b)

FIGURE 8–6
Light pens can be activated with button switches that are (a) mounted on the side or (b) installed as a push tip. Courtesy Interactive Computer Products.

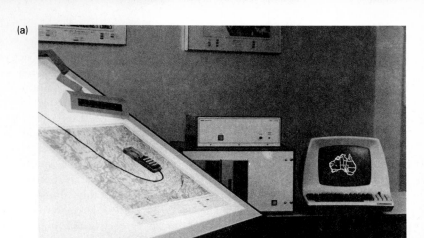

(a)

(b)

Graphics Tablets

Another method for selecting screen positions is by activating a hand cursor or a stylus at corresponding positions on a flat surface, called a **graphics tablet** or **digitizer**. A hand cursor contains cross hairs for sighting positions, while a stylus is a pencil-shaped device that is pointed at positions on the tablet. The two methods for entering data with a graphics tablet are illustrated in Figure 8–7. Graphics tablets provide one of the most accurate methods for selecting coordinate positions. They also have some other advantages. Movement of a stylus over the tablet surface does not block the user's view of any part of the screen, as does a light pen as it is moved over the screen surface. When a selected position is to be input, the hand cursor or stylus is activated by pressing a button. Several buttons are often available to provide options, such as storing a single point or a stream of points as the cursor is moved across the tablet surface.

Many graphics tablets are constructed with a rectangular grid of wires embedded in the tablet surface. Each wire has a slightly different voltage, which is correlated with the coordinate position of the wire. Voltage differences between wires in the horizontal and vertical directions correspond to coordinate differences in these directions on the screen. By activating a stylus or hand cursor at some point on the tablet, a user causes the voltages at that point to be recorded. These voltages are then converted to screen positions for use in the graphics routines. Some tablets employ electromagnetic fields instead of voltages to record positions. With these systems, the stylus is used to detect coded pulses or phase shifts in the wire grid.

Another type of graphics tablet uses sound waves. One such system is constructed with two perpendicular strip microphones (L-frame assembly) to detect the sound emitted by an electrical spark from a stylus tip. The position of the stylus is calculated by timing the arrival of the generated sound at the two microphones. An example of a graphics tablet employing an L-frame microphone assembly is shown in Fig. 8–8 (a). Point microphones, as in Fig. 8–8 (b), are used in some systems to replace the larger strip microphones. The compact size of the point microphone systems make them more portable, but the working area provided can be smaller than that available with an L-frame microphone assembly. A table top, or any other surface, is used as the "tablet" work area with these sonic devices.

Three-dimensional sonic digitizers are constructed with three or more microphones to record positions in space. Figure 8–9 shows such a three-dimensional system using four point microphones to digitize a surface. As the stylus is moved over the solid object, the Cartesian x, y, and z coordinates are calculated at each point by timing the arrival of the sound pulse at three of the microphones. The object is then projected onto the screen, as shown in the figure. A clear line of sight to at least three of the microphones is required to digitize positions on the surface of an object. The fourth microphone is provided for convenience in tracing over surfaces that might obscure the stylus from one of the microphones.

(a)

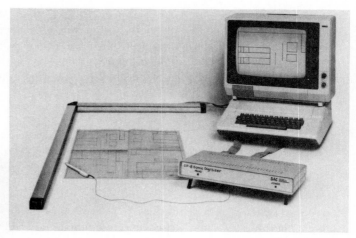

(b)

FIGURE 8–8
Acoustic "tablets": (a) an L-frame microphone assembly; (b) point microphones mounted on the front panel of the cabinet. Courtesy Science Accessories Corp.

FIGURE 8–9
A three-dimensional sonic digitizer, using four point microphones (at the corners of the large white panel). Courtesy Science Accessories Corp.

Joysticks

A **joystick** consists of a small, vertical lever (called the stick) mounted on a base that is used to steer the screen cursor around. Most joysticks select screen positions with actual stick movement; others respond to pressure on the stick. Figure 8–10 shows a movable joystick. The distance that the stick is moved in any direction from its center position corresponds to screen cursor movement in that direction. Potentiometers are used in the joystick to measure the amount of movement, and springs return the stick to the center position when it is released. Sometimes joysticks are constructed with one or more buttons that can be programmed as input switches to signal some type of action once a screen position has been selected.

In another type of movable joystick, the stick is used to activate switches that cause the screen cursor to move at a constant rate in the direction selected. Eight switches, arranged in a circle, are usually provided, so that the stick can select any one of eight directions for cursor movement.

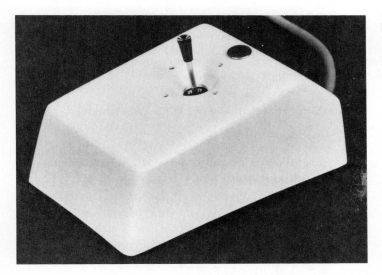

FIGURE 8–10
A movable joystick. Courtesy CalComp Group; Sanders Associates, Inc.

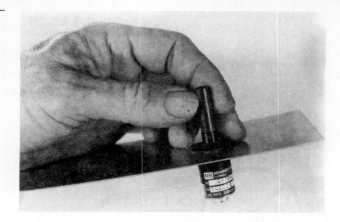

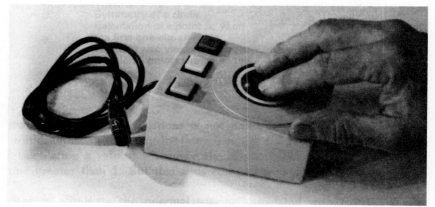

A pressure-sensitive joystick is shown in Fig. 8–11. This device, also called an isometric joystick, has a nonmovable stick. Pressure on the stick is measured with strain gauges and converted to movement of the cursor in the direction specified.

Trackball

The operation of a **trackball** (Fig. 8–12) is similar to that of a joystick. In this case, cursor movement is obtained by moving a sphere instead of a stick. The sphere can be rotated in any direction, and potentiometers measure the amount and direction of rotation.

Mouse

A **mouse** is small hand-held box with wheels or rollers on the bottom, as shown in Fig. 8–13. As the mouse is pushed across a flat surface, the rollers record the amount and direction of motion for conversion to a corresponding movement of the screen cursor. Since a mouse can be picked up and put down at another position without change in cursor movement, it is used for making relative changes in the position of the screen cursor. Buttons on the top of the mouse are used as switches to signal the execution of some operation, such as recording cursor position.

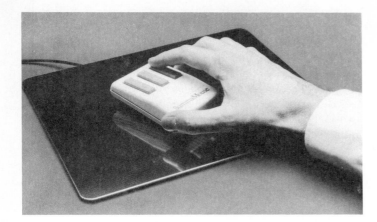

FIGURE 8–13
A mouse. Courtesy
Summagraphics Corp.

Voice Systems

Speech recognizers are used in some graphics workstations as input devices to accept voice commands. The voice input can be used to initiate graphics operations or to enter data. These systems operate by matching an input against a predefined dictionary of words.

A dictionary is set up for a particular operator by having the operator speak the command words to be used into the system. Each word is spoken several times, and the system analyzes the word and establishes a frequency pattern for that word in the dictionary along with the corresponding function to be performed. Later, when a voice command is given, the system searches the dictionary for a frequency-pattern match. Voice input is typically spoken into a microphone on a headset, as in Fig. 8–14. The microphone is designed to minimize input of other background sounds. If a different operator is to use the system, the dictionary must be reestablished with that operator's voice patterns. Voice systems have some advantage over other input devices, since the attention of the operator does not have to be switched from one device to another to enter a command.

FIGURE 8–14
A speech-recognition system.
Courtesy Threshold
Technology, Inc.

8-2 Logical Classification of Input Devices

Graphics programs use a number of types of input data. They include values for coordinate positions, character strings for labeling, scalar values for the transformation parameters, values specifying menu options, and values for segment identification. Any of the devices discussed in the foregoing section can be used to input these various data types. To make graphics packages independent of the particular hardware devices used, input commands can be structured according to the data description to be handled by each command. This approach provides a logical classification for input devices in terms of the kind of data to be input.

The various types of input data are summarized in the following six logical device classifications:

LOCATOR — a device for specifying a coordinate position (x, y)

STROKE — a device for specifying a series of coordinate positions

STRING — a device for specifying text input

VALUATOR — a device for specifying scalar values

CHOICE — a device for selecting menu options

PICK — a device for selecting picture components

In some packages, a single logical device is used for both locator and stroke operations. Some other mechanism, such as a switch, can then be used to indicate whether one coordinate position or a "stream" of positions is to be input.

Each of the six logical input device classifications can be implemented with any of the hardware devices, but some hardware devices are more convenient for certain kinds of data than others. A device that can be pointed at a screen position is more convenient for entering coordinate data than a keyboard, for example. In the following sections, we discuss how the various physical devices are used to provide input within each of the logical classifications.

8-3 Locator Devices

A typical method for establishing interactive coordinate input is by positioning the screen cursor. This can be accomplished with movement of thumbwheels, dials, a trackball, a joystick, a mouse, or a tablet stylus or hand cursor. Movement of each of these physical devices is translated into a corresponding screen cursor movement (Fig. 8–15). When the screen cursor is at the desired location, a button is activated to input the coordinates of that point.

Light pens are also used to input coordinate positions, but some special implementation considerations are necessary. Since light pens operate by detecting light emitted from the screen phosphors, some nonzero intensity level must be present at the coordinate position to be selected. With a raster system, we can paint a color background onto the screen. As long as no black areas are present, a light pen can be used to select any screen position.

When a background color or intensity cannot be provided, a light pen can be used as a locator by creating a small light pattern for the pen to detect. The pattern could be a single point, a single character, or a line pattern that is moved around the screen until it finds the light pen. A straightforward method for carrying out this search is to move the pattern across each scan line in turn until the pattern

FIGURE 8–15
Relative position changes of a
mouse can be used to control
screen cursor movement.

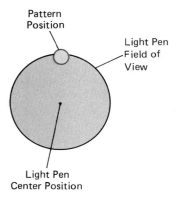

FIGURE 8–16
A small pattern detected by a
light pen at the edge of its field
of view causes a displaced
coordinate position to be input.

Pattern
Position

Light Pen
Field of
View

Light Pen
Center Position

moves into the light pen's field of view. At that instant, the activated pen signals that it has seen the pattern. This light pen interrupt signal causes the coordinate position of the pattern at that instant to be recorded as the input. Since the field of view of a light pen is large compared to the size of a screen pixel, a larger pattern produces more accurate coordinate selections than a small pattern. With a point or other small pattern, a coordinate position could be recorded at the edge of the pen's field of view instead of at the center position, as demonstrated in Fig. 8–16.

A technique used on some vector systems is to have the light pen move a tracking-cross pattern (Fig. 8–17) to the desired coordinate position. The cross is initially displayed at an arbitrary screen location, such as the screen center. To select a coordinate position, the pen first must be pointed at the cross, then moved slowly to the destination position. As the pen moves, each new cross position is calculated from a knowledge of how much of the cross the pen last saw. This is determined by drawing the cross from the outside toward the cross center, as shown in Fig. 8–18. Points along the arms of the cross are "turned on," one at a time, starting with the endpoints. As soon as a point on each of the four arms is detected by the pen, its position is recorded. The average x and y positions of these four points determine the new center position for the cross. When the cross finally reaches its destination, button activation can be used to signal storage of the coordinate position.

If the light pen is moved too rapidly, it could lose the tracking cross. In this case, some mechanism for restarting the tracking procedure could be initiated by the system. A small pattern could be scanned across the screen to find the pen. Once the light pen has been located, the cross can be moved to that position. If the pen has moved off screen and cannot be found, tracking is terminated. Other procedures, such as restarting the tracking process from the beginning, could be used when tracking is lost. To reduce the possibility of losing the tracking cross, a tracking procedure can be set up that attempts to move the cross slightly ahead of the pen. A straight-line prediction of the probable next pen position can be calculated and the cross moved to that position at each step.

Keyboards can be used for locator input in two ways. Coordinate values could be typed in, but this is a slow process in which the user is required to know exact coordinate values. As an alternative, cursor keys can be used to move the screen cursor to the required position. Four keys provide for relative horizontal and vertical cursor movement (up, down, right, left). With an additional four keys, the cursor can be moved diagonally as well. Rapid cursor movement can often be ac-

FIGURE 8–17
A light-pen tracking cross,
formed by two perpendicular
arms drawn with adjacent
screen points.

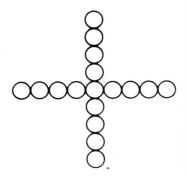

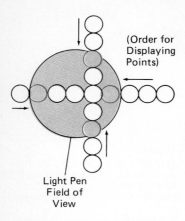

FIGURE 8–18
As a tracking cross is displayed from the outer points to the center, the average position of the first points detected by the light pen (gray dots) determine the new tracking-cross center position.

FIGURE 8–19
(a) A character drawn by plotting points along the path of a moving cursor. (b) A series of drawn letters input as a label.

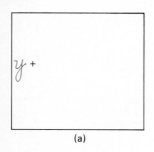

(a)

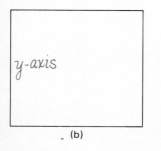

(b)

complished by holding down one of the cursor keys. When the cursor has been positioned properly, the input key is pressed.

8–4 Stroke Devices

This class of logical devices is used to input a sequence of coordinate positions. Stroke-device input is equivalent to multiple calls to a locator device. The set of input points is usually used to display a line section.

Many of the physical devices used for generating locator input can be used as stroke devices. Continuous movement of a mouse, trackball, or joystick is translated into a series of input coordinate values.

One of the most commonly used stroke input devices is the tablet. Button activation can be used to place a tablet hand cursor into "continuous" mode. As the cursor is moved across the tablet surface, a stream of coordinate values is generated. This process is used in paintbrush systems that allow artists to draw scenes on the screen and in engineering systems where layouts can be traced and digitized for storage. A similar procedure is used for stroke input with a light pen. By moving an activated pen across a CRT screen, a sequence of input points can be generated.

8–5 String Devices

The primary physical device used for string input is the keyboard. Input character strings are typically used for labels or program commands.

Other physical devices are sometimes used for generating character patterns in a "text-writing" mode. In these applications, individual characters are drawn on the screen with a stroke or locator-type device. A pattern recognition program then interprets the characters using a stored dictionary of predefined patterns. Figure 8–19 illustrates character patterns input in this way.

8–6 Valuator Devices

This logical class of devices is employed in graphics systems to input scalar values. Valuators are used for setting various graphics parameters, such as rotation angle and scale factors, and for setting physical parameters associated with a particular application (temperature settings, voltage levels, stress factors, etc.).

A typical physical device used to provide valuator input is a set of control dials. Floating-point numbers within any predefined range are input by rotating the dials. Dial rotations in one direction increase the numeric input value, and opposite rotations decrease the numeric value. Rotary potentiometers convert dial rotation into a corresponding voltage. This voltage is then translated into a real number within a defined scalar range, such as −10.5 to 25.5. Instead of dials, slide potentiometers are sometimes used to convert linear movements into scalar values.

Any keyboard with a set of numeric keys can be used as a valuator device. A user simply types the numbers directly in floating-point format. This is a slower method than using dials or slide potentiometers.

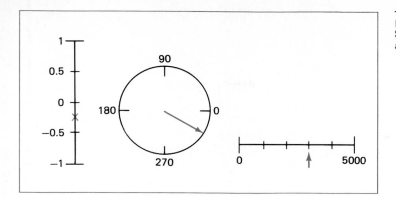

FIGURE 8–20
Scales displayed on a screen
and used for valuator input.

Joysticks, trackballs, tablets, and other such devices can be adapted for valuator input by interpreting movement of the device relative to a scalar range. For one direction of movement, say left to right, increasing scalar values can be input. Movement in the opposite direction decreases the scalar input value.

Another technique for providing valuator input is to display the scale ranges in pictorial form on a video monitor. Figure 8–20 illustrates some possibilities for scale representations. A light pen, joystick, mouse, tablet, or other locator device is used to select a coordinate position on the scale representation. This coordinate value is then converted to a numeric input value. As a feedback mechanism for the user, the selected position can be marked with some symbol. In Fig. 8–20, the **X** symbol marks the value of -0.25 on the vertical scale, while an arrow is used on the horizontal scale at the value 3000. An arrow is used also on the circular scale to indicate a position at 330°. As new positions are selected, these markers are moved to show the new values. The numeric values may also be displayed somewhere on the screen to confirm the selection value.

8–7 Choice Devices

Menu selections are common inputs in many graphics applications. A choice device is defined as one that enters a selection from a list (menu) of alternatives. Packages employ menus to input programming options, parameters, and figures to be used in the construction of a picture. Commonly used choice devices are a set of buttons, a touch panel, and the light pen.

A function keyboard, or "button box," designed as a stand-alone unit, is often used to enter menu selections. Usually each button is programmable, so that its function can be altered to suit different applications. Single-purpose systems have a fixed, predefined function for each button. Programmable function keys and fixed-function buttons are often included with other standard keys on a keyboard.

A touch panel or a light pen is used with many graphics systems for selecting menu options listed on the screen. With a vector system, the activation of a light pen is a signal for the system to record which particular menu item was in the process of being refreshed at that instant. On a raster system, a coordinate position (x, y) is recorded by the light pen or touch panel. This screen location is compared to the area boundaries for each listed menu item to determine which option has been selected. Each menu option can be considered to be bounded by a rectangular area. A menu item with vertical and horizontal boundaries at the coordinate values x_{min}, x_{max}, y_{min}, and y_{max} is selected if the input coordinates (x, y) satisfy the inequalities

$$x_{min} < x < x_{max}, \quad y_{min} < y < y_{max} \tag{8–1}$$

Other devices, such as a tablet, joystick, or mouse, are sometimes used to make menu selections with coordinate input. These devices can move the screen cursor, a character, or some special pattern to the location of an item to be selected. Button activation then signals the input of coordinates at that position.

Alternate methods for choice input include keyboard and voice entry. A standard keyboard can be used to type in commands or menu options. For this method of choice input, some abbreviated format is useful. Menu listings can be numbered or given short identifying names. Similar codings can be used with voice input systems. Voice input is particularly useful when a small number of options (20 or less) are to be used.

8–8 Pick Devices

Segment selection is the function of this logical class of devices. Typical uses for pick input are the application of transformations and manipulation procedures to the selected segments.

The light pen is the standard pick device used with many graphics systems. On a vector system, activation of a light pen causes the display processor to note which segment was being refreshed at that instant. Each segment is refreshed using the set of output primitives defining that segment. When the pen interrupt occurs, a check is made to determine which set of commands was being processed. The easiest way to do this is for the system to use a register to store the name of each segment in turn as it is being refreshed. Then a check of the current contents of the register identifies the segment selected.

With a raster system, refreshing is done from the frame buffer, and light-pen input is a screen coordinate position. This coordinate information must be mapped onto the frame buffer to determine which segment area encompasses that point. Several levels of search may be necessary to identify the correct segment. First, a rectangular boundary area can be established for each segment (Fig. 8–21). If the input coordinates from the pen fall within this area and no segment areas overlap, the desired segment has been identified. Should two or more segment areas overlap, the process is repeated for individual primitives. That is, bounding rectangles

FIGURE 8–21
A picture component (triangle) and corresponding bounding rectangle.

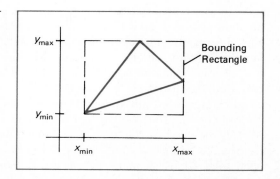

for the component lines in a segment (Fig. 8–22) are used to narrow the search to individual primitives. If the pen coordinates are found to be in the primitive bounding areas of only one segment, the search is over. If the pen coordinates are found to be in overlapping primitive areas from two different segments, calculation of the shortest distance from the input point to each line segment (Fig. 8–23) finally settles the issue.

Other physical devices can be used for segment selection by identifying the segment position with a screen cursor. A coordinate position is selected by moving the screen cursor with a mouse, trackball, joystick, or tablet to the position of a segment and activating a button. This coordinate input is used in the same way as pen coordinates to identify the selected segment.

Keyboards and buttons also are used as segment selection devices in some applications. With a keyboard, the segment name can be typed. A technique for button input is to use one button to highlight successive segments and another button to stop the process when the desired segment is highlighted. If very many segments are to be searched in this way, the process can be speeded up and additional buttons used to help identify the segment. The first button can initiate a rapid successive highlighting of segments. A second button can again be used to stop the process, and a third button can be used to back up more slowly if the desired segment passed before the operator pressed the stop button.

8–9 Interactive Picture-Construction Techniques

There are several techniques that we can incorporate into graphics packages to aid users in interactively constructing pictures. Various input options can be provided to a user, so that coordinate information entered with locator and stroke devices can be interpreted according to the selected option. Input coordinates can establish the position or boundaries for objects to be drawn, or they can be used to rearrange previously displayed objects.

Basic Positioning Methods

Coordinate values supplied by locator input are often used with **positioning** methods to specify a location for displaying an object or a character string. Screen positions can be input with a light pen or by moving the screen cursor to the desired position. Figure 8–24 illustrates object positioning with a cursor. The cursor is moved to the desired screen location; then a button is pressed to signal that the object should be placed at this coordinate position. In a similar way, a text position can be specified. Depending on the options available, the text position can specify the coordinates for the beginning, ending, or middle position of the character string. Figure 8–25 demonstrates text positioning by selecting the center position of a string.

Line drawing with locator input is shown in Fig. 8–26. The first coordinate position selects the starting endpoint, and the second input position indicates the opposite endpoint. A line is then displayed between the two selected endpoints.

As an aid in positioning objects, we can design the package to display coordinate information for the user. Figure 8–27 illustrates how coordinates might be displayed near the cursor position. With this technique, a user can move the cursor until the correct coordinates are shown, then press the button to select this position.

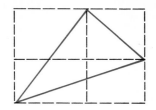

FIGURE 8–22
Bounding rectangles for component lines in an object (triangle).

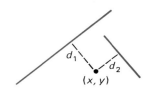

FIGURE 8–23
Distances d_1 and d_2 from a point at (x, y) to two line segments.

FIGURE 8–24
Positioning an object with the screen cursor.

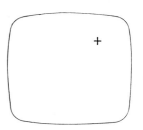

Position Cursor
and Press Button

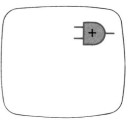

Object Displayed
at Cursor Position

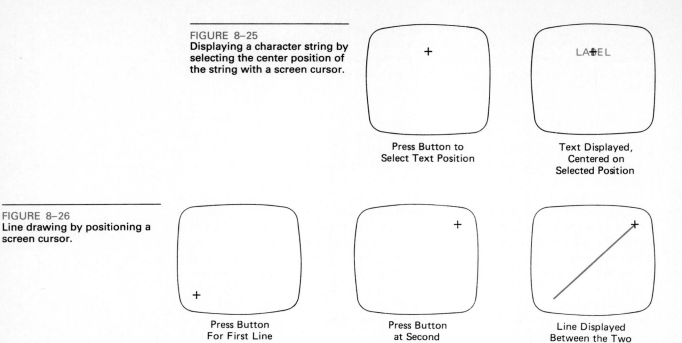

FIGURE 8–25
Displaying a character string by selecting the center position of the string with a screen cursor.

Press Button to
Select Text Position

Text Displayed,
Centered on
Selected Position

FIGURE 8–26
Line drawing by positioning a screen cursor.

Press Button
For First Line
Endpoint

Press Button
at Second
Line Endpoint

Line Displayed
Between the Two
Chosen Endpoints

FIGURE 8–27
Coordinates displayed near a cursor position, as an aid in selecting screen locations.

Constraints

With some applications, certain types of prescribed orientations or object alignments are useful. **A constraint** is a rule for altering input coordinate values to produce a specified orientation or alignment of the displayed coordinates. There are many kinds of constraint functions that can be specified, but the most common constraint is a horizontal or vertical alignment of straight lines. This type of constraint, shown in Figs. 8–28, and 8–29, is useful in forming network layouts. With this constraint, a user can create horizontal and vertical lines without worrying about precise specification of endpoint coordinates.

One method for implementing the line constraints demonstrated in Figs. 8–28 and 8–29 is to allow the package to determine whether any two input coordinate endpoints are more nearly horizontal or more nearly vertical. If the difference in the y values of the two endpoints is smaller than the difference in x values, a horizontal line is displayed. Otherwise, a vertical line is drawn.

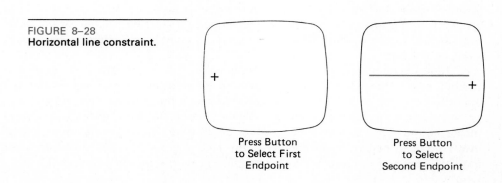

FIGURE 8–28
Horizontal line constraint.

Press Button
to Select First
Endpoint

Press Button
to Select
Second Endpoint

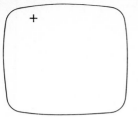
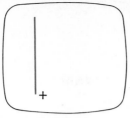

FIGURE 8-29
Vertical line constraint.

Press Button
to Select
First Endpoint

Press Button
to Select
Second Endpoint

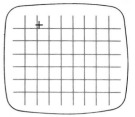

Press Button to
Select First Endpoint

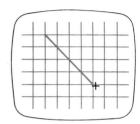

Press Button
to Select
Second Endpoint

FIGURE 8-30
Line drawing using a grid.

Other kinds of constraints can be applied to input coordinates to produce a variety of alignments. Lines could be constrained to have a particular slant, such as 45°, and input coordinates could be constrained to lie along predefined paths, such as circular arcs.

Grids

Another type of constraint is a **grid** of rectangular lines superimposed on the screen coordinate system. When a grid is used, any input coordinate position is rounded to the nearest intersection of two grid lines. Figure 8-30 illustrates line drawing with a grid. Each of the two cursor positions is converted to a grid intersection point, and the line is drawn between these grid points. This technique can help users to draw lines and figures more accurately and neatly. Grids also make the construction of objects easier, since positioning a cursor at an exact coordinate position can be a difficult process.

Grid lines can be used also for positioning and aligning objects or text. The spacing between grid lines is often left as an option for the user, and the grid pattern may or may not be displayed. It is also possible to use partial grids and grids of different sizes in different screen areas.

Gravity Field

In the construction of figures, a user often needs to connect a new line to a previously drawn line. If a grid is available, the grid points could be used for all line intersections. But sometimes a user may want to connect two lines at a position between grid points. Since exact positioning of the screen cursor at the connecting point can be difficult, graphics packages can be designed to convert any input position near a line to a position on the line.

This conversion of input position is accomplished by creating a **gravity field** area around the line. Any selected position within the gravity field of a line is moved ("gravitated") to the nearest position on the line. A gravity field area around a line is illustrated with the shaded region in Fig. 8-31. Areas around the endpoints are enlarged to make it easier for a user to connect lines at their endpoints. The size of gravity fields is chosen large enough to aid the user but small enough to reduce chances of overlap with other lines. If many lines are displayed, gravity areas can overlap, and it may be difficult for a user to specify points correctly. Normally, the boundary for the gravity field is not displayed; the user simply selects points as near to the line as possible.

FIGURE 8-31
Gravity field around a line.

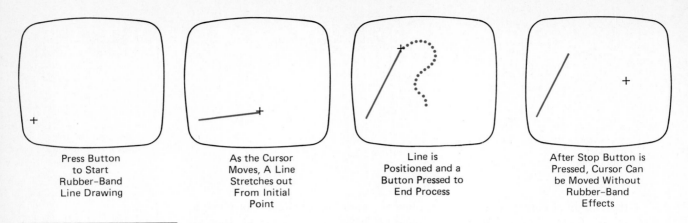

Press Button to Start Rubber–Band Line Drawing	As the Cursor Moves, A Line Stretches out From Initial Point	Line is Positioned and a Button Pressed to End Process	After Stop Button is Pressed, Cursor Can be Moved Without Rubber–Band Effects

FIGURE 8–32
Rubber-band method for drawing and positioning a line.

Rubber-Band Methods

Straight lines can be constructed and positioned by **rubber-band methods**, which stretch out a line from a starting position as the screen cursor is moved. Figure 8–32 demonstrates the rubber-band method. The start of the process is signaled by pressing a start button. As the cursor moves around, the line is displayed from the start position to the current position of the cursor. A stop button is used to signal the termination of the operation and fix the position of the line. On some systems, the rubber-band drawing of a line starts when a button is pressed and stops when the button is released.

Rubber-band methods can be used to construct and position various types of objects. In Fig. 8–33 a circular arc is produced, and Fig. 8–34 demonstrates rubber-band construction of a rectangle.

FIGURE 8–33
Drawing a circular arc using a rubber-band method.

FIGURE 8–34
Rubber-band method for constructing a rectangle.

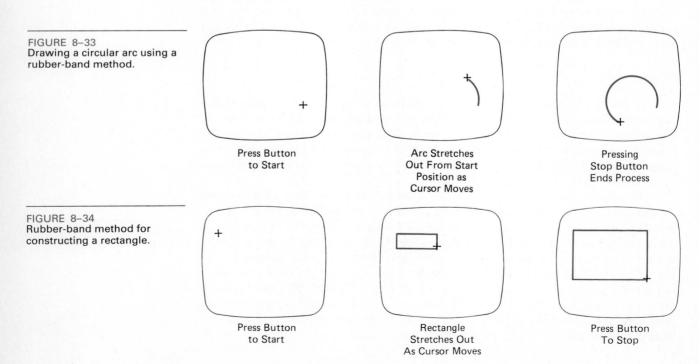

Press Button to Start	Arc Stretches Out From Start Position as Cursor Moves	Pressing Stop Button Ends Process
Press Button to Start	Rectangle Stretches Out As Cursor Moves	Press Button To Stop

Sketching

For many applications it is convenient to be able to **sketch** objects by tracing their outline on the screen. An extension of the rubber-band method can be used to create objects formed with straight line segments. Instead of drawing a single line, a series of connected lines can be drawn before the rubber-band procedure is terminated. As illustrated in Fig. 8–35, two buttons can be used. One button controls the beginning and ending of the overall procedure, and the second button is used to mark the intermediate line endpoints. This type of sketching is useful for facility layouts, circuit diagrams, and various network layouts.

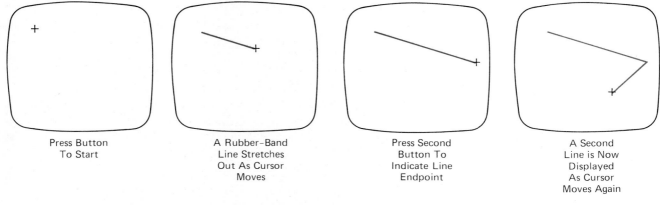

Press Button   A Rubber-Band   Press Second   A Second
To Start   Line Stretches   Button To   Line is Now
                      Out As Cursor   Indicate Line   Displayed
                      Moves   Endpoint   As Cursor
                                                                   Moves Again

Instead of displaying straight line segments, a sketching program could plot individual points along the path of the cursor as it is moved around the screen. Various curved figures can then be displayed, as illustrated in Fig. 8–36. This type of sketching routine is used with paintbrush programs. The artist is furnished with a number of "brushes," which are used to generate lines of varying thickness and style. A color palette provides a menu of colors that can be displayed with the brushes. Lines are erased by retracing them in the background color.

FIGURE 8–35
Sketching with straight line segments. Connecting lines are drawn until the stop button is pressed.

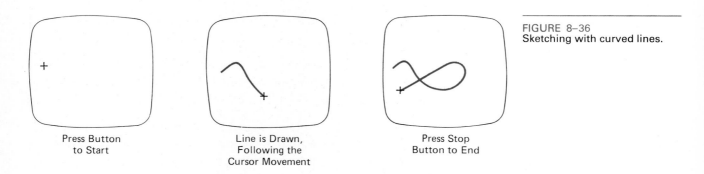

Press Button   Line is Drawn,   Press Stop
to Start   Following the   Button to End
                      Cursor Movement

FIGURE 8–36
Sketching with curved lines.

Dragging

A technique that is often used in interactive picture construction is to move objects into position by **dragging** them with the screen cursor. Usually, a menu of shapes is displayed, and the user selects an item, then drags it into position. This

FIGURE 8–37
Dragging a selected shape into
position.

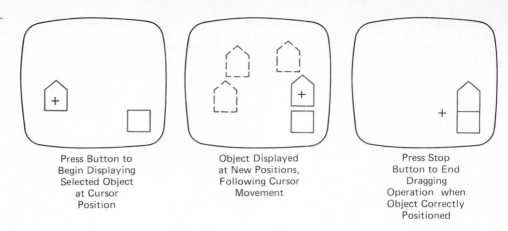

Press Button to Begin Displaying Selected Object at Cursor Position	Object Displayed at New Positions, Following Cursor Movement	Press Stop Button to End Dragging Operation when Object Correctly Positioned

technique is demonstrated in Fig. 8–37. After an object has been selected from the menu, a button can be pressed to initiate the dragging process. When the user is satisfied with the object's position, the button is again pressed to release the object from the cursor.

8–10 Input Functions

We can design a graphics package using the six logical input classifications in various ways. An input statement in an application program could specify both the logical classification and the type of physical device employed to input the data. The other parameters needed depend on the type of data to be input. In addition, there are alternative ways to structure the interaction between an application program and the input devices.

Input Modes

Commands to provide input can be structured to operate in various **input modes,** which specify how the program and input devices interact. Input could be initiated by the program, or the program and input devices both could be operating simultaneously, or data input could be initiated by the devices. These three input modes are referred to as request mode, sample mode, and event mode.

In **request mode,** the application program requests input and suspends processing until the required data are input. The program and the input devices operate alternately. Devices are put into a wait state until an input request is made; then the program waits until the data are delivered.

In **sample mode,** the application program and input devices operate at the same time. Input data are stored and continually updated to current values as the input devices operate. The program samples these current data as it needs input.

In **event mode,** the input devices initiate data input to the application program. A stream of input values is provided to the program, and these data values are processed one at a time by the program. In this mode, the processing is directed by the input data.

Input commands can be defined for each of the three input modes, and a package can allow a user to specify the mode of operation for each logical device class. For example, the command

```
set_locator_mode (ws, device_code, input_mode)
```

specifies that a locator device is to be used in the particular mode set in parameter *input_mode*. The three choices for this parameter are *request, sample,* and *event.* Parameter *ws* identifies the workstation to be used, and parameter *device_code* is assigned a value that identifies which particular physical device is to be used as a locator. One possible assignment of device codes is given in Table 8–1. Using the assignments in this table, the command

```
set_stroke_mode (4, 2, event)
```

designates the graphics tablet as a stroke device in *event* mode on workstation 4.

TABLE 8–1.

Assignment of Device Codes

Device Code	Physical Device Type
1	Keyboard
2	Graphics Tablet
3	Light Pen
4	Touch Panel
5	Thumbwheels
6	Dial
7	Button
8	Joystick
9	Mouse
10	Trackball
11	Voice Entry

Similar commands are issued by a user to set the input mode for the other logical input classes. Devices can operate in only one mode at a time, but several devices could be operating simultaneously in different modes. Once the mode has been set, commands in that mode can be used.

Request Mode

Input commands used in this mode correspond to input commands such as the *read* statement in a programming language. An input request is made, and further processing waits for the input data to be received. After a device has been assigned a request mode, as discussed in the preceding section, input requests can be made to that device. For example, to request input from a locator device, the following command could be used in an application program:

```
request_locator (ws, device_code, x, y)
```

where parameters *x* and *y* are used to store the input coordinates for a single point.

Parameters included in the input commands for each logical classification depend on the type of data to be input. Stroke input is requested with

```
request_stroke (ws, device_code, n, xa, ya)
```

where the coordinates of the *n* input points are to be stored in arrays *xa* and *ya*. Similarly, text could be input in request mode with

        request_string (ws, device_code, nc, text)

where parameter *text* specifies an input string of length *nc* (number of characters). To select a segment, an application program could include the following command, which identifies the segment with parameter *segment_id:*

        request_pick (ws, device_code, segment_id)

Other parameters can be included in the input commands for request mode, depending on the options offered at a particular facility. For instance, it is useful in some applications to be able to identify component parts of segments, such as individual lines. An additional parameter could be included in the pick command to select labeled segment parts. This means, of course, that the segment parts must be labeled as the segment is being created. An activated light pen, pointed at the segment, would then input both the name of the segment and the name of a segment part.

Sample Mode

Once sample mode has been set for one or more physical devices, data input begins without waiting for a program input statement. If a joystick has been designated as a locator device in sample mode, coordinate values for the current position of the activated joystick are immediately stored. As the activated stick position changes, the stored values are continually replaced with the coordinates of the current stick position.

Sampling of the current values from a physical device in this mode begins when a *sample* command is encountered in the application program. A locator device is sampled with a call to

        sample_locator (ws, device_code, x, y)

Sampling the other logical devices is performed with similar commands.

Event mode

When an input device is placed in event mode, the program and device operate simultaneously. Data input from the device can be accumulated in an **event queue,** or **input queue.** All input devices active in event mode can enter data (**events**) into this single event queue, with each device entering data values as they are generated. At any one time, the event queue can contain a mixture of data types, in the order they were input. Data entered into the queue are identified according to logical class, workstation number, and physical device code.

An application program can be directed to check the event queue for any input with the command

        await_event (time, device_class, ws, device_code)

Parameter *time* is used to set a maximum waiting time for the application program. If the queue happens to be empty, processing is suspended until either the number of seconds specified in *time* has elapsed or an input arrives. Should the waiting time run out before data values are input, the parameter *device_class* can be used to return the value *none*. When *time* is assigned the value 0, the program checks the queue and immediately returns to other processing if the queue is empty.

When processing is directed to the event queue with the *await_event* command and the queue is not empty, the first event in the queue is transferred to a **current event record.** The particular logical device class, such as locator or stroke, that made this input is stored in parameter *device_class.* Codes, identifying the particular workstation and physical device that made the input, are stored in parameters *ws* and *device_code,* respectively.

To retrieve a data input from the current event record, an event-mode input command is used. The form of the commands in event mode is similar to those in request and sample modes. However, no workstation and device code parameters are necessary in the commands, since the values for these parameters are stored in the data record. A user could ask for locator data from the current event record with the command

```
get_locator (x, y)
```

As an example of the use of *await_event* and *get* commands, the following program section inputs a set of points from a tablet on workstation 1 and plots a series of straight line segments connecting the input coordinates:

```
set_stroke_mode (1, 2, event); {set tablet to stroke device, event
                                mode}
repeat
   await_event (3600, device_class, ws, device_code)
until device_class = stroke;
get_stroke (n, x, y);
polyline (n, x, y);
```

The *repeat–until* loop bypasses any data from other devices that might be in the queue. Also, the waiting time is set to one hour, which is long enough to ensure that the input data will be received. If the tablet is the only active input device in event mode, this loop is not necessary.

A number of devices can be used at the same time in event mode for rapid interactive processing of displays. The following statements plot input lines from a tablet with attributes specified by a button box:

```
set_polyline_index (1);
set_stroke_mode (1, 2, event); {set tablet to stroke device, event
                                mode}
set_choice_mode (1, 7, event); {set buttons to choice device, event
                                mode}
repeat
   await_event (120, device_class, ws, device_code);
   if device_class = choice then begin
      get_choice (option);
      set_polyline_index (option)
   end
   else
   if device_class = stroke then begin
      get_stroke (n, x, y);
      polyline (n, x, y)
   end
until device_class = none;
```

In this example, we have assumed that only the buttons and tablet are in use. Termination is signaled by a value of *none* for logical device parameter *device_class*. This occurs after a waiting time of two minutes if no event arrives in the queue during this time.

Some additional housekeeping commands can be used in event mode. Commands for clearing the event queue are useful when a process is terminated and a new application is to begin. These commands can be set to clear the entire queue or to clear only data associated with specified input devices and workstations.

Concurrent Use of Input Modes

An example of the simultaneous use of input devices in different modes is given in the following procedure. An object is dragged around the screen with a light pen. When a final position has been decided on, a button is pressed to terminate any further movement of the object. The pen positions are obtained in sample mode, and the button input is sent to the event queue.

```
{drags object in response to light pen input}
{button is used to terminate processing}

begin
    set_locator_mode (1, 3, sample);      {set pen to locator device,
                                           sample mode}
    set_choice_mode (1, 7, event);        {set button to choice device,
                                           event mode}
  repeat
    sample_locator (1, 3, x, y);          {read from pen}

      {translate object to x, y and draw}

      await_event (0, class, ws, code)    {check event queue for input}
    until class = choice                  {stop if button has been used}
end;
```

8–11 Summary

Many types of hardware devices can be used to input data to a graphics program. They include keyboards, buttons and dials, touch panels, light pens, two-dimensional and three-dimensional tablets, joysticks, and trackball, mouse, and voice devices. The type of device used in a particular system depends on the type of application and the data type to be input.

A logical classification of input describes devices in terms of the type of input data. This provides a basis for structuring input routines in a graphics package to make the package independent of the type of physical devices that may be used. Locator devices are any devices used by a program to input a single coordinate position. Stroke devices input a stream of coordinates. String devices are used to input text. Valuator devices are any input devices used to enter a scalar value. Choice devices enter menu selections. Pick devices input a segment name.

Interactive picture-construction methods are used in many design and painting packages. These methods provide users with the capability to position objects, to constrain figures to predefined orientations or alignments, to sketch figures, and to drag objects around the screen. Grids, gravity fields, and rubber-band methods are also used to aid users in constructing pictures.

Commands available in a package can be defined in three input modes. Request mode places input under the control of the application program. Sample mode allows the input devices and program to operate concurrently. Event mode allows input devices to initiate data entry and control processing of data. Once a mode has been chosen for a logical device class and the particular physical device to be used to enter this class of data, input commands in the program are used to enter data values into the program. An application program can make simultaneous use of several physical input devices operating in different modes.

REFERENCES

The evolution of the concept of logical (or virtual) input devices is discussed in Rosenthal, et al. (1982) and in Wallace (1976). An early discussion of input-device classifications is to be found in Newman (1968).

Additional information on GKS operations with input devices is to be found in Enderle, Kansy, and Pfaff (1984) and in Hopgood, et. al. (1983).

EXERCISES

8–1. Suppose the positions of the four microphones for a three-dimensional sonic digitizer have coordinates (x_k, y_k, z_k), where $k = 1, 2, 3, 4$. Solve three of the following four equations to find the input position (x, y, z) of the stylus:
$$(x - x_k)^2 + (y - y_k)^2 + (z - z_k)^2 = r^2_k, \quad k = 1, 2, 3, 4$$
where each r_k is the measured distance to one microphone from the input position (as determined by the time of arrival of the sound from the stylus).

8–2. How can all four equations in Ex. 8–1 be used to provide cross checks on the calculated values for the input coordinates?

8–3. Develop a program to allow a user to position objects on the screen using a locator device. An object menu of geometric shapes is to be presented to a user who is to select an object and a placement position. The program should allow any number of objects to be positioned until a "terminate" signal is given.

8–4. Extend the program of Ex. 8–3 so that selected objects can be scaled and rotated before positioning. The transformation choices and transformation parameters are to be presented to the user as menu options.

8–5. Write a program that allows a user to interactively sketch pictures using a stroke device.

8–6. Discuss the methods that could be employed in a pattern-recognition procedure to match input characters against a stored library of shapes.

8–7. Write a routine that allows a user to select a numeric value from a displayed linear scale. Values are to be chosen by positioning the cursor (or other symbol) along the scale line. Both the position on the line and the scalar value selected are to be displayed after a choice has been made.

8–8. Write the routine in Ex. 8–7 so that angles (in degrees) can be selected from a circular scale. Mark the position selected with a radial arrow.

8–9. Design a program that will produce a picture as a set of line segments drawn between specified endpoints. The coordinates of the individual line segments are to be selected with a locator device.

8–10. Extend the program of Ex. 8–9 so that a gravity field is used to aid the designer in joining line segments.

8–11. Write a procedure to allow a user to design a pattern with a locator device so that all lines are constrained to be horizontal or vertical.

8–12. Develop a program that displays a grid pattern and rounds input screen positions to grid intersections. The program can be used to design patterns or position objects, using a locator device to input positions. Once a picture is complete, the grid pattern can be removed before transferring the picture to a hardcopy device.

8–13. Write a routine that allows a designer to create a picture by sketching straight lines with a rubber-band method.

8–14. Extend the program of Ex. 8–13 so that designers can sketch either straight lines or circular arcs.

8–15. Write a program that allows a user to design a picture from a menu of basic shapes by dragging each selected shape into position with a pick device.

8–16. Design an implementation of the input commands for request mode.

8–17. Design an implementation of the sample mode input commands.

8–18. Design an implementation of the input commands for event mode.

8–19. Combine the implementations of Exs. 8–16, 8–17, and 8–18 into one package.

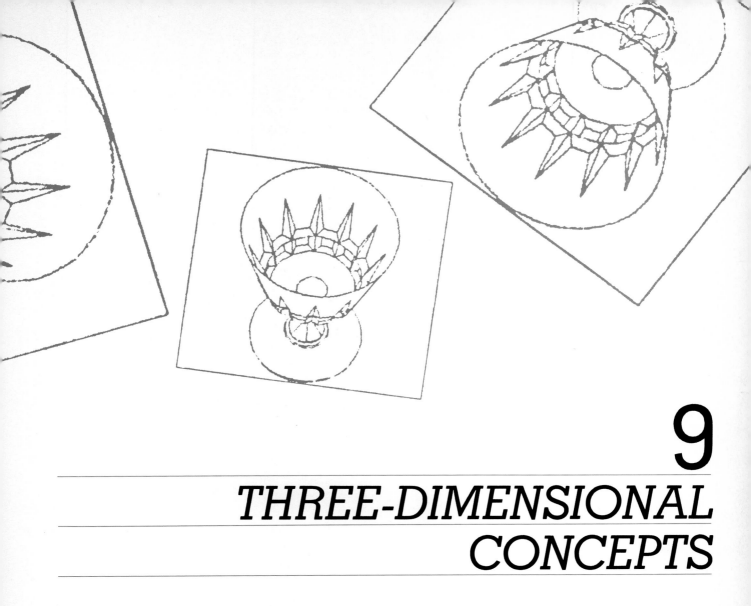

9

THREE-DIMENSIONAL CONCEPTS

We can classify three-dimensional graphics applications according to whether we are dealing with representations of existing ("real") objects or whether we are designing new shapes. A representation for an existing three-dimensional object is an approximate description that we use to construct the display. For example, we could describe a solid object as a framework of lines or as a set of flat surfaces (Fig. 9–1). In another application, we might need to specify a representation that includes curved lines and surfaces, as in Fig. 9–2. In computer-aided design applications, on the other hand, the goal is to create objects by constructing and manipulating patterns to form new three-dimensional shapes. Automobile and aircraft bodies are fashioned by rearranging surface patterns until certain design criteria are satisfied. For either type of application, descriptions of solid objects are specified in a three-dimensional world coordinate system and mapped onto the two-dimensional reference of a video monitor or other output device.

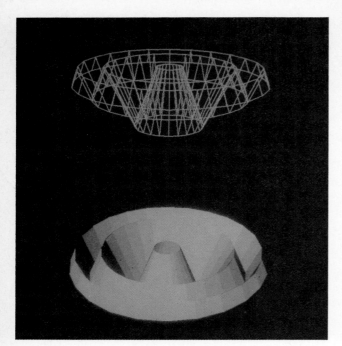

FIGURE 9–1
A three-dimensional object can be represented as a line framework or as a set of plane surfaces. Courtesy Aydin Controls, a division of Aydin Corp.

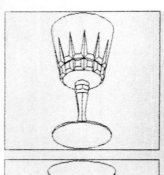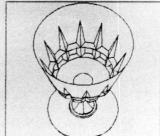

FIGURE 9–2
Representation of a solid object as a combination of plane and curved surfaces. Courtesy Selanar Corp.

9–1 Three-Dimensional Coordinate Systems

Figure 9–3 (a) shows the conventional orientation of coordinate axes in a three-dimensional Cartesian reference system. This is called a right-handed system because the right-hand thumb points in the positive z direction when we imagine grasping the z axis with the fingers curling from the positive x axis to the positive

FIGURE 9–3
Coordinate representation of a point P at position (x, y, z) in a right-handed reference system.

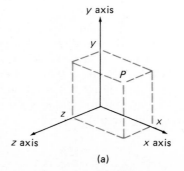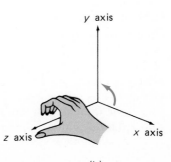

(a)

(b)

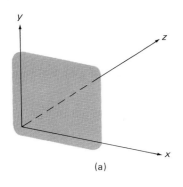

(a)

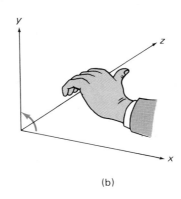

(b)

y axis (through 90°), as illustrated in Fig. 9–3 (b). We will assume that all world coordinate descriptions of objects are to be stated relative to a right-handed reference system.

Another possible arrangement of coordinate axes is the left-handed system shown in Fig. 9–4. For this system, the fingers of the left hand curl from the positive x axis to the positive y axis through 90° when we imagine grasping the z axis so that the left thumb points in the positive z direction. This orientation of axes is convenient in many graphics applications. With the coordinate origin of a left-handed system placed in the lower left screen corner, the first quadrant of the xy plane maps directly to screen coordinates, and positive z values indicate positions behind the screen as in Fig 9–4 (a). This coordinate reference can be used conveniently to specify device coordinates, with the screen in the $z = 0$ plane. Larger values along the positive z axis are then interpreted as being farther from the viewer.

Other coordinate references also can be useful in describing three-dimensional scenes. For some objects, it may be convenient to define coordinate positions using a spherical, cylindrical, or other system that takes advantage of any naturally occurring symmetries. However, for graphics packages that allow only Cartesian world coordinate representations, any non-Cartesian coordinate descriptions must first be converted by the user to corresponding Cartesian coordinates.

Like two-dimensional descriptions, three-dimensional world coordinate descriptions are converted to normalized device coordinates and then displayed in the coordinate reference for a particular output device. Unlike two-dimensional descriptions, a three-dimensional object can be viewed from any position. We can think of this as analogous to photographing the object, where the photographer walks around and chooses a position and orientation for the camera.

9–2 Three-Dimensional Display Techniques

Representations of a solid object on a viewing surface usually contain depth information so that a veiwer can easily identify, for the particular view selected, which is the back and which is the front of the object. Figure 9–5 illustrates the ambiguity that can result when an object is displayed without depth information. There are several techniques that can be used to include depth information in the two-dimensional representation of solid objects; the choice of display technique depends on the requirements of a particular application.

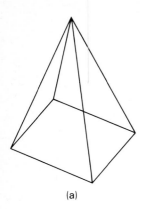

(a)

Parallel Projection

A solid object can be represented in two dimensions by projecting points on the object surface along parallel lines onto a plane viewing surface. By selecting different viewing positions, we can project visible points onto the viewing surface to obtain different two-dimensional views of the object, as in Fig. 9–6. In a parallel projection, parallel lines on the surface of the object project into parallel lines on the two-dimensional viewing plane. This technique is used in engineering and architectural drawings to represent the object with a set of views that maintain relative proportions of the object. The appearance of the solid object can then be reconstructed from the major views.

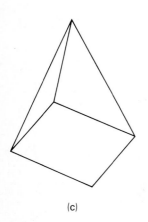

(b)

FIGURE 9–6
Two parallel projection views of an object, used to show relative proportions. Lines on the object that are parallel remain parallel in the projection views.

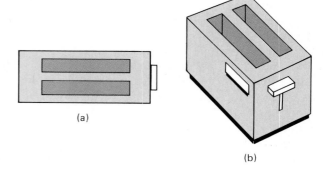

(a)

(b)

Perspective Projection

Another method for representing depth on a two-dimensional viewing surface is perspective projection. Instead of projecting points along parallel lines, perspective projections change the sizes of objects so that those farther from the viewing position are displayed smaller than those nearer the viewing position. Parallel lines on the surface of an object are now projected into lines that tend to converge. Objects displayed as perspective projections appear more natural, since this is the way that the eye and a camera lens form images. In Fig. 9–7 a building and its interior are represented in perspective, with the back lines shorter than the front lines.

(c)

FIGURE 9–5
The wire-frame representation of a pyramid (a) contains no depth information to indicate whether the viewing direction is from above (b) or below the base (c).

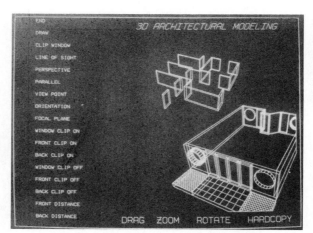

FIGURE 9–7
A perspective layout of a building. Parallel lines on the building are projected onto the screen as converging lines. Courtesy Precision Visuals, Inc., Boulder, Colorado.

Intensity Cuing

A simple method for indicating depth in a display is to vary the intensity of lines according to their distance from the viewing position. Figure 9–8 shows an object with front lines highlighted and drawn wider than back lines. More sophisticated intensity-cuing techniques employ a range of intensities, so that the brightness gradually decreases for lines farther from the viewer.

Hidden-Line Removal

This technique is useful when objects are defined as a set of lines representing the edges of the surfaces of the objects. For a selected view, any lines that are hidden by front surfaces are removed before the object is displayed. Figure 9–2 displays an object with hidden lines removed. Although extensive computation may be required to locate all hidden line segments in a scene, this method gives a more realistic display of depth information in line drawings. For some applications it is helpful to replace hidden edges of objects with dashed lines (Fig. 9–9) rather than remove them all together. In this way more information about back surfaces is provided.

Hidden-Surface Removal and Shading

When objects are defined as surfaces filled by color or shading patterns, hidden-surface removal techniques are used to take out any back surfaces that are hidden by visible surfaces, as in the display of Fig. 9–1. Removing hidden surfaces is generally a complicated and time-consuming process, but it provides a highly realistic method for displaying objects. Added realism is attained by combining hidden-surface removal with perspective projections and by including shadows and surface texture. Figure 9–10 is an example of a three-dimensional scene modeled in this way.

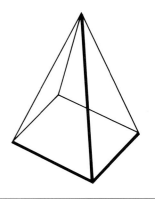

FIGURE 9–8
Highlighting, one form of intensity cuing, can be used to mark the front edges of objects.

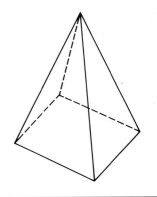

FIGURE 9–9
Displaying hidden edges as dashed lines provides more information about the back surfaces.

FIGURE 9–10
Scene generated using hidden-surface removal, perspective, shading, and surface texture techniques. Courtesy Evans & Sutherland and Daimler-Benz AG, Stuttgart, West Germany.

Exploded and Cutaway Views

Hidden-line and hidden-surface removal techniques can be combined with exploded and cutaway views to give additional information about the structure of three-dimensional objects. The exploded line drawing of Fig. 9–11 clearly shows the structure of component parts, including those that are invisible in the assembled view. An alternative to exploding an object into its component parts is the cutaway view, which removes part of the visible surfaces to show internal structure. Figure 9–12 illustrates the cutaway technique.

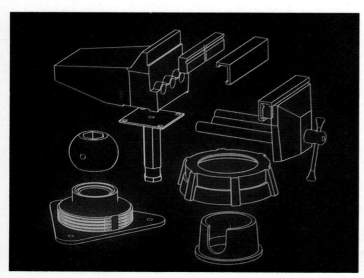

(a)

FIGURE 9–11
Exploded view (a) of an object (b) composed of several parts. Courtesy Evans & Sutherland and Shape Data, Ltd.

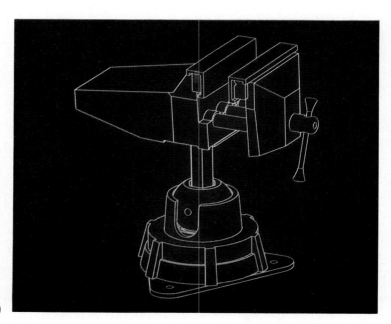

(b)

FIGURE 9–12
Cutaway view of an object
showing the structure of
internal components. Courtesy
Chromatics, Inc.

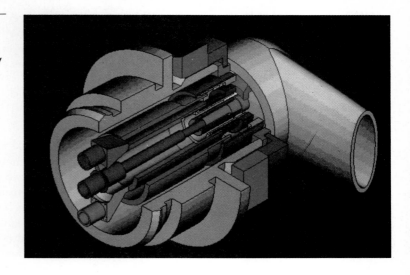

Three-Dimensional and Stereoscopic Views

Instead of presenting a two-dimensional projection to a viewer, three-dimensional and stereoscopic views are sometimes used to give more depth information. As we have seen in Chapter 2, video monitors can be adapted to display such views.

A method for displaying true three-dimensional views is to reflect a CRT image off a vibrating, flexible mirror. The vibrations of the mirror are synchronized with the display of the scene on the CRT. As the mirror vibrates, the focal length varies so that each point in the scene is reflected to a position corresponding to its depth.

Stereoscopic devices present two simultaneous two-dimensional displays to a viewer, one for the left eye and the other for the right eye. The two views are generated by selecting viewing positions that correspond to those for each eye. These two views can be displayed on a single monitor using shutters or polarized filters to present each view to the correct eye. Another method for creating stereoscopic views is to use two small CRTs on a headset, so that each eye of the viewer sees only the display from one of the CRTs.

9–3 Three-Dimensional Graphics Packages

Design of three-dimensional packages requires some considerations that are not necessary with two-dimensional packages. A significant difference between the two packages is that a three-dimensional package must include methods for mapping three-dimensional descriptions onto a flat viewing surface. We need to consider implementation procedures for selecting different views and for using different projection techniques. We also need to consider how surfaces of solid objects are to be modeled, how hidden surfaces can be removed, how transformations of objects are performed in space, and how to describe the additional spatial properties introduced by three dimensions. Later chapters explore each of these considerations in detail.

Other considerations for three-dimensional packages are straightforward extensions from two-dimensional methods. World coordinate descriptions are extended to three dimensions, and users are provided with output and input routines accessed with specifications such as

```
polyline_3 (n, x, y, z)
fill_area_3 (n, x, y, z)
text_3 (x, y, z, string)
get_locator_3 (x, y, z)
```

Algorithms for displaying three-dimensional output primitives on a flat viewing surface are basically the same as for two-dimensional packages, since these procedures are applied after the projection transformations have been accomplished.

Three-dimensional input can be entered by a user with a three-dimensional device, such as the three-dimensional sonic digitizer, but most often two-dimensional input devices, such as a light pen or mouse, are used. When two-dimensional devices are used to input three-dimensional descriptions, coordinate input must be transformed from the device coordinates to three-dimensional world coordinates for processing. For example, if a three-dimensional position is to be input by pointing a light pen at a screen, the selected screen coordinates must be mapped through the inverse transformation back to world coordinates to obtain the "actual" position selected.

Two-dimensional attribute functions that are independent of geometric considerations can be used for both two-dimensional and three-dimensional descriptions. No new attribute functions need be defined for colors, line styles, marker attributes, or text fonts. However, a graphics package with three-dimensional capabilities would need to extend attribute procedures for orienting character strings and for filling defined areas. Text attribute routines associated with the up vector require expansion to include z-coordinate data so that strings can be given any spatial orientation. Area-filling routines, such as those for positioning the pattern reference point and for mapping patterns onto a fill area, would be expanded to accommodate various orientations of the fill-area plane and the pattern plane. Except for transformations, all two-dimensional segment operations can also be carried over to a three-dimensional package.

REFERENCES   Applications of three-dimensional and stereoscopic methods are discussed by Grotch (1983) and by Roese and McCleary (1979).

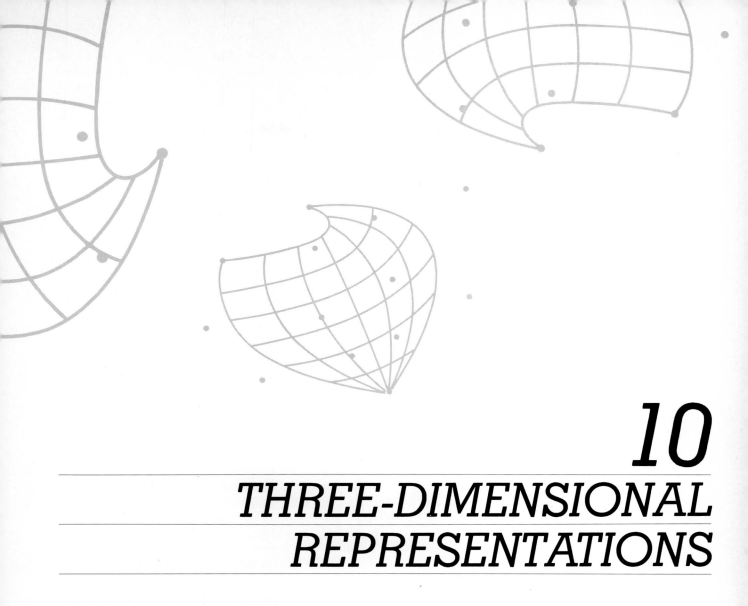

10

THREE-DIMENSIONAL REPRESENTATIONS

Solid objects can be represented for graphics display in a number of ways. In some cases, we may be able to give a precise description of an object in terms of well-defined surfaces. A cube is constructed with six plane faces; a cylinder is a combination of one curved surface and two plane surfaces; and a sphere is formed with a single curved surface. When more complex objects are to be represented, approximation methods are used to define the objects. In design applications, the exact appearance of an object is often not known in advance, and the designer wants to be able to experiment with surface features.

One way for a user to represent an arbitrary object to a graphics package is to approximate its shape with a set of plane, polygon faces. Surfaces of solids could also be described using parametric curve equations or fractal representations. For some applications, definitions of solids are given as construction methods that build the solids from simpler shapes. One technique for building a solid is to sweep a two-dimensional pattern through some region of space, creating a volume. Another construction technique uses solid-geometry methods to combine a basic set of three-dimensional objects, such as blocks, pyramids, and cylinders. Finally, solids can be represented using octree encoding, which defines the properties of each elementary volume of the three-dimensional space containing the solids.

10–1 Polygon Surfaces

Any three-dimensional object can be represented as a set of plane, polygon surfaces. For some objects, such as a polyhedron, this precisely defines the surface features. In other cases, a polygon representation provides an approximate description of the object. Figure 10–1 displays a solid object modeled as a mesh of polygon surfaces. This polygon-mesh representation can be displayed quickly to give a general indication of the object's structure, and the approximation can be improved by dividing object surfaces into smaller polygon faces.

Each polygon in an object can be specified to a graphics package using line or area-fill commands to define the vertex coordinates. CAD packages often allow users to enter vertex positions along polygon boundaries with interactive methods. These vertices can represent the result of digitizing a drawing, or they can be input by a designer who is creating a new shape.

Polygon Tables

Once each polygon surface has been defined by a user, the graphics package organizes the input data into tables that are to be used in the processing and display of the surfaces. The data tables contain the geometric and attribute properties of the object, organized to facilitate processing. Geometric data tables contain boundary coordinates and parameters to identify the spatial orientation of the polygon surfaces. Attribute information for the object includes designations for any color and shading patterns that are to be applied to the surfaces.

Geometric data can be organized in several ways. A convenient method for storing coordinate information is to create three lists: a vertex table, an edge table,

FIGURE 10–1
**Solid object represented as a
set of polygon surfaces.
Courtesy Megatek Corp.**

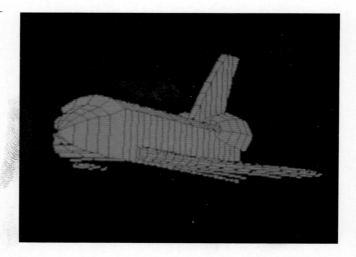

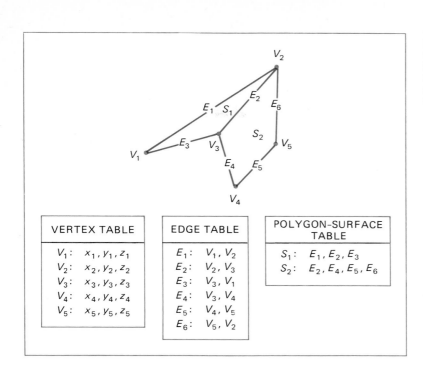

FIGURE 10–2
Geometric data tables for a three-dimensional object represented by two plane polygon surfaces, formed with six edges and five vertices.

VERTEX TABLE

V_1:	x_1, y_1, z_1
V_2:	x_2, y_2, z_2
V_3:	x_3, y_3, z_3
V_4:	x_4, y_4, z_4
V_5:	x_5, y_5, z_5

EDGE TABLE

E_1:	V_1, V_2
E_2:	V_2, V_3
E_3:	V_3, V_1
E_4:	V_3, V_4
E_5:	V_4, V_5
E_6:	V_5, V_2

POLYGON-SURFACE TABLE

S_1:	E_1, E_2, E_3
S_2:	E_2, E_4, E_5, E_6

and a polygon table. Coordinate values for each vertex in the object are stored in the vertex table. The edge table lists the endpoint vertices defining each edge. Each polygon is defined in the polygon table as a list of component edges. This scheme is illustrated in Fig. 10–2 for an object consisting of two polygon surfaces. The polygon table contains pointers back to the edge table, which, in turn, contains pointers back to the coordinate values in the vertex table. When more than one object is to be represented in a scene, each object can be identified in an object table by the set of polygon surfaces in the polygon table defining that object.

Listing the geometric data in three tables, as in Fig. 10–2, provides a convenient reference to the components (vertices, edges, and polygons) of an object. Also, the object can be displayed efficiently by using data from the edge table to draw the component lines. Without the edge table, the object would be displayed using data in the polygon table, and this means that some lines would be drawn twice. If the vertex table were also absent, the polygon table would have to list explicit coordinates for each vertex in each polygon. All information regarding vertices and edges would have to be reconstructed from the polygon table, and coordinate positions would be duplicated for vertices on the border of two or more polygons.

Additional information could be incorporated into the data tables of Fig. 10–2 for faster information extraction. For instance, we could expand the edge table to include pointers into the polygon table so that common edges between polygons could be identified more rapidly (Fig. 10–3). This is particularly useful when shading models are applied to the surfaces, with the shading patterns varying smoothly from one polygon to the next. We could also expand the vertex table by cross-referencing vertices to corresponding edges.

Since the geometric data tables may contain extensive listings of vertices and edges for complex objects, it is important that the data be checked for consistency and completeness. When vertex, line, and polygon definitions are specified, it is

FIGURE 10–3
Expanded edge table for the surface of Fig. 10–2, with pointers to the polygon table.

E_1:	V_1, V_2, S_1
E_2:	V_2, V_3, S_1, S_2
E_3:	V_3, V_1, S_1
E_4:	V_3, V_4, S_2
E_5:	V_4, V_5, S_2
E_6:	V_5, V_2, S_2

possible that certain input errors could be made that would distort the display of the object. The more information included in the data tables, the easier it is to check. Some of the tests that could be performed by a graphics package are (1) that every vertex is listed as an endpoint for at least two lines, (2) that every line is part of at least one polygon, (3) that every polygon is closed, (4) that each polygon has at least one shared edge, and that (5) if the edge table contains pointers to polygons, every edge referenced by a polygon pointer has a reciprocal pointer back to the polygon.

Plane Equations

Parameters specifying the spatial orientation of each polygon are obtained from the vertex coordinate values and the equations that define the polygon planes. These plane parameters are used in viewing transformations, shading models, and hidden-surface algorithms that determine which lines and planes overlap along the line of sight.

The equation for a plane surface can be expressed in the form

$$Ax + By + Cz + D = 0 \tag{10-1}$$

where (x, y, z) is any point on the plane. The coefficients A, B, C, D are constants that can be calculated using the coordinate values of three noncollinear points in the plane. Typically, we use the coordinates of three successive vertices on a polygon boundary to find values for these coefficients. Denoting coordinates for three vertices of a polygon as (x_1, y_1, z_1), (x_2, y_2, z_2), and (x_3, y_3, z_3), we can solve the following set of simultaneous plane equations for the ratios A/D, B/D, and C/D:

$$(A/D)x_i + (B/D)y_i + (C/D)z_i = -1; \quad i = 1, 2, 3 \tag{10-2}$$

Using a solution method such as Cramer's rule, we can write the solution for the plane parameters in determinant form:

$$A = \begin{vmatrix} 1 & y_1 & z_1 \\ 1 & y_2 & z_2 \\ 1 & y_3 & z_3 \end{vmatrix}$$

$$B = \begin{vmatrix} x_1 & 1 & z_1 \\ x_2 & 1 & z_2 \\ x_3 & 1 & z_3 \end{vmatrix}$$

$$C = \begin{vmatrix} x_1 & y_1 & 1 \\ x_2 & y_2 & 1 \\ x_3 & y_3 & 1 \end{vmatrix} \tag{10-3}$$

$$D = - \begin{vmatrix} x_1 & y_1 & z_1 \\ x_2 & y_2 & z_2 \\ x_3 & y_3 & z_3 \end{vmatrix}$$

We can expand the determinants and write the calculations for the plane coefficients in the explicit form:

$$
\begin{aligned}
A &= y_1 (z_2 - z_3) + y_2 (z_3 - z_1) + y_3 (z_1 - z_2) \\
B &= z_1 (x_2 - x_3) + z_2 (x_3 - x_1) + z_3 (x_1 - x_2) \\
C &= x_1 (y_2 - y_3) + x_2 (y_3 - y_1) + x_3 (y_1 - y_2) \\
D &= -x_1 (y_2 z_3 - y_3 z_2) - x_2 (y_3 z_1 - y_1 z_3) - x_3 (y_1 z_2 - y_2 z_1)
\end{aligned}
\tag{10-4}
$$

Values for A, B, C, and D are stored in the data structure containing the coordinate and attribute information about the polygon defined in this plane.

Orientation of a plane surface in space is specified by the normal vector to the plane, as shown in Fig. 10–4. This three-dimensional normal vector has Cartesian coordinates (A, B, C).

Since we are often dealing with polygon surfaces that enclose an object interior, we need to distinguish between the two sides of the surface. The side of the plane that faces the object interior is called the "inside," and the visible or outward side is the "outside." If vertices are specified in a counterclockwise direction when viewing the outer side of the plane in a right-handed coordinate system, the direction of the normal vector will be from inside to outside. This is demonstrated for one plane of a unit cube in Fig. 10–5.

To determine the components of the normal vector for the shaded surface shown in Fig. 10–5, we select three of the four vertices along the boundary of the polygon. These points are selected in a counterclockwise direction as we view from outside the cube toward the origin. The coordinates for these vertices, in the order selected, are used in Eqs. 10–4 to obtain the plane coefficients: $A = 1$, $B = 0$, $C = 0$, $D = -1$. The normal vector for this plane is in the direction of the positive x axis.

Plane equations are used also to identify inside and outside points. Any point (x, y, z) on the outside of a plane satisfies the inequality

$$Ax + By + Cz + D > 0 \qquad (10\text{–}5)$$

Similarly, any points on the inside of the plane produce a negative value for the expression $Ax + By + Cz + D$. For the shaded surface in Fig. 10–5, any point outside the plane satisfies the inequality $x - 1 > 0$, while any point inside the plane has an x-coordinate value less than 1.

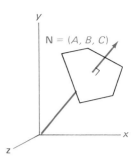

FIGURE 10–4
The vector **N**, normal to the surface of a plane described by the equation $Ax + By + Cz + D = 0$, has Cartesian coordinates (A, B, C).

FIGURE 10–5
The shaded polygon surface of the unit cube has plane equation $x - 1 = 0$ and normal vector $(1, 0, 0)$.

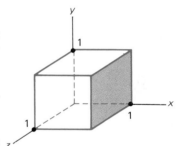

10–2 Curved Surfaces

Three-dimensional displays of curved surfaces can be generated from an input set of mathematical functions defining the surfaces or from a set of user-specified data points. When curve functions are specified, a package can use the defining equations to locate and plot pixel positions along the curve paths, much the same as with two-dimensional curves. An example of the kind of surfaces that can be generated from a functional definition is given in Fig. 10–6. From a set of input data points, a package determines the functional description of the curve that best fits the data points according to the constraints of the application. Figure 10–7 shows an object whose curved surfaces can be defined by an input set of data points.

We can represent a three-dimensional curved line in an analytical form with the pair of functions

$$y = f(x), \qquad z = g(x) \qquad (10\text{–}6)$$

with coordinate x selected as the independent variable. Values for the dependent variables y and z are then determined from Eqs. 10–6 as we step through values for x from one line endpoint to the other endpoint. This representation has some disadvantages. If we want a smooth plot, we must change the independent variable whenever the first derivative (slope) of either $f(x)$ or $g(x)$ becomes greater than 1. This means that we must continually check values of the derivatives, which may become infinite at some points. Also, Eqs. 10–6 provide an awkward format for

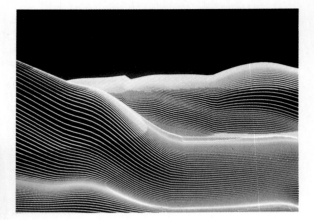

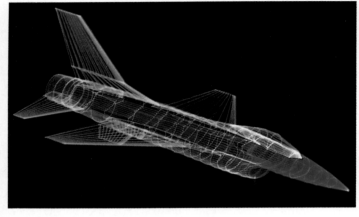

representing multiple-valued functions. A more convenient representation of curves for graphics applications is in terms of parametric equations.

Parametric Equations

By introducing a fourth parameter, u, into the coordinate description of a curve, we can express each of the three Cartesian coordinates in parametric form. Any point on the curve can then be represented by the vector function

$$\boldsymbol{P}(u) = (x(u), y(u), z(u))\qquad(10\text{–}7)$$

Usually, the parametric equations are set up so that parameter u is defined in the range from 0 to 1. For example, a circle in the xy plane with center at the coordinate origin could be defined in parametric form as

$$x(u) = r\cdot\cos(2\pi u),\quad y(u) = r\cdot\sin(2\pi u),\quad z(u) = 0$$

Other parametric forms are also possible for describing circles and circular arcs.

For an arbitrary curve, it may be difficult to devise a single set of parametric equations that completely defines the shape of the curve. But any curve can be approximated by using different sets of parametric functions over different parts of the curve. Usually these approximations are formed with polynomial functions. Such a piecewise construction of a curve must be carefully implemented to ensure that there is a smooth transition from one section of the curve to the next. The smoothness of a curve can be described in terms of curve **continuity** between the sections. Zero-order continuity means simply that the curves meet. First-order continuity means that the tangent lines (first derivatives) of two adjoining curve sections are the same at the joining point. Second-order continuity means that the curvatures (second derivatives) of the two curve sections are the same at the intersection. Figure 10–8 shows examples of the three orders of continuity.

Parametric equations for surfaces are formulated with two parameters, u and v. A coordinate position on a surface is then represented by the parametric vector function

$$P(u, v) = (x(u, v), y(u, v), z(u, v))\qquad(10\text{--}8)$$

The equations for coordinates x, y, and z are often arranged so that parameters u and v are defined within the range 0 to 1. A spherical surface, for example, can be described with the equations

$$\begin{aligned}
x(u, v) &= r\,\sin(\pi u)\,\cos(2\pi v)\\
y(u, v) &= r\,\sin(\pi u)\,\sin(2\pi v)\\
z(u, v) &= r\,\cos(\pi u)
\end{aligned}\qquad(10\text{--}9)$$

where r is the radius of the sphere. Parameter u describes lines of constant latitude over the surface, while parameter v describes lines of constant longitude. By keeping one of these parameters fixed while varying the other over any values within the range 0 to 1, we could plot latitude and longitude lines for any spherical section (Fig. 10–9).

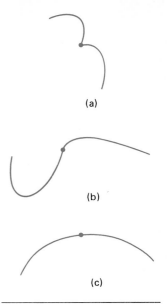

FIGURE 10–8
Piecewise specification of a curve by joining two curve segments with varying orders of continuity: (a) zero-order continuity only, (b) first-order continuity, and (c) second-order continuity.

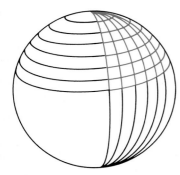

FIGURE 10–9
Section of a spherical surface described by lines of constant u and lines of constant v in Eqs. 10–9.

In design applications, a curve or surface is often defined by interactively specifying a set of **control points,** which indicate the shape of the curve. These control points are used by the package to set up polynomial parametric equations to display the defined curve. When the displayed curve passes through the control points, as in Fig. 10–10, it is said to **interpolate** the control points. On the other hand, the control points are said to be **approximated** if the displayed curve passes near them (Fig. 10–11). Many techniques exist for setting up polynomial parametric equations for curves and surfaces, given the coordinates for the control points. Basic methods for displaying curves specified with control points include the Bézier and the spline formulations.

FIGURE 10–10
A set of six control points interpolated by a curve.

Bézier Curves

This method for constructing curves was developed by the French engineer Bézier for use in the design of Renault automobile bodies. For any input set of

FIGURE 10–11
A set of four control points approximated by a curve.

195

control points, an approximating curve is formed by adding a sequence of polynomial functions formed from the coordinates of the control points.

Suppose $n + 1$ control points are input and designated as the vectors $p_k = (x_k, y_k, z_k)$, for k varying from 0 to n. From these coordinate points, we calculate an approximating Bézier vector function $P(u)$, which represents the three parametric equations for the curve that fits the input control points p_k. This Bézier coordinate function is calculated as

$$P(u) = \sum_{k=0}^{n} p_k \, B_{k,n}(u) \tag{10-10}$$

Each $B_{k,n}(u)$ is a polynomial function defined as

$$B_{k,n}(u) = C(n,k)u^k (1 - u)^{n-k} \tag{10-11}$$

and the $C(n,k)$ represent the binomial coefficients

$$C(n,k) = \frac{n!}{k! \, (n - k)!} \tag{10-12}$$

Equation 10–10 can be written in explicit form as a set of parametric equations for the individual curve coordinates:

$$x(u) = \sum_{k=0}^{n} x_k B_{k,n}(u)$$
$$y(u) = \sum_{k=0}^{n} y_k B_{k,n}(u) \tag{10-13}$$
$$z(u) = \sum_{k=0}^{n} z_k B_{k,n}(u)$$

The polynomials $B_{k,n}(u)$ are called **blending functions** because they blend the control points to form a composite function describing the curve. This composite function is a polynomial of degree one less than the number of control points used. Three points generate a parabola, four points a cubic curve, and so forth. Figure 10–12 demonstrates the appearance of some Bézier curves for various selections of control points in the xy plane ($z = 0$). An important property of any Bézier curve is that it lies within the **convex hull** (polygon boundary) of the control points (Fig. 10–13). This ensures that the curve smoothly follows the control points without erratic oscillations.

In Fig. 10–14 we show the shapes of the four Bézier polynomials used in the construction of a curve to fit four control points. The form of each blending function determines how the control points influence the shape of the curve for values of parameter u. At $u = 0$, the only nonzero blending function is $B_{0,3}$, which has the value 1. At $u = 1$, the only nonzero function is $B_{3,3}$, with a value of 1 at that point. Thus the Bézier curve will always pass through the endpoints p_0 and p_3. The other functions, $B_{1,3}$ and $B_{2,3}$, influence the shape of the curve at intermediate values of the parameter u, so that the resulting curve tends toward the points p_1 and p_2. Blending function $B_{1,3}$ is maximum at $u = 1/3$ and $B_{2,3}$ is maximum at $u = 2/3$.

Bézier curves are useful for a variety of design applications. Closed curves can be generated by specifying the first and last control points at the same position, as in the example shown in Fig. 10–15. Specifying multiple control points at a single position gives more weight to that position. In Fig. 10–16, a single coordinate position is input as two control points, and the resulting curve is pulled nearer to this position.

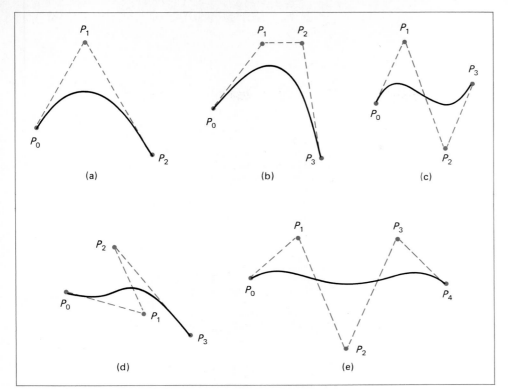

FIGURE 10–12
Examples of Bézier curves generated from three, four, and five control points in the *xy* plane. Dashed lines show the straight-line connection of the control points.

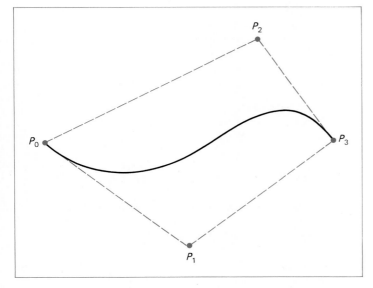

FIGURE 10–13
Convex hull (dashed line) of the control points for a Bézier curve.

In general, any number of control points could be specified for a Bézier curve, but this requires the calculation of polynomial functions of higher degree. When complicated curves are to be generated, they can be formed by piecing several Bézier sections of lower degree together. Piecing together smaller sections also gives a user better control over local variations that may be desired in a curve. Since Bézier curves pass through endpoints, it is easy to match curve sections (zero-

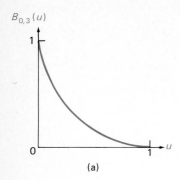

(a)

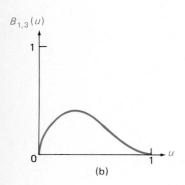

(b)

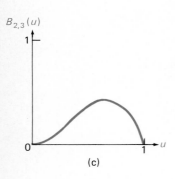

(c)

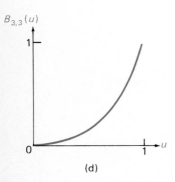

(d)

FIGURE 10–14
The four Bézier functions used in the construction of a curve with four control points.

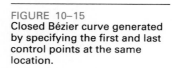

FIGURE 10–15
Closed Bézier curve generated by specifying the first and last control points at the same location.

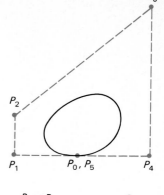

FIGURE 10–16
A Bézier curve can be made to pass closer to a given position by assigning multiple control points to that position.

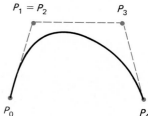

order continuity). Also, Bézier curves have the important property that the tangent to the curve at an endpoint is along the line joining that endpoint to the adjacent control point. Therefore, to obtain first-order continuity between curve sections, a user can pick control points so that the positions p_{n-1} and p_n of one section are along the same straight line as positions p_0 and p_1 of the next section (Fig. 10–17). Bézier curves, in general, do not possess second-order continuity.

The following example program illustrates a method for generating Bézier curves. More efficient algorithms can be developed using recursive calculations to obtain successive points along the curves.

```
procedure bezier (n, m : integer);
  {Uses n + 1 control points. Generates curve by finding
   m + 1 points along the interval of 0 ≤ u ≤ 1}
  type
    {control points}
    control_array = array [0..max_controls, 1..3] of real;
    {n!/(k!(n − k)!)}
    coefficient_array = array [0..max_controls] of integer;
    {points to plot}
    curve_points = array [0..max_points] of real;
  var
    control : control_array;
    c : coefficient_array;
    x, y, z : curve_points;
    j : integer;

procedure get_control_points (n : integer;
                              var controls : control_array);
  begin
    {returns n+1 control points in controls}
```

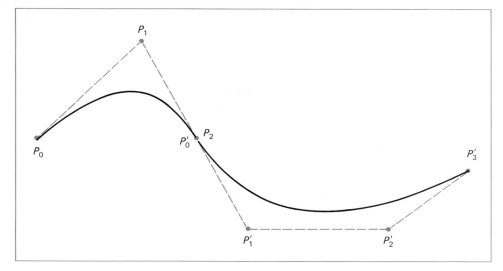

FIGURE 10–17
Curve formed with two Bézier sections. Zero-order and first-order continuity is attained between curve sections by setting $P'_0 = P_2$ and by making the points P_1, P_2, and P'_1 collinear.

```
    end;    {get_control_points}

procedure compute_coefficients (n : integer;
                                   var c : coefficient_array);
  var k, m: integer;
  begin
    for k := 0 to n do begin
        {compute n!/(k!(n − k)!)}
        c[k] := 1;
        for m := n downto k+1 do c[k] := c[k] * m;
        for m := n−k downto 2 do c[k] := c[k] div m
      end {for k}
  end;    {compute_coefficients}

procedure compute_point (n : integer; u : real;
                            controls : control_array;
                            c : coefficient_array;
                            var x, y, z : real);
  var k : integer; b : real;
  function blending_value (n, k : integer; u : real);
    {returns blending value for this control
     point at this point in the interval}
    var bv : real; m : integer;
    begin
      {compute c[k] * (u to kth power) * ((1−u) to (n−k) power)}
      bv := c[k];
      for m := 1 to k do bv := bv * u;
      for m := 1 to n−k do bv := bv * (1 − u);
      blending_value := bv
    end;    {blending_value}

  begin    {compute_point}
    x := 0; y := 0; z := 0;
    for k := 0 to n do begin
        {add in influence of each control point}
```

```
    b := blending_value (n, k, u);
    x := x + controls[k,1] * b;
    y := y + controls[k,2] * b;
    z := z + controls[k,3] * b
  end  {for k}
end;  {compute_point}


begin  {bezier}
  get_control_points (n, controls);
  compute_coefficients (n, c);
  for j := 0 to m do  {generate m+1 points}
    compute_point (n, j/m, controls, c, x[j+1], y[j+1], z[j+1]);
  polyline_3 (m+1, x, y, z)
end;  {bezier}
```

Spline Curves

In drafting terminology, a spline is a flexible strip used to produce a smooth curve through a set of plotted control points. The term **spline curves,** or spline functions, refers to the resulting curves drawn in this manner. Such curves can be described mathematically as piecewise approximations of cubic polynomial functions with all three orders of continuity (zero-order, first-order, and second-order continuity), although many other types of approximating functions are also referred to as spline curves.

B-splines are a class of spline curves that are particularly useful in graphics applications. Given an input set of $n + 1$ control points p_k, with k varying from 0 to n, we define points on the approximating B-spline curve as

$$P(u) = \sum_{k=0}^{n} p_k N_{k,t}(u) \tag{10--14}$$

where the B-spline blending functions $N_{k,t}$ can be defined as polynomials of degree $t - 1$. A method for setting up the polynomial form of the blending functions is to define them recursively over various subintervals of the range for parameter u. This range now depends on the number of control points n and the choice for t, so that u varies from 0 to $n - t + 2$ (instead of from 0 to 1). Setting up $n + t$ subintervals, we define the blending functions recursively as

$$N_{k,1}(u) = \begin{cases} 1 & \text{if } u_k \leqslant u < u_{k+1} \\ 0 & \text{otherwise} \end{cases} \tag{10--15}$$

$$N_{k,t}(u) = \frac{u - u_k}{u_{k+t-1} - u_k} N_{k,t-1}(u) + \frac{u_{k+t} - u}{u_{k+t} - u_{k+1}} N_{k+1,\ t-1}(u)$$

Since the denominators in the recursive calculations can have a value of 0, this formulation assumes that any terms evaluated as 0/0 are to be assigned the value 0.

The defining positions u_j for the subintervals of u are referred to as **breakpoints,** and points on the B-spline curve corresponding to the breakpoints are called **knots.** Breakpoints can be defined in various ways. A uniform spacing of the breakpoints is achieved by setting u_j equal to j. Another method for defining uniform intervals is with breakpoints set to the values

$$u_j = \begin{cases} 0 & \text{if } j < t \\ j - t + 1 & \text{if } t \leqslant j \leqslant n \\ n - t + 2 & \text{if } j > n \end{cases} \tag{10--16}$$

for values of j ranging from 0 to $n + t$.

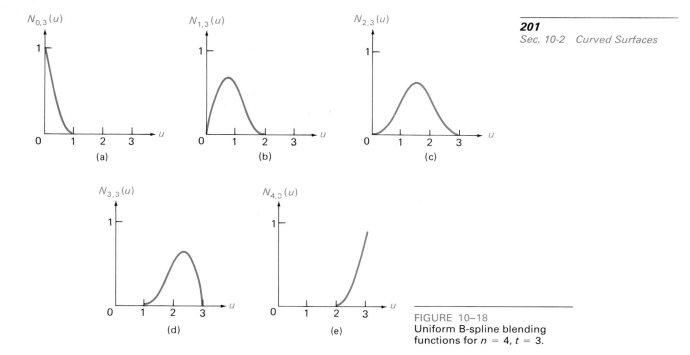

FIGURE 10–18
Uniform B-spline blending functions for $n = 4$, $t = 3$.

Figure 10–18 illustrates the shape of uniform, quadratic B-spline blending functions ($t = 3$) using five control points ($n = 4$) and subintervals as defined in Eq. 10–16. Parameter u is then varied over the interval from 0 to 3, with breakpoints u_0 to u_7 as 0, 0, 0, 1, 2, 3, 3, 3, respectively. An important property of B-spline curves, demonstrated in this example, is that the blending functions are each zero over part of the range of u. Blending function $N_{0,3}$, for instance, is nonzero only in the subinterval from 0 to 1, so the first control point influences the curve only in this interval. Thus B-spline curves allow localized changes to be made easily. If a user changes the position of the first control point, the shape of the curve near that point is changed without greatly affecting other parts of the curve. Figure 10–19 demonstrates this local property using the blending functions of Fig. 10–18.

B-spline curves have the advantage that any number of control points can be specified by a designer without increasing the degree of the curve. A cubic function ($t = 4$) could then be used for many different curve shapes, without the need to

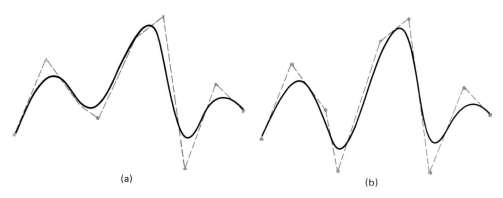

FIGURE 10–19
Local modification of a B-spline curve. Changing one of the control points in (a) produces curve (b), which is modified only in the neighborhood of the altered control point.

FIGURE 10–20
Cubic B-spline curve ($t = 4$)
with multiple control points
specified at the same
coordinate position to
emphasize that position: (a)
one control point at each
position; (b) two control points
at the center position; (c) three
control points at the center
position.

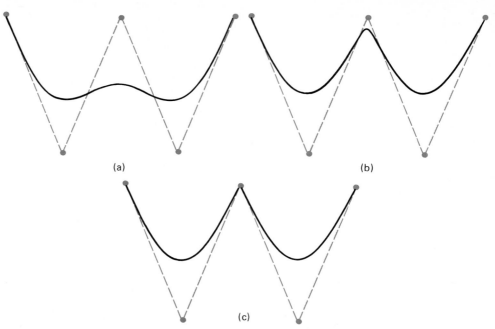

(a)   (b)

(c)

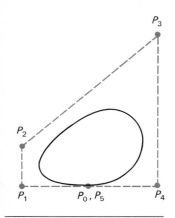

FIGURE 10–21
Closed cubic B-spline curve
($t = 4$), specified by setting the
first and last control points to
the same position.

piece curve segments together. Any number of control points can be added or modified to manipulate the curve shape.

As with Bézier curves, specifying multiple control points at the same coordinate position pulls the B-spline curve closer to that position (Fig. 10–20). Also, closed curves are obtained by specifying the first and last control points at the same position, as in Fig. 10–21. B-splines also lie within the convex hull of the control points. In fact, any B-spline curve with parameter t lies within the convex hull of at most $t + 1$ of its control points, so that this class of curves is tightly bound to the input positions.

Another type of spline curve is the Beta-spline. This spline method introduces two additional parameters, called beta-1 and beta-2, that give the user added capabilities for manipulating curve shapes. The two beta parameters are used to adjust the shape of the curve relative to the convex hull. Depending on the values assigned to these parameters, the curve can be made to move away from the convex hull or toward it. For certain values of beta-1 and beta-2, a Beta-spline curve reduces to a B-spline.

Bézier Surfaces

Two sets of Bézier curves can be used to represent surfaces of objects specified by input control points. The parametric vector function for the Bézier surface is formed as the Cartesian product of Bézier blending functions:

$$\boldsymbol{P}(u,v) = \sum_{j=0}^{m} \sum_{k=0}^{n} \boldsymbol{p}_{j,k} B_{j,m}(u) \, B_{k,n}(v) \tag{10–17}$$

with $\boldsymbol{p}_{j,k}$ specifying the location of the $(m + 1)$ by $(n + 1)$ control points.

Figure 10–22 illustrates two Bézier surface plots. The control points are connected by lighter lines, and the heavier lines show curves of constant u and con-

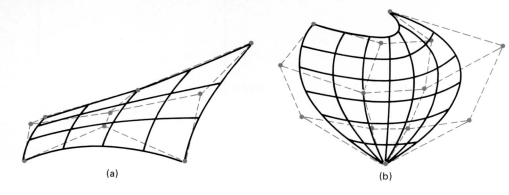

stant v. Each curve of constant u is plotted by varying v over the interval from 0 to 1, with u fixed at one of the values in this unit interval. Curves of constant v are plotted similarly.

Bézier surfaces have the same properties as Bézier curves, and they provide a convenient method for interactive design applications. Figure 10–23 illustrates a surface formed with two Bézier surface sections. As with curves, a smooth transition from one section to the other is assured by establishing both zero-order and second-order continuity at the boundary line. Zero-order continuity is obtained by matching control points at the boundary. First-order continuity is obtained by choosing control points along a straight line across the boundary and by maintaining a constant ratio of collinear line segments for each such line crossing the surface boundary line.

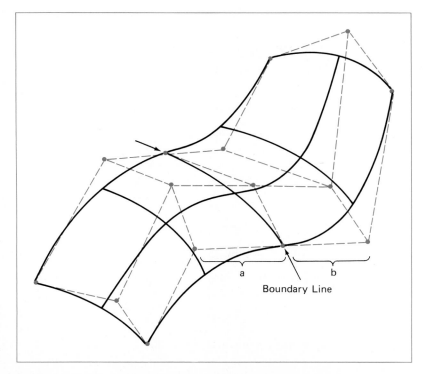

FIGURE 10–23
Bézier surface constructed with two Bézier sections, joined at the indicated boundary line. The dashed lines connect specified control points. First-order continuity is established by making the ratio of length a to length b constant for each collinear line of control points across the boundary line.

Spline Surfaces

Formulation of a B-spline surface is similar to that for a Bézier curve. The Cartesian product of B-spline blending functions defines a parametric vector function over a B-spline surface:

$$P(u, v) = \sum_{j=0}^{m} \sum_{k=0}^{n} p_{j,k} N_{j,s}(u) \, N_{k,t}(v) \tag{10-18}$$

As before, vector values for $p_{j,k}$ specify the $(m + 1)$ by $(n + 1)$ control points.

B-spline surfaces exhibit the same properties as those of their component B-spline curves. A surface is constructed from selected values for parameters s and t (which determine the polynomial degrees to be used) by evaluating the blending functions according to Eqs. 10–15.

Methods for Surface Generation

Since the equations describing Bézier and spline surfaces involve a great many calculations, it is important to devise algorithms that use efficient methods for generating successive points along the curved lines of the surfaces. Several techniques are available for reducing the calculations involved in evaluating parametric polynomial equations.

One method for reducing the number of arithmetic operations in a polynomial equation is Horner's rule, which specifies an order for factoring the terms in the polynomial. The cubic equation, $f(u) = a_0 u^3 + a_1 u^2 + a_2 u + a_3$ for example, is evaluated in the order:

$$f(u) = [(a_0 u + a_1)u + a_2]u + a_3 \tag{10-19}$$

which requires three multiplications and three additions. Although this factoring technique reduces the number of arithmetic operations, it does involve floating-point multiplications.

A more efficient method for evaluating polynomial equations is to recursively generate each succeeding value of the function by incrementing the previously calculated value:

$$f_{i+1} = f_i + \Delta f_i \tag{10-20}$$

where Δf_i is called the **forward difference.** The function f_i is evaluated at u_i, and f_{i+1} is evaluated at $u_{i+1} = u_i + \delta$, where δ is the step size for incrementing parameter u. As an example, the linear equation $f(u) = a_0 u + a_1$ can be incrementally evaluated using Eq. (10–20) and the forward difference $\Delta f = a_0 \delta$. In this case, the forward difference is a constant. With higher-order polynomials, the forward difference is itself a polynomial function of parameter u.

For a cubic curve, the forward difference evaluates to

$$\Delta f_i = 3a_0 \delta u_i^2 + (3a\delta^2 + 2a_1\delta)u_i + a_0\delta^3 + a_1\delta^2 + a_2\delta \tag{10-21}$$

which is a quadratic function of parameter u. However, we can use the same incremental procedure to obtain successive values of Δf. That is,

$$\Delta f_{i+1} = \Delta f_i + \Delta^2 f_i \tag{10-22}$$

where the second forward difference is a linear function of u:

$$\Delta^2 f_i = 6a_0\delta^2 u_i + 6a_0\delta^3 + 2a_1\delta^2 \qquad (10\text{--}23)$$

Repeating this process once more, we can write

$$\Delta^2 f_{i+1} = \Delta^2 f_i + \Delta^3 f_i \qquad (10\text{--}24)$$

with the third forward difference as the constant

$$\Delta^3 f_i = 6a_0\delta^3 \qquad (10\text{--}25)$$

Equations (10–20), (10–22), (10–24), and (10–25) are used to incrementally obtain points along the curve from $u = 0$ to $u = 1$ with a step size δ. The initial values at $i = 0$ and $u = 0$ are

$$
\begin{aligned}
f_0 &= a_3 \\
\Delta f_0 &= a_0\delta^3 + a_1\delta^2 + a_2\delta \\
\Delta^2 f_0 &= 6a_0\delta^3 + 2a_1\delta^2
\end{aligned}
\qquad (10\text{--}26)
$$

Calculations for successive points are then carried out as a series of additions.

To apply this incremental procedure to Bézier and spline curves, three sets of calculations are needed for the coordinates $x(u)$, $y(u)$, and $z(u)$. For surfaces, incremental calculations are applied for both parameter u and parameter v.

10–3 Fractal-Geometry Methods

The techniques discussed in the preceding section generate smooth curves and surfaces. But many objects, such as mountains and clouds, have irregular or fragmented features. Such objects can be modeled using the **fractal-geometry methods** developed by Mandelbrot. Basically, fractal objects are described as geometric entities that cannot be represented with Euclidean-geometry methods. This means that a fractal curve cannot be described as one-dimensional, and a fractal surface is not two-dimensional. Fractal shapes have a fractional dimension.

Smooth curves are one-dimensional objects whose length can be precisely defined between two points. A fractal curve, on the other hand, contains an infinite variety of detail at each point along the curve, so we cannot say exactly what its length is. In fact, as we continue to zoom in on more and more detail, the length of the fractal curve grows longer and longer. An outline of a mountain, for example, shows more variation the closer we get to it (Fig. 10–24). As we near the mountain, the detail in the individual ledges and boulders becomes apparent. Moving even

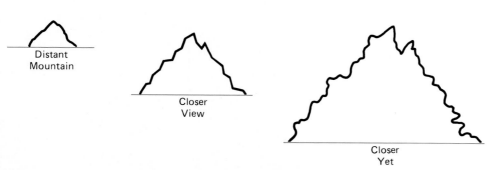

FIGURE 10–24
The ragged appearance of a mountain outline increases as we get closer.

closer, we see the outlines of rocks, then stones, and then grains of sand. At each step, the outline reveals more twists and turns, and the overall length of the curve tends to infinity as we move closer and closer. Similar types of curves describe coastlines and the edges of clouds. Such curves, represented in a two-dimensional coordinate system, can be described mathematically with fractional dimensions between 1 and 2. When a fractal curve is described in a three-dimensional space, it has a dimension between 1 and 3.

A fractal curve is generated by repeatedly applying a specified transformation function to points within a region of space. The amount of detail included in the final display of the curve depends on the number of iterations performed and the resolution of the display system. If $P_0 = (x_0, y_0)$ is a selected initial point, each iteration of a transformation function F generates the next level of detail with the calculations

$$P_1 = F(P_0), \quad P_2 = F(P_1), \quad P_3 = F(P_2), \quad \ldots \quad (10\text{--}27)$$

The transformation function can be specified in various ways to generate either regular or random variations along the curve at each iteration.

An example of a fractal curve generated with a regular pattern is shown in Fig. 10–25. We start with a curve containing the two line segments shown. First the pattern for the original curve is reduced by a factor of 1/3, and this reduced pattern is used to replace the middle third of the two line segments in the original curve. The resulting curve is the second pattern shown in this figure. We then scale the reduced pattern by a factor of 1/3 again and use it to replace the middle

FIGURE 10–25
Producing a fractal curve by repeatedly scaling the original curve and using the reduced pattern to replace the middle third of the line segments in the curve.

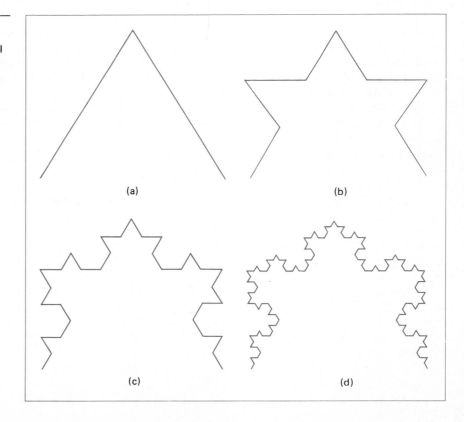

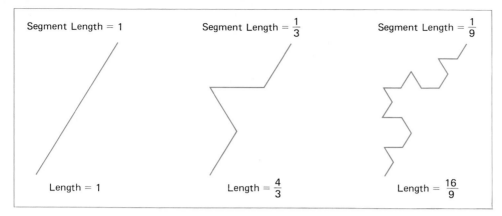

Segment Length = 1	Segment Length = $\frac{1}{3}$	Segment Length = $\frac{1}{9}$
Length = 1	Length = $\frac{4}{3}$	Length = $\frac{16}{9}$

FIGURE 10–26
Length of the fractal line increases by a factor of 4/3 at each iteration, when line-segment lengths are reduced by a factor of 1/3 at each step.

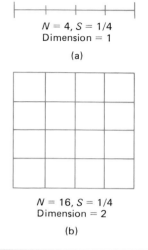

$N = 4$, $S = 1/4$
Dimension = 1

(a)

$N = 16$, $S = 1/4$
Dimension = 2

(b)

FIGURE 10–27
Subdividing a line (a) and a surface (b) into equal parts without changing the size of the objects.

FIGURE 10–28
A unit circle in the complex plane. The function $f(z) = z^2$ moves points that are inside the circle toward the origin, while points outside the circle are moved farther away from the circle.

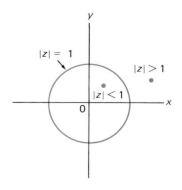

third of the line segments in the transformed curve to produce the third curve shown. This process is continued by repeatedly scaling the original pattern by a factor of 1/3 and using the scaled patterns to modify line segments in the successive curves generated. At each step, the number of lines in the curve is increased by a factor of 4, and the length of each new line segment generated is one-third the length of line segments in the previous curve. This increases the total length of the fractal curve by a factor of 4/3 at each step (Fig. 10–26). Therefore, the length of the fractal curve tends to infinity as more detail is added to the curve.

One method for determining the dimension of a fractal curve such as that in Fig. 10–25 is the calculation

$$D = \frac{\ln N}{\ln (1/S)} \qquad (10\text{--}28)$$

where N is the number of subdivisions at each step and S is the scaling factor. For our example, we subdivided line segments into four parts, so $N = 4$, and we used a scaling factor of $S = 1/3$. This gives the fractal curve in Fig. 10–25 a dimension of $D = \ln 4/\ln 3 = 1.2619$. If we subdivide a line into equal parts without changing its length, $N = 1/S$ and the dimension of the line as calculated by Eq. 10–20 is $D = 1$, as described in Euclidean geometry. Similarly, when a surface is subdivided into N equal parts without changing its area, $N = 1/S^2$ and the dimension of the surface is 2. Figure 10–27 illustrates subdivision of a line and a surface without a change in size.

Although fractal objects, by definition, contain infinite detail, we generate a fractal curve with a finite number of iterations. Therefore, the curves we display with repeated patterns actually have finite length. Our representation approaches a true fractal curve as the number of transformations is increased to produce more and more detail.

Many fractal curves are generated with functions in the complex plane. That is, each two-dimensional point (x, y) is represented as the complex expression $z = x + iy$, where x and y are real numbers and i is used to represent the square root of -1. A complex function $f(z)$ is then used to map points repeatedly from one position to another. Depending on the initial point selected, this iteration could cause points to diverge to infinity, or the points could converge to a finite limit, or the points could remain on some curve. For example, the function $f(z) = z^2$ transforms points according to their relation to the unit circle (Fig. 10–28). Any point z

whose magnitude $|z|$ is greater than 1 is transformed through a sequence of points that tend to infinity. A point with $|z| < 1$ is transformed closer to the origin. Points on the circle, $|z| = 1$, remain on the circle. For some functions, the boundary between those points that move toward infinity and those that tend toward a finite limit is a fractal curve.

A function that is rich in fractal curves is the transformation

$$z' = f(z) = \lambda z(1 - z) \qquad (10\text{--}29)$$

with λ assigned any constant complex value. Testing the behavior of transformed points in the complex plane to determine the position of the fractal curve can be a time-consuming process. A quicker method for calculating points on the fractal curve is to use the inverse of the transformation function. An initial point chosen on the inside or outside of the curve will then converge to points on the fractal curve. We can obtain the inverse function by rewriting Eq. 10–29 as

$$\lambda z^2 - \lambda z + z' = 0 \qquad (10\text{--}30)$$

Solving this quadratic equation for z, we have

$$z = \frac{1}{2}[1 \pm \sqrt{1 - (4z')/\lambda}] \qquad (10\text{--}31)$$

Using complex arithmetic operations, we solve this equation for the real and imaginary parts of z; that is, $x = R(z)$ and $y = I(z)$. Coordinate positions (x, y) are then plotted along the fractal curve.

The following procedure demonstrates plotting of fractal curves generated from Eq. 10–31. Since this inverse function provides two possible transformed positions, we randomly choose one or the other at each step in the iteration. Also, whenever the imaginary part of $-4z'/\lambda$ is negative, one of the possible transformed positions is in the second quadrant ($x < 0$ and $y > 0$). The other position is situated 180° away, in the fourth quadrant ($x > 0$, $y < 0$). Figure 10–29 shows two fractal curves output by this procedure.

FIGURE 10–29
Two fractal curves generated with the inverse of the function $f(z) = \lambda z (1 - z)$ by procedure fractal: (a) $\lambda = 3$; (b) $\lambda = 2 + i$. Each curve is plotted with 10,000 points.

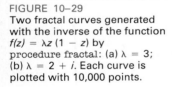

```
{procedure fractal accepts lambda and an initial point
z_prime, and calculates points on a fractal curve using the
inverse of the function z_prime = lambda * z * (1 − z). Random
is a predefined function returning values between 0 and 1}
```

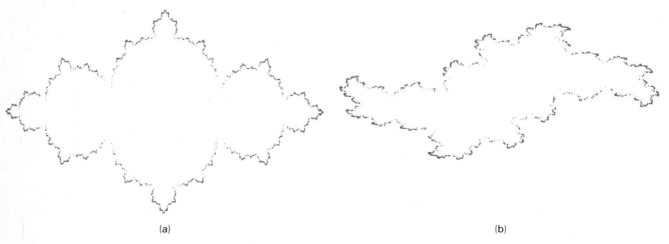

(a)   (b)

```
type
  complex = record
    a : real;
    b : real
  end;  {record}
var  lambda, z_prime, z : complex;

procedure fractal (lambda, z_prime : complex; count : integer);
  var
    k : integer;
    lambda_magnitude : real;
    four_over_lambda : complex;

  {calculate_point accepts a point z_prime and returns
   a point z that satisfies inverse of z' = λz(1−z)}
  procedure calculate_point (z_prime : complex; var z : complex);
    var  save_b : real;

    procedure complex_multiply (c1, c2 : complex;
                                        var result : complex);
      begin
        result.a := c1.a * c2.a − c1.b * c2.b;
        result.b := c1.a * c2.b + c1.b * c2.a
      end;  {complex_multiply}

    procedure complex_square_root (c : complex;
                                        var result : complex);
      var  c_magnitude : real;
      begin
        c_magnitude := sqrt(c.a * c.a + c.b * c.b);
        if (c_magnitude + c.a) < 0 then result.a := 0
          else result.a := sqrt((c_magnitude + c.a) / 2);
        if (c_magnitude − c.a) < 0 then result.b := 0
          else result.b := sqrt((c_magnitude − c.a) / 2)
      end;  {complex_square_root}

    begin  {calculate_point}
      {compute 4 / lambda * z_prime. Return result in z}
      complex_multiply (z_prime, four_over_lambda, z);
      {subtract from 1}
      z.a := 1 − z.a;
      {retain current y part}
      save_b := z.b;
      {take square root of z. Return result in z}
      complex_square_root (z, z);
      {determine correct sign for square root of x part}
      if save_b < 0 then z.a := −z.a;
      {choose one of the two points satisfying inverse function}
      if random < 0.5 then begin
          z.a := −z.a;
          z.b := −z.b
        end;  {if random}
      {subtract from 1}
      z.a := 1 − z.a;
      {divide by 2}
```

```
      z.a := z.a / 2;
      z.b := z.b / 2
   end;  {calculate_point}

procedure plot_point (x, y : real);
  begin
    {device-dependent routine to map point to device}
  end;  {plot_point}
  begin {fractal}
    {compute 4 divided by lambda}
    lambda_magnitude := lambda.a * lambda.a +
                          lambda.b * lambda.b;
    four_over_lambda.a :=  4 * lambda.a / lambda_magnitude;
    four_over_lambda.b := -4 * lambda.b / lambda_magnitude;
    {calculate but don't plot the first few points.
    Gets to a point that's actually on the curve}
    for k := 1 to 10 do begin
        calculate_point (z_prime, z);
        z_prime := z            {update z_prime}
      end;  {for k}
    {calculate successive points (z) on the
    curve.  For each new z, plot the real (z.a)
    and imaginary (z.b) parts as x and y}
    for k := 1 to count do begin
        calculate_point (z_prime, z);
        plot_point (z.a, z.b);
        z_prime := z            {update z_prime}
    end   {for k}
  end;  {fractal}
```

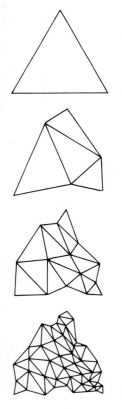

FIGURE 10–30
Creating a fractal mountain
from a triangle by random
displacement of boundary
points.

Fractal surfaces represented in three dimensions can be described as objects with a dimension between 2 and 3. We can create fractal surfaces with procedures similar to those for generating fractal curves. Points on the surface are successively transformed at each step to produce increasingly more detail. In Fig. 10–30, a triangle is turned into a mountain by randomly displacing points on the triangle boundary. First, a random point is selected on each leg of the triangle. Then random displacement distances are applied to each of the three points, and the displaced points are joined with straight lines. As shown, in the second step, this turns the triangle into four smaller contiguous triangles. The process is repeated for each of the new triangles formed at each step. Final display of the object is a surface modeled with a mesh composed of small polygon sections. Many other types of transformations can be used to produce fractal surfaces with different features.

Complex-function transformations, such as Eq. (10–29), can also be extended to produce fractal surfaces and fractal solids. Methods for generating these objects often use quaternion representations for transforming points in three- and four-dimensional space. A quaternion has four components, one real and three imaginary, expressed as

$$q = q_0 + iq_1 + iq_2 + iq_3 \qquad (10\text{–}32)$$

Using this representation and iteration methods to transform points in space, surfaces of fractal objects are generated. As successive points are generated, they are tested to determine whether they are inside or outside the surface. A basic procedure is to start with an interior point and generate successive points until an exterior point is identified. The previous interior point is then retained as a surface point. Neighbors of this surface point are then tested to determine whether they are inside or outside. Any inside point that connects to an outside point is a surface point. In this way, the procedure threads its way along the fractal boundary without generating points that are too far from the surface. When four-dimensional fractals are generated, three-dimensional slices are projected onto the two-dimensional surface of the video monitor.

Procedures for generating fractal objects require considerable computation time for evaluating the iteration function and for testing points. Each point on a surface can be represented as a small cube, giving the inner and outer limits of the surface. Output from such programs for three-dimensional fractal representations typically contain over a million vertices for the surface cubes. Display of the fractal objects is performed by applying illumination models that determine the lighting and color for each surface cube. Hidden-surface methods are then applied so that only visible surfaces of the objects are displayed.

Figure 10–31 illustrates some highly realistic scenes produced with fractal-geometry methods, using a probabilistic function to transform points in space. Frac-

(a)

(b)

(c)

FIGURE 10–31
Scenes generated by fractal-geometry methods, with a random iteration procedure. Courtesy R. V. Voss and B. B. Mandelbrot, adapted from *The Fractal Geometry of Nature* by Benoit B. Mandelbrot (New York: Freeman Press, 1982).

tal-generated displays of natural objects are often used in making movies containing animated scenes. Terrain, clouds, shorelines, and other objects are modeled with the same basic outlines. Differences in the appearances of these objects are due to the kind of lighting model used to provide object shading. Terrain reflects most of the incident light, while clouds allow light to penetrate partially and scatter, producing a diffuse effect.

The infinite detail contained in a description of a three-dimensional fractal is illustrated in the sequence of scenes in Fig. 10–32. As with two-dimensional fractals, each part of a three-dimensional fractal object has the same degree of detail as the entire object, no matter how many times we might enlarge sections of it. The sequence of scenes demonstrates this property of fractals by expanding a section of each display to produce the next display.

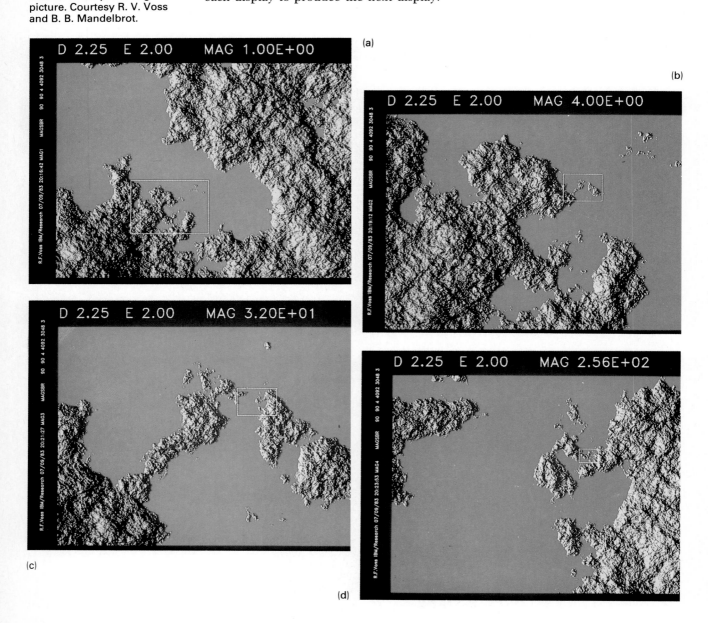

(a)

(b)

(c)

(d)

10–4 Sweep Representations

Graphics design packages can allow solid objects to be constructed from simpler objects in a number of ways. Solids with translational or rotational symmetry can be formed by sweeping a two-dimensional figure through a region of space.

Figure 10–33 shows a translational sweep. A flat object is translated over a specified distance to generate a solid. With this method, a user creates any desired two-dimensional shape and then specifies a translation direction. The volume of space over which the two-dimensional shape is swept defines the solid. Objects with translational symmetry can be defined in this way by specifying a shape that corresponds to a cross-sectional view of the object.

A method for creating a solid with a rotational sweep is shown in Fig. 10–34. Here a hollow tube is described with a specified rotation of a defined plate. Objects

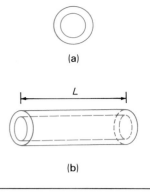

(a)

(b)

FIGURE 10–33
Representing a solid with a translational sweep. By translating the flat ring in (a) through a distance *L,* the hollow tube (b) is described.

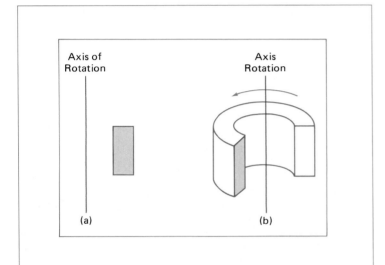

FIGURE 10–34
Representing a solid with a rotational sweep. The flat plate in (a) is rotated about a specified axis of rotation to produce the solid in (b).

with rotational symmetry can be represented with this method by specifying a flat shape corresponding to a cross section of the object parallel to the specified axis of rotation.

Other construction methods based on symmetries can be provided by a design package. For example, the ring in Fig. 10–33 (a) is symmetric about its center. A user could describe the ring with a specification for a quarter section and the symmetry operations for completing the rest of the ring (Fig. 10–35).

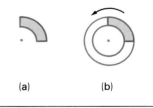

(a)   (b)

FIGURE 10–35
A description for a quarter section of a ring (a) can be used to create the shape in (b) with specified symmetry operations.

10–5 Constructive Solid-Geometry Methods

When a set of three-dimensional primitives, such as blocks, pyramids, cylinders, cones, and spheres, are provided to a user, object definitions are specified as combinations of the primitive solids. To create an object, the user specifies the construction methods to be used and the particular primitives to be combined.

Solid constructions can be accomplished with three-dimensional set operations. A user picks the solids to be combined and the set operation to be performed. Set operations include those for the union, intersection, and difference of two solids. For example, by positioning a block and pyramid as shown in Fig.

10–36 (a) and specifying the union operation, a user creates the solid in Fig. 10–36 (b). Surface definitions of the two original objects are combined to define the new, composite solid, which can then be combined with other objects until the final structure is attained.

FIGURE 10–36
Combining two objects (a) with a union operation joins the two objects to produce a single solid (b).

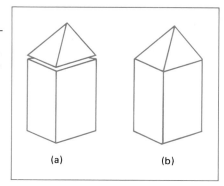

(a)   (b)

An intersection operation describes a solid as the overlap volume of two objects, as demonstrated in Fig. 10–37. The user interactively positions the two objects so that an overlap region is created; then an intersection specification generates a new solid as the common subset of the original objects. This operation can be implemented in a graphics package using a procedure that tests the points within the two objects to determine which points are within the boundaries of both objects. Another implementation technique is based on the octree representation of solids, discussed in Section 10–6. Figure 10–38 illustrates the difference operation. In this case, the volume of the second object specified is subtracted from the volume of the first object.

FIGURE 10–37
An intersection operation specified for the block and cylinder in (a) produces the wedge-shaped solid in (b).

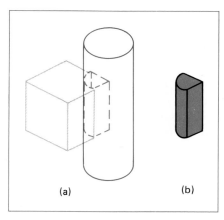

(a)   (b)

FIGURE 10–38
A solid generated with a difference operation applied to the two overlapping objects in Fig. 10–37 (a).

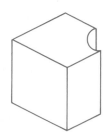

Similar construction methods can be used to generate solids from surfaces. In such packages, the set operations are used to combine various types of surface specifications. Surfaces combined with these operations can include polygons, spherical or cylindrical surfaces, or surfaces defined with polynomial functions.

Hierarchical tree structures, called **octrees,** are used to represent solid objects in some graphics systems. The tree structure is organized so that each node corresponds to a region of three-dimensional space. This representation for solids takes advantage of spatial coherence to reduce storage requirements for three-dimensional objects. It also provides a convenient representation for displaying objects with hidden surfaces removed and for performing various object manipulations.

The octree encoding procedure for a three-dimensional space is an extension of an encoding scheme for two-dimensional space, called **quadtree** encoding. Quadtrees are generated by successively dividing a two-dimensional region into quadrants. Each node in the quadtree has four data elements, one for each of the quadrants in the region (Fig. 10–39). If all pixels within a quadrant have the same color (a homogeneous quadrant), the corresponding data element in the node stores that color. In addition, a flag is set in the data element to indicate that the quadrant is homogeneous. Suppose all pixels in quadrant 2 of Fig. 10–39 are found to be red. The color code for red is then placed in data element 2 of the node. Otherwise the quadrant is said to be heterogeneous, and that quadrant is itself divided into quadrants (Fig. 10–40). The corresponding data element in the node now flags the quadrant as heterogeneous and stores the pointer to the next node in the quadtree.

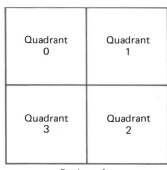

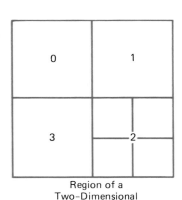

Region of a
Two-Dimensional
Space

Data Elements
in the Representative
Quadtree Node

FIGURE 10–39
Region of a two-dimensional space divided into numbered quadrants and the associated quadtree node with four data elements.

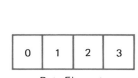

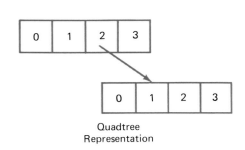

Region of a
Two-Dimensional
Space

Quadtree
Representation

FIGURE 10–40
Region of a two-dimensional space with two levels of quadrant divisions and the associated quadtree representation.

An algorithm for generating a quadtree tests pixel intensity values and sets up the quadtree nodes accordingly. If all quadrants in the original space have a single color specification, the quadtree has only one node. For a heterogeneous region of space, the successive subdivisions into quadrants continues until all quadrants are homogeneous. Figure 10–41 shows a quadtree representation for a region containing one area with a solid color that is different from the uniform color specified for all other areas in the region.

FIGURE 10–41
Quadtree representation for a region containing one foreground-color pixel on a solid background.

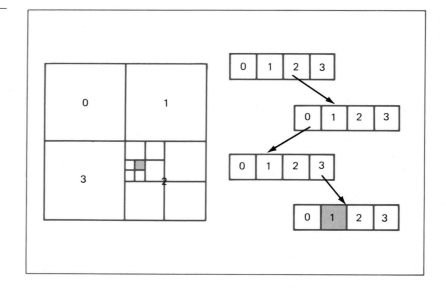

Quadtree encodings provide considerable savings in storage when large color areas exist in a region of space, since a single node can represent a single-color area. For an area containing 2^n by 2^n pixels, a quadtree representation contains at most n levels. Each node in the quadtree has at most four immediate descendants.

An octree encoding scheme divides regions of three-dimensional space into octants and stores eight data elements in each node of the tree (Fig. 10–42). Individual elements of a three-dimensional space are called **volume elements,** or **voxels.** When all voxels in an octant are of the same type, this type value is stored in the corresponding data element of the node. Empty regions of space are represented by voxel type "void." Any heterogeneous octant is subdivided into octants, and the corresponding data element in the node points to the next node in the octree. Procedures for generating octrees are similar to those for quadtrees: Voxels in each octant are tested, and octant subdivisions continue until the region of space contains only homogeneous octants. Each node in the octree can now have from zero to eight immediate descendants.

Algorithms for generating octrees can be structured to accept definitions of objects in any form, such as a polygon mesh, curved surface patches, or solid-geometry constructions. Using the minimum and maximum coordinate values of the object, a box (parallelepiped) can be defined around the object. This region of three-dimensional space containing the object is then tested, octant by octant, to generate the octree representation.

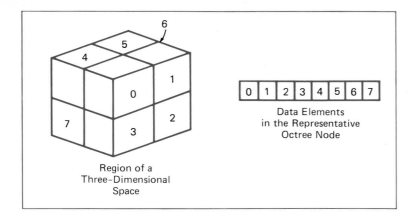

FIGURE 10–42
Region of a three-dimensional
space divided into numbered
octants and the associated
octree node with eight data
elements.

Data Elements
in the Representative
Octree Node

Region of a
Three–Dimensional
Space

Once an octree representation has been established for a solid object, various manipulation routines can be applied to the solid. An algorithm for performing set operations accepts two octree representations as input and performs a specified operation, such as union, intersection, or difference. The octree representation for the resulting solid is output. Other algorithms perform three-dimensional transformations, hidden-surface removal, or shading on a single input octree. When an octree representation of an object is to be displayed on a video monitor, the octree can be converted into a quadtree representation. Then the quadtree structure is mapped into a frame buffer for display.

REFERENCES

Sources of information on parametric curve representations include Barsky (1983 and 1984), Bézier (1972), Burt and Adelson (1983), Farouki and Hinds (1985), Huitrie and Nahas (1985), Kochanek and Bartels (1984), and Pavlidis (1983).

Other solid-modeling references include Casale and Stanton (1985), Requicha (1980), Requicha and Voelcker (1982 and 1983), Tilove (1984), and Weiler (1985).

For further information on fractals see Mandelbrot (1977 and 1982) and Norton (1982). Related methods for modeling objects with irregular outlines are discussed in Fournier, Fussel, and Carpenter (1982) and in Reeves (1983).

Octrees and quadtrees are discussed by Carlbom, Chakravarty, and Vanderschel (1985), Doctor (1981), Frieder, Gordon, and Reynold (1985), Pavlidis (1982), and by Yamaguchi, Kunii, and Fujimura (1984).

EXERCISES

10–1. Set up geometric data tables as in Fig. 10–2 for a unit cube.

10–2. Develop alternate representations for the unit cube in Ex. 10–1 using only: (a) vertex and polygon tables, and (b) a single polygon table. Compare the three methods for representing the unit cube and estimate storage requirements for each.

10–3. Define an efficient polygon representation for a cylinder. Justify your choice of representation.

10–4. Set up a procedure for establishing polygon tables for any input set of data points defining an object.

10–5. Devise routines for checking the data tables in Fig. 10–2 for consistency and completeness.

10–6. Write a program that calculates parameters $A, B, C,$ and D for any set of three-dimensional plane surfaces defining an object.

10–7. Given the plane parameters $A, B, C,$ and D for all surfaces of an object, devise an algorithm to determine whether any specified point is inside or outside the object.

10–8. How would the values for the parameters A, B, C, D in the equation of a plane surface have to be altered if the coordinate reference is changed from a right-handed system to a left-handed system?

10–9. Using Eqs. 10–11 and 10–12, express the Bézier blending functions for four control points as explicit polynomial functions. Plot each function and label the maximum and minimum values.

10–10. Carry out the operations in Ex. 10–9 for five control points.

10–11. Revise the routines for calculating points along a Bézier curve to make use of forward differences. Limit the output to cubic curves.

10–12. Implement the routines in Ex. 10–11 to display Bézier curves for control points specified in the xy plane.

10–13. Using Eqs. 10–15 and 10–16, determine explicit polynomial expressions for uniform, quadratic B-spline blending functions using five control points. Plot each function and label the maximum and minimum values.

10–14. Carry out the operations in Ex. 10–13 for six control points.

10–15. Write a program using forward differences to calculate points along a cubic B-spline curve, given an input set of control points.

10–16. Implement the program in Ex. 10–15 to display cubic B-spline curves using control points defined in the xy plane.

10–17. Develop an algorithm for calculating the normal vector to a Bézier surface at the point $\mathbf{P}(u, v)$.

10–18. Devise an algorithm that uses forward differences to calculate points along a quadratic curve.

10–19. Derive the expressions given in Eqs. (10–21), (10–23), and (10–25) for calculating the three forward differences of a cubic curve.

10–20. Write a program for generating a fractal "snowflake" by applying the procedure shown in Fig. 10–25 to an equilateral triangle.

10–21. Using the method shown in Fig. 10–25 as a guide, develop a fractal curve using a different transformation pattern. What is the dimension of your curve?

10–22. Write a program to generate fractal curves using the equation $f(z) = z^2 + \lambda$, where λ is any selected complex constant.

10–23. Write a program to generate fractal curves using the equation $i(z^2 + 1)$, where $i = \sqrt{-1}$.

10–24. Set up procedures for generating the description of a three-dimensional object from input parameters that define the object in terms of a translational sweep.

10–25. Develop procedures for generating the description of a three-dimensional object using input parameters that define the object in terms of a rotational sweep.

10–26. Devise an algorithm for generating solid objects as combinations of three-dimensional primitive shapes, each defined as a set of surfaces, using constructive solid-geometry methods.

10–27. Develop an algorithm for performing constructive solid-geometry modeling using a primitive set of solids defined in octree structures.

10–28. Develop an algorithm for encoding a two-dimensional scene as a quadtree representation.

10–29. Set up an algorithm for loading a quadtree representation of a scene into a frame buffer for display of the scene.

10–30. Write a routine to convert the polygon definition of a three-dimensional object into an octree representation.

11

THREE-DIMENSIONAL TRANSFORMATIONS

Methods for translating, scaling, and rotating objects in three dimensions are extended from two-dimensional methods by including considerations for the z coordinate. A translation is now accomplished by specifying a three-dimensional translation vector, and scaling is performed by specifying three scaling factors. Extensions for three-dimensional rotations are less straightforward, since rotations can now be performed about axes with any spatial orientation. As in the two-dimensional case, geometric transformation equations can be expressed in terms of transformation matrices. Any sequence of transformations is then represented as a single matrix, formed by concatenating the matrices for the individual transformations in the sequence.

11-1 Translation

In a three-dimensional homogeneous coordinate representation, a point is translated (Fig. 11–1) from position (x, y, z) to position (x', y', z') with the matrix operation

$$[x'\ y'\ z'\ 1] = [x\ y\ z\ 1] \begin{bmatrix} 1 & 0 & 0 & 0 \\ 0 & 1 & 0 & 0 \\ 0 & 0 & 1 & 0 \\ Tx & Ty & Tz & 1 \end{bmatrix} \tag{11-1}$$

Parameters Tx, Ty, Tz, specifying translation distances for the coordinates, are assigned any real values. The matrix representation in Eq. 11–1 is equivalent to the three equations

$$x' = x + Tx, \quad y' = y + Ty, \quad z' = z + Tz \tag{11-2}$$

An object is translated in three dimensions by transforming each defining point of the object. Translation of an object represented as a set of polygon surfaces is carried out by translating the coordinate values for each vertex of each surface (Fig. 11–2). The set of translated coordinate positions for the vertices then defines the new position of the object.

We obtain the inverse of the translation matrix in Eq. 11–1 by negating the translation distances Tx, Ty, and Tz. This produces a translation in the opposite direction, and the product of a translation matrix and its inverse produces the identity matrix.

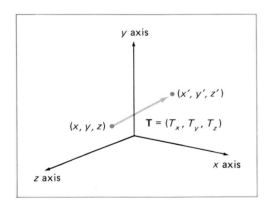

FIGURE 11–1
Translating a point with translation vector *(Tx, Ty, Tz)*.

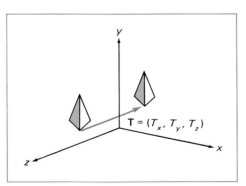

FIGURE 11–2
Translating an object with translation vector *T*.

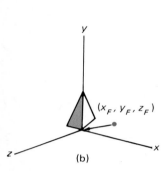

(a)

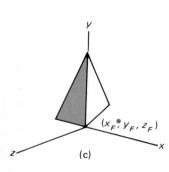

(b)

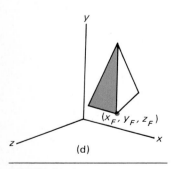

(c)

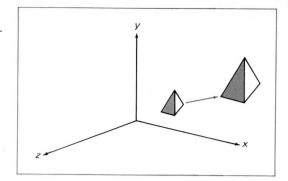

FIGURE 11–3
Doubling the size of an object with transformation 11–3 also moves the object farther from the origin.

11–2 Scaling

The matrix operation for scaling in three dimensions relative to the coordinate origin is

$$[x' \ y' \ z' \ 1] = [x \ y \ z \ 1] \begin{bmatrix} Sx & 0 & 0 & 0 \\ 0 & Sy & 0 & 0 \\ 0 & 0 & Sz & 0 \\ 0 & 0 & 0 & 1 \end{bmatrix} \tag{11-3}$$

where scaling parameters Sx, Sy, and Sz are assigned any positive values. This matrix operation scales a point at (x, y, z) to position (x', y', z') with the scaling equations

$$x' = x \cdot Sx, \quad y' = y \cdot Sy, \quad z' = z \cdot Sz \tag{11-4}$$

When transformation 11–3 is applied to defining points in an object, the object is scaled and moved relative to the coordinate origin. If the transformation parameters are not all equal, relative dimensions in the object are also changed. A uniform scaling ($Sx = Sy = Sz$) preserves the original shape of an object. The result of scaling an object uniformly with each scaling parameter set to 2 is shown in Fig. 11–3.

Scaling with respect to any fixed position (x_F, y_F, z_F) can be obtained by carrying out the following sequence of transformations: (1) translate the fixed point to the origin, (2) scale with Eq. 11–3, and (3) translate the fixed point back to its original position. This sequence of transformations is demonstrated in Fig. 11–4. The transformation matrix for arbitrary fixed-point scaling is formed as the concatenation of these individual transformations:

$$T(-x_F, -y_F, -z_F) \cdot S(Sx, Sy, Sz) \cdot T(x_F, y_F, z_F)$$
$$= \begin{bmatrix} Sx & 0 & 0 & 0 \\ 0 & Sy & 0 & 0 \\ 0 & 0 & Sz & 0 \\ (1 - Sx)x_F & (1 - Sy)y_F & (1 - Sz)z_F & 1 \end{bmatrix} \tag{11-5}$$

where T represents the translation matrix and S the scaling matrix.

We form the inverse scaling matrix for either Eq. 11–3 or Eq. 11–5 by replacing the scaling parameters Sx, Sy, and Sz with their reciprocals. The inverse matrix generates an opposite scaling transformation, so the concatenation of any scaling matrix and its inverse produces the identity matrix.

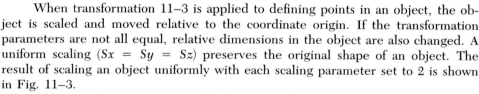

(d)

FIGURE 11–4
Scaling an object relative to a selected fixed point is equivalent to the sequence of transformations shown.

To specify a rotation transformation for an object, we must designate an axis of rotation (about which the object is to be rotated) and the amount of angular rotation. For two-dimensional applications, the axis of rotation is always perpendicular to the xy plane. In three dimensions, an axis of rotation can have any spatial orientation. The easiest rotation axes to handle are those that are parallel to the coordinate axes. Also, we can use rotations about the three coordinate axes to produce a rotation about any arbitrarily specified axis of rotation.

We adopt the convention that counterclockwise rotations about a coordinate axis are produced with positive rotation angles, if we are looking along the positive half of the axis toward the coordinate origin (Fig. 11–5). This convention is in accord with our earlier discussion of rotation equations in two dimensions, which specify rotations about the z axis.

The two-dimensional z-axis rotation equations are easily extended to three dimensions:

$$x' = x \cos\theta - y \sin\theta$$
$$y' = x \sin\theta + y \cos\theta \qquad (11\text{–}6)$$
$$z' = z$$

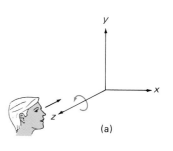

(a)

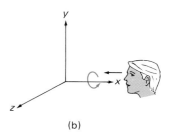

(b)

Parameter θ specifies the rotation angle. In homogeneous coordinate form, the three-dimensional z-axis rotation equations are expressed as

$$[x'\ y'\ z'\ 1] = [x\ y\ z\ 1] \begin{bmatrix} \cos\theta & \sin\theta & 0 & 0 \\ -\sin\theta & \cos\theta & 0 & 0 \\ 0 & 0 & 1 & 0 \\ 0 & 0 & 0 & 1 \end{bmatrix} \qquad (11\text{–}7)$$

Figure 11–6 illustrates rotation of an object about the z axis.

Transformation equations for rotations about the other two coordinate axes can be obtained with a cyclic permutation of the coordinate parameters in Eqs. 11–6. We replace x with y, y with z, and z with x. Using this permutation in Eqs. 11–6, we get the equations for an x-axis rotation:

$$y' = y \cos\theta - z \sin\theta$$
$$z' = y \sin\theta + z \cos\theta \qquad (11\text{–}8)$$
$$x' = x$$

which can be written in the homogeneous coordinate form

$$[x'\ y'\ z'\ 1] = [x\ y\ z\ 1] \begin{bmatrix} 1 & 0 & 0 & 0 \\ 0 & \cos\theta & \sin\theta & 0 \\ 0 & -\sin\theta & \cos\theta & 0 \\ 0 & 0 & 0 & 1 \end{bmatrix} \qquad (11\text{–}9)$$

Rotation around the x axis is demonstrated in Fig. 11–7.

Cyclically permuting coordinates in Eqs. 11–8 gives the transformation equations for a y-axis rotation:

$$z' = z \cos\theta - x \sin\theta$$
$$x' = z \sin\theta + x \cos\theta \qquad (11\text{–}10)$$
$$y' = y$$

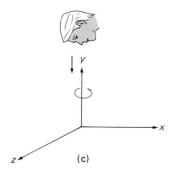

(c)

FIGURE 11–5
Positive rotation directions about the coordinate axes are counterclockwise, as viewed along the positive position of each axis toward the origin.

FIGURE 11–6
Rotation of an object about the z axis.

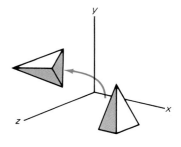

223

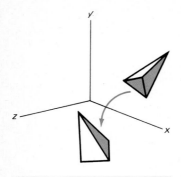

FIGURE 11-7
Rotation of an object about the
x axis.

The matrix representation for y-axis rotation is

$$[x'\ y'\ z'\ 1] = [x\ y\ z\ 1]\begin{bmatrix} \cos\theta & 0 & -\sin\theta & 0 \\ 0 & 1 & 0 & 0 \\ \sin\theta & 0 & \cos\theta & 0 \\ 0 & 0 & 0 & 1 \end{bmatrix} \qquad (11\text{--}11)$$

An example of y-axis rotation is shown in Fig. 11–8.

An inverse rotation matrix is formed by replacing the rotation angle θ by −θ. Negative values for rotation angles generate rotations in a clockwise direction, so the identity matrix is produced when any rotation matrix is multiplied by its inverse. Since only the sine function is affected by the change in sign of the rotation angle, the inverse matrix can also be obtained by interchanging rows and columns. That is, we can calculate the inverse of any rotation matrix R by evaluating its transpose ($R^{-1} = R^T$). This method for obtaining an inverse matrix holds also for any composite rotation matrix.

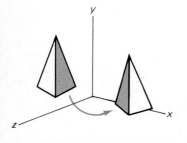

FIGURE 11-8
Rotation of an object about the
y axis.

11–4 Rotation About an Arbitrary Axis

Objects can be rotated about any arbitrarily selected axis by applying a composite transformation matrix whose components perform a sequence of translations and rotations about the coordinate axes. This composite matrix is formed with combinations of the translation matrix and transformations 11–7, 11–9, and 11–11. The correct sequence of transformations can be determined by transforming coordinate positions of the object so that the selected rotation axis is moved onto one of the coordinate axes. Then the object is rotated about that coordinate axis through the

FIGURE 11-9
Sequence of transformations
for rotating an object about an
axis that is parallel to the x
axis.

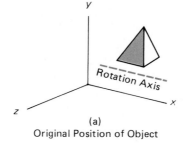

(a)
Original Position of Object

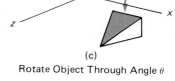

(c)
Rotate Object Through Angle θ

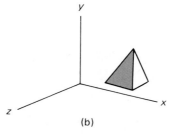

(b)
Translate Rotation Axis onto x axis

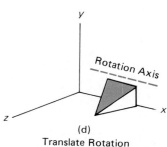

(d)
Translate Rotation
Axis to Original Position

specified rotation angle. The last step is to apply inverse transformations that return the rotation axis to its original position.

In the special case where the selected rotation axis is parallel to one of the coordinate axes, the desired rotation of the object is attained with the equivalent set of three transformations:

1. Translate the object so that the rotation axis coincides with the parallel coordinate axis.
2. Perform the specified rotation.
3. Translate the object so that the rotation axis is moved back to its original position.

The steps in this sequence are illustrated in Fig. 11–9. This procedure is equivalent to the two-dimensional transformation sequence that performs a rotation about an arbitrary pivot point.

When a three-dimensional rotation axis is not parallel to one of the coordinate axes, we need to perform some additional transformations. In this case, we also rotate the rotation axis so as to align it with a coordinate axis and apply inverse rotations to bring the axis back to its original orientation. We can determine the form of the transformation matrices for these alignment rotations using standard vector operations.

Review of Vector Operations

A vector can be defined as a directed line segment between two specified points, as illustrated in Fig. 11–10. Since a line is uniquely defined by two points, an axis of rotation can be defined by specifying any vector along the axis.

For many applications, it is convenient to deal with vectors specified relative to the coordinate origin. An arbitrarily defined vector can be translated so that its beginning position is at the origin of the coordinate system. Such vectors are equivalent to points in the coordinate reference. Figure 11–11 shows two vectors, defined from the coordinate origin, with components specified by their ending endpoints: (x_1, y_1, z_1) and (x_2, y_2, z_2).

Two operations that are useful when manipulating vectors are vector addition and vector multiplication. Vector addition is performed by adding corresponding components of two vectors. The two vectors in Fig. 11–11 can be added to produce the resultant vector with components

$$\mathbf{V}_1 + \mathbf{V}_2 = (x_1 + x_2, \; y_1 + y_2, \; z_1 + z_2) \qquad (11\text{–}12)$$

This resultant vector is shown in Fig. 11–12.

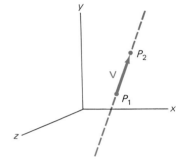

FIGURE 11–10
A vector **V**, defined as the directed line segment from point P_1 to point P_2, can be used to specify an axis of rotation (dashed line).

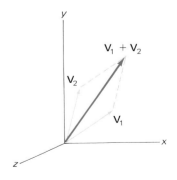

FIGURE 11–12
Vector addition.

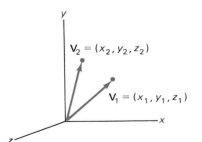

FIGURE 11–11
Vectors **V**₁ and **V**₂ specified from the origin of the coordinate system.

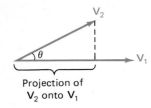

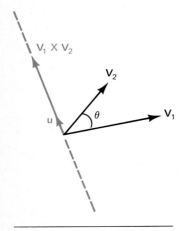

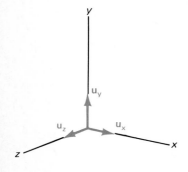

Unlike vector addition, vector multiplication can be performed in two ways. We can multiply two vectors so as to produce a single numeric value (called the scalar product, or dot product), or we can produce another vector (called the vector product, or cross product).

The scalar product of two vectors is defined as

$$V_1 \cdot V_2 = x_1 x_2 + y_1 y_2 + z_1 z_2 \qquad (11\text{–}13)$$

Taking the square root of the scalar product of a vector $V = (x, y, z)$ with itself produces the length of the vector:

$$|V| = (V \cdot V)^{1/2} = (x^2 + y^2 + z^2)^{1/2} \qquad (11\text{–}14)$$

which is a statement of the Pythagorean theorem. An alternate form for the scalar product can be stated in terms of the angle between the two vectors (Fig. 11–13):

$$V_1 \cdot V_2 = |V_1|\, |V_2|\, \cos\theta \qquad (11\text{–}15)$$

In this form, the scalar product can be seen to represent the product of the length of one vector, say V_1, and the projection length of the other vector (V_2 onto V_1 in Fig. 11–13).

With the vector product (or cross product) of two vectors, $V_1 \times V_2$, we get another vector that is perpendicular to each of the original two vectors, as shown in Fig. 11–14. In this figure, the direction for the resultant vector is given by the unit vector u (having a length of 1 unit). We can determine the direction for u by imagining that the perpendicular line (dotted) is grasped by the right hand with the fingers curling from V_1 to V_2. The right thumb then points in the correct direction for u. We can calculate the cross product in terms of the angle between V_1 and V_2 as

$$V_1 \times V_2 = u\, |V_1|\, |V_2|\, \sin\theta \qquad (11\text{–}16)$$

Unit vectors defined along each coordinate axis (Fig. 11–15) are used to express the cross product in terms of Cartesian components:

$$V_1 \times V_2 = \begin{vmatrix} u_x & u_y & u_z \\ x_1 & y_1 & z_1 \\ x_2 & y_2 & z_2 \end{vmatrix} \qquad (11\text{–}17)$$

This determinant form for the cross product produces a vector with components $(y_1 z_2 - z_1 y_2,\ z_1 x_2 - x_1 z_2,\ x_1 y_2 - y_1 x_2)$.

Transformation Matrices

We now make use of the vector operations to determine how a rotation about an arbitrary axis can be expressed in terms of the basic transformation matrices. Given the specifications for the rotation axis and the rotation angle, we can accomplish the required rotation in five steps:

1. Translate the object so that the rotation axis passes through the coordinate origin.
2. Rotate the object so that the axis of rotation coincides with one of the coordinate axes.
3. Perform the specified rotation.
4. Apply inverse rotations to bring the rotation axis back to its original orientation.
5. Apply the inverse translation to bring the rotation axis back to its original position.

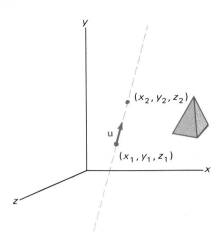

FIGURE 11–16
An axis of rotation (dashed line) for an object is defined by points P_1 and P_2. The unit vector $\boldsymbol{u}$ is established from the coordinates of the two points.

227
Sec. 11-4 Rotation About an Arbitrary Axis

We can transform the rotation axis onto any of the three coordinate axes. The z axis is a reasonable choice, and the following discussion shows how to set up the transformation matrices for getting the rotation axis onto the z axis and returning the rotation axis to its original position after the rotation.

To begin, we assume that the rotation axis is defined by two points, as in Fig. 11–16. These two points are used to define the vector

$$\boldsymbol{V} = (x_2 - x_1,\ y_2 - y_1,\ z_2 - z_1) \tag{11-18}$$

which in turn is used to set up the unit vector $\boldsymbol{u}$ along the rotation axis:

$$\boldsymbol{u} = \frac{\boldsymbol{V}}{|\boldsymbol{V}|} = (a,\ b,\ c) \tag{11-19}$$

where the components a, b and c of vector $\boldsymbol{u}$ are the direction cosines for vector $\boldsymbol{V}$:

$$a = \frac{x}{|\boldsymbol{V}|}, \quad b = \frac{y}{|\boldsymbol{V}|}, \quad c = \frac{z}{|\boldsymbol{V}|} \tag{11-20}$$

Translation of the object so that the rotation axis passes through the coordinate origin is accomplished with the translation matrix

$$T = \begin{bmatrix} 1 & 0 & 0 & 0 \\ 0 & 1 & 0 & 0 \\ 0 & 0 & 1 & 0 \\ -x_1 & -y_1 & -z_1 & 1 \end{bmatrix} \tag{11-21}$$

This sets point $\boldsymbol{P}_1$ at the origin (Fig. 11–17).

Next we need the transformations that will put the rotation axis on the z axis. We can accomplish this transformation in two steps. First, rotate about the x axis so that vector $\boldsymbol{u}$ is in the xz plane. Then rotate about the y axis to bring $\boldsymbol{u}$ onto the z axis. These two rotations are illustrated in Fig. 11–18 for one possible orientation of vector $\boldsymbol{u}$.

We establish the transformation matrix for rotation about the x axis by determining the values for the sine and cosine of the rotation angle necessary to get $\boldsymbol{u}$

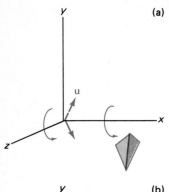

(a)

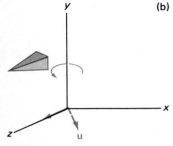

(b)

FIGURE 11–18
Unit vector **u** is rotated about the x axis to bring it into the xz plane (a), then rotated about the y axis to align it with the z axis (b).

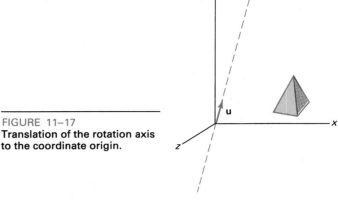

FIGURE 11–17
Translation of the rotation axis to the coordinate origin.

FIGURE 11–19
Rotation of **u** about the x axis into the xz plane is accomplished by rotating **u′** (the projection of **u** in the yz plane) through angle α onto the z axis.

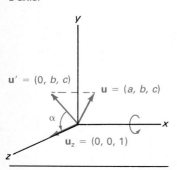

into the xz plane. This rotation angle is the angle between the projection of **u** in the yz plane and the positive z axis (Fig. 11–19). If we designate the projection of **u** in the yz plane as the vector $u′ = (0, b, c)$, then the cosine of the rotation angle α can be determined from the dot product of **u′** and the unit vector u_z along the z axis:

$$\cos\alpha = \frac{u′ \cdot u_z}{|u′|\,|u_z|} = \frac{c}{d} \tag{11–22}$$

where d is the magnitude of **u′**:

$$d = (b^2 + c^2)^{1/2} \tag{11–23}$$

The sine of α can be determined from the cross product of **u′** and u_z in a similar manner. From the definition of cross product, Eq. 11–16, we can write

$$u′ \times u_z = u_x\,|u′|\,|u_z|\,\sin\alpha \tag{11–24}$$

and, using the Cartesian expression for the cross product, Eq. 11–17, we have

$$u′ \times u_z = u_x \cdot b \tag{11–25}$$

Therefore, the sine function can be evaluated as

$$\sin\alpha = \frac{b}{d} \tag{11–26}$$

Now that we have determined the values for cos α and sin α in terms of the components of vector **u,** we can evaluate the rotation matrix about the x axis as

$$Rx(\alpha) = \begin{bmatrix} 1 & 0 & 0 & 0 \\ 0 & c/d & b/d & 0 \\ 0 & -b/d & c/d & 0 \\ 0 & 0 & 0 & 1 \end{bmatrix} \tag{11–27}$$

This matrix rotates unit vector **u** about the x axis into the xz plane.

We next determine the form of the transformation matrix that will swing the unit vector in the xz plane around the y axis onto the positive z axis. The orientation of the unit vector in the xz plane (after rotation about the x axis) is shown in Fig. 11–20. This vector, labeled u'', has the value a for its x component, since the rotation about the x axis must leave the x component unchanged. Its z component is d (the magnitude of u'), since vector u' has been rotated onto the z axis. The y component of u'' is 0, since it now lies in the xz plane. We again determine the trigonometric functions for the rotation angle β from expressions for the vector products between unit vectors u'' and u_z. From the definition of dot product, Eq. 11–15, we have

$$\cos\beta = \frac{u'' \cdot u_z}{|u''|\,|u_z|} = d \qquad (11\text{–}28)$$

since $|u_z| = |u''| = 1$. Using the two equations for the cross product, we can write

$$u'' \times u_z = u_y\,|u''|\,|u_z|\,\sin\beta \qquad (11\text{–}29)$$

and

$$u'' \times u_z = u_y \cdot (-a) \qquad (11\text{–}30)$$

Equating Eqs. 11–29 and 11–30, we have

$$\sin\beta = -a \qquad (11\text{–}31)$$

and the transformation matrix for rotation about the y axis is

$$Ry(\beta) = \begin{bmatrix} d & 0 & a & 0 \\ 0 & 1 & 0 & 0 \\ -a & 0 & d & 0 \\ 0 & 0 & 0 & 1 \end{bmatrix} \qquad (11\text{–}32)$$

With transformation matrices 11–21, 11–27, and 11–32, the rotation axis is aligned with the positive z axis. The specified rotation angle θ can then be applied as a rotation about the z axis:

$$Rz(\theta) = \begin{bmatrix} \cos\theta & \sin\theta & 0 & 0 \\ -\sin\theta & \cos\theta & 0 & 0 \\ 0 & 0 & 1 & 0 \\ 0 & 0 & 0 & 1 \end{bmatrix} \qquad (11\text{–}33)$$

To complete the required rotation about the given axis, we need to transform the rotation axis back to its original position. This is done by applying the inverse of transformations 11–21, 11–27, and 11–32. The transformation matrix for rotation about an arbitrary axis can then be expressed as the composition of these seven individual transformations:

$$R(\theta) = T \cdot Rx(\alpha) \cdot Ry(\beta) \cdot Rz(\theta) \cdot Ry^{-1}(\beta) \cdot Rx^{-1}(\alpha) \cdot T^{-1} \qquad (11\text{–}34)$$

11–5 Other Transformations

There are certain additional transformation methods that are often employed in three-dimensional applications. They include reflections, shears, and transformations of coordinate systems. We have discussed some of these transformations in

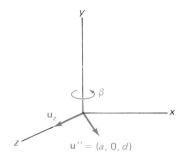

FIGURE 11–20
Rotation of unit vector u'' (vector u after rotation into the xz plane) about the y axis. Positive rotation angle β aligns u'' with vector u_z.

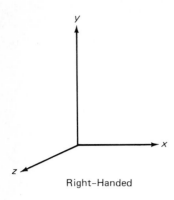

Right-Handed

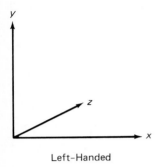

Left-Handed

two-dimensional applications, and their extension to three dimensions is straightforward.

Reflections

This class of transformations produces coordinate reflections about a specified reflection plane. Three-dimensional reflection matrices are set up similarly to those for two dimensions.

A reflection that converts coordinate specifications from a right-handed coordinate system to a left-handed system (or vice versa) is shown in Fig. 11–21. This transformation changes the sign of z coordinates, leaving the x- and y-coordinate values unchanged. The matrix representation for this reflection of points relative to the xy plane is

$$RFz = \begin{bmatrix} 1 & 0 & 0 & 0 \\ 0 & 1 & 0 & 0 \\ 0 & 0 & -1 & 0 \\ 0 & 0 & 0 & 1 \end{bmatrix} \qquad (11\text{–}35)$$

Transformation matrices for inverting x-coordinate and y-coordinate values are defined similarly, as reflections relative to the yz plane and xz plane, respectively. Reflections about other planes can be obtained as a combination of these coordinate-axis reflections and certain rotations, as in the two-dimensional reflections about arbitrary lines.

Shears

For two-dimensional transformations, we have seen that shearing equations can be defined to transform either the x- or y-coordinate values of points to produce shearing distortions in the shapes of objects. We extend these concepts to three dimensions by transforming two of the three coordinate values of defined points.

As an example of three-dimensional shearing, the following transformation produces a z-axis shear:

$$\begin{bmatrix} 1 & 0 & 0 & 0 \\ 0 & 1 & 0 & 0 \\ a & b & 1 & 0 \\ 0 & 0 & 0 & 1 \end{bmatrix} \qquad (11\text{–}36)$$

Parameters a and b can be assigned any real values. The effect of this transformation matrix is to alter x- and y-coordinate values by an amount that is proportional to the z value, while leaving the z coordinate unchanged. Boundaries of planes that are perpendicular to the z axis are thus shifted by an amount proportional to z. An example of the effect of this shearing matrix on a unit cube is shown in Fig. 11–22, for shearing values $a = b = 1$. Shearing matrices for the x axis and y axis are defined similarly.

Transformation of Coordinate Systems

So far, we have discussed transformations as operations applied to points within a single coordinate system. The transformations then move points from one position to another within the same reference frame. There are many times, however, when we are interested in switching coordinates from one system to another.

In three-dimensional modeling packages, objects can be defined in separate coordinate systems and moved to another coordinate system to build a scene. For example, a table might be defined in one coordinate system, and the description of a room might be given in another system. The table is placed in the room by transferring it to the room coordinates. Similar coordinate changes from one system to another are useful in three-dimensional viewing transformations.

An example of the use of multiple coordinate systems is given in Fig. 11–23, which illustrates simulation of tractor movement. As the tractor moves, the tractor coordinate system and front-wheel coordinate system move in the world coordinate system. The front wheels rotate in the wheel system, and the wheel system rotates in the tractor system when the tractor turns.

Coordinate descriptions of objects are transferred from one system to another with transformations that map one set of coordinate axes onto the other set. These transformations are carried out with a translation that brings the two coordinate origins into coincidence, followed by a sequence of rotations that superimpose corresponding coordinate axes. If different scales are used in the two coordinate systems, a scaling transformation may also be necessary to compensate for the differences in coordinate intervals.

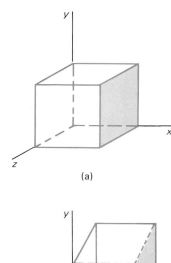

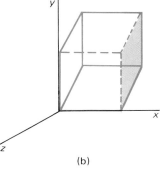

(b)

FIGURE 11–22
A unit cube (a) is sheared (b) by transformation matrix (11–36), with $a = b = 1$.

11–6 Transformation Commands

Functions for performing three-dimensional transformations can be structured as simple extensions of the two-dimensional operations. That is, the parameter list in the two-dimensional *create_transformation_matrix* and *accumulate_transformation_matrix* commands could be expanded to include the additional parameters needed for three-dimensional operations. Graphics packages adopting this approach would use similar commands for both two-dimensional and three-dimensional transformations.

Another approach is to set up separate functions for each of the three basic transformations, translation, scaling, and rotation. Using this approach, we define a command to establish a translation matrix as

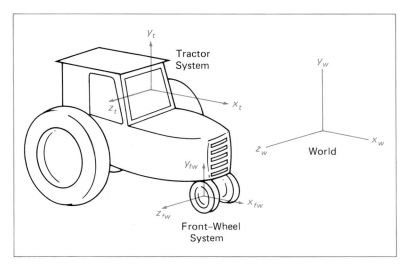

FIGURE 11–23
Possible coordinate systems used in simulating tractor movement. Wheel rotations are described in the front-wheel system. Turning of the tractor is described by a rotation of the front-wheel system in the tractor system. Both the wheel and tractor reference frames move in the world coordinate system.

```
create_translation_matrix_3 (tx, ty, tz, t)
```

Parameters *tx*, *ty*, and *tz* specify the translation distances, and the 4 by 4 translation matrix elements are stored in array *t*.

Similarly, we define the command to set up a scaling matrix *S* as

```
create_scaling_matrix_3 (sx, sy, sz, s)
```

Array *s* contains matrix elements for the scaling transformation specified by parameters *sx*, *sy*, and *sz*.

Three rotation matrices, one for each of the coordinate axes, are defined as

```
create_x_rotation_matrix_3 (a, rx)
```

```
create_y_rotation_matrix_3 (a, ry)
```

```
create_z_rotation_matrix_3 (a, rz)
```

Input angle *a* is used in these commands to create the matrices *rx*, *ry*, or *rz*, for required rotations about the *x*, *y*, or *z* axis.

We define the command to accumulate matrices as

```
accumulate_matrices_3 (m₁, m₂, m)
```

Input matrices m_1 and m_2 are multiplied to form the output matrix, *m*. That is,

$$m \ = \ m_1 \ \cdot \ m_2$$

Finally, a user applies a previously defined transformation matrix to a segment with the command

```
set_segment_transformation_3 (id, m)
```

Parameter *id* identifies the segment, and array *m* specifies the transformation matrix that is to be applied to output primitives defined in the segment.

An example of the use of three-dimensional transformation commands is given in the following program, which produces the transformation matrix for rotation about an arbitrary axis. Input to the program consists of the coordinate values for the two points used to define the axis of rotation, the angle of rotation, and the name of the matrix that is to contain the final transformation matrix.

```
type
   matrix = array [1..4,1..4] of real;

procedure create_3d_rotation_matrix    (x1, y1, z1, x2, y2, z2,
                                         angle : real;
                                         var tm : matrix);
   var
     a, b, c, d, length : real;
     m : matrix;

   procedure set_identity (m : matrix);
      begin   {set m to identity matrix} end;

   begin   {create_3d_rotation_matrix}
      {determine unit vector parallel to axis of rotation}
      a := x2 − x1;  b := y2 − y1;  c := z2 − z1;
      length := sqrt(a * a + b * b + c * c);
```

```
        a := a / length ;  b := b / length;  c := c / length;
        d := sqrt(b * b + c * c);

           {translate to origin}
        create_translation_matrix_3 (-xl, -yl, -zl, tm);

           {rotate around x to lie in xz plane}
        set_identity (m);
        m[2,2] :=   c / d;  m[2,3] := b / d;
        m[3,2] := -b / d;   m[3,3] := c / d;
        accumulate_matrices_3 (tm, m, tm);

           {rotate around y to line up with z axis}
        set_identity (m);
        m[1,1] :=   d;  m[1,3] := a;
        m[3,1] := -a;   m[3,3] := d;
        accumulate_matrices_3 (tm, m, tm);

           {rotate around z axis using input angle}
        create_z_rotation_matrix_3 (angle, m);
        accumulate_matrices_3 (tm, m, tm);

           {do inverse of rotation around y}
        set_identity (m);
        m[1,1] := d;  m[1,3] := -a;
        m[3,1] := a;  m[3,3] :=   d;
        accumulate_matrices_3 (tm, m, tm);

        {do inverse of rotation around x}
        set_identity (m);
        m[2,2] := c / d;  m[2,3] := -b / d;
        m[3,2] := b / d;  m[3,3] :=   c / d;
        accumulate_matrices_3 (tm, m, tm);

           {do inverse of translation}
        create_translation_matrix_3 (xl, yl, zl, m);
        accumulate_matrices_3 (tm, m, tm)
      end;   {create_3d_rotation_matrix}
```

For further discussions of homogeneous coordinates and three-dimensional transformation methods see Blinn (1977), Catmull and Smith (1980), and Pavlidis (1982).

REFERENCES

11-1. Write a program to implement the *accumulate_matrices_3* function by calculating the product of any two input transformation matrices.

EXERCISES

11-2. Extend the program of Ex. 11–1 by allowing the input transformation matrices to be established by the transformation operations for translation, scaling, and rotation. That is, the program is to be expanded to implement the individual routines for setting these transformation matrices.

11-3. Expand the program of Ex. 11–2 to implement the *set_segment_transformation_3* operation. Given a definition of a three-dimensional object and a sequence of transformations, the program is to determine the composite matrix and apply this matrix to the object definition to obtain the transformed object.

11-4. Derive the transformation matrix for scaling an object by a scaling factor S in a direction defined by the direction cosines α, β, γ.

11-5. Develop an algorithm for scaling an object defined in an octree representation.

11-6. Write a procedure for rotating a given object about any specified rotation axis.

11-7. Develop a procedure for animating an object by incrementally rotating it about any specified axis. Use appropriate approximations to the trignometric equations to speed up the calculations, and reset the object to its initial position after each complete revolution about the axis.

11-8. Devise a procedure for rotating an object that is represented in an octree structure.

11-9. Develop a routine to reflect an object about an arbitrarily selected plane.

11-10. Write a program to shear an object with respect to any of the three coordinate axes, using input values for the shearing parameters.

11-11. Develop a procedure for converting an object definition in one coordinate reference to any other coordinate system defined relative to the first system.

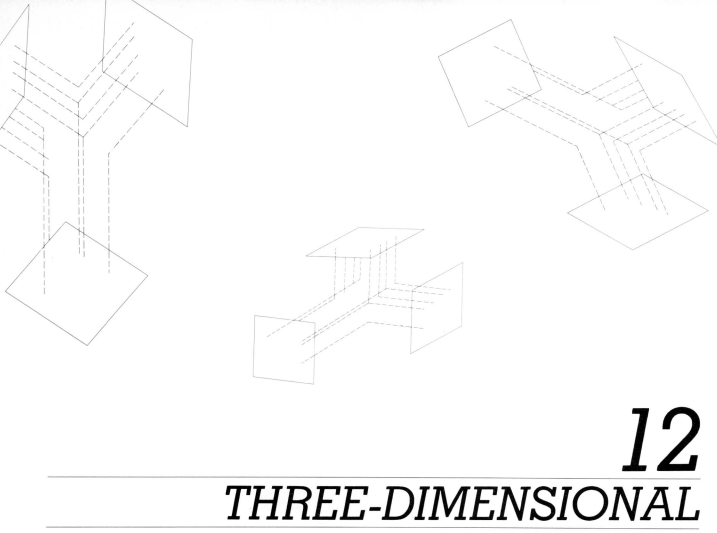

12
THREE-DIMENSIONAL
VIEWING

In two dimensions, viewing operations transfer two-dimensional points in the world coordinate plane to two-dimensional points in the device coordinate plane. Object definitions, clipped against a window boundary, are mapped into a viewport. These normalized device coordinates are then converted to device coordinates, and the object is displayed on the output device. For three dimensions, the situation is a bit more complicated, since we now have some choices as to how views are to be generated. We could view a scene from the front, from above, or from the back. Or we could generate a view of what we would see if we were standing in the middle of a group of objects. Additionally, three-dimensional descriptions of objects must be projected onto the flat viewing surface of the output device. In this chapter, we first discuss the mechanics of projection. Then the operations involved in the viewing transformation are explored, and a full three-dimensional viewing pipeline is developed.

12–1 Projections

There are two basic methods for projecting three-dimensional objects onto a two-dimensional viewing surface. All points of the object can be projected to the surface along parallel lines, or the points can be projected along lines that converge to a position called the **center of projection.** The two methods, called **parallel projection** and **perspective projection,** respectively, are illustrated in Fig. 12–1. In both cases, the intersection of a projection line with the viewing surface determines the coordinates of the projected point on this projection plane. For the present, we assume that the view projection plane is the $z = 0$ plane of a left-handed coordinate system, as shown in Fig. 12–2.

A parallel projection preserves relative dimensions of objects, and this is the technique used in drafting to produce scale drawings of three-dimensional objects. This method is used to obtain accurate views of the various sides of an object, but a parallel projection does not give a realistic representation of the appearance of a three-dimensional object. A perspective projection, on the other hand, produces realistic views but does not preserve relative dimensions. Distant lines are projected as smaller than those closer to the projection plane, as seen in Fig. 12–3.

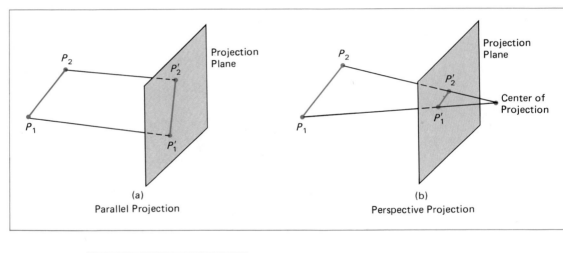

(a)
Parallel Projection

(b)
Perspective Projection

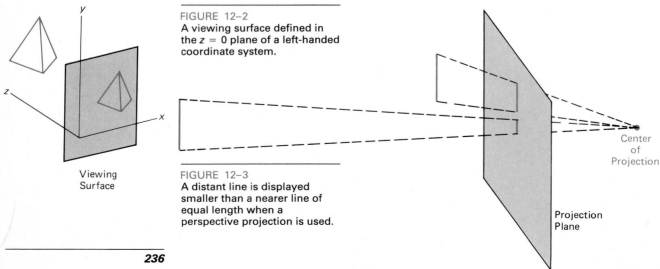

Viewing Surface

FIGURE 12–2
A viewing surface defined in the $z = 0$ plane of a left-handed coordinate system.

FIGURE 12–3
A distant line is displayed smaller than a nearer line of equal length when a perspective projection is used.

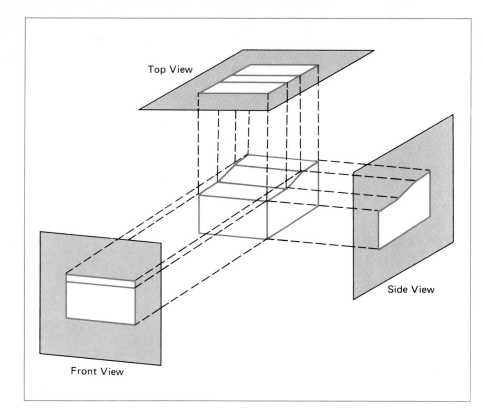

FIGURE 12–4
Three orthographic projections of an object.

Parallel Projections

Views formed with parallel projections can be characterized according to the angle that the direction of projection makes with the projection plane. When the direction of projection is perpendicular to the projection plane, we have an **orthographic projection.** A projection that is not perpendicular to the plane is called an **oblique projection.**

Orthographic projections are most often used to produce the front, side, and top views of an object, as shown in Fig. 12–4. Orthographic front, side, and rear views of an object are called "elevations", and the top views are called "plans". Engineering drawings commonly employ these orthographic projections, since lengths and angles are accurately depicted and can be measured from the drawings.

We can also form orthographic projections that show more than one face of an object. Such views are called **axonometric** orthographic projections. The most commonly used axonometric projection is the **isometric** projection. An isometric projection is obtained by aligning the projection plane so that it intersects each coordinate axis in which the object is defined (called the principal axes) at the same distance from the origin. Figure 12–5 shows an isometric projection. There are eight positions, one in each octant, for obtaining an isometric view. All three principal axes are foreshortened equally in an isometric projection so that relative proportions are maintained. This is not the case in a general axonometric projection, where scaling factors may be different for the three principal directions.

Transformation equations for performing an orthographic parallel projection are straightforward. For any point (x, y, z), the projection point (x_p, y_p, z_p) on the viewing surface is obtained as

$$x_p = x, \qquad y_p = y, \qquad z_p = 0 \qquad (12\text{–}1)$$

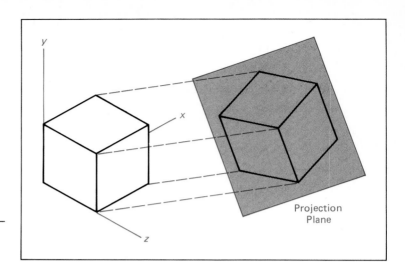

FIGURE 12–5
Isometric projection of an
object onto a viewing surface.

An oblique projection is obtained by projecting points along parallel lines that are not perpendicular to the projection plane. Figure 12–6 shows an oblique projection of a point (x, y, z) along a projection line to position (x_p, y_p). Orthographic projection coordinates on the plane are (x, y). The oblique projection line makes an angle α with the line on the projection plane that joins (x_p, y_p) and (x, y). This line, of length L, is at an angle ϕ with the horizontal direction in the projection plane. We can express the projection coordinates in terms of x, y, L, and ϕ:

$$x_p = x + L \cos\phi$$
$$y_p = y + L \sin\phi \qquad (12\text{–}2)$$

A projection direction can be defined by selecting values for the angles α and ϕ. Common choices for angle ϕ are 30° and 45°, which display a combination view of the front, side, and top (or front, side, and bottom) of an object. Length L is a function of the z coordinate, and we can evaluate this parameter from the relationships

FIGURE 12–6
Oblique projection of point *(x,
y, z)* to position *(x_p, y_p)* on the
projection plane.

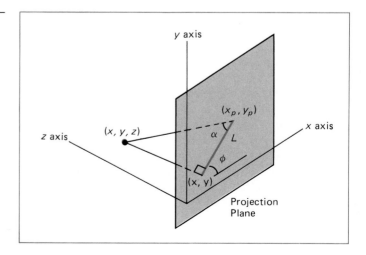

$$\tan \alpha = \frac{z}{L} = \frac{1}{L_1} \qquad (12\text{--}3)$$

where L_1 is the length of the projection line from (x, y) to (x_p, y_p) when $z = 1$. From Eq. 12–3, we have

$$L = z\, L_1 \qquad (12\text{--}4)$$

and the oblique projection equations 12–2 can be written as

$$x_p = x + z(L_1 \cos\phi) \qquad (12\text{--}5)$$
$$y_p = y + z(L_1 \sin\phi)$$

The transformation matrix for producing any parallel projection can be written as

$$P_{\text{parallel}} = \begin{bmatrix} 1 & 0 & 0 & 0 \\ 0 & 1 & 0 & 0 \\ L_1 \cos\phi & L_1 \sin\phi & 0 & 0 \\ 0 & 0 & 0 & 1 \end{bmatrix} \qquad (12\text{--}6)$$

An orthographic projection is obtained when $L_1 = 0$ (which occurs at a projection angle α of 90°). Oblique projections are generated with nonzero values for L_1. Projection matrix 12–6 has a structure similar to that of a z-axis shear matrix. In fact, the effect of this projection matrix is to shear planes of constant z and project them onto the view plane. The x- and y-coordinate values within each plane of constant z are shifted by an amount proportional to the z value of the plane so that angles, distances, and parallel lines in the plane are projected accurately. This effect is shown in Fig. 12–7, where the back plane of the box is sheared and overlapped with the front plane in the projection to the viewing surface. An edge of the box connecting the front and back planes is projected into a line of length L_1 that makes an angle ϕ with a horizontal line in the projection plane.

Two commonly used angles in oblique projections are those for which $\tan \alpha = 1$ and $\tan \alpha = 2$. For the first case, $\alpha = 45°$ and the views obtained are called **cavalier** projections. All lines perpendicular to the projection plane are projected with no change in length. Examples of cavalier projections for a cube are given in Fig. 12–8.

When the projection angle is chosen such that $\tan \alpha = 2$, the resulting view is called a **cabinet** projection. This projection angle of approximately 63.4° causes lines perpendicular to the viewing surface to be projected at one-half their length.

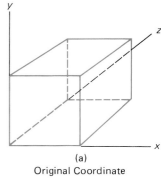

(a)
Original Coordinate
Description of Object

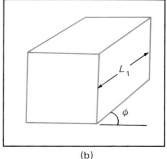

(b)
Projection on the
Viewing Surface

FIGURE 12–7
Oblique projection of a box onto a viewing surface in the $z = 0$ plane.

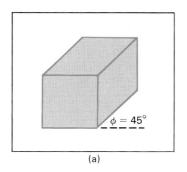

(a)

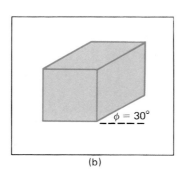

(b)

FIGURE 12–8
Cavalier projections of a cube onto a projection plane for two values of angle ϕ. Depth of the cube is projected equal to the width and height.

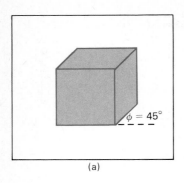

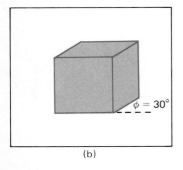

(b)

FIGURE 12–9
Cabinet projections of a cube
onto a projection plane for two
values of angle φ. Depth is
projected as one-half that of
the width and height.

Cabinet projections appear more realistic than cavalier projections because of this reduction in the length of perpendiculars. Figure 12–9 shows a cabinet projection for a cube.

Perspective Projections

To obtain a perspective projection of a three-dimensional object, we project points along projection lines that meet at the center of projection. In Fig. 12–10, the center of projection is on the negative z axis at a distance d behind the projection plane. Any position can be selected for the center of projection, but choosing a position along the z axis simplifies the calculations in the transformation equations.

We can obtain the transformation equations for a perspective projection from the parametric equations describing the projection line from point P to the center of projection in Fig. 12–10. The parametric form for this projection line is

$$
\begin{aligned}
x' &= x - xu \\
y' &= y - yu \\
z' &= z - (z + d)u
\end{aligned}
\qquad (12\text{–}7)
$$

Parameter u takes values from 0 to 1, and coordinates (x', y', z') represent any position along the projection line. When $u = 0$, Eqs. 12–7 yield point P at coordinates (x, y, z). At the other end of the line $u = 1$, and we have the coordinates for the center of projection, $(0, 0, -d)$. To obtain the coordinates on the projection plane, we set $z' = 0$ and solve for parameter u:

$$
u = \frac{z}{z + d}
\qquad (12\text{–}8)
$$

This value for parameter u produces the intersection of the projection line with the projection plane at $(x_p, y_p, 0)$. Substituting Eq. 12–8 into Eqs. 12–7, we obtain the perspective transformation equations

$$
x_p = x\left(\frac{d}{z + d}\right) = x\left(\frac{1}{z/d + 1}\right)
$$

FIGURE 12–10.
Perspective projection of a
point P at coordinates (x, y, z)
to position $(xp, yp, 0)$ on a
projection plane.

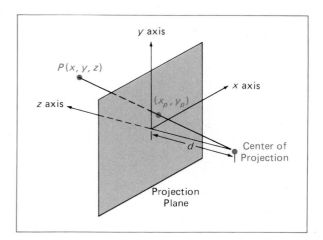

$$y_p = y\left(\frac{d}{z+d}\right) = y\left(\frac{1}{z/d+1}\right)$$ (12–9)

$$z_p = 0$$

Using a three-dimensional homogeneous coordinate representation, we can write the perspective transformation in matrix form:

$$[x_h \ y_h \ z_h \ w] = [x \ y \ z \ 1] \begin{bmatrix} 1 & 0 & 0 & 0 \\ 0 & 1 & 0 & 0 \\ 0 & 0 & 0 & 1/d \\ 0 & 0 & 0 & 1 \end{bmatrix}$$ (12–10)

In this representation,

$$w = \frac{z}{d} + 1$$ (12–11)

and the projection coordinates on the projection plane are calculated from the homogeneous coordinates as

$$[x_p \ y_p \ z_p \ 1] = [x_h/w \ y_h/w \ z_h/w \ 1]$$ (12–12)

When a three-dimensional object is projected onto a plane using perspective transformation equations, any set of parallel lines in the object that are not parallel to the plane are projected into converging lines. Parallel lines that are parallel to the plane project as parallel lines. The point at which a set of projected parallel lines appears to converge is called a **vanishing point**. Each such set of projected parallel lines will have a separate vanishing point.

The vanishing point for any set of lines that are parallel to one of the world coordinate axes is referred to as a principal vanishing point. We control the number of principal vanishing points (one, two, or three) with the orientation of the projection plane, and perspective projections are accordingly classified as one-point, two-point, or three-point projections. The number of principal vanishing points in a projection is determined by the number of world coordinate axes intersecting the projection plane. Figure 12–11 illustrates the appearance of one-point and two-point perspective projections for a cube. In Fig. 12-11 (b), the projection plane has been aligned parallel to the xy plane so that only the z axis is intersected. This orientation produces a one-point perspective projection with a z-axis vanishing point. For the view shown in Fig. 12–11 (c), the projection plane intersects both the x and z axes but not the y axis. The resulting two-point perspective projection contains both x-axis and z-axis vanishing points.

12–2 Viewing Transformation

Generating a view of an object in three dimensions is similar to photographing the object. We can walk around and take its picture from any angle, at various distances, and with varying camera orientations. Whatever appears in the viewfinder is projected onto the flat film surface. The type of camera lens that we use determines what part of the object or scene appears in the final picture. These ideas are incorporated into a graphics package. We ask the user to specify a point from which to view the object and to indicate how much of the scene to include in the final display.

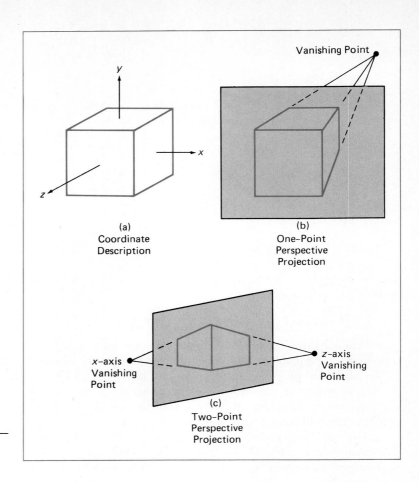

FIGURE 12–11
Perspective views of a cube.

(a)
Coordinate
Description

(b)
One-Point
Perspective
Projection

Vanishing Point

x-axis
Vanishing
Point

z-axis
Vanishing
Point

(c)
Two-Point
Perspective
Projection

Specifying the View Plane

A user specifies a particular view for a scene by defining a **view plane.** The view plane is the surface upon which we project the view of an object. We can think of it as the film in a camera that has been positioned and oriented for a desired shot. The view plane is established by defining a **viewing coordinate system,** as shown in Fig. 12–12. World coordinate positions will be redefined and expressed relative to this coordinate system.

To establish the viewing coordinates, a user picks a world coordinate position to serve as the **view reference point.** This will be the origin of the viewing coordinate system. The orientation of the view plane is defined by specifying the **view plane normal** vector, **N.** This vector establishes the direction for the positive z axis of the viewing coordinate system. A vertical vector **V,** called the **view up** vector, is used to define the direction for the positive y axis. Figure 12–13 illustrates orientation of the viewing coordinate system where the view plane is the xy plane.

The view plane normal **N** can be established by specifying a coordinate position relative to the world coordinate origin. This defines the direction of the normal vector as the line from the origin to the specified coordinate position. Figure 12–14 gives two orientations of the view plane for specified normal vector coordinates. Vector **V** can be specified in a similar manner. It is often difficult for a user to specify two vectors that are precisely perpendicular, so some packages adjust the

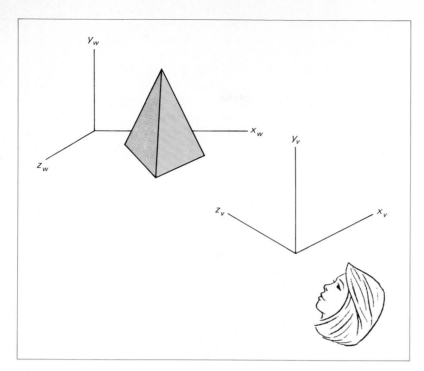

FIGURE 12–12
Viewing coordinate system
with axes x_v, y_v, and z_v. Object
descriptions in world
coordinates are transformed to
viewing coordinates.

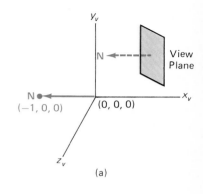

(a)

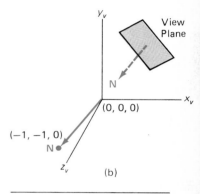

(b)

FIGURE 12–14
Orientation of the view plane
for specified normal vector
coordinates. Position $(-1, 0, 0)$
orients the view plane as in (a),
while $(-1, -1, 0)$ gives the
orientation in (b).

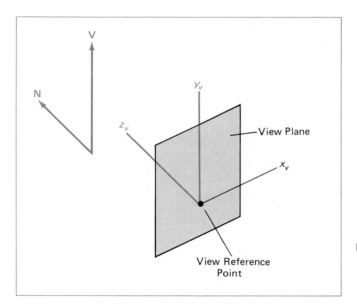

View Reference
Point

FIGURE 12–13
The view reference point and
vectors N and V position and
orient the viewing coordinate
system.

user specification of vector V. As shown in Fig. 12–15, V is projected to a position
perpendicular to the normal vector.

Sometimes a third vector U, is used to indicate the x direction of the viewing
coordinate system. The viewing system can then be described as a uvn system, and
the view plane is called the uv plane. We will assume that positive x is in the
direction shown in Fig. 12–16. The direction of U and V in this picture is consistent

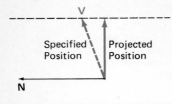

FIGURE 12–15
Adjusting the specification of a view up vector **V** to a position perpendicular to the normal vector **N**.

with the standard orientation of the *x* and *y* axes on a display device. We can think of the view plane in this viewing system as a logical device upon which the picture is to be displayed.

Either a left-handed system (as in Fig. 12–16) or a right-handed system (Fig. 12–17) can be used for the viewing coordinate system. We use a left-handed system in the following discussion because it is somewhat more intuitive. Objects farther away from the viewer have increasing *z*-coordinate values. However, a right-handed system is often used, since it has the same orientation as the world coordinate system. Consequently, conversion between the two systems is simplified slightly.

In establishing the view plane, some packages use an additional parameter called the view distance. The view plane is defined as the plane parallel to the

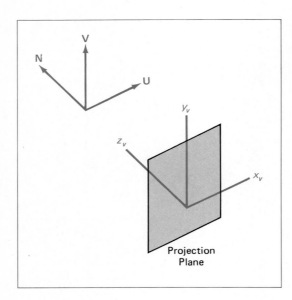

FIGURE 12–16
A *uvn* system defining the directions for the axes of a left-handed viewing coordinate system.

FIGURE 12–17
A right-handed viewing system defined with vectors **U**, **V**, and **N**.

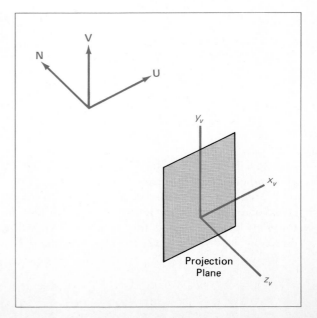

viewing coordinate xy plane that is at a specified distance from the view reference point. For our discussions, we assume that the view plane is the xy plane at the viewing coordinate origin. This allows us to project onto the $z = 0$ plane.

To generate a view from the user-specified vantage point, positions defined relative to the world coordinate origin must be redefined relative to the viewing coordinate origin. That is, we must transform the coordinates from the world coordinate system to the viewing coordinate system. This transformation is accomplished with the sequence of translations and rotations that map the viewing system axes onto the world coordinate axes. When applied to the world coordinate definition of the objects in the scene, this sequence converts them to their positions within the viewing coordinate system. The matrix representing this sequence of transformations can be obtained by concatenating the following transformation matrices:

1. Reflect relative to the xy plane, reversing the sign of each z coordinate. This changes the left-handed viewing coordinate system to a right-handed system.
2. Translate the view reference point to the origin of the world coordinate system.
3. Rotate about the world coordinate x axis to bring the viewing coordinate z axis into the xz plane of the world coordinate system.
4. Rotate about the world coordinate y axis until the z axes of both systems are aligned.
5. Rotate about the world coordinate z axis to align the viewing and world y axes.

The effect of each of these transformations is shown in Fig. 12–18. This sequence has much in common with the transformation sequence that rotates an object about

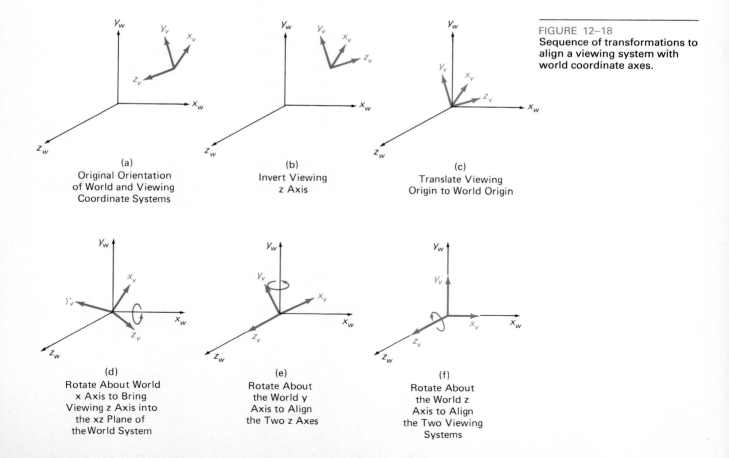

FIGURE 12–18
Sequence of transformations to align a viewing system with world coordinate axes.

(a)
Original Orientation
of World and Viewing
Coordinate Systems

(b)
Invert Viewing
z Axis

(c)
Translate Viewing
Origin to World Origin

(d)
Rotate About World
x Axis to Bring
Viewing z Axis into
the xz Plane of
the World System

(e)
Rotate About
the World y
Axis to Align
the Two z Axes

(f)
Rotate About
the World z
Axis to Align
the Two Viewing
Systems

an arbitrary axis, and the viewing matrix components can be determined using techniques similar to those for arbitrary rotation. For packages that use a right-handed viewing coordinate system, the z coordinate inversion in step 1 is unnecessary.

View Volumes

In the camera analogy, the type of lens used on the camera is one factor that determines how much of the scene is caught on film. A wide-angle lens takes in more of the scene than a regular lens. In three-dimensional viewing, a **projection window** is used to the same effect. The window is defined by minimum and maximum values for x and y on the view plane, as shown in Fig. 12–19. Viewing coordinates are used to give the limits of the window, which may appear anywhere on the view plane.

The projection window is used to define a **view volume**. Only those objects within the view volume are projected and displayed on the view plane. The exact shape of the view volume depends on the type of projection requested by a user. In any case, four sides of the volume pass through the edges of the window. For a parallel projection, these four sides of the view volume form an infinite parallelepiped, as in Fig. 12–20. A truncated pyramid, with apex at the center of projection (Fig. 12–21), is used as the view volume for a perspective projection. This truncated pyramid is called a **frustum.**

Some packages restrict the coordinates of the center of projection to positions along the z axis of the viewing coordinate system. We take a more general approach and allow the center of projection to be located at any position in the viewing system. Figure 12–22 shows two orientations of the view volume pyramid relative to the viewing axes. In Fig. 12–22 (b), no points project to the view plane, since the center of projection and the objects to be viewed are on the same side of the view plane. In this case, nothing is displayed.

In parallel projections, the direction of projection defines the orientation of the view volume. By giving a position relative to the viewing coordinate origin, a user defines a vector that sets the orientation of the view volume relative to the view plane. Figure 12–23 shows the shape of view volumes for both orthographic and oblique parallel projections.

Often, one or two additional planes are used to further define the view volume. Including a **near plane** and a **far plane** produces a finite view volume bounded by six planes, as shown in Fig. 12–24. The near and far planes are always parallel to the view plane, and they are specified by distances from the view plane in viewing coordinates. Alternate names for the near and far planes are hither and yon planes and front and back planes.

With these planes, the user can eliminate parts of the scene from the viewing

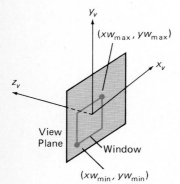

FIGURE 12–19
Window specification on the view plane, with minimum and maximum coordinates given in the viewing reference system.

FIGURE 12–20
View volume for a parallel projection.

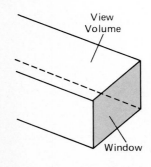

FIGURE 12–21
View volume for a perspective projection.

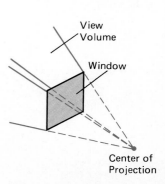

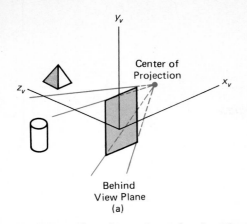

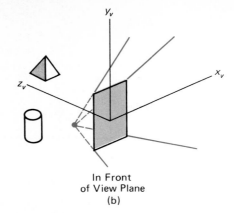

Center of
Projection

Behind
View Plane
(a)

In Front
of View Plane
(b)

operations based on their depth. This is a particularly good idea when using a perspective projection. Objects that are very far from the view plane might project to only a single point. Very near objects could block out the other objects that a user wants to view. Or, when projected, near objects could be so large that they extend beyond the window boundaries and cannot be recognized.

Clipping

An algorithm for three-dimensional clipping identifies and saves all line segments within the view volume for projection onto the view plane. All line segments outside the view volume are discarded. Clipping can be accomplished using an extension of two-dimensional line-clipping or polygon-clipping methods. The plane equations defining each boundary of the view volume can be used to test the relative positions of line endpoints and to locate intersection points.

By substituting the coordinates of a line endpoint into the plane equation of a boundary, we can determine whether the endpoint is inside or outside the boundary. An endpoint (x, y, z) of a line segment is outside a boundary plane if $Ax + By + Cz + D > 0$, where A, B, C, and D are the plane parameters for that boundary. Similarly, the point is inside the boundary if $Ax + By + Cz + D < 0$. Lines with both endpoints outside a boundary plane are discarded, and those with both endpoints inside all boundary planes are saved. The intersection of a line with a boundary is found using the line equations along with the plane equation. Intersection coordinates (x_I, y_I, z_I) are values that are on the line and that satisfy the plane equation $Ax_I + By_I + Cz_I + D = 0$.

Once the system has identified the objects that are interior to the view volume, they are projected to the view plane. All objects in the view volume will fall within the projection window. As in two dimensions, the contents of the window are mapped to a user-specified projection viewport. This normalizes the coordinates, which are then converted to the appropriate device coordinates for a particular display.

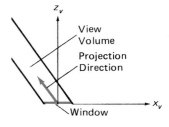

View
Volume

Projection
Direction

Window

Oblique Projection
(a)

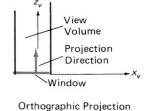

View
Volume

Projection
Direction

Window

Orthographic Projection
(b)

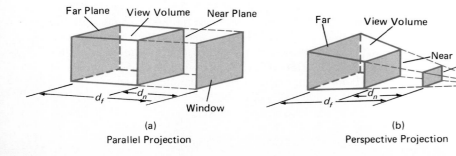

Far Plane   View Volume   Near Plane

d_f d_n

Window

(a)
Parallel Projection

Far   View Volume

Near

Window

d_f d_n

Center of
Projection

(b)
Perspective Projection

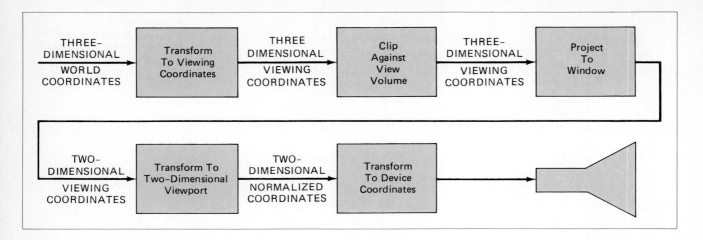

FIGURE 12-25
Logical operations in three-
dimensional viewing.

12-3 Implementation of Viewing Operations

We can conceptualize a sequence of operations for performing viewing as in Fig. 12-25. First, world coordinate descriptions are converted to viewing coordinates. Next, the scene to be viewed is clipped against a view volume and projected into the window area defined on the view plane. This window is then mapped onto a viewport, designated in normalized device coordinates. The final step is to convert the normalized coordinate description into device coordinates and display the view on an output device.

The model presented in Fig. 12-25 is useful as a programmer's model or for first conceptualizing three-dimensional viewing operations. However, to provide efficiency, the actual implementation of three-dimensional viewing in a graphics package takes on a considerably different form. In this section, we look at those places where implementation concerns lead us to diverge from the basic model of three-dimensional viewing.

Normalized View Volumes

Clipping in two dimensions is generally performed against an upright rectangle; that is, the window is aligned with the x and y axes. This greatly simplifies the clipping calculations, since each window boundary is defined by one coordinate value. For example, the intersections of all lines crossing the left boundary of the window have an x coordinate equal to the left boundary.

In the three-dimensional programmer's model, clipping is performed against the view volume as defined by the projection window, the type of projection, and the near and far planes. Since the near and far planes are parallel to the view plane, each has a constant z-coordinate value. The z coordinate of the intersections of lines with these planes is simply the z coordinate of the corresponding plane. But the other four sides of the view volume can have arbitrary spatial orientations. To find the intersection of a line with one of these sides requires finding the equation for the plane containing the view volume side. This becomes unnecessary, however, if we convert the view volume before clipping to a regular parallelepiped.

Clipping against a regular parallelepiped is simpler because each surface is now perpendicular to one of the coordinate axes. As seen in Fig. 12-26, the top

FIGURE 12-26
A regular parallelepiped view
volume.

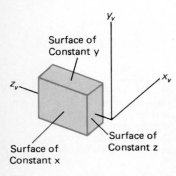

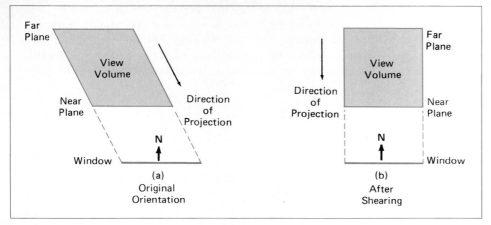

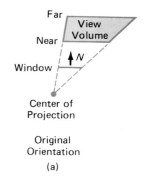

FIGURE 12–27
Shearing an oblique, parallel projection view volume into a regular parallelepiped (top view).

and bottom of such a view volume are planes of constant y, the sides are planes of constant x, and the near and far planes have a fixed z value. All lines intersecting the top plane of the parallelepiped, for example, now have the y-coordinate value of that plane. In addition to simplifying the clipping operation, converting to a regular parallelepiped reduces the projection process to a simple orthogonal projection. We first consider how to convert a view volume to a regular parallelepiped, then discuss the projection operation.

In the case of an orthographic parallel projection, the view volume is already a rectangular parallelepiped. For an oblique parallel projection, we shear the view volume to align the projection direction with the view plane normal vector, **N**. This shearing transformation brings the sides of the view volume perpendicular to the view surface, as seen in Fig. 12–27.

For the view volume in a perspective projection, shearing and scaling transformations are needed to produce the rectangular parallelepiped. We first shear in x and y directions to bring the center of projection onto the line that is normal to the center of the window (Fig. 12–28). With the apex at this point, the opposing sides of the frustum (left versus right and top versus bottom) have the same dimensions. We then apply a scaling transformation to convert the sides of the frustum into the rectangular sides of a regular parallelepiped.

Figure 12–29 shows a side view of the frustum for a parallel projection. To convert this frustum into the regular parallelepiped with height equal to that of the window, we apply a scaling transformation relative to the fixed point $(x_F, y_F, 0)$ at the window center. This transformation must scale points in the frustum that are

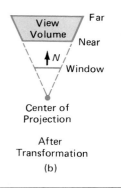

FIGURE 12–28
Shearing a perspective projection view volume to bring the center of projection onto the line perpendicular to the center of the window (top view).

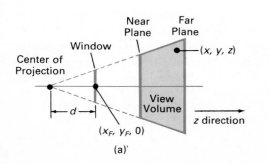

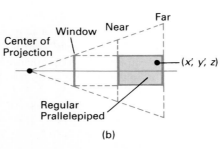

FIGURE 12–29
Side view of a frustum view volume and the resulting regular parallelepiped. A point (x, y, z) is scaled into the position (x', y', z) by the scaling transformation (12–13).

farther from the window more than points that are closer to the window to bring them into the parallelepiped region. In fact, the amount of scaling required is inversely proportional to the distance from the window. For a center of projection at a distance d behind the window, the required scaling factor is $d/(z + d)$, with z as the distance of a point from the window. The matrix representation for this scaling is

$$\begin{bmatrix} S & 0 & 0 & 0 \\ 0 & S & 0 & 0 \\ 0 & 0 & 1 & 0 \\ (1 - S)x_F & (1 - S)y_F & 0 & 1 \end{bmatrix} \qquad (12\text{--}13)$$

where the scaling parameter is $S = d/(z + d)$. All x- and y-coordinate values in a scene are scaled by this transformation. Those points that are in the volume are mapped into points in the parallelepiped with no change in z value (Fig. 12–29).

Converting to a regular parallelepiped has another important benefit. The transformations applied accomplish a large measure of the work required to project the original points onto the view plane. For example, the transformation to convert the frustum to a regular parallelepiped essentially performs the perspective transformation. Coordinate positions are converted to the projection x and y values but retain nonzero z values. Points that fall within the z values for the near and far plane can be projected by simply removing the z coordinate. Thus by converting the view volume to a regular parallelepiped, the projection operation is reduced to a simple orthogonal projection.

We can make the viewing operations still more efficient. Converting the view volume to a regular parallelepiped (which is like doing the projection operation) occurs immediately following the mapping from world coordinates to viewing coordinates. If we concatenate the matrices to do each of these operations, each coordinate position can be transformed from its position in world coordinates to the proper position within the parallelepiped in one step.

Some graphics packages perform clipping operations using the regular parallelepiped as just described. Object parts that are within the parallelepiped are projected to the front plane and then mapped to a two-dimensional viewport.

Other packages map the regular parallelepiped onto the **unit cube** (Fig. 12–30) before clipping and projection. The unit cube is a volume defined by the following planes:

$$x = 0, \; x = 1, \; y = 0, \; y = 1, \; z = 0, \; z = 1 \qquad (12\text{--}14)$$

Since the unit cube is defined by values within the range of 0 to 1, it can be referred to as a **normalized view volume**. As with a regular parallelepiped, once the volume interior has been projected to the front plane, those points are mapped to a two-dimensional viewport.

As another alternative, the regular parallelepiped, defined by the view plane window, can be mapped to a **three-dimensional viewport** before clipping. This viewport is a regular parallelepiped defined in normalized coordinates. The three-dimensional window-to-viewport mapping required is accomplished with a transformation combining scaling and translation operations similar to those for a two-dimensional window-to-viewport mapping. We can express the three-dimensional transformation matrix for these operations in the form

$$\begin{bmatrix} D_x & 0 & 0 & 0 \\ 0 & D_y & 0 & 0 \\ 0 & 0 & D_z & 0 \\ K_x & K_y & K_z & 1 \end{bmatrix} \qquad (12\text{--}15)$$

FIGURE 12–30
Transformation of a regular parallelepiped (a) to a unit cube (b).

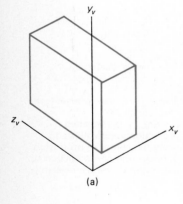

(a)

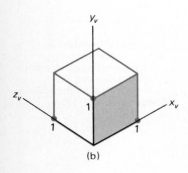

(b)

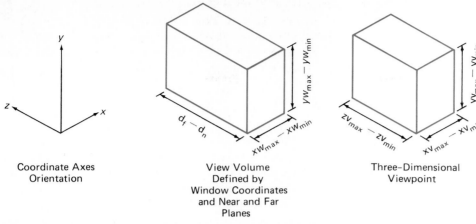

FIGURE 12–31
Dimensions of the view volume
and three-dimensional
viewport.

Coordinate Axes
Orientation

View Volume
Defined by
Window Coordinates
and Near and Far
Planes

Three-Dimensional
Viewpoint

Factors D_x, D_y, and D_z are the ratios of the dimensions of the viewport and regular parallelepiped view volume in the x, y, and z directions (Fig. 12–31):

$$D_x = \frac{xv_{\max} - xv_{\min}}{xw_{\max} - xw_{\min}}$$

$$D_y = \frac{yv_{\max} - yv_{\min}}{yw_{\max} - yw_{\min}} \qquad (12\text{–}16)$$

$$D_z = \frac{zv_{\max} - zv_{\min}}{d_f - d_n}$$

where the view volume boundaries are established by the window limits ($xw_{\min}$, $xw_{\max}$, $yw_{\min}$, $yw_{\max}$), and the positions d_n and d_f of the near and far planes. Viewport boundaries are set with the coordinate values $xv_{\min}$, $xv_{\max}$, $yv_{\min}$, $yv_{\max}$, $zv_{\min}$, and $zv_{\max}$. The additive factors K_x, K_y, and K_z in the transformation are

$$K_x = xv_{\min} - xw_{\min} \cdot D_x$$
$$K_y = yv_{\min} - yw_{\min} \cdot D_y \qquad (12\text{–}17)$$
$$K_z = zv_{\min} - d_n \cdot D_z$$

Performing the window-to-viewport mapping before clipping orders the operations as in Fig. 12–32. The advantage of this is that the normalization transformation matrix (view volume–to–viewport mapping) can be concatenated with the matrix that converts world coordinate positions to positions within the parallelepi-

FIGURE 12–32
Implementing the viewing
transformation so that
operations can be combined
into a single transformation
matrix, applied before clipping.

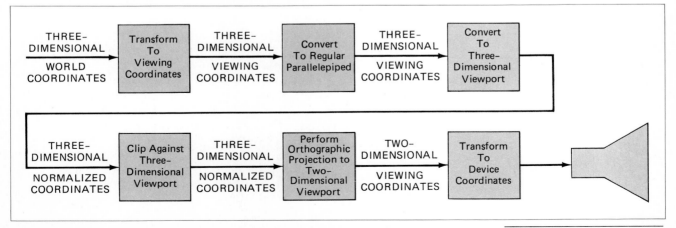

ped. This resultant matrix converts positions within world coordinates to their x and y projection coordinates within the viewport. Each coordinate of the original scene needs to be transformed only once. These transformed points are clipped against the viewport. The x and y values of points inside the viewport volume are then converted to device coordinates for display (Fig. 12–33).

Clipping Against a Normalized View Volume

Surfaces can be clipped against the viewport boundaries with procedures similar to those used for two dimensions. Either line-clipping or polygon-clipping procedures could be adapted to three-dimensional viewport clipping. Curved surfaces are processed using the defining equations for the surface boundary and locating the intersection lines with the parallelepiped planes. We now consider how two-dimensional clipping procedures can be modified to account for the third dimension.

The two-dimensional concept of region codes can be extended to three dimensions by considering positions in front and in back of the three-dimensional viewport, as well as positions that are left, right, below, or above the volume. For two-dimensional clipping, we used a four-digit binary region code to identify the position of a line endpoint relative to the window boundaries. For three-dimensional points, we need to expand the region code to six bits. Each point in the description of a scene is then assigned a six-bit region code that identifies the relative position of the point with respect to the viewport. For a line endpoint at position (x, y, z), we assign the bit positions in the region code from right to left as

$$
\begin{aligned}
\text{bit } 1 &= 1 & &\text{if } x < xv_{\min} \text{ (left)} \\
\text{bit } 2 &= 1 & &\text{if } x > xv_{\max} \text{ (right)} \\
\text{bit } 3 &= 1 & &\text{if } y < yv_{\min} \text{ (below)} \\
\text{bit } 4 &= 1 & &\text{if } y > yv_{\max} \text{ (above)} \\
\text{bit } 5 &= 1 & &\text{if } z < zv_{\min} \text{ (front)} \\
\text{bit } 6 &= 1 & &\text{if } z > zv_{\max} \text{ (back)}
\end{aligned}
$$

For example, a region code of 101000 identifies a point as above and behind the viewport, while the region code 000000 indicates a point within the volume.

A line segment can be immediately identified as completely within the viewport if both endpoints have a region code of 000000. If either endpoint of a line segment does not have a region code of 000000, we perform the logical *and* operation on the two endpoint codes. The result of this *and* operation will be non-

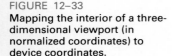

FIGURE 12–33

Mapping the interior of a three-dimensional viewport (in normalized coordinates) to device coordinates.

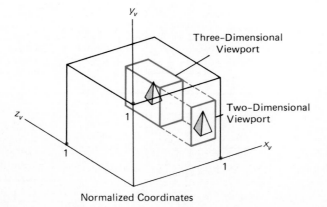

Normalized Coordinates

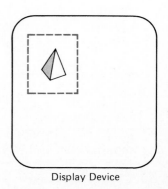

Display Device

zero for any line segment completely outside the viewport volume. If we cannot identify a line segment as completely inside or completely outside the volume, we test for intersections with the bounding planes of the volume.

As in two-dimensional line clipping, we use the calculated intersection of a line with a viewport plane to determine how much of the line can be thrown away. The remaining part of the line is checked against the other planes, and we continue until either the line is totally discarded or a section is found inside the volume.

Determination of intersection points in line clipping, and in polygon-clipping procedures as well, should be done efficiently. Equations for three-dimensional line segments are conveniently expressed in parametric form. For a line segment with endpoints $P_1 = (x_1, y_1, z_1)$ and $P_2 = (x_2, y_2, z_2)$, we can write the parametric line equations as

$$
\begin{aligned}
x &= x_1 + (x_2 - x_1)u \\
y &= y_1 + (y_2 - y_1)u \\
z &= z_1 + (z_2 - z_1)u
\end{aligned}
\tag{12–18}
$$

Coordinates (x, y, z) represent any point on the line between the two endpoints, and parameter u varies from 0 to 1. The value $u = 0$ produces the point P_1, and $u = 1$ gives point P_2.

To find the intersection of a line with a plane of the viewport, we substitute the value of the coordinate that is constant for the plane into the appropriate parametric expression of Eqs. 12–18 and solve for u. For instance, suppose we are testing a line against the front plane of the viewport. Then $z = zv_{min}$, and

$$
u = \frac{zv_{min} - z_1}{z_2 - z_1}
\tag{12–19}
$$

When the value for u as calculated by Eq. 12–19 is not in the range from 0 to 1, this means that the line segment does not intersect the front plane at any point between endpoints P_1 and P_2 (line A in Fig. 12–34). If the calculated value for u is in the interval from 0 to 1, we calculate the intersection's x and y coordinates as

$$
\begin{aligned}
x_I &= x_1 + (x_2 - x_1)\left(\frac{zv_{min} - z_1}{z_2 - z_1}\right) \\
y_I &= y_1 + (y_2 - y_1)\left(\frac{zv_{min} - z_1}{z_2 - z_1}\right)
\end{aligned}
\tag{12–20}
$$

If either x_I or y_I is not in the range of the boundaries of the viewport, then this line intersects the front plane beyond the boundaries of the volume (line B in Fig. 12–34).

The Liang-Barsky line-clipping algorithm discussed in Chapter 6 can be extended to three-dimensions by considering the effects of the near and far planes. These planes add two additional tests in the processing of the intersection parameters u_1 and u_2.

12–4 Hardware Implementations

Graphics chip sets, employing VLSI (very large scale integration) circuitry techniques, are used in some systems to perform the viewing operations. These customized chip sets are designed to transform, clip, and project objects to the output device for either three-dimensional or two-dimensional applications.

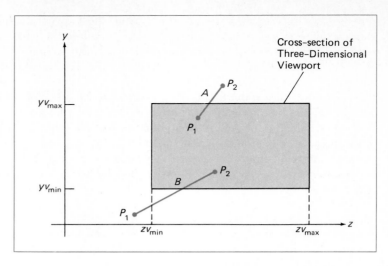

FIGURE 12-34
A side view in the yz plane of
two line segments that are to
be clipped against the front
plane of the viewport. For line
A, Eq. (12-19) produces a value
of u that is outside the range
from 0 to 1. For line B, Eqs.
(12-20) produce intersection
coordinates that are outside the
range from yv_{min} to yv_{max}.

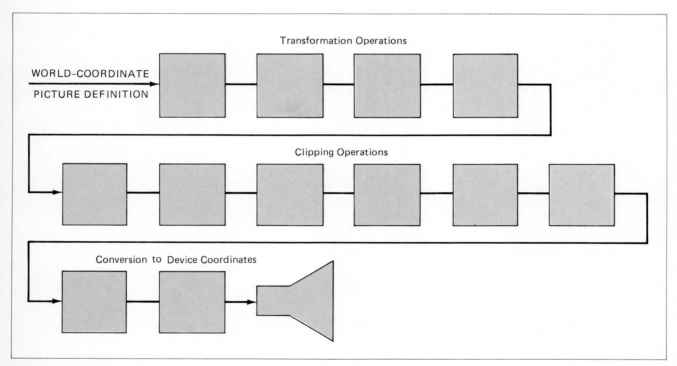

FIGURE 12-35
A graphics chip set with 12
chips to perform the various
viewing operations.

Figure 12-35 shows the components in one type of graphics chip set. The chips are organized into a pipeline for accomplishing the transformation, clipping, and coordinate-conversion operations. Four initial chips are provided for matrix operations involving scaling, translation, rotation, and the transformations needed for orthographic and perspective projections. Each of the next six chips performs clipping against one of the viewport boundaries. Four of these chips are used in two-dimensional applications, and the other two are needed for clipping against the near and far planes of the three-dimensional viewport. The last two chips in the pipeline convert viewport coordinates to output device coordinates.

Several commands can be provided in three-dimensional graphics packages to enable an application program to set the parameters for viewing transformations. With parameters specified relative to the world coordinate origin, the matrix for transforming world coordinate descriptions to the viewing system coordinates is established using

```
create_view_matrix (xo, yo, zo, xn, yn, zn, xv, yv, zv, view_matrix)
```

Parameters *xo*, *yo*, and *zo* specify the origin (view reference point) of the viewing system. The positive *z* axis of the viewing system is established in the direction of the vector from the world coordinate origin to the point (*xn*, *yn*, *zn*). And coordinate position (*xv*, *yv*, *zv*) specifies the view up vector. The projection of this vector onto the view plane defines the positive *y* axis of the viewing coordinate system. These parameters are used to construct a *view_matrix* for transforming world coordinate positions to viewing coordinates.

To specify a second viewing coordinate system, the user can redefine some or all of the coordinate parameters and invoke *create_view_matrix* with a new matrix designation. In this way, any number of world coordinate to viewing coordinate mappings can be defined.

Once a matrix for transforming world to viewing coordinates has been defined, the projection parameters can be specified with the function

```
set_view_representation (view_index, view_matrix,
    projection_type, xp, yp, zp, xw_min, xw_max,
    yw_min, yw_max, near, far, xv_min, xv_max,
    yv_min, yv_max, zv_min, zv_max)
```

Parameter *view_index* serves as an identifying number for the viewing transformation. The transformation matrix for mapping world coordinates to viewing coordinates is specified in *view_matrix*, and *projection_type* is assigned a value of either *parallel* or *perspective*. Coordinate position (*xp*, *yp*, *zp*) establishes either the direction of projection or the center of projection, depending on the input value for parameter *projection_type*. The projection window limits are defined with coordinate values *xw_min*, *xw_max*, *yw_min*, and *yw_max*, specified relative to the viewing coordinate origin. Parameters *near* and *far* specify the location of the corresponding planes. Finally, the three-dimensional viewport boundaries are given with parameters *xv_min*, *xv_max*, *yv_min*, *yv_max*, *zv_min*, and *zv_max*, specified in normalized coordinates. An additional parameter could be included in this function to allow a user to position the view plane at any distance from the view origin. Any number of viewing transformations can be defined with this function, using different *view_index* values.

A user selects a particular viewing transformation with

```
set_view_index (vi)
```

View index number *vi* identifies the set of viewing transformation parameters that are to be applied to subsequently specified output primitives.

Clipping routines in the viewing transformation can be made optional. When a scene is to be viewed in its entirety, it is more efficient to bypass clipping since no part of the scene is to be eliminated. Or the user may know that the scene is completely on the inside of, for example, the far plane. To allow a user selectively

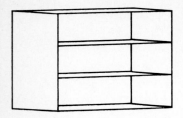

FIGURE 12–36
Object displayed by procedure drawcase using viewing index 2.

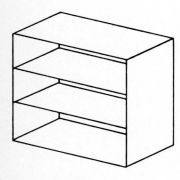

FIGURE 12–37
Object displayed by procedure drawcase using viewing index 3.

to enable and disable clipping against various planes of the view volume, additional parameters can be included in the *set_view_representation* function.

In the following program example, the use of viewing commands is illustrated by generating two perspective views of an object. The two views (shown in Figs. 12–36 and 12–37) are referenced by viewing indices 2 and 3.

```
type
  matrix = array [1..4,1..4] of real;
  projtype = (parallel, perspective);

procedure bookcase;
  begin
    { Defines bookcase with calls to        }
    { fill_area  for the back, sides, top,  }
    { bottom, and 2  shelves. Bookcase is   }
    { defined in feet, as 3'  wide, 4' high,}
    { and 1' deep, with the back,  bottom,  }
    { left corner at (0, 0, 0).             }
  end;  { bookcase }

procedure establish_views;
  var  viewtr1, viewtr2 : matrix;
  begin
    { first view --                         }
    { view reference point is (−8, 3, 6)    }
    { view plane normal is (−1, 0, 1)       }
    { view up vector is (0, 0, 1)           }
    { Store world-to-viewing transformation }
    { matrix in viewtr1.                    }

    create_view_matrix (−8,3,6,  −1,0,1, 0,0,1, viewtr1);

    { Use this world-to-viewing transformation }
    { and additional projection parameters to  }
    { fully specify view 2.                    }
    { center of projection is (−12, 3, 12)     }
    { window goes from (2,2) to (8,8)          }
    { put near plane at 10 and far at 12       }
    { viewport is (.5,.5,0) to (1,1,1)         }

    set_view_representation (2, viewtr1, perspective,  −12,3,12,
        2,8,2,8, 10,12, 0.5,1, 0.5,1, 0,1);

    { second view -                         }
    { view reference point is now (8, 10, 6)  }
    { view plane normal is now (1, 1, 1)      }
    { Store matrix in viewtr2.                }

    create_view_matrix (8,10,6, 1,1,1, 0,0,1, viewtr2);

    { Use viewtr2 and projection para-     }
    { meters to fully specify view 3.      }
    { center of projection is now (20, 20, 20) }

    set_view_representation (3, viewtr2, perspective, 20,20,20,
        2,8,2,8, 10,12, 0.5,1, 0.5,1, 0,1)
```

```
      end;   { establish_views }

   procedure drawcase;
     begin
       establish_views;
       set_view_index (2);      { generate view using transform 2 }
       bookcase;
              .
              .
              .
       set_view_index (3);      { generate view using transform 3 }
       bookcase
     end;   { drawcase }
```

12–6 Extensions to the Viewing Pipeline

To this point, our discussion has concentrated on the central part of the viewing operation, often referred to as the viewing transformation. This includes mapping to the viewing coordinate system, projecting, and clipping. We turn now to operations that may come before or after the viewing transformation and that affect the final view of an object.

Graphics packages that allow transformation matrices to be associated with segments typically apply the matrices before the viewing operations. We can think of this as rotating or repositioning the object in front of the camera. If a number of segments are to be transformed, each is transformed by the appropriate matrix, and the collection of objects is then projected by the viewing transformation to form the final view. When the transformation matrix associated with any segment is changed, the entire viewing process must be repeated.

In some situations, the user may only want to vary the appearance of the view on the output device. Maybe an engineer wants to rotate the cutaway view of some three-dimensional part that has been projected. Or perhaps an animation application needs to move an object from one area of the screen to another. The engineer could use a segment transformation or request a new view of the part using new viewing parameters. In both cases, a second trip through the entire viewing pipeline would be necessary. For such situations, graphics systems sometimes provide for **image transformations:** changes that are applied to the final two-dimensional projection. Image transformations are applied in two dimensions, allowing a user to relocate an object on the monitor but not to turn it around to see its back side. Since these changes do not require three-dimensional viewing or clipping, they are accomplished quickly.

For further discussions of three-dimensional clipping and viewing transformations, see Blinn and Newell (1978), Cyrus and Beck (1978), Liang and Barsky (1984), Michener and Carlbom (1980), and Pavlidis (1982).

REFERENCES

EXERCISES

12–1. Set up the definition of a polyhedron (solid formed with plane surfaces) in the first octant of a left-handed coordinate system (that is, all coordinate values defining the vertices of the object are to be positive). Develop a procedure for performing any specified parallel projection of the object onto the *xy* plane.

12-2. Extend the procedure of Ex. 12-1 to obtain different views of the object by first performing specified rotations of the object about rotation axes that are parallel to the projection plane, then projecting the object onto the viewing surface.

12-3. Set up the procedure in Ex. 12-1 to generate a one-point perspective projection of the object onto the projection plane, using Eq. 12-10 and any specified viewing distance d along the negative z axis.

12-4. Extend the transformation matrix in Eq. 12-10 so that the center of projection can be selected at any position $(x, y, -d)$ behind the projection plane.

12-5. Set up the procedure in Ex. 12-1 to generate a one-point perspective projection of the object onto the projection plane, using the transformation matrix of Ex. 12-4.

12-6. Assuming that a projection surface is defined as the xy plane of a left-handed coordinate system, set up the coordinate definition of a rectangular parallelepiped in this system so that it is in front of the projection plane. Using the projection matrix of Ex. 12-4, orient the block to obtain one-point and two-point perspective projections. Write a program to display these two perspective views on your system. Which of the two perspective views appears more realistic?

12-7. Extend the routine in Ex. 12-6 to obtain a three-point perspective projection. Can you detect much difference between the two-point and three-point projections?

12-8. Develop a set of routines to convert an object description in world coordinates to specified viewing coordinates. That is, implement the function for setting the *view_matrix,* given the coordinates for the view reference point, normal vector, and view up vector.

12-9. Expand the procedures in Ex. 12-8 to obtain a specified parallel projection of the object onto a defined window in the xy plane of the viewing system. Then transform the window to a viewpoint area on the screen. Assume that the object is in front of the view plane and that no clipping against a view volume is to be performed.

12-10. Expand the procedures in Ex. 12-8 to obtain a specified perspective projection of the object onto a defined window in the xy plane of the viewing system, followed by a transformation to a viewport area on the screen. Assume that the object is in front of the view plane and that no clipping against a view volume is to be performed.

12-11. Devise an algorithm to clip objects in a scene against a defined frustum. Compare the operations needed in this algorithm to those needed in an algorithm that clips the scene against a regular parallelepiped.

12-12. Write a program to convert a perspective projection frustum to a regular parallelepiped.

12-13. Modify the two-dimensional Liang-Barsky line-clipping algorithm to clip three-dimensional lines against a specified parallelepiped.

12-14. Extend the algorithm of Ex. 12-13 to clip a specified polyhedron against a parallelepiped.

12-15. For both parallel and perspective projections, discuss the conditions under which three-dimensional clipping followed by projection onto the view plane would be equivalent to first projecting then clipping against the window.

12–16. Using any clipping procedure, write a program to perform a complete viewing transformation from world coordinates to the viewport for an orthographic parallel projection of an object.

12–17. Extend the procedure of Ex. 12–16 to perform any specified parallel projection of an object onto a defined viewport.

12–18. Develop a program to implement a complete viewing operation for a perspective projection. The program is to transform the world coordinate specification of an object onto a defined two-dimensional viewport for display on a section of a video monitor.

12–19. Implement the *set_view_representation* and *set_view_index* functions to perform any specified projection operation on a defined object in world coordinates to obtain the viewport display on the screen.

12–20. Modify the routines in Ex. 12–19 to allow clipping against any view volume plane to be optional. This can be accomplished with additional parameters to set the clipping condition for each plane as either *clip* or *noclip*.

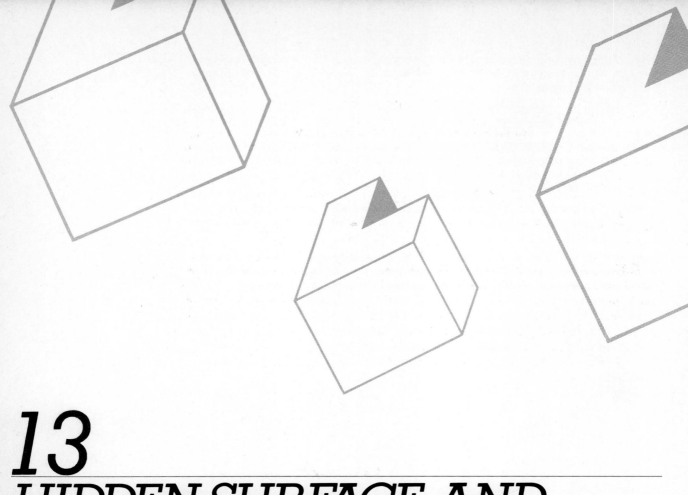

13

HIDDEN-SURFACE AND
HIDDEN-LINE REMOVAL

A major consideration in the generation of realistic scenes is the identification and removal of the parts of the picture definition that are not visible from a chosen viewing position. There are many approaches we can take to solve this problem, and numerous algorithms have been devised to remove hidden parts of scenes efficiently for different types of applications. Some methods require more memory, some involve more processing time, and some apply only to special types of objects. The method chosen for a particular application depends on such factors as the complexity of the scene, type of objects to be displayed, available equipment, and whether static or animated displays are to be generated. In this chapter, we explore some of the most commonly used methods for removing hidden surfaces and lines.

13–1 Classification of Algorithms

Hidden-surface and hidden-line algorithms are often classified according to whether they deal with object definitions directly or with their projected images. These two approaches are called **object-space** methods and **image-space** methods, respectively. An object-space method compares objects and parts of objects to each other to determine which surfaces and lines, as a whole, should be labeled as invisible. In an image-space algorithm, visibility is decided point by point at each pixel position on the projection plane. Most hidden-surface algorithms use image-space methods, but object-space methods can be used effectively in some cases. Hidden-line algorithms generally employ object-space methods, although many image-space hidden-surface algorithms can be readily adapted to hidden-line removal.

Although there are major differences in the basic approach taken by the various hidden-surface and hidden-line algorithms, most use sorting and coherence methods to improve performance. Sorting is used to facilitate depth comparisons by ordering the individual lines, surfaces, and objects in a scene according to their distance from the view plane. Coherence methods are used to take advantage of regularities in a scene. An individual scan line can be expected to contain intervals (runs) of constant pixel intensities, and scan-line patterns often change little from one line to the next. Animation frames contain changes only in the vicinity of moving objects. And constant relationships can often be established between objects and surfaces in a scene.

13–2 Back-Face Removal

A simple object-space method for identifying the **back faces** of objects is based on the equation of a plane:

$$Ax + By + Cz + D = 0 \qquad (13–1)$$

As we noted in Chapter 10, any point (x', y', z') specified in a right-handed coordinate system is on the "inside" of this plane if it satisfies the inequality

$$Ax' + By' + Cz' + D < 0 \qquad (13–2)$$

If the point (x', y', z') is the viewing position, then any plane for which inequality 13–2 is true must be a back face. That is, it is one that we cannot see from the viewing position.

We can perform a simpler back-face test by looking at the normal vector to a plane described by equation 13–1. This normal vector has Cartesian components (A, B, C). In a right-handed viewing system with the viewing direction along the negative z_v axis (Fig. 13–1), the normal vector has component C parallel to the viewing direction. If $C < 0$, the normal vector points away from the viewing position, and the plane must be a back face.

Similar methods can be used in packages that employ a left-handed viewing system. In these packages, plane parameters A, B, C, and D can be calculated from vertex coordinates specified in a clockwise direction (instead of the counterclockwise direction used in a right-handed system). Inequality 13–2 then remains a valid test for inside points. Also, back faces have normal vectors that point away from the viewing position and are identified by $C > 0$ when the viewing direction is

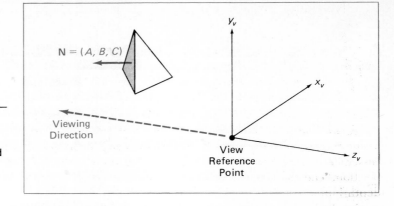

FIGURE 13–1

A plane with parameter $C < 0$ in a right-handed viewing coordinate system is identified as a back face when the viewing direction is along the negative z_v axis.

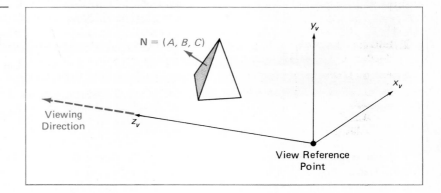

FIGURE 13–2

In a left-handed viewing system with viewing direction along the positive z_v axis, a back face is one with plane parameter $C > 0$.

along the positive z_v axis (Fig. 13–2). For all further discussions in this chapter, we assume that a left-handed viewing system is to be used.

By examining parameter C for the different planes defining an object, we can immediately identify all the back faces. For a single convex polyhedron, such as the pyramid in Fig. 13–1, this test identifies all the hidden surfaces on the object, since each surface is either completely visible or completely hidden. For other objects, more tests need to be carried out to determine whether there are additional faces that are totally or partly hidden (Fig. 13–3). Also, we may need to determine whether some objects are partially or completely obscured by other objects. In general, back-face removal can be expected to eliminate about half of the surfaces in a scene from further visibility tests.

FIGURE 13–3

View of an object with one face partially hidden.

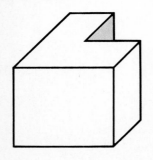

13–3 Depth-Buffer Method

A commonly used image-space approach to eliminating hidden surfaces is the **depth-buffer** method, also called the **z-buffer** method. Basically, this algorithm tests the visibility of surfaces one point at a time. For each pixel position (x, y) on the view plane, the surface with the smallest z coordinate at that position is visible. Figure 13–4 shows three surfaces at varying depths with respect to position (x, y) in a left-handed viewing system. Surface S_1 has the smallest z value at this position, so its intensity value at (x, y) is saved.

Two buffer areas are required for implementation of this method. A depth buffer is used to store z values for each (x, y) position as surfaces are compared, and the refresh buffer stores the intensity values for each position.

This method can be implemented conveniently in normalized coordinates, with depth values varying from 0 to 1. Assuming that a projection volume has been mapped into a normalized parallelepiped view volume, the mapping of each surface onto the view plane is an orthographic projection. The depth at points over the surface of a polygon is calculated from the plane equation. Initially, all positions in the depth buffer are set to 1 (maximum depth), and the refresh buffer is initialized to the background intensity. Each surface listed in the polygon tables is then processed, one scan line at a time, calculating the depth, or z value, at each (x, y) position. The calculated z value is compared to the value previously stored in the depth buffer at that position. If the calculated z value is less than the value stored in the depth buffer at that position, the new z value is stored, and the surface intensity at that position is placed in the same location in the refresh buffer.

We can summarize the steps of a depth-buffer algorithm as follows:

1. Initialize the depth buffer and refresh buffer so that for all coordinate positions (x, y), $depth(x, y) = 1$ and $refresh(x, y) = background$.

2. For each position on each surface, compare depth values to previously stored values in the depth buffer to determine visibility.
   a. Calculate the z value for each (x, y) position on the surface.
   b. If $z < depth (x, y)$, then set $depth(x, y) = z$ and $refresh(x, y) = i$, where i is the value of the intensity on the surface at position (x, y).

In the last step, if z is not less than the value of the depth buffer for that position, the point is not visible. When this process has been completed for all surfaces, the depth buffer contains z values for the visible surfaces and the refresh buffer contains only the visible intensity values.

Depth values for a position (x, y) are calculated from the plane equation for each surface:

$$z = \frac{-Ax - By - D}{C} \qquad (13\text{--}3)$$

For any scan line (Fig. 13–5), x coordinates across the line differ by 1 and y values between lines differ by 1. If the depth of position (x, y) has been determined to be z, then the depth z' of the next position $(x + 1, y)$ along the scan line is obtained from Eq. 13–3 as

$$z' = \frac{-A(x + 1) - By - D}{C} \qquad (13\text{--}4)$$

or

$$z' = z - \frac{A}{C}$$

The ratio A/C is constant for each surface, so succeeding depth values across a scan line are obtained from preceding values with a single subtraction.

We can obtain depth values between scan lines in a similar manner. Again, suppose that position (x, y) has depth z. Then at position $(x, y - 1)$ on the scan line immediately below, the depth value is calculated from the plane equation as

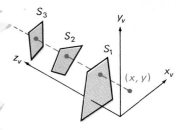

FIGURE 13–4
At position (x, y), surface S_1 has the smallest depth value and so is visible at that position.

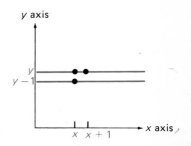

FIGURE 13–5
From position (x, y) on a scan line, the next position across the line has coordinates $(x + 1, y)$, and the position immediately below on the next line has coordinates $(x, y - 1)$.

$$z'' = \frac{-Ax - B(y - 1) - D}{C}$$

or   (13–5)

$$z'' = z + \frac{B}{C}$$

which requires a single addition of the constant B/C to the previous depth value z.

The depth-buffer method is easy to implement, and it requires no sorting of the surfaces in a scene. But it does require the availability of a second buffer in addition to the refresh buffer. A system with a resolution of 1024 by 1024, for example, would require over a million positions in the depth buffer, with each position containing enough bits to represent the number of z-coordinate increments needed. One way to reduce storage requirements is to process one section of the scene at a time, using a smaller depth buffer. After each view section is processed, the buffer is reused for the next section.

13–4 Scan-Line Method

This image-space method for removing hidden surfaces is an extension of the scan-line algorithm for filling polygon interiors. Instead of filling just one surface, we now deal with multiple surfaces. As each scan line is processed, all polygon surfaces intersecting that line are examined to determine which are visible. At each position along a scan line, depth calculations are made for each surface to determine which is nearest to the view plane. When the visible surface has been determined, the intensity value for that position is entered into the refresh buffer.

As we saw in Chapter 10, representation for the polygon surfaces in a three-dimensional scene can be set up to include both an edge table and a polygon table. The edge table contains coordinate endpoints for each line in the scene, the inverse slope of each line, and pointers into the polygon table to identify the surfaces bounded by each line. The polygon table contains coefficients of the plane equation for each surface, intensity information for the surfaces, and possibly pointers into the edge table.

To facilitate the search for surfaces crossing a given scan line, we can set up an active list of edges from information in the edge table. This active list will contain only edges that cross the current scan line, sorted in order of increasing x. In addition, we define a flag for each surface that is set *on* or *off* to indicate whether a position along a scan line is inside or outside of the surface. Scan lines are processed from left to right. At the leftmost boundary of a surface, the surface flag is turned on; and at the rightmost boundary, it is turned off.

Figure 13–6 illustrates the scan-line method for locating visible portions of surfaces along a scan line. The active list for scan line 1 contains information from the edge table for edges AB, BC, HE, and EF. For positions along this scan line between edges AB and BC, only the flag for surface S_1 is on. Therefore, no depth calculations are necessary, and intensity information for surface S_1 is entered from the polygon table into the refresh buffer. Similarly, between edges HE and EF, only the flag for surface S_2 is on. No other positions along scan line 1 intersect surfaces, so the intensity values in the other areas are set to the background intensity. The background intensity can be loaded throughout the buffer in an initialization routine.

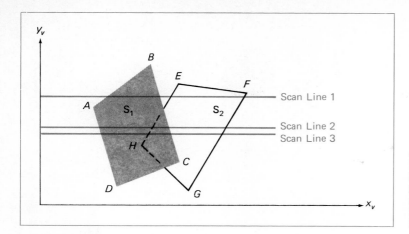

FIGURE 13–6
Scan lines crossing the
projection of two surfaces, S_1
and S_2, in the view plane.
Dashed lines indicate the
boundaries of hidden surfaces.

The active list for scan lines 2 and 3 in Fig. 13–6 contain edges *DA*, *HE*, *BC*, and *FG*. Along scan line 2 from edge *DA* to edge *HE*, only the flag for surface S_1 is on. But between edges *HE* and *BC*, the flags for both surfaces are on. In this interval, depth calculations must be made using the plane coefficients for the two surfaces. For this example, the depth of surface S_1 is assumed to be less than that of S_2, so intensities for surface S_1 are loaded into the refresh buffer until boundary *BC* is encountered. Then the flag for surface S_1 goes off, and intensities for surface S_2 are stored until edge *FG* is passed.

We can take advantage of coherence along the scan lines as we pass from one scan line to the next. In Fig. 13–6, scan line 3 has the same active list of edges as scan line 2. Since no changes have occured in line intersections, it is unnecessary again to make depth calculations between edges *HE* and *BC*. The two surfaces must be in the same orientation as determined on scan line 2, so the intensities for surface S_1 can be entered without further calculations.

Any number of overlapping polygon surfaces can be processed with this scan-line method. Flags for the surfaces are set to indicate whether a position is inside or outside, and depth calculations are performed when surfaces overlap. In some cases, it is possible for surfaces to obscure each other alternately (Fig. 13–7). When coherence methods are used, we need to be careful to keep track of which surface section is visible on each scan line. One way of dealing with this situation is to divide the surfaces so that conflicts are resolved. For instance, plane *ABC* in Fig. 13–8 could be divided into the three surfaces *ABED*, *DEGF*, and *CFG*. Each can be treated as a distinct surface, so that no two planes can be alternately hidden and visible.

FIGURE 13—7
Examples of surface
orientations that alternately
obscure one another.

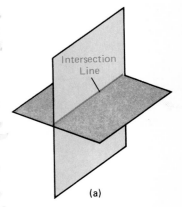

(a)

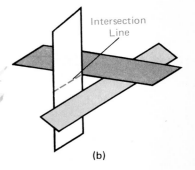

(b)

13–5 Depth-Sorting Method

It is possible to use both image-space and object-space operations in a hidden-surface algorithm. The **depth-sorting** method is a combination of these two approaches that performs the following basic functions:

1. Surfaces are sorted in order of decreasing depth.
2. Surfaces are scan-converted in order, starting with the surface of greatest depth.

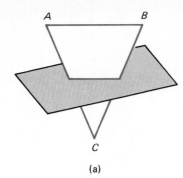

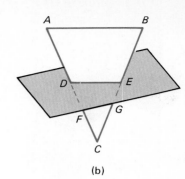

C

(a)

C

(b)

FIGURE 13–8
Dividing a surface into multiple surfaces to avoid alternate visibility and invisibility problems between the two planes.

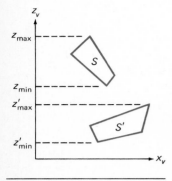

FIGURE 13–9
Two surfaces with no depth overlap.

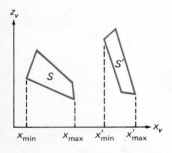

FIGURE 13–10
Two surfaces with depth overlap but no overlap in the x direction.

FIGURE 13–11
Surface S is completely "outside" the overlapping surface S', relative to the view plane.

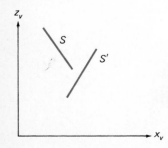

Sorting operations are carried out in object space, and the scan conversion of the polygon surfaces is performed in image space.

This method for solving the hidden-surface problem is sometimes referred to as the **painter's algorithm.** In creating an oil painting, an artist first paints the background colors. Next, the most distant objects are added. Finally, the foreground objects are painted on the canvas over the more distant objects. Each layer of paint covers up the previous layer. Using a similar technique, we first sort surfaces according to their distance from the view plane. The intensity values for the farthest surface are then entered into the refresh buffer. Taking each succeeding surface in turn (in decreasing-depth order), we "paint" the surface intensities onto the frame buffer over the intensities of the previously processed surfaces.

Painting polygon surfaces onto the frame buffer according to depth is carried out in several steps. On the first pass, surfaces are ordered according to the largest z value on each surface. The surface with the greatest depth (call it S) is then compared to the other surfaces in the list to determine whether there are any overlaps in depth. If no depth overlaps occur, S is scan converted. Figure 13–9 shows two surfaces with no depth overlap that have been projected onto the xz plane. This process is then repeated for the next surface in the list. As long as no overlaps occur, each surface is processed in depth order until all have been scan-converted. If a depth overlap is detected at any point in the list, we need to make some additional comparisons to determine whether any of the surfaces should be reordered.

For each surface that overlaps with S, we make the following tests. If any one of these tests is true, no reordering is necessary for that surface. The tests are listed in order of increasing difficulty:

1. The bounding rectangles in the xy plane for the two surfaces do not overlap.
2. Surface S is on the "outside" of the overlapping surface, relative to the view plane.
3. The overlapping surface is on the "inside" of surface S, relative to the view plane.
4. The projections of the two surfaces onto the view plane do not overlap.

As soon as one test is found to be true for an overlapping surface, we know that surface is not behind S. So we proceed to the next surface that overlaps S. If all the overlapping surfaces pass at least one of these tests, no reordering is necessary and S can be scan-converted.

Test 1 is performed in two parts. We first check for overlap in the x direction, then for overlap in the y direction. If either of these directions shows no overlap,

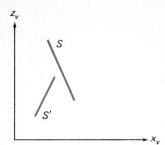

FIGURE 13–12
Overlapping surface S' is
completely "inside" surface S,
relative to the view plane.

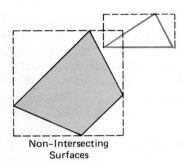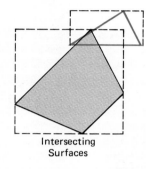

Non-Intersecting
Surfaces

Intersecting
Surfaces

FIGURE 13–13
Two surfaces with overlapping
bounding rectangles in the xy
plane.

the two planes cannot obscure each other. An example of two surfaces that overlap in the z direction but not in the x direction is shown in Fig. 13–10.

We can perform test 2 by substituting the coordinates for all vertices of S into the plane equation for the overlapping surface and testing the sign of the result. Suppose that the overlapping surface has plane coefficients A', B', C', and D'. If $A'x + B'y + C'z + D' > 0$ for each vertex of S, then surface S is "outside" the overlapping surface (Fig. 13–11). As noted earlier, the coefficients A', B', C', and D' must be specified so that the normal to the overlapping surface points away from the view plane.

Inside test 3 is carried out using the plane coefficients A, B, C, and D for surface S. If the coordinates for all vertices of the overlapping surface satisfy the condition $Ax + By + Cz + D < 0$, then the overlapping surface is "inside" surface S (providing the surface normal to S points away from the view plane). Figure 13–12 shows an overlapping surface S' that satisfies this test. In this example, surface S is not "outside" S' (test 2 is not true).

If tests 1 through 3 have all failed, we try test 4 by checking for intersections between the bounding edges of the two surfaces using line equations in the xy plane. As demonstrated in Fig. 13–13, two surfaces may or may not intersect even though their bounding volumes overlap in the x, y, and z directions.

Should all four tests fail with a particular overlapping surface S', we interchange surfaces S and S' in the sorted list. An example of two surfaces that would be reordered with this procedure is given in Fig. 13–14. However, we still do not know for certain that we have found the farthest surface from the view plane. Figure 13–15 illustrates a situation in which we would first interchange S and S''. But since S'' obscures part of S', we need to interchange S'' and S' to get the three surfaces into the correct depth order. Therefore, we need to repeat the testing process for each surface that is reordered in the list.

It is possible for the algorithm just outlined to get into an infinite loop if two or more surfaces alternately obscure each other, as in Fig. 13–7. In such situations,

FIGURE 13–14
Surface S has greater depth but
obscures surface S'.

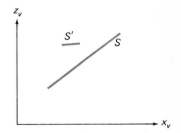

FIGURE 13–15
Three surfaces entered into the
sorted surface list in the order
S, S', S'' should be reordered
S', S'', S.

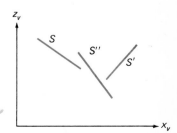

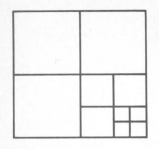

the algorithm would continually reshuffle the positions of the overlapping surfaces. To avoid such loops, we can flag any surface that has been reordered to a farther depth position so that it cannot be moved again. If an attempt is made to switch the surface a second time, we divide it into two parts at the intersection line of the two planes that are under comparison. The original surface is then replaced by the two new surfaces, and we continue processing as before.

13–6 Area-Subdivision Method

This technique for hidden-surface removal is essentially an image-space method, but object-space operations can be used to accomplish depth ordering of surfaces. The **area-subdivision** method takes advantage of area coherence in a scene by locating those view areas that represent part of a single surface. We apply this method by successively dividing the total viewing area into smaller and smaller rectangles until each small area is the projection of part of a single visible surface or no surface at all.

To implement this method, we need to establish tests that can quickly identify the area as part of a single surface or tell us that the area is too complex to analyze easily. Starting with the total view, we apply the tests to determine whether we should subdivide the total area into smaller rectangles. If the tests indicate that the view is sufficiently complex, we subdivide it. Next, we apply the tests to each of the smaller areas, subdividing these if the tests indicate that visibility of a single surface is still uncertain. We continue this process until the subdivisions are easily analyzed as belonging to a single surface or until they are reduced to the size of a single pixel. One way to subdivide an area is successively to divide the dimensions of the area by 2, as shown in Fig. 13–16. This approach is similar to that used in constructing a quadtree. A viewing area with a resolution of 1024 by 1024 could be subdivided ten times in this way before a subdivision is reduced to a point.

Tests to determine the visibility of a single surface within a specified area are made by comparing surfaces to the boundary of the area. There are four possible relationships that a surface can have with a specified area boundary. We can describe these relative surface characteristics in the following way (Fig. 13–17):

A **surrounding surface** is one that completely encloses the area.
An **overlapping surface** is one that is partly inside and partly outside the area.
An **inside surface** is one that is completely inside the area.
An **outside surface** is one that is completely outside the area.

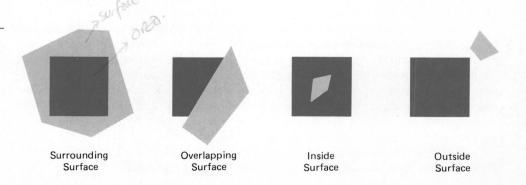

Surrounding Surface

Overlapping Surface

Inside Surface

Outside Surface

The tests for determining surface visibility within an area can be stated in terms of these four classifications. No further subdivisions of a specified area are needed if one of the following conditions is true:

1. All surfaces are outside the area.
2. Only one inside, overlapping, or surrounding surface is in the area.
3. A surrounding surface obscures all other surfaces within the area boundaries.

Test 1 can be carried out by checking the bounding rectangles of all surfaces against the area boundaries. Test 2 can also use the bounding rectangles in the xy plane to identify an inside surface. For other types of surfaces, the bounding rectangles can be used as an initial check. If a single bounding rectangle intersects the area in some way, additional checks are used to determine whether the surface is surrounding, overlapping, or outside. Once a single inside, overlapping, or surrounding surface has been identified, its pixel intensities are transferred to the appropriate area within the frame buffer.

One method for implementing test 3 is to order surfaces according to their minimum depth. For each surrounding surface, we then compute the maximum z value within the area under consideration. If the maximum z value of one of these surrounding surfaces is less than the minimum z value of all other surfaces within the area, test 3 is satisfied. Figure 13–18 shows an example of the conditions for this method.

Another method for carrying out test 3 that does not require depth sorting is to use plane equations to calculate z values at the four vertices of the area for all surrounding, overlapping, and inside surfaces. If the calculated z values for one of the surrounding surfaces is less than the calculated z values for all other surfaces, test 3 is true. Then the area can be filled with the intensity values of the surrounding surface.

For some situations, both methods of implementing test 3 will fail to identify correctly a surrounding surface that obscures all the other surfaces. Further testing could be carried out to identify the single surface that covers the area, but it is faster to subdivide the area than to continue with more complex testing. Once

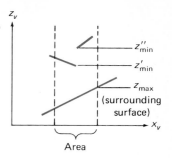

FIGURE 13–18
A surrounding surface with a maximum depth of z_{max} within an area obscures all surfaces that have a minimum depth greater than z_{max}.

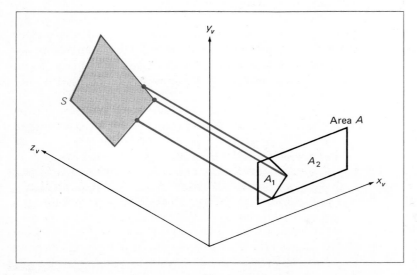

FIGURE 13–19
Area A is subdivided into A_1 and A_2 using the boundary of surface S on the view plane.

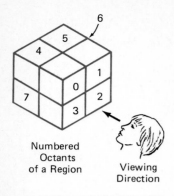

Numbered
Octants
of a Region

Viewing
Direction

FIGURE 13–20
Objects in octants 0, 1, 2, and 3
obscure objects in the back
octants (4, 5, 6, 7) when the
viewing direction is as shown.

FIGURE 13–21
Octant divisions for a region of
space and the corresponding
quadrant plane.

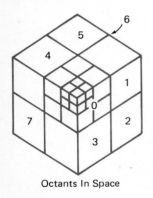

Octants In Space

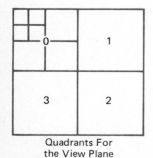

Quadrants For
the View Plane

outside and surrounding surfaces have been identified for an area, they will remain outside and surrounding surfaces for all subdivisions of the area. Furthermore, some inside and overlapping surfaces can be expected to be eliminated as the subdivision process continues, so that the areas become easier to analyze. In the limiting case, when a subdivision the size of a pixel is produced, we simply calculate the depth of each relevant surface at that point and transfer the intensity of the nearest surface to the frame buffer.

As a variation on the basic subdivision process, we could subdivide areas along surface boundaries instead of dividing them in half. If the surfaces have been sorted according to minimum depth, we can use the surface of smallest z value to subdivide a given area. Figure 13–19 illustrates this method for subdividing areas. The projection of the boundary of surface S is used to partition the original area into the subdivisions A_1 and A_2. Surface S is then a surrounding surface for A_1 and visibility tests 2 and 3 can be applied to determine whether further subdividing is necessary. In general, fewer subdivisions are required using this approach, but more processing is needed to subdivide areas and to analyze the relation of surfaces to the subdivision boundaries.

13–7 Octree Methods

When an octree representation is used for the viewing volume, hidden-surface elimination is accomplished by projecting octree nodes onto the viewing surface in a front-to-back order. In Fig. 13–20, the front face of a region of space (the side toward the viewer) is formed with octants 0, 1, 2, and 3. Surfaces in the front of these octants are visible to the viewer. Any surfaces toward the rear of the front octants or in the back octants (4, 5, 6, and 7) may be hidden by the front surfaces.

Back surfaces are eliminated, for the viewing direction given in Fig. 13–20, by processing data elements in the octree nodes in the order 0, 1, 2, 3, 4, 5, 6, 7. This results in a depth-first traversal of the octree, so that nodes representing octants 0, 1, 2, and 3 for the entire region are visited before the nodes representing octants 4, 5, 6, and 7. Similarly, the nodes for the front four suboctants of octant 0 are visited before the nodes for the four back suboctants. The traversal of the octree continues in this order for each octant subdivision.

When a color value is encountered in an octree node, the pixel area in the frame buffer corresponding to this node is assigned that color value only if no values have previously been stored in this area. In this way, only the front colors are loaded into the buffer. Nothing is loaded if an area is void. Any node that is found to be completely obscured is eliminated from further processing, so that its subtrees are not accessed.

Different views of objects represented as octrees can be obtained by applying transformations to the octree representation that reorient the object according to the view selected. We assume that the octree representation is always set up so that octants 0, 1, 2, and 3 of a region form the front face, as in Fig. 13–20.

A method for displaying an octree is first to map the octree onto a quadtree of visible areas by traversing octree nodes from front to back in a recursive procedure. Then the quadtree representation for the visible surfaces is loaded into the frame buffer. Figure 13–21 depicts the octants in a region of space and the corresponding quadrants on the view plane. Contributions to quadrant 0 come from octants 0 and 4. Color values in quadrant 1 are obtained from surfaces in octants 1 and 5, and values in each of the other two quadrants are generated from the pair of octants aligned with each of these quadrants.

Recursive processing of octree nodes is demonstrated in procedure *convert_oct_to_quad*, which accepts an octree description and creates the quadtree representation for visible surfaces in the region. In most cases, both a front and a back octant must be considered in determining the correct color values for a quadrant. However, we can dispense with processing the back octant if the front octant is homogeneously filled with some color. For heterogeneous regions, the procedure is recursively called, passing as new arguments the child of the heterogeneous octant and a newly created quadtree node. If the front is empty, it is necessary only to process the child of the rear octant. Otherwise, two recursive calls are made, one for the rear octant and one for the front octant.

```
type
   oct_node_ptr  =  ↑ oct_node;
   oct_entry  =  record
     case homogeneous : boolean of
       true  :  (color : integer);
       false  :  (child : oct_node_ptr)
     end;  {record}
   oct_node  =  array [0..7] of oct_entry;

   quad_node_ptr  =  ↑ quad_node;
   quad_entry  =  record
     case homogeneous : boolean of
       true  :  (color : integer);
       false  :  (child : quad_node_ptr)
     end;  {record}
   quad_node  =  array [0..3] of quad_entry;

var
   newquadtree : quad_node_ptr;
   backcolor : integer;

{Assumes a frontal view of an octree (with octants 0, 1, 2,
 and 3 in front) and, as preparation for display, converts
 it to a quadtree. Accepts an octree as input, where each
 element of the octree is either a color value (homogeneous
 = true and the octant is filled with this color), the
 number −1 (homogeneous = true and the octant is empty), or
 a pointer to a child octant node (homogeneous is false).}
procedure convert_oct_to_quad (octree : oct_node;
                                      var quadtree : quad_node);
   var  k : integer;
   begin
     for k := 0 to 3 do begin
         quadtree[k].homogeneous := true;
         if octree[k].homogeneous then
           if (octree[k].color > −1) then          {front octant full}
             quadtree[k].color := octree[k].color
           else                                    {front octant empty}
             if octree[k+4].homogeneous then
               if (octree[k+4].color > −1) then{front empty, back full}

                 quadtree[k].color := octree[k+4].color
               else                             {front & back empty}
                 quadtree[k].color := backcolor
             else begin                      {front empty, back hetero}
               quadtree[k].homogeneous := false;
```

```
        new(newquadtree);
        quadtree[k].child := newquadtree;
        convert_oct_to_quad (octree[k+4].child ↑ , newquadtree ↑ )
    end
  else begin                              {front hetero, back unknown}
      quadtree[k].homogeneous := false;
      new(newquadtree);
      quadtree[k].child := newquadtree;
      convert_oct_to_quad (octree[k+4].child ↑ , newquadtree ↑ );
      convert_oct_to_quad (octree [k   ].child ↑ , newquadtree ↑ )
    end
  end   {for}
end;
```

13–8 Comparison of Hidden-Surface Methods

The effectiveness of a hidden-surface method depends on the characteristics of a particular application. If the surfaces in a scene are spread out in the z direction so that there is very little overlap in depth, a depth-sorting method may be best. For scenes with surfaces fairly well separated horizontally, a scan-line or area-subdivision method might be the best choice. In this way methods can be chosen that use sorting and coherence techniques to take advantage of the natural properties of a scene.

Because sorting and coherence considerations are important to the overall efficiency of a hidden-surface method, techniques for performing these operations should be chosen carefully. Whenever objects are known to be in approximate order, such as the list for an active edge table used in the scan-line method, a bubble sort can be employed effectively to perform the few exchanges required. Similarly, coherence techniques applied to scan lines, areas, or frames can be powerful tools for increasing the efficiency of hidden-surface methods.

As a general rule, the depth-sorting method is a highly effective approach for scenes with only a few surfaces. This is due to the fact that these scenes usually have few surfaces that overlap in depth. The scan-line method also performs well when a scene contains a small number of surfaces. Either the scan-line method or the depth-sorting method can be used effectively for scenes with several thousand faces. With scenes that contain more than a few thousand surfaces, the depth-buffer method or octree approach performs best. The depth-buffer method has a nearly constant processing time, independent of the number of surfaces in a scene. This is because the size of the surface areas decreases as the number of surfaces in the scene increases. Therefore, the depth-buffer method exhibits relatively low performance with simple scenes and relatively high performance with complex scenes. This approach is simple to implement, but it does require more memory than most methods. For that reason, another method, such as octrees or area subdivision, might be preferred for scenes with many surfaces.

When octree representations are used in a system, the hidden-surface elimination process is fast and simple. Only integer additions and subtractions are used in the process, and there is no need to perform sorting or intersection calculations. Another advantage of octrees is that they store more than surfaces. The entire solid region of an object is available for display, which makes the octree representation useful for obtaining cross-sectional slices of solids.

It is possible to combine and implement the various hidden-surface methods in various ways. In addition, algorithms are implemented in hardware, and special systems utilizing parallel processing are employed to increase the efficiency of these methods. Special hardware systems are usually used when processing speed is an especially important consideration, as in the generation of animated views for flight simulators.

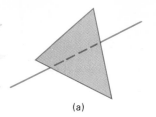

13–9 Hidden-Line Elimination

When only the outline of an object is to be displayed, hidden-line methods are used to remove the edges of objects that are obscured by surfaces closer to the view plane. Methods for removing hidden lines can be developed by considering object edges directly or by adapting hidden-surface methods.

A direct approach to eliminating hidden lines is to compare each line to each surface in a scene. The process involved here is similar to clipping lines against arbitrary window shapes, except that we now want to clip out the parts hidden by surfaces. For each line, depth values are compared to the surfaces to determine which line sections are not visible. We can use coherence methods to identify hidden line segments without actually testing each coordinate position. If both line intersections with the projection of a surface boundary have greater depth than the surface at those points, the line segment between the intersections is completely hidden, as in Fig. 13–22 (a). When the line has greater depth at one boundary intersection and less depth than the surface at the other boundary intersection, the line must penetrate the surface interior, as in Fig. 13–22 (b). In this case, we calculate the intersection point of the line with the surface using the plane equation and display only the visible sections.

Some hidden-surface methods are readily adapted to hidden-line removal. Using a back-face method, we could identify all the back surfaces of an object and display only the boundaries for the visible surfaces. With a depth-sorting method, surfaces can be painted into the refresh buffer so that surface interiors are in the background color, while boundaries are in the foreground color. By processing the surfaces from back to front, hidden lines are erased by the nearer surfaces. An area-subdivision method can be adapted to hidden-line removal by displaying only the boundaries of visible surfaces. Scan-line methods can be used to display visible lines by setting points along the scan line that coincide with boundaries of visible surfaces. Any hidden-surface method that uses scan conversion can be modified to a hidden-line method in a similar way.

FIGURE 13–22
Hidden-line sections (dashed) for lines that (a) pass behind a surface and (b) penetrate a surface.

13–10 Curved Surfaces

An effective method for handling hidden-surface elimination for objects with curved surfaces is the octree representation. Once the octrees have been established from the input definition of the objects, all hidden-surface eliminations are carried out with the same processing procedures. No special considerations need be given to curved surfaces.

Another method for dealing with hidden parts of a scene containing curved surfaces is to approximate each object as a set of plane, polygon surfaces. In the list of surfaces, we then replace each curved surface with its polygon representation and use one of the other hidden-surface methods previously discussed. This same approach can be used with Bézier and spline surfaces, where each surface section is divided into polygons. A scan-line method can then be used to load visible intensities into the refresh buffer.

We can also deal directly with the curve equations defining the surface boundaries. For most objects of interest, such as spheres, ellipsoids, cylinders, and cones, we can use quadratic equations to describe surfaces. Spherical and cylindrical surfaces are commonly used in modeling applications involving molecules, roller bearings, rings, and shafts. The quadratic equations can be expressed in parametric form, and numerical approximation techniques are often used to locate intersections of the curved surface with a scan line.

13–11 Hidden-Line and Hidden-Surface Command

A three-dimensional graphics package can accommodate several hidden-line or hidden-surface algorithms by providing a command to select the method that is to be used in a particular application. The following function is defined for this purpose:

    set_hlhs_method_index (i)

Parameter i is assigned an integer code to identify the hidden-line or hidden-surface method to be used in displaying visible parts of objects. In an implementation of this function, an index table is used to define the range of allowable values for i and the type of algorithms available.

For some applications, it is useful to display hidden lines as dashed or dotted. This technique sometimes can give a better indication of the structure of complex objects than simply erasing all back parts. A system can accommodate this technique by expanding the index table to include these options.

REFERENCES   Additional sources of information on hidden-surface methods include Atherton (1983), Carpenter (1984), Crocker (1984), Frieder, Gordon, and Reynold (1985), Hamlin and Gear (1977), Sutherland, Sproull, and Schumacker (1973 and Mar. 1974), and Weiler and Atherton (1977).

EXERCISES

13–1. Develop a procedure, based on a back-face removal technique, for identifying all the front faces of a convex polyhedron with different-colored surfaces relative to a viewing plane. Assume that the object is defined in a left-handed viewing system with the *xy* plane as the viewing surface.

13–2. Implement the procedure of Ex. 13–1 in a program to orthographically project the visible faces of the object onto a window in the view plane. To simplify the procedure, assume that all parts of the object are in front of the view plane. Map the window onto a screen viewport for display.

13–3. Implement the procedure of Ex. 13–1 in a program to produce a perspective projection of the visible faces of the object in the view plane window, assuming that the object lies completely in front of the view plane. Map the window onto a screen viewport for display.

13–4. Write a program to implement the procedure of Ex. 13–1 for an animation application that incrementally rotates the object about an axis that passes through the object and is parallel to the view plane. Assume that the object lies completely in front of the view plane. Use an orthographic parallel projection to map the views successively onto the view screen.

13–5. Use the depth-buffer method to display the visible faces of any object that is defined in normalized coordinates in front of the viewport. Equations (13–4) and (13–5) are to be used to obtain depth values for all points on each surface once an initial depth has been determined. How can the storage requirements for the depth buffer be determined from the definition of the objects to be displayed?

13–6. Develop a program to implement the scan-line algorithm for displaying the visible surfaces of any object defined in front of the viewport. Use polygon and edge tables to store the definition of the object, and use coherence techniques to evaluate points along and between scan lines.

13–7. Set up a program to display the visible surfaces of a convex polyhedron using the painter's algorithm. That is, surfaces are to be sorted on depth and painted on the screen from back to front.

13–8. Extend the program of Ex. 13–7 to display any defined object with plane faces, using the depth-sorting checks to get surfaces in their proper order.

13–9. Give examples of situations where the two methods discussed for test 3 in the area-subdivision algorithm will fail to identify correctly a surrounding surface that obscures all other surfaces.

13–10. Develop an algorithm that would test a given plane surface against a rectangular area to decide whether it is a surrounding, overlapping, inside, or outside surface.

13–11. Extend the methods in Ex. 13–10 into an algorithm for generating a quadtree representation for the visible surfaces of an object by applying the area-subdivision tests to determine the values of the quadtree elements.

13–12. Set up an algorithm to load the quadtree representation of Ex. 13–11 into a raster for display.

13–13. Write a program on your system to display an octree representation for an object so that hidden surfaces are removed.

13–14. Discuss how antialiasing methods can be incorporated into the various hidden-surface elimination algorithms.

13–15. Develop an algorithm for hidden-line removal by comparing each line in a scene to each surface.

13–16. Discuss how hidden-line removal can be accomplished with the various hidden-surface methods.

13–17. Set up a procedure for displaying the hidden edges of an object with plane faces as dashed lines.

13–18. Develop an algorithm for displaying a set of three-dimensional primitives (block, sphere, and cylinder) in any relative positions so that hidden parts of objects are not displayed.

14
SHADING
AND COLOR MODELS

Realistic displays of objects are obtained by generating perspective projections with hidden surfaces removed and then applying shading and color patterns to the visible surfaces. A **shading model** is used to calculate the intensity of light that we should see when we view a surface. These intensity calculations are based on the optical properties of surfaces, the relative positions of the surfaces, and their orientation with respect to light sources. We first consider how intensity calculations can be modeled from the laws of optics, then explore some of the techniques for applying calculated intensities to surfaces. Finally, we discuss the structure and applications of color models useful in graphics packages.

14-1 Modeling Light Intensities

The intensity of light seen on each surface of an object depends on the type of light sources in the vicinity and the surface characteristics of the object. Some objects have shiny surfaces, and some have dull, or matte, surfaces. In addition, some objects are constructed of opaque materials, while others are more or less transparent. A shading model to produce realistic intensities over the surfaces of an object must take these various properties into consideration.

Light Sources

When we view an object, we see the intensity of reflected light from the surfaces of the object. The light reflected from the surfaces comes from the various light sources around the object. If the object is transparent, we also see light from any sources that may be behind the object.

Light sources that illuminate an object are of two basic types, **light-emitting sources** and **light-reflecting sources** (Fig. 14–1). Light-emitting sources include light bulbs and the sun. Light-reflecting sources are illuminated surfaces of other objects, such as the walls of a room, that are near the object we are viewing. A surface that is not exposed directly to a light-emitting source will still be visible if nearby objects are illuminated. The multiple reflections of light from such nearby objects combine to produce a uniform illumination called **ambient light**, or **background light.**

When the dimensions of a light source are small compared to the size of an object, we can model it as a **point source**, as in Fig. 14–1. This approximation is used for most sources, such as the sun, that are sufficiently far from the object. In other cases, we have a **distributed light source**. This occurs when we have a large, nearby source, such as the long neon light in Fig. 14–2, whose area cannot be considered as infinitely small compared to the size of the illuminated object. Shading models based on the intensity laws for ambient light and point sources provide highly effective surface shading for objects with distant light sources. Only slight modifications to this model are needed to accommodate most distributed sources that may be included in a scene.

A shading model for calculating the intensity of light reflected from a surface can be established by considering contributions from the ambient light sources and point sources in the vicinity of the surface. Both of these sources produce light reflections that are scattered in all directions. This scattered light is called **diffuse reflection,** and it results from the surface roughness, or graininess. A matte surface produces primarily diffuse reflections, so that the surface appears equally bright from all viewing directions. In addition to diffuse reflection, point sources create highlights, or bright spots, called **specular reflection.** This highlighting effect is more pronounced on shiny surfaces than on dull surfaces. These two types of reflections are illustrated in Fig. 14–3.

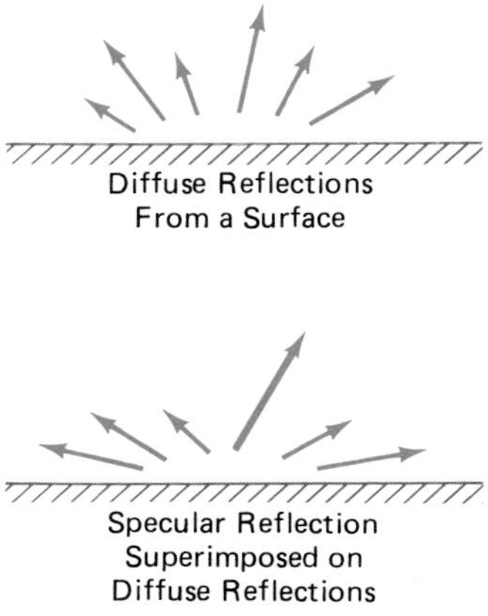

For transparent objects, we can expand the reflection-shading model to include light transmission effects. As in reflection, both diffuse and specular transmission of light occur.

Diffuse Reflection

We first consider the effects of ambient light. Since this background light is the result of multiple reflections from nearby objects, we can consider it to be of uniform intensity I_a in all directions. When ambient light is reflected from a sur-

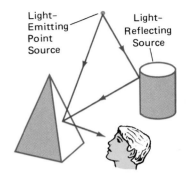

FIGURE 14–1
Surfaces of objects are illuminated by both light-emitting and light-reflecting sources.

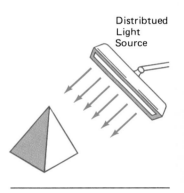

FIGURE 14–2
An object illuminated with a distributed light source.

FIGURE 14–3
Diffuse and specular reflections.

Diffuse Reflections
From a Surface

Specular Reflection
Superimposed on
Diffuse Reflections

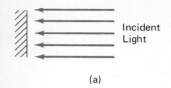

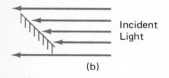

FIGURE 14–4
A surface perpendicular to the direction of the incident light (a) is more illuminated (appears brighter) than a surface at an angle (b) to the light direction.

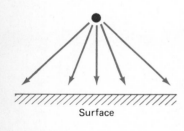

FIGURE 14–5
A nearby light source illuminates a surface with nonparallel rays of incident light.

FIGURE 14–6
Angle of incidence θ between the light direction L and the surface normal N.

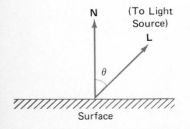

face, it produces a uniform illumination of the surface at any viewing position from which the surface is visible. If a surface is exposed only to ambient light, we can express the intensity of the diffuse reflection at any point on the surface as

$$I = k_d I_a \qquad (14\text{–}1)$$

Parameter k_d is the **coefficient of reflection,** or **reflectivity,** for the surface. It is assigned a constant value in the interval 0 to 1, according to the reflecting properties of the surface. Highly reflective surfaces have a reflectivity near 1, so that the intensity of the reflected light is nearly that of the incident light. Surfaces that absorb most of the incident light have a reflectivity near 0.

Rarely are surfaces illuminated with ambient light alone. A shading model that calculates intensities according to Eq. 14–1 would shade all visible surfaces of an object with the same intensity. More realistic shading is obtained by including the effects of point sources in the shading model.

The calculation of diffuse reflection due to a point source of light is based on Lambert's cosine law, which states that the intensity of the reflected light depends on the angle of illumination. A surface that is perpendicular to the direction of the incident light appears brighter than a surface that is at an angle to the direction of the incoming light. As the angle increases, less of the incident light falls on the surface, as shown in Fig. 14–4. This figure shows a group of parallel light rays incident on two surfaces with different spatial orientations relative to the incident light direction from a distant source. A light source that is close to the surface, however, produces incident light rays that are not parallel (Fig. 14–5). To simplify calculations in our model, we assume that each point source in a scene is sufficiently far from the surface so that the light rays from that source are parallel as they strike the surface. Later we consider extensions to the model for other types of sources.

We can describe the orientation of a surface with a unit normal vector N and the direction to the light source with a unit vector L. The angle θ between these two vectors is called the **angle of incidence** (Fig. 14–6), and Lambert's cosine law states that the intensity of reflected light is proportional to cos θ. We can calculate cos θ from the dot product of these two unit vectors:

$$\cos\theta = N \cdot L \qquad (14\text{–}2)$$

A surface is illuminated by a point source only if the angle of incidence is between 0° and 90° (cos θ is in the interval from 0 to 1). When cos θ is negative, the light source is "behind" the surface.

We can expect the brightness of an illuminated surface to depend on the distance to the light source, since more distant sources are fainter than those that are nearer. If d represents the distance from a light source to a point on the surface and I_p is the intensity of the source, the intensity of the diffuse reflection at that position on the surface can be modeled as

$$I = \frac{k_d I_p}{d + d_0}(N \cdot L) \qquad (14\text{–}3)$$

where parameter d_0 is a constant that is included to prevent the denominator from approaching zero when d is small. In an implementation of this intensity calculation, it is often convenient to assume that a point source at the viewer's position is illuminating a scene. Then d can be set to the distance from the surface position to the projection reference point, and d_0 can be adjusted until satisfactory shading patterns are obtained.

Equation 14–3 is an adaptation of Lambert's cosine law that has been found to produce realistic shading of surfaces. Theoretically, the light intensity arriving at a surface is proportional to $1/d^2$, where d is the distance from the surface to the point source. However, most light sources are larger than points, and we can expect the intensity to decrease less rapidly. The factor $d + d_0$ in the denominator of Eq. 14–3 more accurately models the intensity reflections for surfaces at varying distances from a nearby light source.

Total diffuse reflection for a surface illuminated by ambient light and one point source is given by

$$I = k_d I_a + \frac{k_d I_p}{d + d_0}(\mathbf{N} \cdot \mathbf{L}) \qquad (14\text{–}4)$$

If more than one point source is to be included in a scene, Eq. 14–4 is expanded to include terms for the additional light sources.

When color is to be included in a scene, Eq. 14–4 must be expressed in terms of the color components of the intensity. For an RGB video monitor, color components are red, green, and blue. Parameters for intensity and reflectivity then become three-element vectors, with one element for each of the color components. The vector representing the coefficient of reflection has components (k_{dr}, k_{dg}, k_{db}). A green surface, for example, has a nonzero value for the green reflectivity component, k_{dg}, while the red and blue components are set to zero ($k_{dr} = k_{db} = 0$). For any light falling on this surface, the red and blue components of the light are absorbed, and only the green component is reflected. The intensity calculation for this example reduces to the single expression

$$I_g = k_{dg} I_{ag} + \frac{k_{dg} I_{pg}}{d + d_0}(\mathbf{N} \cdot \mathbf{L}) \qquad (14\text{–}5)$$

using the green components of the intensity and reflectivity vectors. In general, a surface can reflect all three color components of the incident light, and three equations would be needed to calculate the three color components of the reflected light. Calculated intensity levels for each color component are then used to adjust the corresponding electron gun in the RGB monitor.

Specular Reflection

At certain viewing angles, a shiny surface reflects all incident light, independently of the reflectivity values. This phenomenon, called specular reflection, produces a spot of reflected light that is the same color as the incident light. Normally, objects are illuminated with white light, so that the specular reflection is a bright white spot. For an ideal reflector (perfect mirror), the angle of incidence and the angle of specular reflection are the same (Fig. 14–7). We use unit vector $\mathbf{R}$ to represent the direction for specular reflection. Unit vector $\mathbf{V}$ points in the direction of the viewer, and unit vector $\mathbf{L}$ points to the light source. Specular reflection can be seen with a perfect reflector only when $\mathbf{V}$ and $\mathbf{R}$ coincide ($\phi = 0$).

Real objects exhibit specular reflection over a range of positions about the

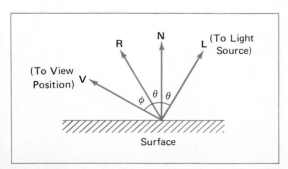

FIGURE 14–7

For a perfect reflector, angle of incidence θ is the same as the angle of reflection.

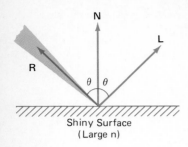

Shiny Surface
(Large n)

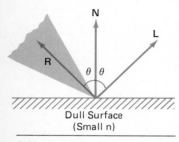

Dull Surface
(Small n)

FIGURE 14–8
Modeling specular reflection
(shaded area) with parameter
n.

FIGURE 14–9
Vector **B** is along the bisector
of the angle between vectors **V**
and **L**.

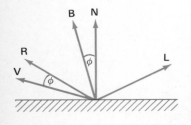

vector **R**. Shiny surfaces have a narrow reflection range, and dull surfaces have a wider reflection range. Specular-reflection models must produce the highest intensity in the direction of **R**, with the intensity decreasing rapidly as the viewing angle ϕ increases.

One method for modeling specular reflection, developed by Phong Bui Tuong and called the Phong model, sets the intensity of specular reflection proportional to $\cos^n\phi$. The value assigned to *n* determines the type of surface that is to be viewed. A very shiny surface is modeled with a large value for *n* (200 or more), and smaller values (down to 1) are used for duller surfaces. For a perfect reflector, *n* is infinite. A rough surface, such as cardboard, might be assigned a value near 1. The effect of *n* on the angular range for viewing specular reflection is shown in Fig. 14–8.

Specular reflection also depends on the angle of incidence. In general, the intensity increases as the angle of incidence increases. This effect is incorporated into the specular-reflection model by making the intensity proportional to a reflection function $W(\theta)$, so that the complete reflection model is written as

$$I = k_d I_a + \frac{I_p}{d + d_0}[k_d(N \cdot L) + W(\theta)\cos^n\phi] \qquad (14\text{–}6)$$

The functional form for $W(\theta)$ depends on the surface material. Some materials, such as glass, exhibit very little specular reflection at smaller angles of incidence but increase the intensity of the specular reflection as θ approaches 90°. For these materials, W should vary from a value near 0 up to a value of 1 as the angle of incidence varies from 0° to 90°. Some materials have nearly constant specular reflection for all incidence angles, so that W could be assigned a constant value in the interval 0 to 1.

Since **V** and **R** are unit vectors in the viewing and reflection directions, we can set $\cos\phi = V \cdot R$ in Eq. 14–6. Also, for many applications, we can simplify the intensity calculations by setting $W(\theta)$ to a constant value k_s for the surface. The complete intensity model for reflection, due to ambient light and a single point source, can then be written as

$$I = k_d I_a + \frac{I_p}{d + d_o}[k_d (N \cdot L) + k_s (V \cdot R)^n] \qquad (14\text{–}7)$$

In this model, constant values are assigned to parameters k_d, k_s, and d_o for each illuminated surface. Intensity values for the ambient light and the point sources are set, and values for the unit vectors are established. For each point on an illuminated surface, we calculate the relevant dot products and determine the intensity of the reflected light.

If the point source is far from a plane surface, the dot product $N \cdot L$ is approximately constant over the surface. Similarly, if the view reference point is sufficiently far from the surface, the product $V \cdot R$ is constant. When these simplifications can be made, the number of calculations is significantly reduced. If one or both of these simplifications cannot be made, dot products must be evaluated at each point. Since we can expect the values of these products to change only slightly from one point to the next, coherence methods can be used to calculate the dot products across a scan line.

Vectors **L** and **N** can be used to determine vector **R** for the calculation of $\cos\phi$. Alternatively, we can evaluate $\cos\phi$ directly in terms of vectors **L**, **N**, and **V** as follows. The direction of the normal vector **N** is along the bisector of the angle between **R** and **L**, and we can define a vector **B** along the bisector of the angle between **V** and **L** (Fig. 14–9) as

$$B = \frac{V + L}{|V + L|}$$
(14–8)

Then, vector B can then be used to calculate $\cos \phi$, since

$$V \cdot R = N \cdot B$$
(14–9)

Other methods for modeling light intensities have been developed. One technique, developed by Torrance and Sparrow and adapted to graphics applications by Blinn, divides each surface in a scene into a set of tiny planes. Each of the small planes is assumed to be an ideal reflector, and the planes are oriented randomly over the total surface. A Gaussian distribution function is used to set the orientation of each plane. The specular reflection for the surface is calculated as the total contribution from the small planes as a function of the intensity I_p from a distant point source and the vectors N, V, and L.

Refracted Light

When a transparent object is to be modeled, the intensity equations must be modified to include contributions from light sources in back of the object. In most cases, these sources are light-reflecting surfaces of other objects, as in Fig. 14–10. Reflected light from these surfaces passes through the transparent object and modifies the object intensity, as calculated by Eq. 14–6 or Eq. 14–7. Light passing through a surface is called **transmitted light** or **refracted light**.

Both **diffuse refraction** and **specular refraction** can take place at the surfaces of an object. Diffuse effects are important when a partially transparent surface, such as frosted glass, is to be modeled. Light passing through such materials is scattered so that a blurred image of background objects is obtained. Diffuse refractions can be generated by decreasing the intensity of the refracted light and spreading intensity contributions at each point on the refracting surface onto a finite area. These manipulations are time-consuming, and most shading models employ only specular effects.

Realistic models of transparent materials, such as clear glass, can be developed by adding specular-refraction contributions to the reflected intensity calculations. When light is incident upon a transparent surface, part of it is reflected and

FIGURE 14–10
A transparent object, modeled here as a thin sheet of paper, transmits some light from surfaces behind the object. From Panasonic "Glider," courtesy Robert Abel & Associates.

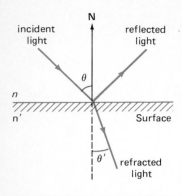

FIGURE 14–11
A ray of light incident upon a surface is partially reflected and partially refracted.

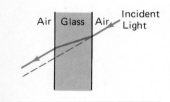

FIGURE 14–12
Refraction of light through a glass object. The emerging refracted ray travels along a path that is parallel to the incident light path (dashed line).

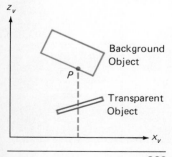

FIGURE 14–13
The intensity of a background object at point P can be added to the intensity of a transparent object along a projection line (dashed).

part is refracted (Fig. 14–11). Because the speed of light is different in different materials, the path of the refracted light is different from that of the incident light. The direction of the refracted light, specified by the **angle of refraction,** is a function of the **index of refraction** of a material. Specifically, the angle of refraction θ' is calculated from the angle of incidence θ, the index of refraction n of the material outside the surface (usually air), and the index of refraction n' of the surface material according to the law of refraction:

$$n \sin\theta = n' \sin\theta' \qquad (14\text{–}10)$$

Actually, the index of refraction of a material is a function of the wavelength of the incident light, so that the different color components of a light ray will be refracted at different angles. For most applications, we can use an average index of refraction for the different materials that are modeled in a scene. The index of refraction of air is approximately 1, and that of crown glass is about 1.5. Using these values in Eq. 14–10 with an angle of incidence of 30° yields an angle of refraction of about 19°. Figure 14–12 illustrates the changes in the path direction for a light ray refracted through a glass object. The overall effect of the refraction is to shift the incident light to a parallel path. Since the calculations of the trigonometric functions in Eq. 14–10 are time-consuming, refraction effects could be modeled by simply shifting the path of the incident light a small amount.

A simpler procedure for modeling transparent objects is to ignore the path shifts altogether. In effect, this approach assumes that there is no change in the index of refraction from one material to another, so that the angle of refraction is always the same as the angle of incidence. This method speeds up the calculation of intensities and produces realistic displays for thin objects, such as champagne glasses.

We can modify the reflection-shading model to include refraction effects by projecting the intensity of background objects to the front surface of the transparent object, as shown in Fig. 14–13. The intensity I_b of a background object is added to the intensity I_t of the transparent object. A more realistic shading pattern is obtained by using a "refraction coefficient" r to weight the reflected and refracted intensity contributions to produce a total intensity I, calculated as

$$I = rI_t + (1 - r)I_b \qquad (14\text{–}11)$$

For highly transparent objects, we assign r a value near 0. Opaque objects transmit no light from background objects, and we can set $r = 1$ for these materials. It is also possible to allow r to be a function of position over the surface, so that different parts of an object can transmit more or less background intensity according to the values assigned to r.

Background objects relative to a transparent object can be identified with a hidden-surface method that sorts surfaces according to depth. Once the surfaces have been sorted, those that are visible through the transparent object are identified. Then the intensity of corresponding points along the viewing direction is combined according to Eq. 14–11 to produce the total shading pattern for the transparent object.

An example of the application of an intensity model to the surfaces of an automobile is shown in Fig. 14–14. The surfaces of the car display specular reflections (bright spots and lines), diffuse reflections, and refracted light through the windows. An intensity model employing multiple light sources and "light controls" was used to reproduce the lighting effects typically available in a photography studio. The light controls allowed the light direction and the light concentration to be varied so that both spotlight and floodlight effects could be simulated.

FIGURE 14–14
Illumination patterns produced
with an intensity model,
displaying diffuse reflections,
specular reflections, and
refracted light. Courtesy David
Warn, General Motors
Research Lab.

Texture and Surface Patterns

The shading model we have discussed for calculating light intensities provides a smooth shading for every surface in a scene. However, many objects do not have smooth surfaces. Surface texture is needed to model accurately such objects as brick walls, gravel roads, and shag carpets. In addition, some surfaces contain patterns that must be included in the shading model. The surface of a vase could contain a painted design; a water glass might have the family crest engraved into the surface; a tennis court contains markings for the alleys, service areas, and base line; and a four-lane highway has dividing lines and other markings, such as oil spills and tire skids. Figure 14–15 illustrates the display of surfaces modeled with texture and patterns.

Intensity values furnished by a shading model can be adjusted to accommodate surface texture by altering the surface normal so that it is a function of position over the surface. If we allow the surface normal to vary randomly, we can obtain an irregularly textured surface such as that of a raisin. A repeating function can be used to model a more regular surface, such as a sculptured carpet that contains a repeated texture pattern. An irregular surface can also be modeled by dividing the surface into a collection of small, randomly oriented surfaces. In addition, we could allow the coefficient of reflection to vary with position so as to obtain greater variations in intensity.

FIGURE 14–15
Combining surface patterns
and textures with an intensity
model. Courtesy Robert Abel &
Associates.

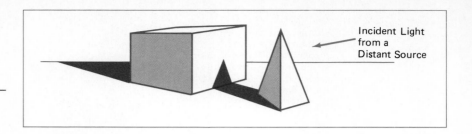

FIGURE 14–16
Objects modeled with
shadows.

Texture-mapping methods are also used to model objects. Patterns can be applied to surfaces of three-dimensional objects with methods similar to those for applying patterns to two-dimensional objects. A shading pattern is defined in an array, and the array is mapped onto an object at a designated position. The array pattern can be treated as a plane surface, and the position and orientation of the pattern specified relative to the object to contain the texture pattern. This is accomplished with commands in a graphics package to set the pattern reference point and two vectors defining the orientation of the array plane, such as the x-axis and y-axis directions of the array. The difference between two-dimensional and three-dimensional objects is that now the pattern must be wrapped around the three-dimensional object. Pattern planes can be stored and linked to the appropriate object surfaces so that they can be processed by a hidden-surface method along with the object surfaces. Intensity values stored in pattern arrays are used to modify or replace intensity values calculated in the shading model.

Shadows

Hidden-surface methods can be used to locate areas where light sources produce shadows. By applying a hidden-surface method with a light source at the view position, we can determine which surface sections cannot be "seen" from the light source. These are the shadow areas. Once we have determined the shadow areas for all light sources, the shadows could be treated as surface patterns and stored in pattern arrays. Figure 14–16 illustrates the generation of shading patterns for two objects on a table and a distant light source. All shadow areas in this figure are surfaces that are not visible from the position of the light source. An example of a scene modeled with shadows (and surface patterns) is given in Fig. 14–17.

The shadow patterns generated by a hidden-surface method are valid for any selected viewing position, so long as the light source positions are not changed. Surfaces that are visible from the view position are shaded according to the intensity model, with surface patterns and shadow patterns added. Visible surfaces that are not illuminated by a point source have only ambient light intensity applied. Visible surfaces that are illuminated by a point source are shaded by combining the intensity model and the pattern arrays. Projected shadow areas are shaded with the ambient light intensity only.

14–2 Displaying Light Intensities

Values of intensity calculated by a shading model for each surface in a scene must be converted to one of the allowable intensity levels for the particular graphics system in use. Some systems are capable of displaying several intensity levels di-

FIGURE 14–17
A scene modeled with various intensities, surface patterns, and shadows. Courtesy Evans & Sutherland and Rediffusion Simulation.

rectly, while others are capable of only two levels for each pixel (on or off). In the first case, we convert intensities from the shading model into one of the available levels for storage in the refresh buffer. For bilevel systems, we can represent shading intensities with a **halftoning** method that converts the intensity of each point on a surface into a rectangular pixel grid that can display a number of intensity levels. The number of intensity levels that can be displayed with this method depends on how many pixels we include in the grid.

Assigning Intensity Levels

Allowable pixel intensity levels in a system are usually distributed over the range from 0 to 1. The value 0 indicates that a pixel position is off, and the value 1 signifies maximum intensity. All remaining values are spaced over the range 0 to 1 so that the ratio of successive intensities is constant. This method of assigning intensity levels is chosen so that intensity changes on a video screen correspond to the way our eyes perceive changes in intensity. If n intensity levels are to be assigned in this way, with the lowest level (above 0) called I_1 and the highest I_n, we require that

$$\frac{I_2}{I_1} = \frac{I_3}{I_2} = \cdots = \frac{I_n}{I_{n-1}} = r \tag{14-12}$$

The constant ratio r is determined from the values for I_1 and n by expressing I_n in terms of I_1:

$$I_n = r^{n-1} I_1 \tag{14-13}$$

But $I_n = 1$, so

$$r = \left(\frac{1}{I_1}\right)^{1/(n-1)} \tag{14-14}$$

with I_1 chosen as any convenient value near 0. For example, we could set $I_1 = 1/8$ for a system with four intensity levels (above 0). Since $n - 1 = 3$, we have $r = 2$, and the five possible intensity levels for a pixel are assigned the values 0, 1/8, 1/4, 1/2, and 1.

(a)

(b)

The number of intensity levels above zero is usually chosen to be a multiple of 2. A four-level system provides minimum shading capability, and high-quality shading patterns are generated on systems that are capable of from 32 to 256 different intensity levels per pixel.

An intensity value calculated from a shading model is converted to the nearest allowable level, I_k, for the system. If there are very many allowable intensity levels, a binary search could be used to locate the nearest level. Since an intensity value must be converted to a control grid voltage for the video monitor in use, there are several alternatives for storing intensity levels in the refresh buffer. We could store the intensity value I_k, or we could simply store the level number k. Another possibility is to store a value that is directly proportional to the control grid voltage. If a voltage value is not stored in the raster, a lookup table is used to convert the raster entry into a voltage value.

Halftoning

When a graphics output device is capable of displaying only two intensity levels per pixel (on and off), a halftoning method can be used to furnish the intensity variations in a scene. Each intensity position in the original scene is replaced with a rectangular pixel grid. This method is used in printing to reproduce photographs for publication in magazines, newspapers, or books. Figure 14–18 illustrates a photograph reproduced with a halftone technique.

A graphics package employing a halftoning technique displays a scene by replacing each position in the original scene with an n by n grid of pixels. The number of pixels that are turned on in each grid is determined by the intensity level of the corresponding position in the scene. Using this technique, we can turn a two-level system into one with the five possible intensitities shown in Fig. 14–19. These

FIGURE 14–19
A 2 by 2 pixel grid can be used to produce five intensity levels for a halftone representation of a scene.

0   1   2   3   4

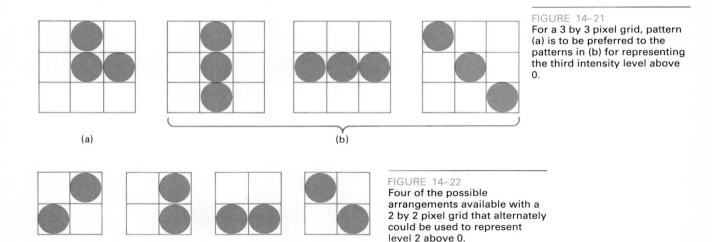

levels are labeled 0 through 4. For any n by n grid, we obtain n^2 intensity levels above zero with this technique. Figure 14–20 illustrates a range of gray shades generated with a halftoning method. Also shown are some color variations obtained by halftoning, where the number of color pixels turned on in the grid controls the color shade to be displayed.

As a general rule, symmetrical pixel arrangements in a grid are to be avoided whenever possible. Otherwise, patterns can be introduced into the halftone representation that were not in the original picture. This is especially important for larger pixel grids. For a 3 by 3 pixel grid, the third intensity level above zero would be better represented by the pattern in Fig. 14–21 (a) than by any of the symmetrical arrangements in Fig. 14–21 (b). The symmetrical patterns in this figure would produce either vertical, horizontal, or diagonal streaks in a halftone representation. One method for avoiding the introduction of such patterns is randomly to select different pixel arrangements for the representation of an intensity level. The four possibilities in Fig. 14–22 can be alternately selected to represent the second intensity level above zero instead of using only a single arrangement for this level. Another method that has been used to minimize extraneous patterns is to form successive grid patterns with the same pixels turned on. That is, if a pixel is on for one grid level, it is on for all higher levels. This scheme was used to set pixel

(a)

(b)

FIGURE 14–21
For a 3 by 3 pixel grid, pattern (a) is to be preferred to the patterns in (b) for representing the third intensity level above 0.

FIGURE 14–22
Four of the possible arrangements available with a 2 by 2 pixel grid that alternately could be used to represent level 2 above 0.

patterns in Fig. 14–19, where the pixel in the lower left corner is on for level 2 and for all subsequent levels.

Halftoning techniques can also be used to increase the number of intensity options on systems that are capable of displaying more than two intensities per pixel. For example, on a system that can display four intensity levels per pixel, we can extend the available intensity levels from four to 13 by employing a halftoning method with 2 by 2 pixel grids. In Fig. 14–19, the four grids above zero now represent several levels each, since each pixel can take three intensity values above zero. Figure 14–23 shows one way to assign the pixel intensities to obtain the 13 distinct levels. Intensity levels for individual pixels are labeled 0 through 3, and the overall levels for the system are labeled 0 through 13.

Normally 2 by 2 or 3 by 3 grids are used in halftoning representations. Although larger grids provide more intensity levels, they tend to introduce new patterns into a scene, and the overall resolution of the output is reduced. A video monitor with a resolution of 1024 by 1024 would be reduced to 512 by 512 when 2 by 2 grids are used, while 4 by 4 grids reduce the resolution to 256 by 256.

Since the use of pixel grids reduces resolution, halftoning methods are more easily applied when the resolution of the original scene is less than that of the output device. When the resolution of the scene is equal to or greater than that of the output device, intensity areas of the scene can be mapped into the pixel grid. A simple method for accomplishing this is to divide the scene into enough rectangular areas to correspond to the pixel grid resolution. The average intensity in each area is then mapped into one of the allowable intensity levels.

Dithering techniques are used with halftoning methods to smooth the edges of displayed objects. We can accomplish this by adding a **dither intensity,** or **dither noise,** to the calculated intensity of points. The amount of dither noise added to the intensity can be determined with a random process or with a calculation based on the coordinate position of the point. Adding a dither value to calculated intensities tends to break up the contours of objects, and the overall appearance of a scene is improved.

Another way to apply a dithering method is to compare the intensity of a point in a scene to a dither value. The corresponding pixel on the output device is turned on if the intensity is greater than the dither value. As with dither noise, these dither values can be generated using a random process, or they can depend on the coordinates of the point. As an example of this approach, suppose 2 by 2 pixel grids are to be used in the halftone process. We can define a dither matrix as

$$D = \begin{bmatrix} 3 & 1 \\ 0 & 2 \end{bmatrix}$$

(14–15)

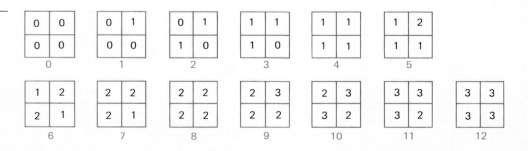

FIGURE 14–23
Intensity levels 0 through 12 obtained with halftoning techniques using 2 by 2 pixel grids on a four-level system.

The sequence of integers 0 through 3 has been assigned to matrix positions in D in the same order that pixels were added to the 2 by 2 grid in Fig. 14–19. Suppose (x, y) is the coordinate position of a point in a scene with intensity I. We calculate a position (i, j) in the dither matrix as

$$i = x \bmod 2, \qquad j = y \bmod 2 \qquad (14-16)$$

If $I > D(i, j)$, we turn on the pixel at position (x, y). Otherwise it is not turned on. Higher-order dither matrices can be used to display greater intensity ranges.

14–3 Surface-Shading Methods

An intensity model can be applied to surface shading in various ways, depending on the type of surface and the requirements of a particular application. Objects with plane surfaces can sometimes be shaded realistically with a single intensity for each surface. For a curved surface, we could apply the intensity model to each point on the surface. This can produce a highly realistic display, but it is a time-consuming process. If we wish to speed up the intensity calculations, we could represent a curved surface as a set of polygon planes and apply the shading model to each plane. Each of these polygon surfaces could then be shaded with constant intensity, or we could vary the shading with interpolated intensity values.

Constant Intensity

Under certain conditions, an object with plane surfaces can be shaded realistically using constant surface intensities. In the case where a surface is exposed only to ambient light and no surface designs, textures, or shadows are to be applied, constant shading generates an accurate representation of the surface. For a surface illuminated by a point source, the shading model produces a constant surface intensity, provided that the point source and the view reference point are sufficiently far from the surface. When the point source is far from the surface, there is no change in the direction to the source ($N \cdot L$ is constant). Similarly, the direction to a distant viewing point will not change over a surface, so $V \cdot R$ is constant.

A curved surface that is represented as a set of plane surfaces can be shaded with constant surface intensities if the planes subdividing the surface are made small enough. This can generate a reasonably good display in many cases, especially when surface curvature changes gradually and light sources and view position are far from the surface. Figure 14–24 shows an object modeled with constant shading. With this method, the intensity is calculated at an interior point of each plane, and the entire surface is shaded with the calculated intensity. When the orientation between adjacent planes changes abruptly, the difference in surface intensities can produce a harsh and unrealistic effect. We can smooth the intensity discontinuities in these cases by varying the intensity over each surface according to some interpolation scheme.

Gouraud Shading

This **intensity interpolation** scheme, developed by Gouraud, removes intensity discontinuities between adjacent planes of a surface representation by linearly varying the intensity over each plane so that intensity values match at the plane boundaries. In this method, intensity values along each scan line passing through a

FIGURE 14–24
Solid modeling using constant
shading over polygon surfaces.
Courtesy Megatek Corp.

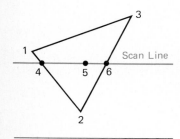

FIGURE 14–25
For interpolated shading, the
intensity value at point 4 is
determined from intensity
values at points 1 and 2,
intensity at point 6 is
determined from values at
points 2 and 3, and intensities
at other points (such as 5)
along the scan line are
interpolated between values at
points 4 and 6.

FIGURE 14–26
The normal vector at the
common vertex point P is
calculated as the average of the
surface normals for each plane:
$N_p = (N_1 + N_2 + N_3) / 3.$

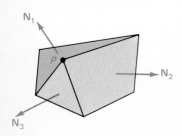

surface are interpolated from the intensities at the intersection points with the surface.

Figure 14–25 demonstrates this interpolation scheme. Intensity values at the
vertices of each polygon are determined from a shading model. All other intensities
for the surface are then calculated from these values. In Fig. 14–25, the intensity
at the left intersection of the scan line with the polygon (point 4) is interpolated
from the intensities at vertices 1 and 2 with the calculation

$$I_4 = I_1 \frac{y_4 - y_2}{y_1 - y_2} + I_2 \frac{y_1 - y_4}{y_1 - y_2} \tag{14-17}$$

For this example, the intensity at point 4 has a value that is closer to the intensity
of point 1 than that of point 2. Similarly, intensity at the right intersection of the
scan line (point 6) is interpolated from intensity values at vertices 2 and 3. Once
these bounding intensities are established for a scan line, an interior point (such as
point 5) is interpolated from the bounding intensities at points 4 and 6 with the
calculation

$$I_5 = I_4 \frac{x_6 - x_5}{x_6 - x_4} + I_6 \frac{x_5 - x_4}{x_6 - x_4} \tag{14-18}$$

This process is repeated for each scan line passing through the polygon.

With this interpolation method, surface normals must first be approximated
at each vertex of a polygon. This is accomplished by averaging the surface normals
for each polygon containing the vertex point, as shown in Fig. 14–26. These vertex
normal vectors are then used in the shading model to generate the vertex intensity
values. When color is used to shade a surface, the intensity of each color component is calculated at the vertices. The method can be combined with a hidden-
surface algorithm to fill in the visible polygons along each scan line. An example of
an object shaded with the Gouraud method appears in Fig. 14–27.

Gouraud shading removes the intensity discontinuities associated with the
constant shading model, but it has some other deficiencies. Highlights on the surface are sometimes displayed with anomalous shapes, and the linear intensity interpolation can cause bright or dark intensity streaks, called Mach bands, to appear
on the surface. These effects can be reduced by dividing the surface into a greater

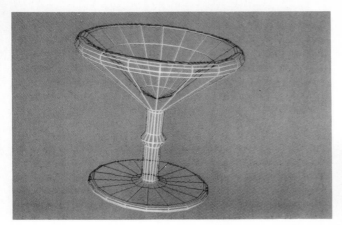

(a)

FIGURE 14–27
An example of Gouraud shading. The object is divided into the planes shown in (a) and shaded with the intensity interpolation method (b). Courtesy Megatek Corp.

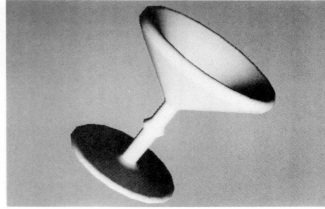

(b)

number of polygon faces or by using other methods, such as Phong shading, that require more calculations.

Phong Shading

Improvements in the Gouraud shading patterns can be accomplished by approximating the surface normal at each point along a scan line, then calculating the intensity using the approximated normal vector at that point. This method, developed by Phong Bui Tuong, is also referred to as a **normal-vector interpolation** scheme. It displays more realistic highlights on a surface and greatly reduces the Mach-band effect.

Phong shading first interpolates the normal vectors at the bounding points along a scan line. For the polygon shown in Fig. 14–25, the normal vector at point 4 is interpolated from the calculated normals at points 1 and 2. The normal at point 6 is calculated similarly from the normals at points 2 and 3. All interior points along the scan line are then assigned normal vectors that are interpolated from those at points 4 and 6. Intensity calculations using an approximated normal vector at each point along the scan line produce more accurate results than the direct interpolation of intensities from the vertex intensity values. However, the trade-off is that Phong shading requires considerably more calculations. The automobile shown in Fig. 14–14 is an example of the application of Phong shading.

Ray-Tracing Algorithms

Since an infinite number of intensity points could be generated over the various surfaces in a scene, an effective method for determining the specular intensities at visible surface positions is to trace rays backward from the viewing position

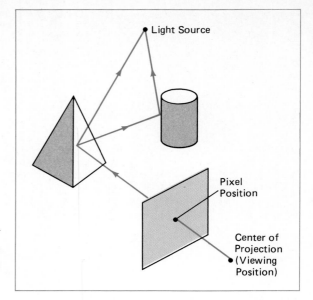

FIGURE 14–28
Tracing a ray from the center of
projection to a light source with
multiple reflections from the
objects in a scene.

to the light source. This technique, referred to as **ray tracing,** is illustrated in Fig.
14–28.

Starting from the viewing position (or center of projection), the ray passing
through each pixel in the view plane is traced back to a surface in the three-dimensional scene. The ray is then reflected backward from this surface to determine
whether it came from another surface or from a point source. This backward tracing
continues until the ray ends at a light source or passes out of the scene. Each pixel
is processed in this way, and the number of rays that must be traced is equal to
the number of pixels to be displayed.

When transparent objects are encountered in the ray-tracing process, the intensity contributions from both specular reflection and specular refraction are taken
into account. At a transparent surface, the ray is divided into the two components
shown in Fig. 14–29. Each ray is then traced individually to its source.

After a ray has been processed to determine all specular intensity contributions, the intensity of the corresponding pixel is set. Ray tracing requires

FIGURE 14–29
Ray tracing follows both
reflected and refracted paths at
the surface of a transparent
object.

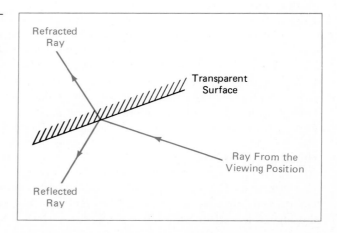

(a)   (b)

FIGURE 14–30
Scenes generated with ray-
tracing methods, using (a) a
pinhole camera at the viewing
position and (b) a finite-
aperture camera. Courtesy
Gould Inc., Imaging & Graphics
Division and Michael Potmesil,
Rensselaer Polytechnic
Institute.

considerable computation, but it produces highly realistic results. Figure 14–30 shows two views of a scene generated with ray-tracing techniques. The view in Fig. 14–30 (a) was generated with rays emanating from the center of projection (a single point), while Fig. 14–30 (b) simulates a camera with a lens of finite area. That is, instead of projecting rays back from a single viewing point (a pinhole camera), we suppose that a camera with a finite lens aperture is at the viewing position. By including lens parameters in the viewing model, the projected view can be focused at any plane in the scene. This provides a more realistic projection, as in Fig. 14–30 (b), where the background and near foreground are not focused as sharply as the surface of the vase.

Octree Methods

The application of an intensity model to scenes represented in octrees requires some special considerations. Each volume element, or voxel, in a scene contains information about the type of material at that position, but no information about surface orientations is explicitly stored in the octree. However, we have seen that intensity calculations depend on the surface normals. To include surface shading, we therefore need to modify the procedures that map an octree onto a quadtree for display.

Surface orientation information can be extracted from the octree by examining the regions around each voxel as it is processed for display. If some of the neighboring regions are void, the voxel is part of a surface. Also, the surface normal must have some component in the direction of the void region. An algorithm for testing regions around a voxel can start with the front of the octree (as discussed previously) and examine the four neighboring regions (left, right, top, and bottom) shown in Fig. 14–31. The data stored in the octree for the voxel and its four neighbors are passed to an intensity illumination procedure that first checks to see whether the voxel is part of a surface. If it is, surface normals are determined, and the voxel illumination is calculated from an intensity model.

Assuming that all octree data elements are homogeneous, the intensity for a visible, nonvoid voxel is stored in the quadtree for display. This intensity is calculated by the intensity illumination function using information about the regions

FIGURE 14–31
A voxel and four neighboring
regions in an octree.

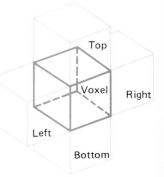

around the voxel. Transparent materials are handled by superimposing intensities for transparent voxels and background voxels in the same quadtree position. A refraction coefficient, r, with a value between 0 and 1, is used in Eq. 14–11 to combine the intensity values of the transparent and background voxels.

Fractal Surfaces

As we have seen, fractal surfaces are generated by nonrandom or random iteration processes that are used to model objects with irregular features, such as clouds and terrain. To determine intensity settings for the various points over the surface of a fractal object, we need some method for determining surface normals. One method for accomplishing this is to represent a fractal surface as a number of small planes, with a surface normal set for each plane.

In general, however, fractal representations contain infinite detail at each surface point of the object. This means that we cannot precisely define a surface normal at any point. For these representations, approximate surface normals can be calculated using the coordinate differences between neighboring points on the surface. Figure 14–32 shows the relationship between a point P at position (x, y, z) and a neighboring point P' at (x', y', z') for a cross-sectional view in the yz plane. We assume that the component N_{yz} of a surface normal at P makes an angle α with the surface at that point. The tangent of this angle can be calculated as the ratio of the z-coordinate and y-coordinate differences of the two points:

$$\tan\alpha = \frac{\Delta z}{\Delta y} \qquad (14\text{–}19)$$

where $\Delta z = z - z'$ and $\Delta y = y - y'$. A similar calculation determines the other component N_{xz} of the normal vector. This determines a normal vector at P relative to point P'. We can then repeat this process for the other points around P and average the various normal-vector directions to obtain the final approximation for the normal at P. Once the approximate surface normal has been established for the points over the fractal surface, the intensity model is applied.

Antialiasing Surface Boundaries

We have seen that lines and polygon edges can be smoothed with antialiasing techniques that either adjust pixel positions (pixel phasing) or set the pixel intensities according to the percent of pixel-area coverage at each point. Similar antialiasing methods can be applied to smooth out the bondaries in a scene containing a collection of surfaces.

FIGURE 14–32
Approximating the fractal
surface normal at position *P* by
examining the position of
neighboring surface points.

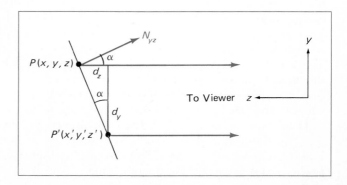

When multiple objects are to be displayed in a scene, we can expect that some pixel areas will be overlapped by two or more surface boundaries, as in Fig. 14–33. The intensity to be assigned to such pixels is determined by sampling the intensities of all such overlapping surfaces. Contributions from the individual overlapping surfaces can be combined according to the percent of the pixel area that each surface covers. Any of the methods discussed in Chapter 4 for estimating pixel coverage could be used to determine the percent of intensity contribution from each overlapping surface.

A method that provides better estimates of interior pixel areas is to treat the rectangular area of a pixel as a small window. Polygons are then clipped against each of these windows, and the area of a polygon inside the pixel window is calculated. This antialiasing technique could also be applied to surfaces with curved boundaries.

Some other approaches to antialiasing have been used to take advantage of the capabilities of a particular intensity method, such as ray tracing or the shading of fractal surfaces. In ray tracing, instead of projecting each ray through the center of the corresponding pixel to be displayed, rays can be projected through the corners of the pixel (Fig. 14–34). The average of the four intensities obtained in this way is assigned to the pixel. This averaging method antialiases the pixels along surface boundaries. When a pixel area projects onto a part of the scene containing a great deal of detail, the area can be further subdivided so that more projection rays are used in the averaging process.

With fractal objects, each cube used to represent a three-dimensional surface can be treated as slightly transparent. This allows cubes behind illuminated cubes to receive some incident light. Intensities over the fractal surface can then have contributions from more than one cube, and the stairstep appearance of boundaries can be reduced, especially when the incident direction of light is parallel to one surface of the cubes.

14–4 Color Models

Our discussions of color up to this point have concentrated on the mechanisms for generating color displays with combinations of red, green, and blue light. This model is helpful in understanding how color is represented on a video monitor, but several other color models are useful as well in graphics applications. Some models are used to describe color output on printers and plotters, and other models provide a more intuitive color-parameter interface for the user.

A **color model** is a method for explaining the properties or behavior of color within some particular context. No single color model has yet been devised that explains all aspects of color, so we make use of different models to help describe the different perceived characteristics of color.

Properties of Light

What we perceive as "light," or different colors, is a narrow frequency band within the electromagnetic spectrum. A few of the other frequency bands within this spectrum are called radio waves, microwaves, infrared waves, and X-rays. Figure 14–35 shows the approximate frequency ranges for some of the electromagnetic bands.

Each frequency value within the visible band corresponds to a distinct color. At the low-frequency end is a red color (4.3×10^{14} hertz), and the highest fre-

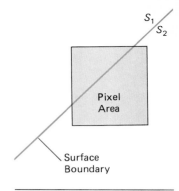

FIGURE 14–33
A boundary line between two surfaces passing through a pixel area. Surface S_1 covers about one-third of the pixel area, and surface S_2 covers the other two-thirds.

FIGURE 14–34
Rays projected through the corners of a pixel area provide four intensities that are averaged to a value for that pixel.

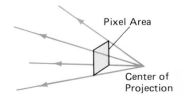

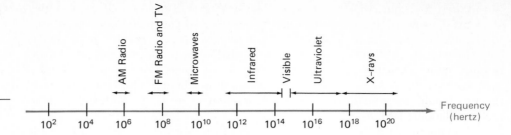

FIGURE 14-35
Electromagnetic spectrum.

quency we can see is a violet color (7.5 × 10^{14} hertz). Between these frequency limits, the human eye can distinguish nearly 400,000 different colors. These colors range from the reds through orange and yellow at the low frequency end to greens, blues, and violet at the high end.

Since light is an electromagnetic wave, we can describe the various colors in terms of either the frequency or the wavelength of the wave. The two quantities are inversely proportional to each other, with the proportionality constant as the speed of light in the material in which the light is traveling. Light at the red end of the spectrum has a wavelength of approximately 700 nanometers (nm), and the wavelength of the violet light at the other end of the spectrum is about 400 nm.

A light source such as the sun or a light bulb emits all frequencies within the visible range to produce white light. When white light is incident upon an object, some frequencies are reflected and some are absorbed by the object. The combination of frequencies present in the reflected light determines what we perceive as the color of the object. If low frequencies are predominant in the reflected light, the object is described as red. In this case, we say the perceived light has a **dominant frequency** (or **dominant wavelength**) at the red end of the spectrum. The dominant frequency is also called the **color,** or **hue,** of the light.

Other properties besides frequency are useful for describing the characteristics of light. When we view a source of light, our eyes respond to the color (or dominant frequency) and two other basic sensations. One of these we call the **luminance,** or **brightness** of the light. Brightness is related to the intensity of the light: The higher the intensity (or energy), the brighter the source appears. The other characteristic is the **purity,** or **saturation,** of the light. Purity describes how washed out or how "pure" the color of the light appears. Pastels and pale colors are described as less pure. These three characteristics—dominant frequency, brightness, and purity—are commonly used to describe the different properties we perceive in a source of light. The term **chromaticity** is used to refer collectively to the two properties describing the color characteristics, purity and dominant frequency.

The energy emitted by a white-light source has a distribution over the visible frequencies as shown in Fig. 14–36. Each frequency component within the range from red to violet contributes more or less equally to the total energy, and the color of the source is described as white. When a dominant frequency is present, the energy distribution for the source takes a form such as that in Fig. 14–37. We would now describe the light as having the color corresponding to the dominant frequency. The energy of the dominant light component is labeled as E_D in this figure, and the contributions from the other frequencies produce white light of intensity E_W. The brightness of the source can be calculated as the area under the curve, giving the total energy emitted. Purity depends on the difference between

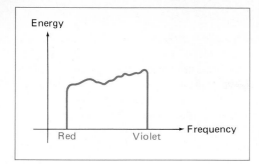

FIGURE 14–36
Energy distribution of a white-light source.

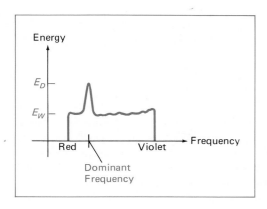

FIGURE 14–37
Energy distribution of a light source with a dominant frequency.

E_D and E_W. The larger the energy E_D of the dominant frequency compared to the white light component E_W, the more pure the light. We have a purity of 100 percent when $E_W = 0$ and a purity of 0 percent when $E_W = E_D$.

When we view light that has been formed by a combination of two or more sources, we see a resultant light with characteristics determined by the original sources. Two different-color light sources with suitably chosen intensities can be used to produce a range of other colors. If the two color sources combine to produce white light, they are referred to as **complementary colors.** Examples of complementary color pairs are red and cyan, green and magenta, and blue and yellow. With a judicious choice of two or more starting colors, we can form a wide range of other colors. Typically, color models that are used to describe combinations of light in terms of dominant frequency (the hue or color) use three colors to obtain a reasonably wide range of colors, called the **color gamut** for that model. The two or three colors used to describe other colors in such a color model are referred to as **primary colors.**

No unique set of primary colors exists that will describe all possible frequencies within the visible spectrum. More colors could be added to the list of primaries to widen the color gamut, but it would still require an infinite number of primaries to include all possible colors. However, three primaries are sufficient for most purposes, and colors not in the color gamut for a specified set of primaries can still be described by extended methods. For example, if a certain color cannot be obtained from three given primaries, we can mix one or two of the primaries with that color to obtain a match with the remaining primaries. In this extended sense, a set of primary colors can be considered to describe all colors.

An international standard for primary colors was established in 1931 by the International Commission on Illumination (Commission Internationale de l'Éclairage, also called the CIE). The purpose of this standard is to allow all other colors to be defined as the weighted sum of the three primaries. Since no three colors in the visible spectrum are able to accomplish this, the standard primary "colors" established by the CIE do not correspond to any real colors. The fact that these primaries represent imaginary colors is not really important, since any real color is only defined by the amounts of each primary needed mathematically to produce that color. Each primary in this international standard is defined by its energy distribution curve.

If we let A, B, and C represent the amounts of the standard primaries needed to match a given color within the visible spectrum, we can express the components of the color with the calculations

$$x = \frac{A}{A + B + C}, \quad y = \frac{B}{A + B + C}, \quad z = \frac{C}{A + B + C} \quad (14\text{--}20)$$

Since $x + y + z = 1$, any two of these three quantities are sufficient to define a color. This makes it possible for us to represent all colors on a two-dimensional diagram. When we plot x and y values for colors in the visible spectrum, we obtain the tongue-shaped curve shown in Fig. 14–38. This curve is called the CIE **chromaticity diagram.** Color points are labeled along the curve according to wavelength in nanometers, from the red end to the violet end of the spectrum. Point C in the diagram corresponds to the white-light position. Actually, this point is plotted for a white-light source known as **illuminant C,** which is used as a standard approximation for "average daylight."

The curve in Fig. 14–38 is called the chromaticity diagram because it provides a means for quantitatively defining purity and dominant wavelength. For any color point, such as C_1 in Fig. 14–39, we define the purity of the color as the relative distance of the color point from the white-light point C along the straight line joining C to the curve (representing colors in the visible spectrum). Color C_1 in this figure is about 25 percent pure, since it is situated at about one-fourth the

FIGURE 14–39
Defining purity and dominant wavelength on the chromaticity diagram.

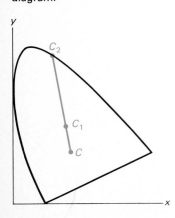

FIGURE 14–38
The CIE chromaticity diagram, with color positions within the visible spectrum labeled in wavelength units (nm).

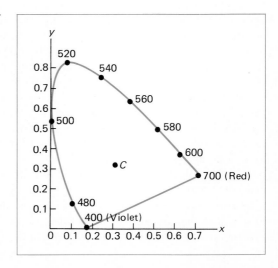

total distance from C to C_2. Dominant wavelength of any color is defined as the wavelength on the spectral curve that intersects the line joining C and that color point. For color point C_1, the dominant wavelength is at C_2, since the line joining C and C_1 intersects the spectral curve at point C_2.

Complementary colors are represented by the two endpoints of a line passing through point C, as in Fig. 14–40. When the two colors C_1 and C_2 are combined in proper proportions, white light results.

Color gamuts are represented on the chromaticity diagram with lines joining the color points defining the gamut. All colors along the line joining points C_1 and C_2 in Fig. 14–41 can be obtained by mixing amounts of the colors represented by the endpoints. If a greater proportion of C_1 is used, the resultant color is closer to C_1 than to C_2. The color gamut for the three points C_3, C_4, and C_5 is the shaded triangle formed with vertices for the three colors. These three colors can be used to generate any color within the triangle, but no points outside the triangle could be generated with these colors. Thus the chromaticity diagram helps us understand why no set of three primaries can be used to generate all colors, since no triangle within the diagram can encompass all colors. Such triangular color gamuts are typically defined on chromaticity diagrams for video monitors and hard-copy devices. This provides a convenient means for comparing the color gamuts for the various devices.

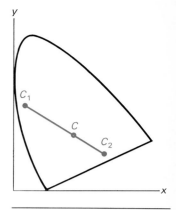

FIGURE 14–40
Representing complementary colors on the chromaticity diagram.

Intuitive Color Concepts

An artist creates a color painting by mixing color pigments with white and black pigments to form the various shades, tints, and tones in the scene. Starting with the pigment for a "pure color" (or "pure hue"), a black pigment is added to produce different **shades** of that color. The more black pigment the artist adds, the darker the shade produced. Similarly, different **tints** of the color are obtained by adding a white pigment to the original color, making it lighter as more white is added. **Tones** of the color are produced by adding both black and white pigments.

To many, these color concepts are more intuitive than describing a color as a set of three numbers that give the relative proportions of the primary colors. It is generally much easier to think of making a color lighter by adding white and making a darker color by adding black. Therefore, graphics packages providing color palettes to a user often employ two or more color models. One model provides an intuitive color interface for the user, and the others describe the color components for the output devices.

RGB Color Model

Our eyes perceive color through the stimulation of three visual pigments in the cones of the retina. These visual pigments have a peak sensitivity at wavelengths of about 630 nm (red), 530 nm (green), and 450 nm (blue). By comparing intensities in a light source, we perceive the color of the light. This tri-stimulus theory of vision is the basis for displaying color output on a video monitor using the three color primaries red, green, and blue, referred to as the RGB color model.

We can represent this model with the unit cube defined on R, G, and B axes, as shown in Fig. 14–42. The origin represents black, and the vertex with coordinates (1, 1, 1) is white. Vertices of the cube on the axes represent the primary colors, and the remaining vertices represent the complementary color for each of the primary colors.

FIGURE 14–41
Color gamuts defined on the chromaticity diagram for a two-color and a three-color system of primaries.

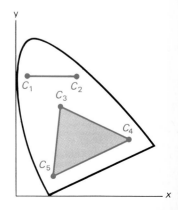

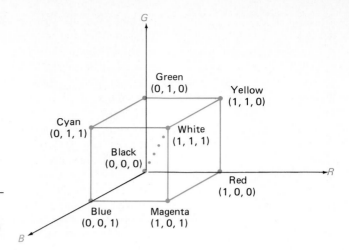

FIGURE 14–42

The RGB color model, defining
colors with an additive process
within a unit cube.

This color scheme is an additive model: Intensities of the primary colors are
added to produce other colors. Each color point within the bounds of the cube can
be represented as the triple (R, G, B), where values for R, G, and B are assigned
in the range from 0 to 1. The magenta vertex is obtained by adding red and blue
to produce the triple $(1, 0, 1)$, and white at $(1, 1, 1)$ is the sum of the red, green,
and blue vertices. Shades of gray are represented along the main diagonal of the
cube from the origin (black) to the white vertex. Each point along this diagonal has
an equal contribution from each primary color, so that a gray shade halfway between black and white is represented as $(0.5, 0.5, 0.5)$. The color graduations along
the front and top planes of the RGB cube are illustrated in Fig. 14–43.

When only a few color choices are available on an RGB system, the color
options can be expanded by using halftoning methods. This approach with colors is
similar to that for developing gray patterns, but now we can set the individual RGB
color dots within each pixel as well. For example, suppose we have a bilevel system, so that the intensity of each color dot within a pixel is either on or off. Without
halftoning, we have eight color combinations. But if we expand each position in a

FIGURE 14–43

Three planes of the RGB color
cube defined in Fig. 14–42.
Shown are the front two planes
(red-magenta-white-yellow and
blue-cyan-white-magenta) and
the top plane (green-yellow-
white-cyan). Courtesy Diablo
Systems Inc., A Xerox
Company.

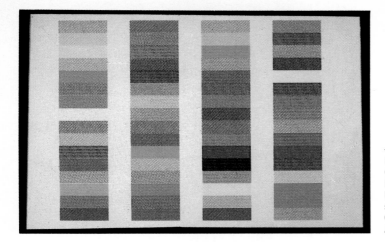

FIGURE 14–44
Color patterns obtained with a halftoning technique on an RGB system with two intensity settings for each RGB color dot. Courtesy Diablo Systems Inc., A Xerox Company.

scene to a 2 by 2 pixel grid, we now have five possible settings for the red color dots within the 2 by 2 grid, five possible settings for the green dots, and five for the blue dots. This gives us a total of 125 different color combinations. An example of the color patterns possible with this method is shown in Fig. 14–44. This color technique is commonly referred to as dithering, although the term is also applied to the halftoning methods previously discussed for extending the intensity levels of a scene with resolution equal to that of the output device.

CMY Color Model

A color model defined with the primary colors cyan, magenta, and yellow (CMY) is useful for describing color output to hard-copy devices. Unlike video monitors, which produce a color pattern by combining light from the screen phosphors, hard-copy devices such as plotters produce a color picture by coating a paper with color pigments. We see the colors by reflected light, a subtractive process.

As we have noted, cyan can be formed by adding green and blue light. Therefore, when white light is reflected from cyan-colored ink, the reflected light must have no red component. That is, red light is absorbed, or subtracted, by the ink. Similarly, magenta ink subtracts the green component from incident light, and yellow subtracts the blue component. A unit cube representation for the CMY model is illustrated in Fig. 14–45.

In the CMY model, the point (1, 1, 1) represents black, because all components of the incident light are subtracted. The origin represents white light. Equal amounts of each of the primary colors produce grays, along the main diagonal of the cube. A combination of cyan and magenta ink produces blue light, because the red and green components of the incident light are absorbed. Other color combinations are obtained by a similar subtractive process.

The printing process often used with the CMY model generates a color point with a collection of four ink dots, somewhat as an RGB monitor uses a collection of three phosphor dots. One dot is used for each of the primary colors (cyan, magenta, and yellow), and one dot is black. A black dot is included because the combination of cyan, magenta, and yellow inks typically produce dark gray instead of black. Some plotters produce different color combinations by spraying the ink for the three primary colors over each other and allowing them to mix before they dry.

FIGURE 14–45
The CMY color model, defining colors with a subtractive process inside a unit cube.

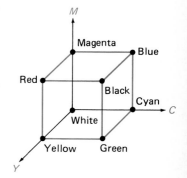

Conversion Between RGB and CMY Models

When an RGB representation is to be converted to the CMY model, each RGB primary value can be subtracted from the RGB representation (1, 1, 1) for white light to give the corresponding CMY components. We write this in a vector form as

$$\begin{bmatrix} C \\ M \\ Y \end{bmatrix} = \begin{bmatrix} W \\ W \\ W \end{bmatrix} - \begin{bmatrix} R \\ G \\ B \end{bmatrix} \qquad (14\text{--}21)$$

For example, $C = (1, 1, 1) - R$, and the other primaries are converted similarly.

Conversion from CMY to RGB can be performed by subtracting CMY components from the CMY representation (1, 1, 1) for black. In vector form, this is expressed as

$$\begin{bmatrix} R \\ G \\ B \end{bmatrix} = \begin{bmatrix} B \\ B \\ B \end{bmatrix} - \begin{bmatrix} C \\ M \\ Y \end{bmatrix} \qquad (14\text{--}22)$$

For the red component, we have $R = (1, 1, 1) - C$, with similar calculations for the other primaries.

HSV Color Model

This model employs color descriptions that have a more intuitive appeal to a user. Instead of choosing colors according to their RGB components, users can specify a hue (or color) and the amount of white and black to add to the color to obtain different shades, tints, and tones. The three color parameters in this model that are presented to a user are called *hue*, *saturation*, and *value* (HSV).

The three-dimensional representation of the HSV model is derived from the RGB cube. If we imagine viewing the cube along the diagonal from the white vertex to the origin (black), we see an outline of the cube that has the hexagon shape shown in Fig. 14–46. The boundary of the hexagon represents the various hues, and it is used as the top of the HSV hexcone (Fig. 14–47). In the hexcone, saturation is measured along a horizontal axis, and value is along a vertical axis through the center of the hexcone.

Hue is represented as an angle about the vertical axis, ranging from 0° at red through 360°. Vertices of the hexagon are separated by 60° intervals. Yellow is at 60°, green at 120°, and cyan opposite red at $H = 180°$. Complementary colors are 180° apart.

Saturation S varies from 0 to 1. It is represented in this model as the ratio of the purity of a selected hue to its maximum purity at $S = 1$. A selected hue is said to be one-quarter pure at the value $S = 0.25$. At $S = 0$, we have the gray scale.

Value V varies from 0 at the apex of the hexcone to 1 at the top. The apex represents black. At the top of the hexcone, colors have their maximum intensity. When $V = 1$ and $S = 1$, we have the "pure" hues. White is the point at $V = 1$ and $S = 0$.

This is a more intuitive model for most users. Starting with a selection for a pure hue, which specifies the hue angle H and sets $V = S = 1$, the user describes the color desired in terms of adding either white or black to the pure hue. Adding black decreases the setting for V while S is held constant. To get a dark blue, V could be set to 0.4 with $S = 1$ and $H = 240°$. Similarly, when white is to be added

FIGURE 14–46
When the RGB color cube (a) is viewed along the diagonal from white to black, a hexagon outline (b) is seen.

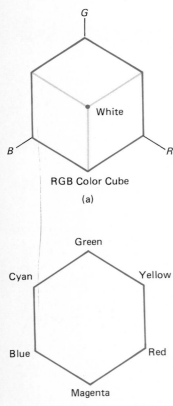

RGB Color Cube

(a)

Color Hexagon

(b)

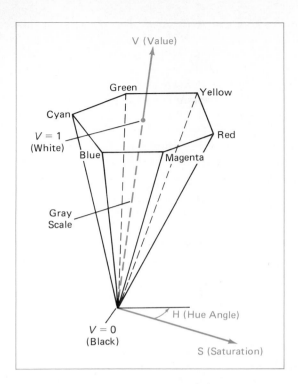

FIGURE 14-47
The HSV hexcone.

to the hue selected, parameter S is decreased while keeping V constant. A light blue could be designated with $S = 0.3$ while $V = 1$ and $H = 240°$. If a user wants some black and some white added, both V and S are decreased. An interface for this model typically presents the HSV parameter choices in a color palette.

Color concepts associated with the terms *shades*, *tints*, and *tones* are represented in a cross-sectional plane of the HSV hexcone (Fig. 14–48). Adding black to a pure hue decreases V down the side of the hexcone. Thus various shades are represented with values $S = 1$ and $0 \leq V \leq 1$. Adding white to a pure tone produces different tints across the top plane of the hexcone, where parameter values are $V = 1$ and $0 \leq S \leq 1$. Various tones are specified by adding both black and white, producing color points within the triangular cross-sectional area of the hexcone.

The human eye can distinguish about 128 different hues and about 130 different tints (saturation levels). For each of these, a number of shades (value settings) can be detected, depending on the hue selected. About 23 shades are discernible with yellow colors, and about 16 different shades can be seen at the blue end of the spectrum. This means that we can distinguish about $128 \times 130 \times 23 = 382,720$ different colors. For most graphics applications, 128 hues, 8 saturation levels, and 15 value settings are sufficient. With this range of parameters in the HSV color model, 16,384 colors would be available to a user, and the system would need 14 bits of color storage per pixel. Color lookup tables could be used to reduce the storage requirements per pixel and to increase the number of available colors.

Conversion Between HSV and RGB Models

If HSV color parameters are made available to a user of a graphics package, these parameters are transformed to the RGB settings needed for the color monitor. To determine the operations needed in this transformation, we first consider

FIGURE 14-48
Cross section of the HSV hexcone, showing the regions representing shades, tints, and tones.

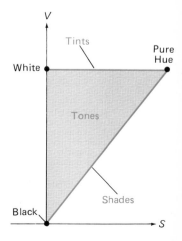

how the HSV hexcone can be derived from the RGB cube. The diagonal of this cube from black (the origin) to white corresponds to the V axis of the hexcone. Also, each subcube of the RGB cube corresponds to a hexagonal cross-sectional area of the hexcone. At any cross section, all sides of the hexagon and all radial lines from the V axis to any vertex have the value V. For any set of RGB values, V is equal to the maximum value in this set. The HSV point corresponding to the set of RGB values lies on the hexagonal cross section at value V. Parameter S is then determined as the relative distance of this point from the V axis. Parameter H is determined by calculating the relative position of the point within each sextant of the hexagon. An algorithm for mapping any set of RGB values into the corresponding HSV values is given in the following procedure.

```
{Converts a color specification given in rgb parameters to the
 equivalent specification in hsv parameters. As input, r, g, and
 b are in the range from 0 to 1}
procedure convert_rgb_to_hsv (r, g, b : real; var h, s, v : real);
  var  m, rl, gl, bl : real;
  begin
    v := max(r, g, b);                      {set v}
    m := min(r, g, b);
    if v <> 0 then s := (v - m) / v
      else s = 0;                           {set s}
    if s <> 0 then begin
      rl := (v - r) / (v - m);    {distance of color from red}
      gl := (v - g) / (v - m);    {distance of color from green}
      bl := (v - b) / (v - m);    {distance of color from blue}
      if v = r then if m = g then h := 5 + bl
                        else h := 1 - gl;
      if v = g then if m = b then h := 1 + rl
                        else h := 3 - bl;
      else if m = r then h := 3 + gl
                 else h := 5 - rl;
      h := h * 60                  {convert to degrees}
    end   {if s <> 0}
  else
     {return h as undefined}
  end; {convert_rgb_to_hsv}
```

We obtain the transformation from HSV parameters to RGB parameters by determining the inverse of the equations in the above procedure. These inverse operations are carried out for each sextant of the hexcone. The resulting transformation equations are summarized in the following algorithm.

```
{Converts a color specification given in hsv parameters to
 the equivalent specification in rgb parameters. As input,
 h is in the range 0 to 360, s and v are in the range 0 to 1.}
procedure convert_hsv_to_rgb (h, s, v : real; var r, g, b : real);
  var  pl, p2, p3 : real;
  begin
    if h = 360 then h := 0;
    h := h / 60;            {convert h to be in [0,6)}
    i := floor(h);          {i = greatest integer <= h}
    f := h - i;             {f = fractional part of h}
    pl := v * (1 - s);
    p2 := v * (1 - (s * f));
    p3 := v * (1 - (s * (1 - f)));
    case i of
```

```
0 : begin
        r := v;   g := p3;  b := p1 end;
1 : begin
        r := p2;  g := v;   b := p1 end;
2 : begin
        r := p1;  g := v;   b := p3 end;
3 : begin
        r := p1;  g := p2;  b := v   end;
4 : begin
        r := p3;  g := p1;  b := v   end;
5 : begin
        r := v;   g := p1;  b := p2  end
    end   {case}
end;  {convert}
```

HLS Color Model

Another model based on intuitive color parameters is the HLS system used by Tektronix. This model has the double-cone representation shown in Fig. 14–49. The three color parameters in this model are called *hue*, *lightness*, and *saturation* (HLS).

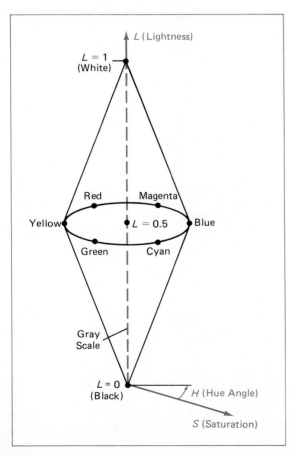

FIGURE 14–49
The HLS double cone.

Hue has the same meaning as in the HSV model. It specifies an angle about the vertical axis that locates a chosen hue. In this model, $H = 0°$ corresponds to blue. The remaining colors are specified around the perimeter of the cone in the same order as in the HSV model. Magenta is at 60°, red is at 120°, and cyan is located at $H = 180°$. Again, complementary colors are 180° apart on the double cone.

The vertical axis in this model is called lightness, L. At $L = 0$, we have black, and white is at $L = 1$. Gray scale is along the L axis, and the "pure hues" lie on the $L = 0.5$ plane.

Saturation parameter S again specifies relative purity of a color. This parameter varies from 0 to 1, and pure hues are those for which $S = 1$ and $L = 0.5$. As S decreases, the hues are said to be less pure. At $S = 0$, we have the gray scale.

This model, like the HSV model, allows a user to think in terms of making a selected hue darker or lighter. A hue is selected with hue angle H, and the desired shade, tint, or tone is obtained by adjusting L and S. Colors are made lighter by increasing L and made darker by decreasing L. When S is decreased, the colors move toward gray.

Color Selection

A graphics package can provide color capabilities to a user in a way that aids the user in making color selections. The color model in the package can allow users freely to select any color combinations, but the system can be designed to help the user to select harmonizing colors. In addition, the designer of a package can follow some basic color rules when designing the color displays that are to be presented to the user.

One method for obtaining a set of coordinating colors is to generate the set from some subspace of a color model. If colors are selected at regular intervals along any straight line within the RGB or CMY cube, for example, we can expect to obtain a set of well-matched colors. Randomly selected hues can be expected to produce harsh and clashing color combinations. Another consideration in color displays is the fact that we perceive colors at different depths. This occurs because our eyes focus on colors according to their frequency. Blues, in particular, tend to recede. Displaying a blue pattern next to a red pattern can cause eye fatigue, since we continually need to refocus when our attention is switched from one area to the other. This problem can be reduced by separating these colors or by using colors from one-half or less of the color hexagon in the HSV model. With this technique, a display contains either blues and greens or reds and yellows.

As a general rule, the use of a smaller number of colors produces a more pleasing display than a large number of colors, and tints and shades blend better than pure hues. For a background, gray or the complement of one of the foreground colors is usually best.

REFERENCES

Additional information on intensity models is to be found in Blinn (1977, 1978, and 1982), Blinn and Newell (1976), Phong (1975), Cook (1984), Cook and Torrance (1982), Potmesil and Chakravarty (1983), Torrance and Sparrow (1967), and Warn (1983). Methods for modeling shadows are discussed in Brotman and Badler (1984) and in Crow (1977). For further information on texturing see Blinn (1976), Crow (1984), Haruyama and Barsky, and Schweitzer (1983).

Ray-tracing techniques are discussed in Cook, Porter, and Carpenter (1984), Glassner (1984), Hanrahan (1983), Kajiya (1983), Potmesil and Chakravarty (1982), and in Weghorst, Hooper, and Greenberg (1984).

Halftoning algorithms are presented in Jarvis and Roberts (1976), Jarvis, Judice, and Ninke (1976), and Judice, Jarvis, and Ninke (1974).

Sources of information on color models include Baldwin (1984), Joblove and Greenberg (1978), Murch (1984), and Smith (1978 and 1979).

14-1. Write a routine to implement the shading model of Eq. 14–7 assuming that the light source and view position are "infinitely" far from the object to be shaded.

14-2. Develop an algorithm for shading a surface using the calculations in Eq. 14–7 when the light source and view position cannot be assumed to be infinitely far from the surface.

14-3. Devise a scan-line algorithm that takes advantage of coherence to evaluate the dot products in Eq. 14–7 along the scan lines.

14-4. Devise an algorithm for identifying surfaces that are visible through a transparent object.

14-5. Outline a scan-line method for obtaining the intensity values over the surface of a transparent object that is in front of one or more background objects.

14-6. Discuss how the different hidden-surface removal methods can be combined with an intensity model for displaying objects with opaque surfaces.

14-7. Discuss how the various hidden-surface removal methods can be modified to process transparent objects. Are there any hidden-surface methods that cannot handle transparent surfaces?

14-8. Modify the routine of Ex. 14–1 to include a texture function. Apply both a random and a repeating texture function to display two different types of surfaces.

14-9. Develop an algorithm for mapping a specified texture-intensity pattern onto a defined surface.

14-10. Set up an algorithm, based on one of the hidden-surface removal methods, that will display shadow areas around an object illuminated by a distant point source.

14-11. For a system with n intensity levels above zero, show that any calculated intensity value I, between 0 and 1, can be mapped onto one of the n discrete levels by calculating the integer level number:
$$k = \text{round} (\log_r (I/I_1)) + 1$$

14-12. How many intensity levels can be displayed with a halftoning method using n by n pixel grids where each pixel can be displayed with m different intensities?

14-13. Given a surface of intensity values, write a routine to display the surface using a 3 by 3 halftoning method with two intensity levels per pixel.

14-14. Develop an algorithm that uses 3 by 3 dither matrices to set intensity values over the surface of an object.

14-15. Write a routine to implement a constant shading method for the surfaces of a defined polyhedron.

14-16. Write a procedure for implementing Gouraud shading over the surfaces of a specified polyhedron.

14-17. Implement the Phong shading method for an object with plane faces.

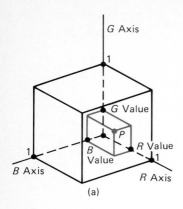

(a)

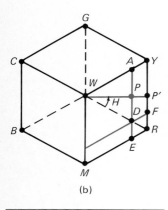

(b)

FIGURE 14–50
Mapping point P in the RGB
color space (a) into the
corresponding position (b) on a
hexagon cross section of the
HSV hexcone.

14–18. Set up an algorithm that determines surface intensities using a ray-tracing method for a scene containing a single object illuminated by a single point source.

14–19. Devise an algorithm to process an intensity model and an octree representation of an object, storing visible surface intensity values in a quadtree.

14–20. How many different color combinations can be generated using halftoning on a two-level RGB system with a 2 by 2 pixel grid? How many combinations can be obtained with a 3 by 3 pixel grid?

14–21. Derive the expressions for converting RGB color parameters to HSV values using the diagrams in Fig. 14–50. Position P in this diagram marks a color point specified by assigned values for R, G, and B. In this example, R is assumed to have the maximum value and B the minimum value, so that color point P is mapped onto the first sextant of an HSV hexagon cross section as shown in Fig. 14–50 (b). The length of each side of this hexagon is equal to the value of parameter V, which is equal to the maximum of the RGB values. This value is also equal to each of the distances from the hexagon center W (the white point) to the color vertices. Parameter S is calculated as the relative distance of point P from the center point W of the hexagon: $S = |WP|/|WP'| = |WA|/|WY| = (|WY| - |AY|)/|WY| = (R - B)/R = [\max(R,G,B) - \min(R,G,B)]/\max(R,G,B)$. Similarly, parameter H can be calculated as a number between 0 and 1 by determining the relative distance of P from the line WR. That is, $H = |DP|/|DA| = (|EP| - |ED|)/(|EA| - |ED|) = (G - B)/(R - B) = [G - \min(R,G,B)]/[\max(R,G,B) - \min(R,G,B)]$. Perform a similar analysis for each of the other sextants of the hexagon to obtain the complete transformation calculations for any input set of RGB values.

14–22. Derive the inverse operations of the procedures in Ex. 14–21 to obtain the expressions for converting HSV color values to RGB values. As an example of this approach, consider a color point in the first sextant of the HSV hexagon (Fig. 14–50). For this case, parameter S can be written as $(V - B)/V$. The inverse of this expression yields: $B = V(1 - S)$. Using this expression in $H = (G - B)/(V - B)$, we obtain $G = V[1 - S(1 - H)]$. Similar methods can be applied in each of the other sextants.

14–23. Write a procedure that would allow a user to select HSV color parameters from a displayed menu, then convert the color choices to RGB values for storage in a raster.

14–24. Revise the procedures outlined in Ex. 14–21 to convert a set of RGB color values to HLS color parameters.

14–25. Set up an algorithm for converting the HLS color parameters to RGB color parameters. The proper conversion procedures can be determined by obtaining the inverse operations of the procedures in Ex. 14–24.

14–26. Implement the algorithm of Ex. 14–25 in a program that allows a user to select HLS values from a color menu then converts these values to corresponding RGB values.

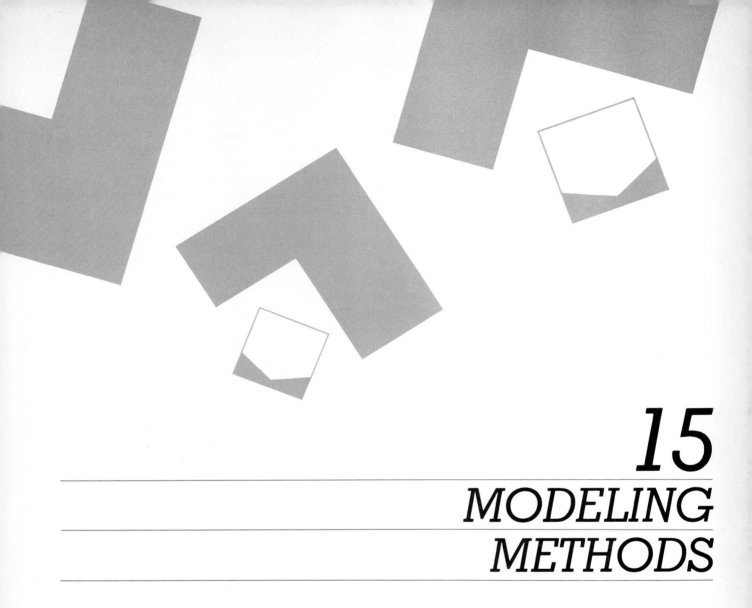

15

MODELING
METHODS

An important use of graphics is in the design and representation of different types of systems. Architectural and engineering systems, such as building layouts and electronic circuit schematics, are commonly put together using computer-aided design methods. Graphical methods are used also for representing economic, financial, organizational, scientific, social, and environmental systems. Representations for these systems are often constructed to simulate the behavior of a system under various conditions. The outcome of the simulation can serve as an instructional tool or as a basis for making decisions about the system. To be effective in these various applications, a graphics package must possess efficient methods for constructing and manipulating the graphical system representations.

15-1 Basic Modeling Concepts

The creation and manipulation of a system representation is termed **modeling.** Any single representation is called a **model** of the system. Models for a system can be defined graphically, or they can be purely descriptive, such as a set of equations that define the relationships between system parameters. Graphical models are often referred to as **geometric models,** because the component parts of a system are represented with geometric entities such as lines, polygons, or circles. We are concerned here only with graphics applications, so we will use the term *model* to mean a computer-generated, geometric representation of a system.

Model Representations

Figure 15-1 shows a representation for a logic circuit, illustrating the features common to many system models. Component parts of the system are displayed as geometric structures, called **symbols,** and relationships between the symbols are represented in this example with a network of connecting lines. Three standard symbols are used to represent logic gates for the Boolean operations: AND, OR, and NOT. The connecting lines define relationships in terms of input and output flow (from left to right) through the system parts. One symbol, the AND gate, is displayed at two different positions within the logic circuit. Repeated positioning of a few basic symbols is a common method for building complex models. Each such occurrence of a symbol within a model is called an **instance** of that symbol. We have one instance for the OR and NOT symbols in Fig. 15-1, and two instances of the AND symbol.

In many cases, the particular symbols chosen to represent the parts of a system are dictated by the system description. For circuit models, standard electrical or logic symbols are used. With models representing abstract concepts, such as political, financial, or economic systems, symbols may be any convenient geometric pattern.

Information describing a model is usually provided as a combination of geometric and nongeometric data. Geometric information includes coordinate positions for locating the component parts, output primitives and attribute functions to define the structure of the parts, and data for constructing connections between the parts. Nongeometric information includes text labels, algorithms describing the operating characteristics of the model, and rules for determining the relationships or connections between component parts, if these are not specified as geometric data.

The information needed to construct and manipulate a model is often stored in some type of data structure, such as a table or linked list. This information could also be specified in procedures. In general, a model specification will contain both

FIGURE 15-1
Model of a logic circuit.

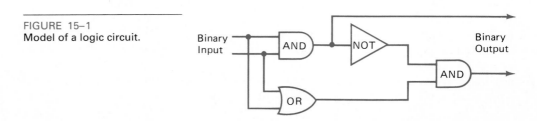

SYMBOL CODE	GEOMETRIC DESCRIPTION	IDENTIFYING LABEL
Gate 1	(Coordinates and other Parameters)	AND
Gate 2	⋮	OR
Gate 3	⋮	NOT
Gate 4	⋮	AND

FIGURE 15–2
A data table defining the structure and position of each gate in the circuit of Fig. 15–1.

data structures and procedures, although some models are defined completely with data structures and others use only procedure specifications. An application to perform solid modeling of objects might use mostly information taken from some data structure to define coordinate positions, with very few procedures. A weather model, on the other hand, may need mostly procedures to calculate plots of temperature and pressure variations.

As an example of how combinations of data structures and procedures can be used, we consider some alternative model specifications for the logic circuit of Fig. 15–1. One method is to define the logic components in a data table (Fig. 15–2), with processing procedures used to specify how the network connections are to be made and how the circuit operates. Geometric data in this table include coordinates and parameters necessary for drawing and positioning the gates. These symbols could all be drawn as polygon shapes, or they could be formed as combinations of straight line segments and elliptical arcs. Labels for each of the component parts also have been included in the table, although the labels could be omitted if the symbols are displayed as commonly recognized shapes. Procedures would then be used to display the gates and construct the connecting lines, based on the coordinate positions of the gates and a specified order for connecting them. An additional procedure is used to produce the circuit output (binary values) for any given input. This procedure could be set up to display only the final output, or it could be designed to display intermediate output values to illustrate the internal functioning of the circuit.

Another method for specifying the circuit model is to define as much of the system as possible in data structures. The connecting lines, as well as the gates, could be defined in a data table, which explicitly lists endpoints for each of the lines in the circuit. A single procedure might then display the circuit and calculate the output. Going to the other extreme, the model could be defined completely in procedures using no external data structures.

Symbol Hierarchies

Many models can be organized as a hierarchy of symbols. The basic "building blocks" for the model are defined as simple geometric shapes appropriate to the type of model under consideration. These basic symbols can be used to form composite objects, called **modules,** which themselves can be grouped to form higher-level modules, and so on, for the various components of the model. In the simplest case, we can describe a model by a one-level hierarchy of component parts, as in Fig. 15–3. For this circuit example, we assume that the gates are positioned and connected to each other with straight lines according to connection rules that are

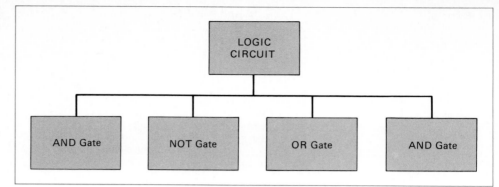

FIGURE 15–3
A one-level hierarchical
description of a circuit formed
with logic gates.

specified with each gate description. The basic symbols in this hierarchical description are the logic gates. Although the gates themselves could be described as hierarchies—formed from straight lines, elliptical arcs, and text—that sort of description would not be a convenient one for constructing logic circuits, in which the simplest building blocks are gates. For an application in which we were interested in designing different geometric shapes, the basic symbols could be defined as straight line segments and arcs.

An example of a two-level symbol hierarchy appears in Fig. 15–4. Here a facility layout is planned as an arrangement of work areas. Each work area is outfitted with a collection of furniture. The basic symbols are the furniture items: worktable, chair, shelves, file cabinet, and so forth. Higher-order objects are the work areas, which are put together with different furniture organizations. An instance of a basic symbol is defined by specifying its size, position, and orientation within each work area. For a facility layout package with fixed sizes for objects, only position and orientation need be specified by a user. Positions are given as coordinate locations in the work areas, and orientations are specified as rotations that determine which way the symbols are facing. At the second level up the hierarchy, each work area is defined by specifying its size, position, and orientation within the facility layout. The boundary for each work area might be fitted with a divider, which encloses the work area and provides aisles within the facility.

More complex symbol hierarchies are formed by repeated grouping of symbol clusters at each higher level. The facility layout of Fig. 15–4 could be extended to

FIGURE 15–4
A two-level hierarchical
description of a facility layout.

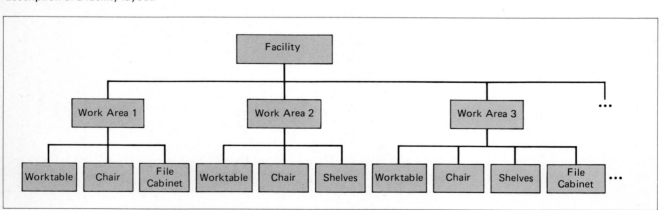

include symbol clusters that form different rooms, different floors of a building, different buildings within a complex, and different complexes at widely separated physical locations.

Modeling Packages

Standard general-purpose graphics systems are usually not designed to accommodate extensive modeling applications. Routines necessary to handle modeling procedures and data structures are often set up as separate **modeling packages,** and standard graphics packages then can be adapted to interface with the modeling package. The purpose of graphics routines is to provide methods for generating and manipulating final output displays. Modeling routines, by contrast, provide a means for defining and rearranging model representations in terms of symbol hierarchies, which are then processed by the graphics routines for display. Systems designed specifically for modeling may integrate the modeling and graphics functions into one package.

Symbols available in a modeling package are defined and structured according to the type of application the package has been designed to handle. Modeling packages can be designed for either two-dimensional or three-dimensional displays. Figure 15–5 illustrates a two-dimensional layout used in circuit design. A three-dimensional molecular modeling display is shown in Fig. 15–6. Three-dimensional facility

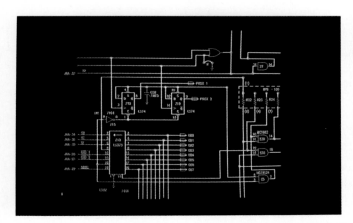

FIGURE 15–5
Two-dimensional modeling layout used in circuit design. Courtesy Summagraphics.

FIGURE 15–6
MIDAS molecular modeling system display of a color-coded, three-dimensional representation of a component of adenosine triphosphate as it is rotated about the glycosyl bond. Courtesy Evans & Sutherland and Computer Graphics Laboratory, University of California at San Francisco.

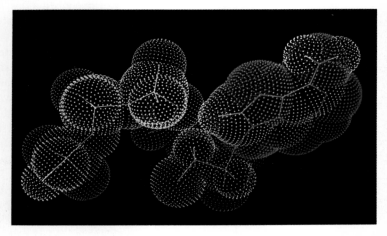

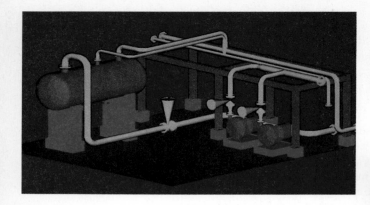

FIGURE 15-7
Three-dimensional, color-coded layout used in plant design. Courtesy Intergraph Corp.

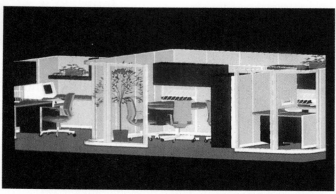

FIGURE 15-8
Office facility design using three-dimensional displays. Courtesy Intergraph Corp.

layouts are demonstrated in Figs. 15–7 and 15–8, which illustrate models for plant design and office design. Such three-dimensional displays can give a designer a better appreciation of the appearance of a layout. In the following sections, we explore the characteristic features of modeling packages and the methods for interfacing or integrating modeling functions with graphics routines.

15-2 Master Coordinates and Modeling Transformations

In many design applications, models are constructed with instances (transformed copies) of the geometric shapes that are defined in a basic symbol set. Instances are created by positioning the basic symbols within the world coordinate reference of the model. Since we do not know in advance where symbol instances are to be placed in the world coordinate system, the definition of a basic symbol must be stated in an independent coordinate reference, which is then transformed to world coordinates. This independent reference is called the **master coordinate** system for each symbol. Figure 15–9 illustrates master coordinate definitions for two symbols that could be used in a two-dimensional facility-layout application. Arrays *worktable* and *chair* are used to store the master coordinate definitions. An example of instance placement within a facility world coordinate reference is shown in Fig. 15–10, where the worktable and chair of Fig. 15–9 have been rotated and translated.

Any transformations applied to the master coordinate definition of a symbol are referred to as **modeling transformations.** A particular kind of modeling transformation, the creation of an instance in world coordinates from a master coordinate symbol definition, is termed an **instance transformation.** In general, modeling packages allow applications programs to perform both instance transformations (master to world coordinates) and transformations within a symbol master system (master to master coordinates).

Arrays for Chair
Coordinates

x_chair	y_chair
−3	−3
−3	3
3	3
3	−3
1	3
2	0
1	−3

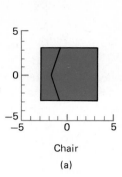

Chair

(a)

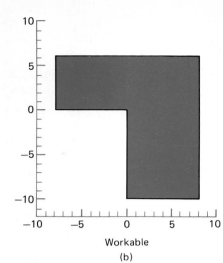

Workable

(b)

Arrays for
Workable Coordinates

x_worktable	y_worktable
0	0
−8	0
−8	6
8	6
8	−10
0	−10

FIGURE 15–9
Master coordinate definitions
of two symbols for use in a
two-dimensional facility design
package.

Modeling Transformations

Master coordinate symbol definitions are typically transformed by a modeling package into world coordinates using matrix transformation methods. These packages are designed to concatenate individual transformations into a homogeneous coordinate **modeling transformation matrix, *MT***. An instance transformation is carried out by applying *MT* to points in the master coordinate definition of a symbol to produce the corresponding world coordinate position of the object:

$$(x_{world}, y_{world}, z_{world}, 1) = (x_{master}, y_{master}, z_{master}, 1) \cdot MT \qquad (15\text{–}1)$$

A matrix can be designated as the modeling transformation matrix in a modeling package with

    set_modeling_transformation (mt)

This matrix can be used to produce instance transformations, as in Eq. 15–1, or to generate a master-to-master transformation, if the original size or orientation of a symbol is to be altered.

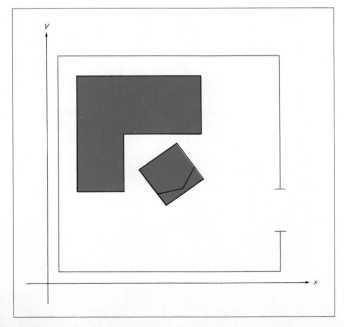

FIGURE 15–10
Instances of furniture symbols
(Fig. 15–9) in the world
coordinates of a facility layout.

315

A set of routines to perform individual transformations can be designated in a modeling package as

```
set_modeling_translation (tx, ty, tz)
set_modeling_scale_factors (sx, sy, sz)
set_modeling_rotation (ax, ay, az)
```

Translation distances *tx*, *ty*, and *tz* are applied to a master coordinate definition to move an object into the world coordinate description of a module. If the object is to be scaled or rotated, these transformations are applied relative to the master coordinate origin. Scaling parameters are designated as *sx*, *sy*, and *sz*, and rotation angles about the master coordinate axes are denoted as *ax*, *ay*, and *az*.

Transformation routines are used to update the current modeling transformation matrix. An update is performed by concatenating the matrix representation for the specified individual transformation with the modeling matrix. This composition of matrices is carried out in a modeling package with the individual transformation matrix on the left. For example, a translation specification would produce an updated modeling matrix *MT* through the operation

$$MT = T \cdot MT$$

As we shall see, multiplying matrices in this order facilitates processing of multilevel hierarchies. However, this arrangement requires that we reverse the logical order of the calls to the transformation routines. Suppose an object is to be rotated and then translated to a world coordinate system. This means that the order of the transformation calls should be translate first, then rotate. If we denote the transformation matrices for translation and rotation as *T* and *R*, this sequence of calls would update the transformation matrix in the order

$$MT = T \cdot MT$$
$$MT = R \cdot MT$$
$$MT = R \cdot T \cdot MT$$

so that the object symbol is first rotated, then translated.

To demonstrate the use of modeling transformations, we consider a method for creating instances of basic symbols for a solid-modeling application. Basic symbols available in this package are the three-dimensional primitives, such as a block, cylinder, sphere, cone, and other solids. These symbols can be defined in procedures that contain the output primitives for constructing the object in master coordinates. We assume that a user can move any number of symbols into a world coordinate system. Once the transformation of symbols from master coordinates to world coordinates is completed, solid-construction operations are to be performed on the instances to form new objects as the union, intersection, or difference of those symbols that have been transformed to world coordinates.

When a user selects a symbol and the associated transformation parameters, this information is stored in an array of records, which we shall call *instances*. Figure 15–11 shows the structure of records in this array. The record entries include a code field, identifying the symbol to be instanced, and the instance transformation parameters for converting the symbol master coordinates into world coordinates. An interactive process could be used to create this array. A pick device might select a symbol from a symbol menu. Then scaling and rotations parameters could be selected from transformation-parameter menus. Finally, the desired position of the instance (scaled and rotated symbol) within a displayed world coordinate representation would be selected. The parameters for the symbol code, scaling factors, rotation angles, and translation distances are then entered into the *instances* array.

FIGURE 15–11
Record fields for the array instances, used by procedure display_ instances.

| Symbol Code $(1,2,3,\cdots)$ |
| Translation Parameters (T_x, T_y, T_z) |
| Scaling Parameters (S_x, S_y, S_z) |
| Rotation Angles (A_x, A_y, A_z) |

Once the *instances* array is complete, the modeling package can transform the master coordinate definition of each symbol and pass the new instance to the graphics package for display. The following procedures illustrate one way in which this might be done.

```
type
  instance = record
    symbol                              : integer;
    tx, ty, tz, sx, sy, sz, ax, ay, az : real
  end;   {instance}
var
  instances : array [1..max_instances] of instance;

procedure display_instance;
  var k : integer;
  begin
    for k := 1 to max_instances do begin
        create_segment (k);
        with instances [k] do begin
            set_modeling_transformation (identity);
            set_modeling_translation (tx, ty, tz);
            set_modeling_rotation (ax, ay, az);
            set_modeling_scale_factors (sx, sy, sz);
            case symbol of
                1 : cylinder;
                2 : block;
                    .
                    .
                    .
            end   {case}
        end;   {with instances}
        close_segment
    end   {for k}
  end;   {display_instance}

procedure cylinder;
  begin   {definition of cylinder}   end;

procedure block;
  begin   {definition of block}   end;
```

In this example, each instance (in world coordinates) is stored in a separate segment. When segments are passed to the graphics package, they are further modified by the viewing transformation. The object is transformed to viewing coordinates, then clipped and mapped into device coordinates for display. In some systems, these viewing transformations are combined with the modeling transformations to form a single transformation operation.

Our example procedure for creating instance segments first scales and rotates a given symbol within its master coordinate reference. Then the object is translated to world coordinates. This is accomplished by specifying the transformation operations in the reverse order: first translate, then rotate, then scale. This ordering of the transformation routines combines the matrix representations for these operations in the order

$$MT = S \cdot R \cdot T \cdot MT$$

so that the final matrix is equivalent to scaling followed by rotation then translation.

As we have seen, modeling applications may require the composition of basic symbols into groups, called modules; these modules may be combined into higher-level modules; and so on. Figure 15–12 illustrates the tree structure for a three-level symbol hierarchy. Such symbol hierarchies can be handled by applying the methods of our previous solid-modeling example to each succeeding level in the tree. We first define a module as a list of symbol instances and their transformation parameters. At the next level, we define each higher-level module as a list of the lower-module instances and their transformation parameters. This process is continued up to the root of the tree, which represents the total picture in world coordinates.

To illustrate a technique for setting up the definition of a symbol hierarchy, we extend the solid-modeling application of our previous example to a two-level hierarchy. Transformations must now be applied at two levels. Instances are positioned within a module, and modules are positioned within the overall picture. We assume that the modules represent subassemblies that are to be fitted together to form the composite structure (piece of equipment). The subassemblies (modules) are created by combining the basic symbols to obtain the shapes needed for the component parts of the total assembly.

Transformation matrices must now be constructed for each module, as well as for each instance within each module. To transform a symbol into its proper position in the total assembly, it is first instanced into the subassembly, then moved into final position using the module-transformation parameters specified for that subassembly. This process can be performed by concatenating the module transformation with the instance transformation necessary to place a symbol in the module, so that the modeling transformation at each step is calculated as

$$MT = MT_{\text{master,module}} \cdot MT_{\text{module,world}} \qquad (15\text{–}2)$$

Applying this modeling transformation matrix MT to a symbol is then equivalent to first performing the instance transformation (master to module coordinates), then moving the symbol into the final assembly (module to world coordinates).

The module transformation matrix $MT_{\text{module,world}}$ must be applied to all instances making up the subassembly. To be able repeatedly to apply this module transformation matrix to its component instances, the module matrix must be saved

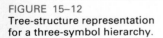

FIGURE 15–12
Tree-structure representation
for a three-symbol hierarchy.

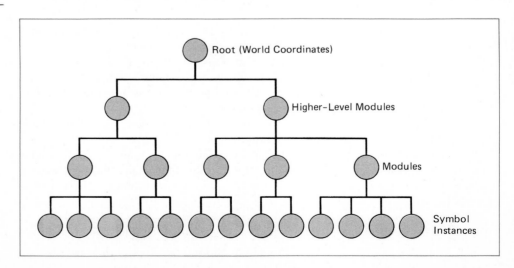

so that the modeling matrix *MT* can be restored to its original form after each instance has been moved into final position. For this purpose, two additional routines are used in the modeling package:

```
save_modeling_transformation (mt, m_stack)
restore_modeling_transformation (mt, m_stack)
```

The first routine saves the current modeling transformation matrix for later use. When the modeling matrix is to be restored to its original form, the second routine is called to retrieve the stored matrix from the designated stack area. These two operations allow the modeling package to combine symbols into modules and then transform the modules into the final world coordinate representation.

An example of how a two-level hierarchy can be implemented for a solid-modeling application is given in the following procedures. The record array *modules* lists the modeling transformation parameters for positioning each module within the facility, using a pointer *(instance_start)* to instances comprising the module. *Instances* is a list of the symbols and transformation parameters needed to form the instances within the module.

```
type
   instance = record
      symbol_type                  : integer;
      tx, ty, tz, sx, sy, sz, ax, ay, az : real
   end;   {instance}
   module = record
      tx, ty, tz, sx, sy, sz, ax, ay, az : real;
      instance_count               : integer;
      instance_start               : integer
   end;   {module}
var
   instances : array [1..max_instances] of instance;
   modules   : array [1..max_modules] of module;

procedure display_picture;
   var j : integer;
   begin
      for j := 1 to max_modules do begin
         create_segment (j);   {put each module in a segment}
         set_modeling_transformation (identity);
         with modules [j] do begin
            set_modeling_translation (tx, ty, tz);
            set_modeling_rotation (ax, ay, az);
            set_modeling_scale_factor (sx, sy, sz);
            display_module (instance_start,
                        instance_start + instance_count − 1)
         end;   {with modules}
         close_segment
      end   {for j}
   end;   {display_picture}

procedure display_module (start, finish : integer);
   var  k : integer;
   begin
      for k := start to finish do begin
         save_modeling_transformation (mt, m_stack);
         with instances [k] do begin
```

```
set_modeling_translation (tx, ty, tz);
set_modeling_rotation (ax, ay, az);
set_modeling_scale_factors (sx, sy, sz);
case symbol of
    1 : cylinder;
    2 : block;
        .
        .
        .

    end   {case}
  end;   {with instances [k]}
   restore_modeling_transformation (mt, mt_stack)
  end   {for k}
end;   {display_module}
```

The first procedure in this example opens a new segment and creates a module transformation matrix. Scaling, rotation, and translation parameters for this transformation are obtained, as in the previous example, from the array of module records. Each module record also points to the record array for the symbol instances forming that module. The second procedure concatenates the module transformation matrix with the transformation matrices for each symbol instance, with the instance transformation matrix on the left. This produces the composite matrix needed to transform symbols into a module and then to world coordinates. Since the same module-to-world transformation must be used with each symbol that is moved into the module reference system, the module-to-world transformation is saved so that it can be restored for application to each succeeding symbol.

FIGURE 15–13
Record layouts for (a) modules, (b) instances, and (c) symbol arrays.

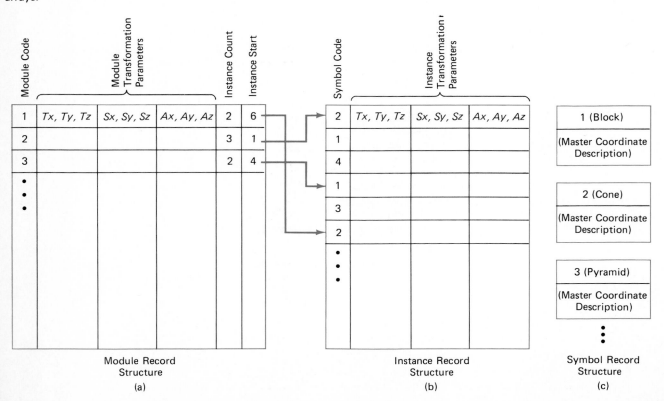

Module Record Structure
(a)

Instance Record Structure
(b)

Symbol Record Structure
(c)

In addition to the two procedures listed, the modeling package would also need the individual symbol-definition procedures for the three-dimensional primitives (block, cone, etc.). Figure 15–13 illustrates how the data structures that supply data to the display procedures could be set up for this two-level symbol hierarchy. One array is used for listing the modules and one for listing symbol instances, and the several symbol arrays provide master coordinate definitions. The modules could be predefined, or they could be user-defined at the time the picture is created.

An alternative arrangement for storing the module and instance data is to set up the data records in a linked list. The records could be linked so as to represent the tree structure of the symbol hierarchy. This would provide greater flexibility for reorganizing the modules within a picture. New symbol or module instances could be inserted more easily, and existing instances are deleted by changing pointer fields.

We can generalize this two-level hierarchy to include additional levels by setting up procedures for handling the further transformations needed to move instances to the final world coordinate representation. Starting at the top of the tree, appropriate transformation matrices at each level are concatenated to the left of the current transformation matrix to produce a new modeling matrix. This matrix is stored on the stack for subsequent use, and modules at the next lower level are processed. At the lowest level, the matrix applied to the output primitives will be a composite matrix formed from all the higher levels. When a branch of the tree has been completed, the tree is ascended back through the various levels until the start of an unprocessed branch is reached. As processing moves back up the tree, previously stored transformation matrices are restored (popped from the stack).

Display Procedures

The steps required to create a symbol instance within a module can be summarized as

1. Save the current modeling transformation matrix.
2. Combine the instance transformations with the current modeling transformation matrix.
3. Call the symbol procedure.
4. Restore the original modeling transformation matrix.

Since these operations are standard for each symbol instance to be created, a modeling package could provide a single routine to accomplish the same results. This routine is referred to as a **display procedure,** and the call to this routine is termed a **display procedure call.**

A display procedure call specifies the symbol name and the instance transformation parameters in some convenient format, such as

```
display (symbol_name, sx, sy, sz, ax, ay, az, tx, ty, tz)
```

In this form, the name of the symbol becomes a parameter that is passed to the procedure *display.* Other formats could be set up for this operation.

Display procedure calls provide a convenient shorthand for creating symbol instances. However, some flexibility in specifying the order of transformations could be sacrificed. For the format stated, the display procedure might carry out the instance transformation operations in the fixed order: scaling first, followed by rotation, then translation. A particular implementation could allow the order of the transformations to be changed to fit different application needs.

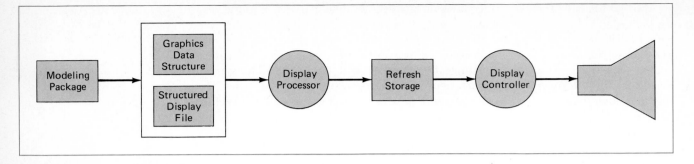

FIGURE 15–14
A structured display file formed
from the graphical data
structure by a modeling
package.

15–3 Structured Display Files

When models formed with symbol hierarchies are to be displayed on a refresh monitor, a modeling package can build a display file that reflects the symbol and module relationships employed in the model. This **structured display file** is accessed by the display processor, which uses the file to create and update the display information in the refresh storage area (Fig. 15–14). Refresh information can be organized either as a linear arrangement of segments or as a frame buffer, depending on whether a vector or a raster monitor is in use. A display controller then refreshes the screen using the contents of the refresh storage area.

The structured display file is organized so that the display processor can make rapid changes to the refresh area without processing through all the nongeometric data that may be in the graphical data structure representation of the model. Segments in this display file contain only master coordinate geometric data and the transformation parameters needed to position instances. These segments are organized into a hierarchical relationship that represents the tree structure of the model. The display processor accesses the structured display file, performing the instance transformations, viewing operations, and clipping necessary for displaying the model on the video monitor.

15–4 Symbol Operations

We have seen how hierarchical models can be constructed using standard procedures to set up symbol and module specifications. Another method that can be used in a modeling package is to allow symbols and modules to be defined with operations similar to those used with segments. For example, the following operations could be used to set up the definition of a symbol in exactly the same way that segments are created:

```
create_symbol (id);
        .
        .
        .
close_symbol;
```

Once a symbol has been defined with *create_symbol*, it can be included in a segment using an *insert_symbol* operation in the same way that we previously called a symbol procedure. This method is illustrated in the following segment definition:

```
create_segment (12);
        .
        .
        .
save_modeling_transformation (mt);
        .
    {perform instance transformations}
        .
insert_symbol (5);
restore_modeling_transformation (mt);
        .
        .
        .
close_segment;
```

Here symbol 5 is inserted into a larger structure defined within segment 12.

In a similar way, commands can be provided to form groups (or modules) of symbols. The following statements could be used for this purpose:

```
create_group (id);
        .
        .
        .
close_group;
```

Groups could be formed with symbols or other groups, using *insert* routines and transformation operations in much the same way that we previously used procedures. In the following example, group 8 is defined as a combination of group 7 and symbol 10:

```
create_group (8);
        .
        .
        .
insert_group (7);
        .
        .
        .
insert_symbol (10);
        .
        .
        .
close_group;
```

Instance transformations would be used to position group 7 and symbol 10 within group 8, and the *insert* operations set pointers to the corresponding symbol and group definitions.

Creating symbols and groups with the preceding modeling routines provides a convenient method for setting up hierarchies and has some advantages over procedure definitions. Permanent symbol libraries can be created and stored with this approach. A user could define an individual symbol library, and a general facility symbol library also could be available to all users at any time. Attributes and other options can be specified for defined symbols. For example, the *insert* operation could include specification of the transformation parameters for the symbol or module referenced, as is done with display procedure calls.

In designing a modeling package, symbol management considerations must be taken into account. As with segments, we need efficient methods for assigning

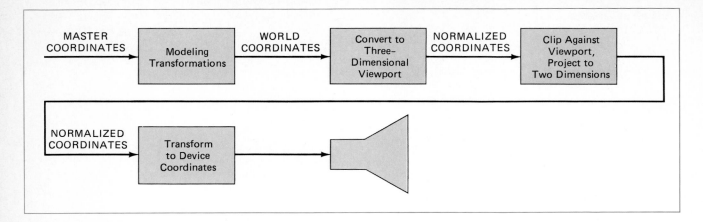

FIGURE 15–15
Transformation of master
coordinates into device
coordinates.

storage and for conducting symbol searches. Routines to accomplish these functions can be designed as part of the modeling package. If a host system is to be used, these tasks could be performed either by the operating system resource management routines or by a relational database system.

15–5 Combining Modeling and Viewing Transformations

Modeling transformations turn master coordinate definitions into world coordinates, which then are passed to the graphics package for the final transformation into device coordinates (clipping and window-to-viewport mapping). Figure 15–15 shows a sequence for transforming a master coordinate definition into device coordinates when modeling routines are interfaced to a graphics package. It is possible to perform the various operations shown in a different order, depending on the structure of the packages and whether the system is designed for two-dimensional or three-dimensional applications.

Master Coordinate Clipping

When modeling routines are built into a graphics package, the instance transformations can be combined with the viewing transformations. In many cases, it is then possible to carry out the clipping operations before any transformations are applied (Fig. 15–16). This can be an efficient approach, since unnecessary processing of clipped primitives by the transformation routines is avoided. For two-dimen-

FIGURE 15–16
Combined modeling and
viewing transformations with
clipping performed first.

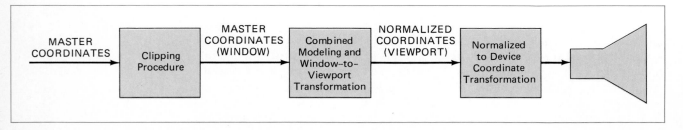

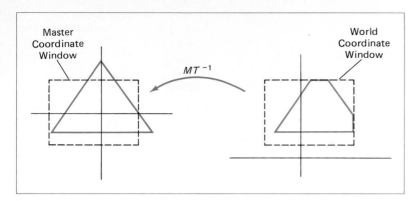

FIGURE 15–17
**Mapping a world coordinate
window onto the master
coordinate reference of a
symbol.**

sional applications with no rotations and standard window and viewport rectangles, clipping can easily be done in master coordinates. The package calculates the inverse of the instance transformation (MT^{-1}) and maps the window boundary onto the master coordinate definition of each symbol to be displayed. This process is illustrated in Fig. 15–17. Each instance in the model is clipped in master coordinates; then the modeling and windowing transformations are applied as one transformation matrix operation.

When rotations are involved, it is more efficient to transform first, then clip. A two-dimensional graphics package that allows rotated windows could make checks to determine whether a rotated window or any rotation transformations are to be used. If either a rotated window or a rotation transformation has been specified, clipping is performed after the transformations. Otherwise, clipping can be performed first, as in Fig. 15–16.

Bounding Rectangles for Symbols

To speed up the clipping process, symbols (and symbol groups) can be processed through a first clipping pass using bounding rectangles, as shown in Fig. 15–18. This provides a fast identification of the symbols that are completely inside or outside the window. The same process can be used for groups of symbols by determining the outer boundaries of the group.

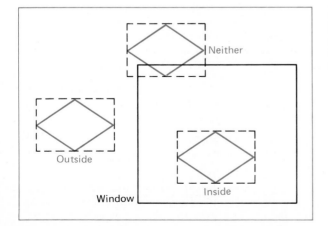

FIGURE 15–18
**Bounding rectangles used to
determine whether a symbol is
completely inside or outside a
window.**

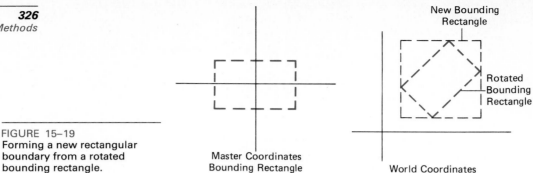

FIGURE 15–19
Forming a new rectangular
boundary from a rotated
bounding rectangle.

As each symbol and module is created, the bounding rectangle can be determined and stored with the symbol or module definition. When clipping is applied, these bounding rectangles are referenced by the clipping routines. The bounding rectangles can be used also for fast pick identification of symbols or groups.

When rotations are involved in the instance transformations, new boundary rectangles can be calculated after the transformation. Figure 15–19 illustrates how a new rectangle is formed from a rotated one.

REFERENCES   Modeling methods and applications are discussed in the following papers: Clark (1976) and Renfrow (1977).

EXERCISES   15–1. Discuss the model representations that would be appropriate for several distinctly different types of systems. Also discuss how each system might be implemented in a graphics modeling package.

15–2. For a logic-circuit modeling application, such as that in Fig. 15–1, give a detailed description of the data structures needed for specifying all modeling information. Then describe how the same information could be given in procedures and compare the advantages and disadvantages of each approach.

15–3. Develop a modeling package for electrical design that will allow a user to position electrical symbols within a circuit network. Only translations need be applied to place an instance of one of the electrical menu shapes into the network. Once a component has been placed in the network, it is to be connected to other specified components with straight line segments.

15–4. Write a two-dimensional facility layout package. A menu of furniture shapes is to be provided to the user, who can place the objects in any location within a single room. A one-level hierarchy is to be used, and instance transformations are limited to rotations and translations.

15–5. Expand the package of Ex. 15–4 to generate a two-level hierarchy. The furniture objects are to be placed into work areas, and the work areas are to be arranged within a larger area.

15–6. Expand the package of Ex. 15–4 to generate a three-level hierarchy. Furniture objects are arranged into work areas, which are then combined into department areas, and the various departments are fitted into a larger area.

15–7. Develop a complete algorithm for implementing the procedures for constructive solid modeling by combining three-dimensional primitives to generate subassemblies, then combining the subassemblies into the final assembly. As the last step, the created assemblies are to be mapped onto a designated area of a video monitor.

15–8. Write routines to implement a display procedure, given a set of input transformation parameters and a symbol identification.

15–9. Develop a procedure for maintaining and updating a structured display file.

15–10. Write a routine for converting the contents of a structured display file into appropriate intensity values in a frame buffer.

15–11. Develop implementation routines for the commands to create symbol definitions.

15–12. Devise an implementation for the commands to create groups as combinations of symbols and other groups.

15–13. Set up a clipping procedure to clip objects in master coordinates by mapping a given window boundary into the master coordinate system, given the transformation parameters.

15–14. Develop an algorithm for the steps in a modeling package that first transforms objects, then clips.

15–15. Devise a clipping procedure using bounding rectangles around the symbol groups.

15–16. Develop a two-dimensional modeling package that combines modeling and viewing transformations.

15–17. Extend the package of Ex. 15–16 to three dimensions.

16

DESIGN OF
THE USER INTERFACE

In designing a graphics package, we need to consider not only the graphics operations to be performed but also how these operations are to be made available to a user. This interface should be designed so as to provide a convenient and efficient means for the user to access basic graphics functions, such as displaying objects, setting attributes, or performing transformations. The graphics package might be set up to produce engineering designs, architectural plans, drafting layouts, or business graphs; or it could be designed as an artist's paintbrush program. Whatever the type of application intended, we need to decide on the interactive dialogue that best suits the intended user, the kind of manipulation routines that are to be used, and the output devices that are appropriate for the type of applications involved. A poorly designed interface increases the chances for user error and can significantly increase the time it takes a user to complete a task.

16–1 Components of a User Interface

There are many factors to be considered in the design of a user interface. In addition to the specific operations that are to be made available to the user, we must consider how menus are to be organized, how the graphics package is to respond to input and errors, how the output display is to be organized, and how the package is to be documented and explained to the user. To aid us in exploring these factors, we consider the design of a user interface in terms of the following components:

> User model
> Command language
> Menu formats
> Feedback methods
> Output formats

The **user model** provides the definition of the concepts involved in the graphics package. This model helps the user to understand how the package operates in terms of application concepts. It explains to the user what type of objects can be displayed and how they can be manipulated.

Operations available to a user are defined in the **command language,** which specifies the object manipulation functions and file operations. Typical object manipulation functions are those for rearranging and transforming objects in a scene. File operations can provide for the creation, renaming, and copying of segments. How the user commands are to be structured will depend on the type of input and output devices chosen for the graphics system.

Processing options can be presented to a user in a **menu format.** The menus could be used to list both the available operations and the objects to be manipulated.

An important consideration in the design of an interface is how the system is to respond, or give **feedback,** to user input. Feedback assists a user in operating the system by acknowledging the receipt of commands, by sending various messages to the user, and by signaling when menu selections have been received. Some types of feedback are an integral part of the structure of the command language, while other forms of feedback are provided to help a user understand the operation of the system.

How information is to be presented to the user is determined by the **output formats.** An output picture should be organized so as to provide information to the user in the most effective manner possible. Factors to be considered in the design of the output formats include the choice of geometric patterns that are used to represent objects and the overall arrangement of the output on a display device.

16–2 User Model

Design of a user interface starts with the user model. This determines the conceptual framework that is to be presented to a user. The model describes what the system is designed to accomplish and what graphics operations are available. For example, if the graphics system is to be used as a tool for architectural design, the model describes how the package can be used to construct and display views of buildings. Once the user model has been established, the other components of the interface can be developed. The final step in the design of the model is to prepare the user manual, which explains the system and provides help in using it.

Basically, the user model defines the graphics system in terms of objects and the operations that can be performed on objects. For a facility layout system, objects could be defined as a set of furniture items (tables, chairs, etc.), and the available operations would include those for positioning and removing different pieces of furniture within the facility layout. Similarly, a circuit design program might use electrical or logic elements for objects, with positioning operations available for adding or deleting elements within the overall circuit design.

Such objects as furniture items and circuit elements are referred to as **application objects.** In addition to these objects, the user model could contain other objects that are used to control graphics operations. These are called **control objects.** Examples of control objects are cursors for selecting screen positions, menu selection symbols, and positioning grids (Fig. 16–1). Operations available in a package allow for manipulation of both the application objects and the control objects. Users can be provided with the capability to move the control objects around, to delete these objects, or to change their size.

Only familiar concepts should be employed in the user model. If we are setting up a graphics package as an aid to architectural design, the operation of the package should be described in terms of the positioning of walls, doors, windows, and other building components to form the architectural structures. The model should not contain references to concepts that may be unfamiliar to a user. There is no reason to assume, for example, that an architect would be familiar with data structure terms. Introducing detailed information concerning the operation of the system in terms of tree structures, linked lists, and segments would place an unnecessary burden on the user. All information in the user model should be presented in the language of the application.

Overall, the user model should be as simple and consistent as possible. A complicated model is difficult for a user to understand and to work with in an effective way. The number of objects and graphics operations in the model should be minimized to only those that are necessary to the application. This makes it easier for the user to learn the system. On the other hand, if the package is oversimplified, it can be easy to learn but difficult to apply. The designer of the user model should also strive for consistency. Objects and operations should not be defined in different ways when used in different contexts. A single symbol, for example, should not serve both as an application object and as a control object, depending on the interaction mode. This can make it difficult for a user to keep track of symbol meanings. It is much easier for a user to apply the package if objects and operations are defined and used in a consistent manner.

As a starting point for developing a user model, a task analysis is often performed. The task analysis is a study of the user's environment and needs. This study is typically carried out by interviewing prospective users and observing how they perform their tasks. Conclusions from the task analysis can form the basis for deciding on the type of objects and operations needed and the way that the graphics package should be presented to the user.

16–3 Command Language

The interactive language chosen for a graphics package should be as natural as possible for the user to learn, with all operations specified in terms relating to the application area. A circuit design package specifies operations in terms of manipu-

FIGURE 16–1
Examples of control objects.

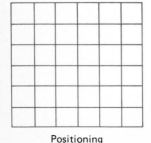

+
Screen Cursor

Menu Selection Symbol

Positioning
Grid

lating circuit elements, while the operations in a drafting package are those for drawing geometric figures. The commands should be designed so that the user does not have to learn new concepts, as well as the new language.

Minimizing Memorization

Each operation in the command language should be structured so that it is easy for a user to understand and remember the purpose of the operation. Obscure, complicated, inconsistent, and abbreviated command formats should be avoided. They only confuse a user and reduce the effectiveness of the graphics package. A command such as *select_object* is much easier for a user to remember than the abbreviated format *so*. One key, or button, that deletes any command is easier to use than a number of delete keys for different operations. In addition, the command language should be structured so that the user is not required constantly to shift attention from one input device to another.

For a less experienced user, a command language with a few easily understood operations is usually more effective than a large, comprehensive language set. A simplified command set is easy to learn and remember, and the user can concentrate on the application instead of on the language. However, an experienced user might find some applications hard to handle with a small command set designed for the novice. To accommodate a range of users, command languages can be designed in several levels. Beginners can use the lowest level, which contains the minimum command set, and experts can use the larger command sets at the higher levels. As experience is gained, a beginner can move up the levels, expanding the command language a little at a time.

User Help Facilities

It is very important that help facilities be included in the command language. Different levels of help allow beginners to obtain detailed instructions, while more experienced users can get short prompts that do not interrupt their concentration.

Help facilities can include a tutorial session that provides instruction in how to use the system. A beginner can sit down with the package and get an overview of what the package is designed to do and how the basic command set operates. Several example applications can be provided so that the user can see how the operations really work in typical applications.

If different help levels are available, a beginner can select the lowest level and receive detailed prompts and explanations at each step during the application of the package. The prompts can tell the beginner exactly what to do next. An experienced user could select less prompting or turn off the prompting altogether. Prompts can be given in the form of menus or displayed messages. For the expert user, more subtle prompts can be given. A blinking cursor could indicate when a coordinate input is required, and a scale could be displayed when a scalar value is to be selected.

Backup and Error Handling

During any sequence of operations, some easy mechanism for backing up, or aborting, should be available. Often an operation can be canceled before execution is completed, with the system restored to the state it was in before the operation was started. With the ability to back up at any point, a user can confidently explore the capabilities of the system, knowing that the effects of any mistake can be erased.

Backup can be provided in many forms. Positions of windows and viewports can be tested, and objects can be dragged into different positions before deciding on the final placement. Sometimes a system can be backed up through several operations, allowing the user to reset the system to some specified point. In a system with extensive backup capabilities, all inputs could be saved so that a user can back up and "rerun" any part of a session.

In the absence of a backup facility, other methods can be used to help users overcome the effects of errors. A user could be asked to verify some commands before executing the instructions. It would be too time-consuming to ask the user *Are you sure you want to do this?* after every input, but it would be appropriate for actions that either cannot be undone or would take too great an effort to restore.

Good diagnostics and error messages should be incorporated into the command language to allow users to avoid errors and to understand what went wrong when an error has been made. Obscure error messages cannot help a user correct an error. The error message should provide a clear statement of what is wrong and what needs to be done to correct the situation. Typically, the recovery system will reject an incorrect input and inform the user of the error in a way that helps the user determine the proper input at that point.

Response Time

The time that it takes the system to respond to a user input depends on the complexity of the task requested. For many routine input requests, the system is able to respond immediately. When a user inputs a complicated processing request, some delay can be expected, and this delay time could be used to plan the next phase of the application.

Regardless of the complexity of the input request, users expect systems to make some type of immediate response; otherwise, they cannot be sure that the input was received and that the system is processing. A graphics package should be designed to make this "instantaneous" response to user input in about one-tenth of a second. A response time longer than this can disrupt a user's train of thought, since the user begins wondering what the system is doing instead of thinking about the next step in the application. If processing time is to be longer than one-tenth of a second, the immediate response simply lets the user know that the input has been received. For the beginning user, this response could be a message stating that the input is being processed. With experienced users, a blinking cursor or a change in color or intensity can serve the same purpose.

Some systems are designed so that the variability in response times between different types of processing is not too great. A system that alternates between instantaneous responses and delays of several seconds (or minutes) could be more disconcerting to a user than a slower-responding system with less variability in response times.

Command Language Styles

There are several possible styles for the command language, and the choice of format for the input commands depends on a number of factors. These factors include the design goals of the package, the type of input devices to be used, and the type of anticipated user.

Overall, the command language can be set up so that the sequence of input actions is directed either by the graphics package or by the user. When the package directs the input, the user is told what type of action is expected at each step. This is a particularly effective approach for beginners, where prompts and menus are used to explain what is required and how to enter the input. In some cases, users may be restricted to a limited number of responses, such as replying with *yes, no,* or a numeric value. With other systems, a user may be directed to select an action from a list of alternatives. This selection could be made from a displayed menu, using a light pen or cursor control from a keyboard, or the selection could be made using function keys. Once the action has been chosen, such as selecting an object, the user is directed to enter appropriate parameters (coordinates, transformation values, etc.).

For user-initiated languages, the system actions are directed by inputs from the user. Little or no prompting is given to the user, who independently selects the type of action to be performed at each step. This approach provides the greatest flexibility and is best suited to the experienced user. Some menus and prompts could be used to remind the user of options available with any selected operation, but in general the user is free to explore the capabilities of the system without following a preset action sequence.

When a package is designed only to carry on a dialogue, no input command set is made available to the user. Input is achieved by selecting options from displayed menus and by making simple responses to prompts. This method for obtaining input is suitable for beginners but is inefficient for those with more experience, who can better utilize the capabilities of a package with an input command set. The commands can be designed to be input with function keys or by typing them on a standard keyboard.

To minimize user learning time, the syntax of input commands should be simple and straightforward. For example, to remove an object from a display, a user could enter the command *delete_object,* followed by the parameter values that identify the object to be deleted. Parameter designations could give an object number or the object name. Alternatively, the user might point to the object with a light pen or move the screen cursor to the location of the object. Commands that specify the action first, as in the example just given, are called prefix commands. Postfix commands specify parameters first and the action second. When postfix commands are used, the parameter list can be corrected in case of an error before the action is given.

In some applications, user input can be reduced by selecting a command syntax that allows for multiple parameter specifications. For example, instead of a separate delete command for each object, a user could enter a single delete command that allows several objects to be deleted:

```
delete
  object_name1
  object_name2
  object_name3

  .

  .

  .
```

The action of the delete command would be terminated when the next operation is entered.

Another possibility for reducing user input is to eliminate the parameter list within commands. Instead of the command *delete_object* followed by the object

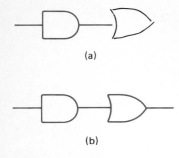

FIGURE 16–2
An input symbol (a) sketched by a designer is identified by the pattern recognition program and replaced with the corresponding circuit element shape (b).

FIGURE 16–3
An input pattern (a) sketched by a parts designer is matched against the library of existing parts to locate a similar shape (b).

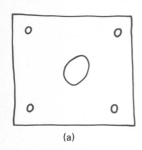

(a)

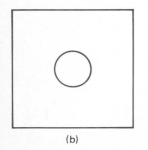

(b)

designation, the name of the object could be incorporated into the command. This requires a separate command for each object, but the commands could be implemented as function keys, so that only one input is required to enter the command. As an example, a facility layout package could allow each furniture item to be deleted with a separate command, such as *delete_worktable*, *delete_shelves*, and so forth.

A sketch pattern is another form of input that is useful in many design applications. Here the user draws a pattern with a stroke device, such as a graphics tablet; the pattern is displayed on a video monitor and processed by the design program. The input pattern could be used with a pattern recognition program to select a shape, or this type of input could be the basis for a painting package that allows a user to create a design or picture.

Pattern recognition programs take an input pattern and match it against a library of predefined shapes. A logic circuit designer could use such a program to sketch circuit layouts. Each circuit element is sketched, as in Fig. 16–2 (a), and the program replaces the sketched element with the corresponding library shape, as in Fig. 16–2 (b). This technique can be faster than selecting a shape from a menu and positioning it within the circuit if the library of stored shapes is not too large (about 20 times or less) and no rotations are involved.

A pattern recognition program is used with some systems to allow a parts designer to determine whether a needed part already exists or could be produced by modifying a similar part. Figure 16–3 illustrates a designer's sketch of a plate with five holes and a matching part found by the program. In this example, the designer might decide that the matching part is close enough so that it could be modified by adding the four smaller holes. To establish the size of input patterns, the user could be required to sketch objects within the bounds of a displayed grid.

Painting programs can be useful for displaying some types of networks (piping and wiring layouts) and for creative art applications. In network drawing, the user sketches the connecting lines, and the program adjusts the sketch into a layout of horizontal and vertical connections (Fig. 16–4). For art applications, the user can be provided with two menus and an area in which to create the picture, as shown in Fig. 16–5. One menu presents a set of brushes allowing the creation of different line sizes and line textures (sharp lines, airbrush, etc.). The other menu lists a palette of available colors and shades. By selecting different brushes and colors, an artist can produce pictures like the creative art examples in Chapter 1.

16–4 Menu Design

Most graphics packages make use of menus. In some cases, all user input is specified with menu selections. When menus are employed in a program, the user is relieved of the burden of remembering input options. Not only does this cut down on the amount of memorization required of the user by listing the range of available options, but it also prevents the user from electing options that are not valid at that point. In addition, menus can easily be changed to accommodate different applications, whereas function keys or buttons must be reprogrammed and relabeled if they are to be changed. Menus can be used as the input mechanism for both operations and parameter values.

Interactive menu selection can be accomplished with most types of input devices. The light pen and touch panel are used to make very rapid selections,

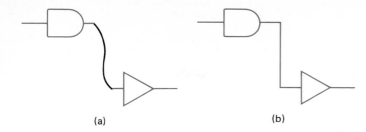

(a)   (b)

FIGURE 16–4
In a network drawing program, a user's sketch of a connecting line (a) is adjusted to a set of horizontal and vertical lines (b).

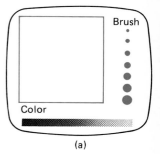

(a)

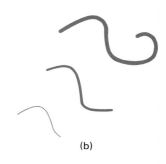

(b)

FIGURE 16–5
(a) Menus used in a painting program to select colors and brush textures and sizes. (b) Lines drawn with different-sized brushes.

since the user simply touches the screen area containing the menu option to be selected. Keyboards, joysticks, and other devices can be used to make selections by positioning a cursor or other symbol at a menu position. A keyboard can also be used to type in the identifying name or number of a menu item. For a small number of menu items, a voice entry system can provide an efficient method for selecting options.

In general, menus with fewer options are more effective, since they reduce the amount of searching time needed to find a particular option, and they take up less screen space. Usually, menus are placed to one side of the screen so that they do not interfere with the displayed picture. When an extensive menu with long descriptions for each option is to be presented, it may have to occupy the entire screen so that the picture and menu are alternately displayed. This can have a very disruptive effect on the user's train of thought, since visual continuity with the picture is lost each time a menu selection is to be made. Such full-screen menus should be avoided by shortening the descriptions of the menu options and breaking the selections into two or more submenus.

One method for organizing a menu into smaller submenus is to arrange the menu options into a multilevel structure. A selection from the first menu brings up a menu at the second level, and so on. This is an effective method for dealing with operations and parameters. Once an action is selected from the operation menu, a parameter menu (scales or dials) can be presented. More than two or three levels should be avoided; otherwise, the menu structure could confuse the user.

Items listed in a menu can be presented either as character strings or as graphical icons (geometric shapes). Such symbols are useful in presenting menus for circuit design and facility layout planning. Icons can also be used to describe the meanings of some actions, as illustrated in Fig. 16–6. A straight arrow is used in this example to indicate a translation direction, and a curved arrow indicates rotation direction. Advantages of icons are that they generally take up less space and are more quickly recognized than corresponding text descriptions. A beginning user may find icons more difficult to use initially, but once the icon set is learned, inputs can be made faster and with fewer errors.

For most applications, menus are always placed in one position, such as at the side or bottom of the screen. Items are always placed in the same position, so that the user gets used to making each selection in a fixed location. Another possibility is to use a "movable" (or "pop-up") menu that is placed near the current position of the screen cursor (Fig. 16–7). Since the user is assumed to be working with the screen cursor, the movable menus allow selections to be made with a minimum of eye and hand movement. The movable menu is placed over part of the picture and so should be displayed only when needed. Movable menus can be implemented on a raster system by replacing a rectangular part of the picture with

FIGURE 16–6
Icons that could be used to select directions for translation and rotation.

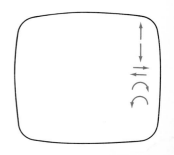

the menu information. With a vector system, the menu and picture may overlap and make it difficult for the user to identify menu items.

FIGURE 16–7
A movable menu placed near the current position of the screen cursor.

16–5 Feedback

An important part of any graphics system is the amount of feedback supplied to a user. The system needs to carry on a continual interactive dialogue and inform the user what the system is doing at each step. This is particularly important when the response time is high. Without feedback, a user may begin to wonder what the system is doing and whether the input should be given again.

As each input is received from the user, a response should immediately appear on the screen. The message should be brief and clearly indicate the type of processing in progress. This not only informs the user that the input has been received, but it also tells the user what the system is working on so that any input errors can be corrected. If processing cannot be completed within a few seconds, several feedback messages might be displayed to keep the user informed of the progress of the system. In some cases this could be a flashing message to tell the user that the system is still working on the input request. It may also be possible for the system to display partial results as they are completed, so that the final display is built up a piece at a time. The system might also allow the user to input other commands or data while one instruction is being processed.

Feedback messages should be given clearly enough so that they have little chance of being overlooked. On the other hand, they should not be so overpowering that the user's concentration is interrupted. With function keys, feedback can be given as an audible click or by lighting up the key that has been pressed. Audio feedback has the advantage that it does not use up screen space, and the user does not have to take attention from the work area to receive the message. When messages are displayed on the screen, a fixed message area can be used so that the user always knows where to look for messages. In some cases, it may be advantageous to place feedback messages in the user work area near the cursor. Different colors can be used to distinguish the feedback from other objects in the display.

To speed system response, feedback techniques can be chosen to take advantage of the operating characteristics of the type of devices in use. With a raster display, pixel intensities are easily inverted (Fig. 16–8), so this method can be used to provide rapid feedback for menu selections. Other methods that could be used for menu selection feedback include highlighting, changing the color, and blinking the item selected.

Special symbols can be designed for different types of feedback. For example, a cross or a "thumbs down" symbol could be used to indicate an error, and a blinking "at work" sign could be used to tell the user that the system is processing the input. This type of feedback can be very effective with a more experienced user, but the beginner may need more detailed feedback that not only clearly indicates what the system is doing but also what the user should input next.

With some types of input, **echo** feedback is desirable. Typed characters can be displayed on the screen as they are input so that a user can detect and correct errors immediately. Button and dial input can be echoed in the same way. Scalar values that are selected with dials or from displayed scales are usually echoed on the screen to let the user check input values for accuracy. Position selections could be echoed with a cursor or other symbol that appears at the selected position. If positions are selected with the screen cursor, coordinate values of the cursor location can be displayed to indicate precisely which position has been selected.

FIGURE 16–8
Inverting pixel intensities as a means for providing feedback to confirm a menu selection.

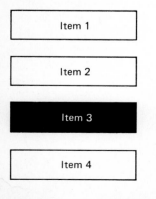

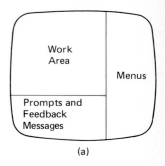

Information presented to the user of a graphics package includes a combination of output pictures, menus, messages, and other forms of dialogue generated by the system. There are many possibilities for arranging and presenting this output information to the user, and the designer of a graphics package must consider how best to design the output formats to achieve the greatest visual effectiveness. Considerations in the design of output formats include menu and message structures, icon and symbol shapes, and the overall screen layouts. As previously discussed, the menu and message structures depend on a number of factors. Besides the experience level of the user and the type of application, the structure of menus and messages will be influenced by the layout chosen for screen output.

Icon and Symbol Shapes

The structure of many symbols used in a graphics package depends on the type of application for which the package is intended, such as electrical design, architectural planning, or facility layouts. Shapes of the symbols are chosen so that they provide a simple yet clear picture of the object or operation they are meant to represent. Other symbols, such as cursors or menu pointers, should be designed so that they are clearly different from the other icons. In some cases, a package may allow a user to specify the shape of some symbols.

Screen Layout

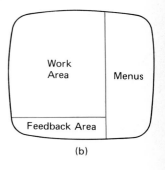

FIGURE 16–9
Screen layout possibilities: (a) large message area; (b) reduced message area.

Three basic components of the screen layout are the user work area, the menu area, and the area for displaying prompts and feedback messages. Fixed sections of the screen can be designated for each of these three areas, as shown in Fig. 16–9 (a). In this layout, menus are always presented at the right, and messages are displayed at the bottom of the screen. To make the work area as large as possible, the menu and message areas should be minimized. If a very large work area is desirable, the menu and message areas could be deleted when not needed so that the work area can expand to fill the screen. One way to allow maximum use of the screen is to give the user some control over the size of the menu and message areas. An experienced user, for example, could reduce the size of the message area by eliminating unnecessary prompting, as in Fig. 16–9 (b).

Greater flexibility in organizing screen layouts can be provided to the user by allowing any number of overlapping window areas to be set up. In this scheme, the user specifies the area of the screen in which to display a menu or picture. As each new window is positioned on the screen, it may overlap and obscure previously created windows. Figure 16–10 shows a layout with several overlapping windows. A set of operations must be provided to the user for creating, deleting, and positioning the window areas.

FIGURE 16–10
Screen layout with overlapping windows.

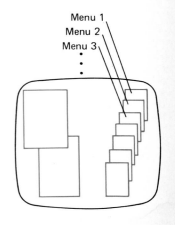

With some applications, it is convenient to have a zoom capability available. This allows a user to expand selected parts of a picture or to show a wider view of a scene, as if the user were moving away from the screen. The zoom feature can be used to blow up a small region of a larger picture so that it fills the work area. Enlargement can be carried out to display additional detail that cannot be seen in the total picture. Sometimes the user would like to view both the entire picture and the expanded section at the same time. One way to do this is to superimpose

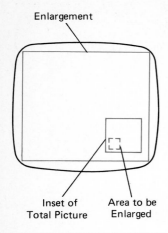

Enlargement

Inset of
Total Picture

Area to be
Enlarged

FIGURE 16–11
Enlarged picture section
containing an inset showing
the total picture.

the total picture as a small window inset on the screen, as shown in Fig. 16–11. Another method is to include two video monitors in the graphics system. A DVST can be used to display the total picture, and a refresh display can be used to show enlargements.

In addition to a zoom capability, it is convenient in some modeling applications to be able to simplify a display by removing some of the detail to provide a better presentation of the essential structure. For example, a layout of a city could be shown with all streets or with only the major streets. By displaying only larger streets, the major thoroughfares in the city can be emphasized (Fig. 16–12).

Overall, the screen layouts chosen should avoid a cluttered appearance. Menus and other areas should be kept simple and easy to understand, and the user should be presented with familiar patterns in a consistent way. As an aid to making the screen layout easy to understand, different colors and line styles can help to distinguish the different menus, prompts, feedback messages, and other display items.

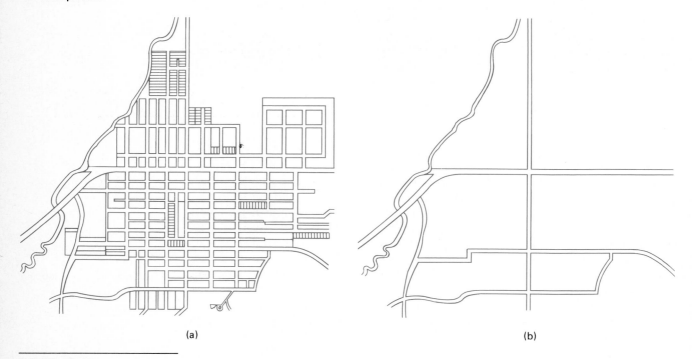

(a)

(b)

FIGURE 16–12
Display of the street layout for
a city: (a) all streets included;
(b) only major thoroughfares
displayed for emphasis.

REFERENCES Techniques for user-interface design are presented in Carroll and Carrithers (1984), Foley, Wallace, and Chan (1984), Good, Whiteside, Wixon, and Jones (1984), Goodman and Spence (1978), Lodding (1983), Phillips (1977), and in Swezey and Davis (1983).

16–1. Select some graphics application with which you are familiar and set up a user model that will serve as the basis for the design of a user interface for graphics applications in that area.

16–2. Summarize the possible formats for the command language and discuss the relative advantages and disadvantages of each for three different applications areas.

16–3. List the possible help facilities that can be provided in a user interface and explain the type of facilities that would be appropriate for different levels of users.

16–4. Summarize the possible ways of handling backup and errors. State which approaches are more suitable for the beginner and which are better suited to the experienced user.

16–5. List the possible formats for presenting menus to a user and explain under what circumstances each might be appropriate.

16–6. Discuss alternatives for feedback in terms of the various levels of users.

16–7. For several applications areas, devise a screen layout that would be suitable for each application area.

16–8. List the various considerations in the choice of icon and symbol shapes.

16–9. Design a user interface for a paintbrush program.

16–10. Design a user interface for a two-level hierarchical modeling package.

16–11. For any area with which you are familiar, design a complete user interface to the graphics package providing capabilities to any users in that area.

BIBLIOGRAPHY

AMANTIDES, J. (July 1984). "Ray Tracing with Cones," SIGGRAPH '84 proceedings, *Computer Graphics,* 18(3), 129–135.

ANDERSON, D. P. (July 1983). "Techniques for Reducing Pen Plotting Time," *ACM Transactions on Graphics,* 2(3), 197–212.

ANGEL, I. O. (1981). *A Practical Introduction to Computer Graphics.* New York: Halstead Press.

APPEL, A. (1968). "Some Techniques for Shading Machine Renderings of Solids," *AFIPS Conference Proceedings,* 32, 37–45.

ARTWICK, B. A. (1984). *Applied Concepts in Microcomputer Graphics.* Englewood Cliffs, N.J.: Prentice-Hall.

ATHERTON, P., K. WEILER, AND D. GREENBERG (Aug. 1978). "Polygon Shadow Generation," SIGGRAPH '78 proceedings, *Computer Graphics,* 12(3), 275–281.

ATHERTON, P. R. (July 1983). "A Scan-Line Hidden Surface Removal Procedure for Constructive Solid Geometry," SIGGRAPH '83 proceedings, *Computer Graphics,* 17(3), 73–82.

BADLER, N., J. O'ROURKE, AND B. KAUFMAN (July 1980). "Special Problems in Human Movement Simulation," SIGGRAPH '80 proceedings, *Computer Graphics,* 14(3), 189–197.

BALDWIN, L. (Sept. 1984). "Color Considerations," *BYTE,* 9(10), 227–246.

BARNHILL, R. E., AND R. F. RIESENFELD, eds. (1974). *Computer-Aided Geometric Design.* New York: Academic Press.

BARNHILL, R. E., J. H. BROWN, AND I. M. KLUCEWICZ (Aug. 1978). "A New Twist in Computer-Aided Geometric Design," *Computer Graphics and Image Processing,* 8(1), 78–91.

BARRETT, R. C., AND B. W. JORDAN (March 1974). "Scan-Conversion Algorithms for a Cell-Organized Raster Display," *Communications of the ACM,* 17(3), 157–163.

BARSKY, B. A., AND J. C. BEATTY (April 1983). "Local Control of Bias and Tension in Beta-Splines," *ACM Transactions on Graphics,* 2(2), 109–134.

BARSKY, B. A. (Jan. 1984). "A Description and Evaluation of Various 3-D Models," *IEEE Computer Graphics and Applications,* 4(1), 38–52.

BEATTY, J. C., J. S. CHIN, AND H. F. MOLL (Aug. 1979). "An Interactive Documentation System," SIGGRAPH '79 proceedings, *Computer Graphics,* 13(2), 71–82.

BÉZIER, P. (1972). *Numerical Control: Mathematics and Applications.* A. R. Forrest, trans. London: Wiley.

BLINN, J. F., AND M. E. NEWELL (Oct. 1976). "Texture and Reflection in Computer-Generated Images," *Communications of the ACM,* 19(10), 542–547.

BLINN, J. F. (Summer 1977). "A Homogeneous Formulation for Lines in 3-Space," SIGGRAPH '77 proceedings, *Computer Graphics,* 11(2), 237–241.

——— (Summer 1977). "Models of Light Reflection for Computer-Synthesized Pictures," SIGGRAPH '77 proceedings, *Computer Graphics,* 11(2), 192–198.

BLINN, J. F., AND M. E. NEWELL, (Aug. 1978). "Clipping Using Homogeneous Coordinates," SIGGRAPH '78 proceedings, *Computer Graphics* 12(3), 245–251.

BLINN J. F. (Aug. 1978). "Simulation of Wrinkled Surfaces," SIGGRAPH '78 proceedings, *Computer Graphics,* 12(3), 286–292.

——— (July 1982). "A Generalization of Algebraic Surface Drawing," *ACM Transactions on Graphics,* 1(3), 235–256.

——— (July 1982). "Light Reflection Functions for Simulation of Clouds and Dusty Surfaces," SIGGRAPH '82 proceedings, *Computer Graphics,* 16(3), 21–29.

BONO, P. R., ET AL. (July 1982). "GKS: The First Graphics Standard," *IEEE Computer Graphics and Applications,* 2(5), 9–23.

BORUFKA, H. G., H. W. KUHLMANN, AND P. J. W. TEN HAGEN (July 1982). "Dialog Cells: A Method for Defining Interactions," *IEEE Computer Graphics and Applications,* 2(5), 25–33.

BOUKNIGHT, W. J. (Sept. 1970). "A Procedure for Generation of Three-Dimensional Halftoned Computer Graphics Representations," *Communications of the ACM,* 13(9), 537–545.

BOUQUET, D. L. (Aug. 1978). "An Interactive Graphics Application to Advanced Aircraft Design," SIGGRAPH '78 proceedings, *Computer Graphics,* 12(3), 330–335.

BOYSE, J. W., AND J. E. GILCHRIST (March 1982). "GMSolid: Interactive Modeling for Design and Analysis of Solids," *IEEE Computer Graphics and Applications,* 2(2), 27–40.

BRESENHAM, J. E. (1965). "Algorithm for Computer Control of Digital Plotter," *IBM Systems Journal,* 4(1), 25–30.

——— (Feb. 1977). "A Linear Algorithm for Incremental Digital Display of Circular Arcs," *Communications of the ACM,* 20(2), 100–106.

BREWER, J. A., AND D. C. ANDERSON (Summer 1977). "Visual Interaction with Overhauser Curves and Surfaces," SIGGRAPH '77 proceedings, *Computer Graphics,* 11(2), 132–137.

BRODLIE, K. W., ed. (1980). *Mathematical Methods in Computer Graphics and Design.* London: Academic Press.

BROTMAN, L. S., AND N. I. BADLER (Oct. 1984). "Generating Soft Shadows with a Depth Buffer Algorithm," *IEEE Computer Graphics and Applications,* 4(10), 5–12.

BROWN, M. H. (July 1984). "A System for Algorithm Animation," SIGGRAPH '84 proceedings, *Computer Graphics,* 18(3), 177–186.

BURT, P. J., AND E. H. ADELSON (Oct. 1983). "A Multiresolution Spline with Application to Image Mosaics," *ACM Transactions on Graphics,* 2(4), 217–236.

CARLBOM, I., I. CHAKRAVARTY, AND D. VANDERSCHEL, (April 1985). "A Hierarchical Data Structure for Representing the Spatial Decomposition of 3-D Objects," *IEEE Computer Graphics and Applications,* 5(4), 24–31.

CARPENTER, L. (July 1984). "The A-Buffer: An Antialiased Hidden-Surface Method," SIGGRAPH '84 proceedings, *Computer Graphics,* 18(3), 103–108.

CARROLL, J. M., AND C. CARRITHERS (Aug. 1984). "Training Wheels in a User Interface," *Communications of the ACM,* 27(8), 800–806.

CARSON, G. S. (Sept. 1983). "The Specification of Computer Graphics Systems," *IEEE Computer Graphics and Applications,* 3(6), 27–41.

CARUTHERS, L. C., J. VAN DEN BOS, AND A. VAN DAM (Summer 1977). "GPGS: A Device-Independent General-Purpose Graphic System for Stand-Alone and Satellite Graphics," SIGGRAPH '77 proceedings, *Computer Graphics,* 11(2), 112–119.

CASALE, M. S., AND E. L. STANTON (Feb. 1985). "An Overview of Analytic Solid Modeling," *IEEE Computer Graphics and Applications,* 5(2), 45-56.

CATMULL, E. (May 1975). "Computer Display of Curved Surfaces," *Proceedings of the IEEE Conference on Computer Graphics, Pattern Recognition, and Data Structure.*

——— (Aug. 1978). "A Hidden-Surface Algorithm with Antialiasing," SIGGRAPH '78 proceedings, *Computer Graphics,* 12(3), 6–11.

——— (Aug. 1978). "The Problems of Computer-Assisted Animation," SIGGRAPH '78 proceedings, *Computer Graphics,* 12(3), 348–353.

——— AND A. R. SMITH (July 1980). "3-D Transformations of Images in Scanline Order," SIGGRAPH '80 proceedings, *Computer Graphics,* 14(3), 279–285.

——— (July 1984). "An Analytic Visible Surface Algorithm for Independent Pixel Processing," SIGGRAPH '84 proceedings, *Computer Graphics,* 18(3), 109–115.

CHASEN, S. H. (1978). *Geometric Principles and Procedures for Computer Graphic Applications.* Englewood Cliffs, N.J.: Prentice-Hall.

CLARK, J. H. (Oct. 1976). "Hierarchical Geometric Models for Visible Surface Algorithms," *Communications of the ACM,* 19(10), 547–554.

——— (July 1982). "The Geometry Engine: A VLSI Geometry System for Graphics," SIGGRAPH '82 proceedings, *Computer Graphics,* 10(3), 127–133.

COOK, R. L., AND K. E. TORRANCE (Jan. 1982). "A Reflectance Model for Computer Graphics," *ACM Transactions on Graphics,* 1(1), 7–24.

COOK, R. L., T. PORTER, AND L. CARPENTER (July 1984). "Distributed Ray Tracing," SIGGRAPH '84 proceedings, *Computer Graphics,* 18(3), 137–145.

COOK R. L. (July 1984). "Shade Trees," SIGGRAPH '84 proceedings, *Computer Graphics,* 18(3), 223–231.

COONS, S. A. (June 1967). *Surfaces for Computer-Aided Design of Space Forms,* Project MAC, M.I.T., TR–41.

CROCKER, G. A. (July 1984). "Invisible Coherence for Faster Scan-Line Hidden-Surface Algorithms," SIGGRAPH '84 proceedings, *Computer Graphics,* 18(3), 95–102.

CROW, F. C. (Summer 1977). "Shadow Algorithms for Computer Graphics," SIGGRAPH '77 proceedings, *Computer Graphics,* 11(2), 242–248.

——— (Nov. 1977). "The Aliasing Problem in Computer-Synthesized Shaded Images," *Communications of the ACM,* 20(11), 799–805.

——— (Aug. 1978). "The Use of Grayscale for Improved Raster Display of Vectors and Characters," SIGGRAPH '78 proceedings, *Computer Graphics,* 12(3), 1–5.

——— (Jan. 1981). "A Comparison of Antialiasing Techniques," *IEEE Computer Graphics and Applications,* 1(1), 40–49.

—— (July 1984). "Summed-Area Tables for Texture Mapping," SIGGRAPH '84 proceedings, *Computer Graphics,* 18(3), 207–212.

CYRUS, M., AND J. BECK (1978). "Generalized Two- and Three-Dimensional Clipping," *Computers and Graphics,* 3(1), 23–28.

DOCTOR, L. J., AND J. G. TORBERG (July 1981). "Display Techniques for Octree-Encoded Objects," *IEEE Computer Graphics and Applications,* 1(3), 29–38.

DUNGAN, W., A. STENGER, AND G. SUTTY (Aug. 1978). "Texture Tile Considerations for Raster Graphics," SIGGRAPH '78 proceedings, *Computer Graphics,* 12(3), 130–134.

DUNLAVEY, M. R. (Oct. 1983). "Efficient Polygon-Filling Algorithms for Raster Displays," *ACM Transactions on Graphics,* 2(4), 264–274.

EASTMAN, C., AND M. HENRION (Summer 1977). "GLIDE: A Language for Design Information Systems," SIGGRAPH '77 proceedings, *Computer Graphics,* 11(2), 24–33.

ENCARNAÇAO, J. (July 1980). "The Workstation Concept of GKS and the Resulting Conceptual Differences to the GSPC CORE System," SIGGRAPH '80 proceedings, *Computer Graphics,* 14(3), 226–230.

ENDERLE, G., K. KANSY, AND G. PFAFF, (1984). *Computer Graphics Programming: GKS—The Graphics Standard.* Berlin: Springer-Verlag.—

FAROUKI, R. T., AND J. K. HINDS, (May 1985). "A Hierarchy of Geometric Forms," *IEEE Computer Graphics and Applications,* 5(5), 51–78.

FISHKIN, K. P., AND B. A. BARSKY (July 1984). "A Family of New Algorithms for Soft Filling," SIGGRAPH '84 proceedings, *Computer Graphics,* 18(3), 235–244.

FOLEY, J. D., AND A. VAN DAM (1982). *Fundamentals of Interactive Computer Graphics,* Reading, Mass.: Addison-Wesley.

FOLEY, J. D., V. L. WALLACE, AND P. CHAN (Nov. 1984). "The Human Factors of Computer Graphics Interaction Techniques," *IEEE Computer Graphics and Applications,* 4(11), 13–48.

FORREST, A. R. (Dec. 1972). "On Coons and Other Methods for the Representation of Curved Surfaces," *Computer Graphics and Image Processing,* 1(4), 341–354.

FOURNIER, A., D. FUSSEL, AND L. CARPENTER (June 1982). "Computer Rendering of Stochastic Models," *Communications of the ACM,* 25(6), 371–384.

FRIEDER, G., D. GORDON, AND R. A. REYNOLD (Jan. 1985). "Back-to-Front Display of Voxel-Based Objects," *IEEE Computer Graphics and Applications,* 5(1), 52–60.

FU, K. S., AND A. ROSENFELD (Oct. 1984). "Pattern Recognition and Computer Vision," 17(10), 274–282.

FUCHS, H., G. D. ABRAM, AND E. D. GRANT (July 1983). "Near Real-Time Shaded Display of Rigid Objects," SIGGRAPH '83 proceedings, *Computer Graphics,* 17(3), 65–72.

FUJIMOTO, A., AND K. IWATA (Dec. 1983). "Jag-Free Images on Raster Displays," *IEEE Computer Graphics and Applications,* 3(9), 26–34.

FUJIMOTO, A., C. G. PERROT, AND K. IWATA (June 1984). "A 3-D Graphics Display System with Depth Buffer and Pipeline Processor," *IEEE Computer Graphics and Applications,* 4(6), 11–23.

GARDNER, T. N., AND H. R. NELSON (March-April 1983). "Interactive Graphics Developments in Energy Exploration," *IEEE Computer Graphics and Applications,* 3(2), 33–44.

GILOI, W. K. (1978). *Interactive Computer Graphics: Data Structures, Algorithms, Languages.* Englewood Cliffs, N.J.: Prentice-Hall.

GLASSNER, A. S. (Oct. 1984). "Space Subdivision for Fast Ray Tracing," *IEEE Computer Graphics and Applications,* 4(10), 15–22.

GLINERT, E. P., AND S. L. TANIMOTO (Nov. 1984). "Pict: An Interactive Graphical Programming Environment," *IEEE Computer Graphics and Applications,* 17(11), 7–25.

GOOD, M. D., ET AL. (Oct. 1984). "Building a User-Derived Interface," *Communications of the ACM,* 27(10), 1032–1043.

GOODMAN, T., AND R. SPENCE (Aug. 1978). "The Effect of System Response Time on Interactive Computer-Aided Problem Solving," SIGGRAPH '78 proceedings, *Computer Graphics,* 12(3), 100–104.

GRAPHICS STANDARDS PLANNING COMMITTEE (1977). "Status Report of the Graphics Standards Planning Committee," *Computer Graphics,* 11.

—— (Aug. 1979). "Status Report of the Graphics Standards Committee," *Computer Graphics,* 13(3).

GROTCH, S. L. (Nov. 1983). "Three-Dimensional and Stereoscopic Graphics for Scientific Data Display and Analysis," *IEEE Computer Graphics and Applications,* 3(8), 31–43.

GUIBAS, L. J., AND J. STOLFI (July 1982). "A Language for Bitmap Manipulation," *ACM Transactions on Graphics,* 1(3), 191–214.

HABER, R. N., AND L. WILKINSON (May 1982). "Perceptual Components of Computer Displays," *IEEE Computer Graphics and Applications,* 2(3), 23–35.

HACKATHORN, R. J. (Summer 1977). "Anima II: A 3-D Color Animation System," SIGGRAPH '77 proceedings, *Computer Graphics,* 11(2), 54–64.

HALL, R. A., AND D. P. GREENBERG (Nov. 1983). "A Testbed for Realistic Image Synthesis," *IEEE Computer Graphics and Applications,* 3(8), 10–20.

HAMLIN, G., AND C. W. GEAR (Summer 1977). "Raster-Scan Hidden-Surface Algorithm Techniques," SIGGRAPH '77 proceedings, *Computer Graphics,* 11(2), 206–213.

HANNA, S. L., J. F. ABEL, AND D. P. GREENBERG (Oct. 1983). "Intersection of Parametric Surfaces by Means of Lookup Tables," *IEEE Computer Graphics and Applications,* 3(7), 39–48.

HANRAHAN, P. (July 1983). "Ray Tracing Algebraic Surfaces," SIGGRAPH '83 proceedings, *Computer Graphics,* 17(3), 83–90.

HARRINGTON, S. (1983). *Computer Graphics: A Programming Approach.* New York: McGraw-Hill.

HARUYAMA, S., AND B. A. BARSKY (March 1984). "Using Stochastic Modeling for Texture Generation," *IEEE Computer Graphics and Applications,* 4(3), 7–19.

HATFIELD, L., AND B. HERZOG (Jan. 1982). "Graphics Software: From Techniques to Principles," *IEEE Computer Graphics and Applications,* 2(1), 59–79.

HAWRYLYSHYN, P. A., R. R. TASKER, AND L. W. ORGAN (Summer 1977). "CASS: Computer-Assisted Stereotaxic Surgery," SIGGRAPH '77 proceedings, *Computer Graphics,* 11(2), 13–17.

HECKBERT, P. (July 1982). "Color Image Quantization for Frame Buffer Display," SIGGRAPH '82 proceedings, *Computer Graphics,* 16(3), 297–307.

——— AND P. HANRAHAN (July 1984). "Beam Tracing Polygonal Objects," SIGGRAPH '84 proceedings, *Computer Graphics,* 18(3), 119–127.

HERBISON-EVANS, D. (Nov. 1982). "Real-Time Animation of Human Figure Drawings with Hidden Lines Omitted," *IEEE Computer Graphics and Applications,* 2(9), 27–33.

HOPGOOD, F. R. A., ET AL. (1983). *Introduction to the Graphical Kernel System (GKS).* London: Academic Press.

HUBSCHMAN, H., AND S. W. ZUCKER (April 1982). "Frame-to-Frame Coherence and the Hidden Surface Computation: Constraints for a Convex World," *ACM Transactions on Graphics,* 1(2), 129–162.

HUITRIC, H., AND M. NAHAS (March 1985). "B-Spline Surfaces: A Tool for Computer Painting," *IEEE Computer Graphics and Applications,* 5(3), 39–47.

IKEDO, T. (May 1984). "High-Speed Techniques for a 3-D Color Graphics Terminal," *IEEE Computer Graphics and Applications,* 4(5), 46–58.

JARVIS, J. F., C. N. JUDICE, AND W. H. NINKE (March 1976). "A Survey of Techniques for the Image Display of Continuous Tone Pictures on Bilevel Displays," *Computer Graphics and Image Processing,* 5(1), 13–40.

JARVIS, J. F., AND C. S. ROBERTS (Aug. 1976). "A New Technique for Displaying Continuous Tone Images on a Bilevel Display," *IEEE Transactions,* COM-24(8), 891–898.

JOBLOVE, G. H., AND D. GREENBERG (Aug. 1978). "Color Spaces for Computer Graphics," SIGGRAPH '78 proceedings, *Computer Graphics,* 12(3), 20–25.

JORDAN, B. W., AND R. C. BARRETT (Nov. 1973). "A Scan Conversion Algorithm with Reduced Storage Requirements," *Communications of the ACM,* 16(11), 676–679.

JUDICE, J. N., J. F. JARVIS, AND W. NINKE (Oct.–Dec. 1974). "Using Ordered Dither to Display Continuous Tone Pictures on an AC Plasma Panel," *Proc. SID,* 161–169.

KAJIYA, J. T. (July 1983). "New Techniques for Ray Tracing Procedurally Defined Objects," *ACM Transactions on Graphics,* 2(3), 161–181.

KAY, D. S., AND D. GREENBERG (Aug. 1979). "Transparency for Computer-Synthesized Images," SIGGRAPH '79 proceedings, *Computer Graphics,* 13(2), 158–164.

KOCHANEK, D. H. U., AND R. H. BARTELS (July 1984). "Interpolating Splines with Local Tension, Continuity, and Bias Control," SIGGRAPH '84 proceedings, *Computer Graphics,* 18(3), 33–41.

KOREIN, J., AND N. I. BADLER (July 1983). "Temporal Antialiasing in Computer-Generated Animation," SIGGRAPH '83 proceedings, *Computer Graphics,* 17(3), 377–388.

LANTZ, K., AND W. I. NOWICKI (Jan. 1984). "Structured Graphics for Distributed Systems," *ACM Transactions on Graphics,* 3(1), 23–51.

LEVOY, M. (Summer 1977). "A Color Animation System Based on the Multiplane Technique," SIGGRAPH '77 proceedings, *Computer Graphics,* 11(2), 65–71.

LEVY, H. M. (Jan. 1984). "VAXstation: A General-Purpose Raster Graphics Architecture," *ACM Transactions on Graphics,* 3(1), 70–83.

LIANG, Y. -D., AND B. A. BARSKY (Nov. 1983). "An Analysis and Algorithm for Polygon Clipping," *Communications of the ACM,* 26(11), 868–877.

——— (Jan. 1984). "A New Concept and Method for Line Clipping," *ACM Transactions on Graphics,* 3(1), 1–22.

LIEBERMAN, H. (Aug. 1978). "How to Color in a Coloring Book," SIGGRAPH '78 proceedings, *Computer Graphics,* 12(3), 111–116.

LIPKIE, D. E., ET AL. (July 1982). "Star Graphics: An Object-Oriented Implementation," SIGGRAPH '82 proceedings, *Computer Graphics,* 16(3), 115–124.

LIPPMAN, A. (July 1980). "Movie-Maps: An Application of the Optical Videodisc to Computer Graphics," SIGGRAPH '80 proceedings, *Computer Graphics.* 14(3), 32–42.

343

LODDING, K. N. (March–April 1983). "Iconic Interfacing," *IEEE Computer Graphics and Applications,* 3(2), 11–20.

LOOMIS, J., ET AL. (July 1983). "Computer Graphic Modeling of American Sign Language," SIGGRAPH '83 proceedings, *Computer Graphics,* 17(3), 105–114.

MAGNENAT-THALMANN, N., AND D. THALMANN (Dec. 1983). "The Use of High-Level 3-D Graphical Types in the Mira Animation System," *IEEE Computer Graphics and Applications,* 3(9), 9–16.

MANDELBROT, B. B. (1977). *Fractals: Form, Chance, and Dimension.* San Francisco: Freeman Press.

———— (1982). *The Fractal Geometry of Nature.* New York: Freeman Press.

MARCUS, A. (July 1983). "Graphic Design for Computer Graphics," *IEEE Computer Graphics and Applications,* 3(4), 63–70.

MARGOLIN, B. (Feb. 1985) "New Flat Panel Displays," *Computers and Electronics,* 23(2), 66–108.

MATHERAT, P. (Aug. 1978). "A Chip for Low-Cost Raster-Scan Graphic Display," SIGGRAPH '78 proceedings, *Computer Graphics,* 12(3), 181–186.

McILROY, M. D. (Oct. 1983). "Best Approximate Circles on Integer Grids," *ACM Transactions on Graphics,* 2(4), 237–263.

McKEOWN, K., AND N. I. BADLER (July 1980). "Creating Polyhedral Stellations," SIGGRAPH '80 proceedings, *Computer Graphics,* 14(3), 19–24.

MEHL, M. E., AND S. J. NOLL (Aug. 1984). "A VLSI Support for GKS," *IEEE Computer Graphics and Applications,* 4(8), 52–55.

MICHENER, J. C., I. B. CARLBOM (July 1980). "Natural and Efficient Viewing Parameters," SIGGRAPH '80 proceedings, *Computer Graphics,* 14(3), 238–245.

MINSKY, A. R. (July 1984). "Manipulating Simulated Objects with Real-World Gestures Using a Force and Position Sensitive Screen," SIGGRAPH '84 proceedings, *Computer Graphics,* 18(3), 195–203.

MITROO, J. B., N. HERMAN, AND N. I. BADLER (Aug. 1979). "Movies from Music: Visualizing Musical Compositions," SIGGRAPH '79 proceedings, *Computer Graphics,* 13(2), 218–225.

MURCH, G. M. (Nov. 1984). "Physiological Principles for the Effective Use of Color," *IEEE Computer Graphics and Applications,* 4(11), 49–54.

MYERS, W. (July 1984). "Staking Out the Graphics Display Pipeline," *IEEE Computer Graphics and Applications,* 4(7), 60–65.

NEWMAN, W. M. (1968). *A System for Interactive Graphical Input.* SJCC, Washington, D.C.: Thompson Books, 47–54.

———— (Oct. 1971). "Display Procedures," *Communications of the ACM,* 14(10), 651–660.

———— AND R. F. SPROULL (1974). "An Approach to Graphics System Design," *Proceedings of the IEEE,* IEEE.

———— (1979). *Principles of Interactive Computer Graphics.* New York: McGraw-Hill.

NG, N., AND T. MARSLAND (1978). "Introducing Graphics Capabilities to Several High-Level Languages," *Software Practice and Experience,* 8, 629–639.

NIIMI, H., ET AL. (July 1984). A Parallel Processor System for Three-Dimensional Color Graphics," SIGGRAPH '84 proceedings, *Computer Graphics,* 18(3), 67–76.

NORTON, A. (July 1982). "Generation and Display of Geometric Fractals in 3-D," SIGGRAPH '82 proceedings, *Computer Graphics,* 16(3), 61–67.

PAO, Y. C. (1984). *Elements of Computer-Aided Design.* New York: Wiley.

PARKE, F. I. (July 1980). "Adaptation of Scan and Slit-Scan Techniques to Computer Animation," SIGGRAPH '80 proceedings, *Computer Graphics,* 14(3), 178–181.

———— (Nov. 1982). "Parameterized Models for Facial Animation," *IEEE Computer Graphics and Applications,* 2(9), 61–68.

PAVLIDIS, T. (Aug. 1978). "Filling Algorithms for Raster Graphics," SIGGRAPH '78 proceedings, *Computer Graphics,* 12(3), 161–166.

———— (Aug. 1981). "Contour Filling in Raster Graphics," SIGGRAPH '81 proceedings, *Computer Graphics,* 15(3), 29–36.

———— (1982). *Algorithms for Graphics and Image Processing.* Rockville, Md.: Computer Science Press.

———— (Jan. 1983). "Curve Fitting with Conic Splines," *ACM Transactions on Graphics,* 2(1), 1–31.

PHILLIPS, R. L. (Summer 1977). "A Query Language for a Network Data Base with Graphical Entities," SIGGRAPH '77 proceedings, *Computer Graphics,* 11(2), 179–185.

PHONG B. T. (June 1975). "Illumination for Computer-Generated Images," *Communications of the ACM,* 18(6), 311–317:

PIKE, R. (April 1983). "Graphics in Overlapping Bitmap Layers," *ACM Transactions on Graphics,* 2(2), 135–160.

PITTEWAY, M. L. V., AND D. J. WATKINSON, (Nov. 1980). "Bresenham's Algorithm with Gray Scale," *Communications of the ACM,* 23(11), 625–626.

PITTMAN, J. H., AND D. P. GREENBERG (July 1982). "An Interactive Graphics Environment for Architectural Energy Simulation," SIGGRAPH '82 proceedings, *Computer Graphics,* 16(3), 233–241.

POTMESIL, M., AND I. CHAKRAVARTY (April 1982). "Synthetic Image Generation with a Lens and Aperture Camera Model," *ACM Transactions on Graphics,* 1(2), 85–108.

—— (July 1983). "Modeling Motion Blurs in Computer-Generated Images," SIGGRAPH '83 proceedings, *Computer Graphics,* 17(3), 389–399.

PREISS, R. B. (Nov. 1978). "Storage CRT Display Terminals: Evolution and Trends," *Computer,* 11(11), 20–28.

PRESTON, K., ET AL. (Oct. 1984). "Computing in Medicine," *Computer,* 17(10), 294–313.

PROSSER, C. J., AND A. C. KILGOUR (July 1983). "An Integral Method for the Graphical Output of Conic Sections," *ACM Transactions on Graphics,* 2(3), 182–191.

REEVES, W. T. (April 1983). "Particle Systems: A Technique for Modeling a Class of Fuzzy Objects," *ACM Transactions on Graphics,* 2(2), 91–108.

REISENFELD, R. F. (1973). *Applications of B-Spline Approximation to Geometric Problems of Computer-Aided Design,* Ph.D. dissertation, Syracuse University.

RENFROW, N. V. (Summer 1977). "Computer Graphics for Facilities Management," SIGGRAPH '77 proceedings, *Computer Graphics,* 11(2), 42–47.

REQUICHA, A. A. G. (Dec. 1980). "Representations of Rigid Solids: Theory, Methods, and Systems," *ACM Computing Surveys,* 12(4), 437–464.

—— AND H. B. VOELCKER (March 1982). "Solid Modeling: A Historical Summary and Contemporary Assessment," *IEEE Computer Graphics and Applications,* 2(2), 9–24.

—— (Oct. 1983). "Solid Modeling: Current Status and Research Directions," *IEEE Computer Graphics and Applications,* 3(7), 25–37.

REYNOLDS, C. W. (July 1982). "Computer Animation with Scripts and Actors," SIGGRAPH '82 proceedings, *Computer Graphics,* 16(3), 289–296.

RHODES, M. L., ET AL. (Aug. 1983). "Computer Graphics and an Interactive Stereotactic System for CT-Aided Neurosurgery," *IEEE Computer Graphics and Applications,* 3(5), 31–37.

ROESE, J. A., AND L. E. McCLEARY (Aug. 1979). "Stereoscopic Computer Graphics for Simulation and Modeling," SIGGRAPH '79 proceedings, *Computer Graphics,* 13(2), 41–47.

ROGERS, D. F., AND J. A. ADAMS (1976). *Mathematical Elements for Computer Graphics.* New York: McGraw-Hill.

ROGERS, D. F. (1985). *Procedural Elements for Computer Graphics.* New York: McGraw-Hill.

ROSENTHAL, D. S. H., ET AL. (July 1982). "The Detailed Semantics of Graphics Input Devices," SIGGRAPH '82 proceedings, *Computer Graphics,* 16(3), 33–38.

RUBIN, S. M., AND T. WHITTED (July 1980). "A 3-Dimensional Representation for Fast Rendering of Complex Scenes," SIGGRAPH '80 proceedings, *Computer Graphics,* 14(3), 110–116.

SAKURAI, H., AND D. C. GOSSARD (July 1983). "Solid Model Input Through Orthographic Views," SIGGRAPH '83 proceedings, *Computer Graphics,* 17(3), 243–252.

SCHACTER, B. J., ed. (1983). *Computer Image Generation.* New York: Wiley.

SCHWEITZER, D. (July 1983). "Artificial Texturing: An Aid to Surface Visualization," SIGGRAPH '83 proceedings, *Computer Graphics,* 17(3), 23–29.

SCOTT, J. E. (1982). *Introduction to Interactive Computer Graphics.* New York: Wiley.

SECHREST, S., AND D. P. GREENBERG (Jan. 1982). "A Visible Polygon Reconstruction Algorithm," *ACM Transactions on Graphics,* 1(1), 25–42.

SHERR, S. (1979). *Electronics Displays.* New York: Wiley.

SINGH, B., ET AL. (July 1983). "A Graphics Editor for Benesh Movement Notation," SIGGRAPH '83 proceedings, *Computer Graphics,* 17(3), 51–62.

SLOTTOW, H. G. (July 1976). "Plasma Displays," *IEEE Transactions on Electron Devices,* ED–23(7).

SMITH, A. R. (Aug. 1978). "Color Gamut Transform Pairs," SIGGRAPH '78 proceedings, *Computer Graphics,* 12(3), 12–19.

—— (Aug. 1979). "Tint Fill," SIGGRAPH '79 proceedings, *Computer Graphics,* 13(2), 276–283.

—— (July 1984). "Plants, Fractals, and Formal Languages," SIGGRAPH '84 proceedings, *Computer Graphics,* 18(3), 1–10.

SORENSEN, P. R. (Sept. 1984). "Fractals," *BYTE,* 157–172.

SPROULL, R. F., AND I. E. SUTHERLAND (1968). *A Clipping Divider.* AFIPS Fall Joint Computer Conference.

SPROULL, R. F., ET AL. (Jan 1983). "The 8 by 8 Display," *ACM Transactions on Graphics,* 2(1), 32–56.

SUTHERLAND, I. E. (1963). "Sketchpad: A Man-Machine Graphical Communication System," *AFIPS Spring Joint Computer Conference,* 23, pp. 329–346.

——, R. F. SPROULL, AND R. A. SCHUMACKER (1973). "Sorting and the Hidden-Surface Problem," *National Computer Conference Proceedings.*

SUTHERLAND, I. E., AND G. W. HODGMAN (Jan. 1974). "Reentrant Polygon Clipping," *Communications of the ACM,* 17(1), 32–42.

SUTHERLAND, I. E., R. SPROULL, AND R. SCHUMACKER (March 1974). "A Characterization of Ten Hidden Surface Algorithms," *ACM Computing Surveys,* 6(1), 1–55.

SWEZEY, R. W., AND E. G. DAVIS (Nov. 1983). "A Case Study of Human Factors Guidelines in Computer Graphics," *IEEE Computer Graphics and Applications,* 3(8), 21–30.

TANNAS, L. (July 1978). "Flat Panel Displays: A Critique," *IEEE Spectrum,* 15(7).

TILLER, W. (Sept. 1983). "Rational B-Splines for Curve and Surface Representation," *IEEE Computer Graphics and Applications,* 3(6), 61–69.

TILOVE, R. (July 1984). "A Null-Object Algorithm for Constructive Solid Geometry," *Communications of the ACM,* 27(7), 684–694.

TORRANCE, K. E., AND E. M. SPARROW (Sept. 1967). "Theory for Off-Specular Reflection from Roughened Surfaces," *J. Opt. Soc. Am.,* 57(9), 1105–1114.

TURKOWSKI, K. (July 1982). "Antialiasing Through the Use of Coordinate Transformations," *ACM Transactions on Graphics,* 1(3), 215–234.

VICKERS, D. (1970). "Head-Mounted Display Terminal," *Proceedings of the 1970 IEEE International Computer Group Conference,* IEEE.

VOELCKER, H., ET AL. (Aug. 1978). "The PADL-1.0/2 System for Defining and Displaying Solid Objects," SIGGRAPH '78 proceedings, *Computer Graphics,* 12(3), 257–263.

WALLACE, B. (Aug. 1981). "Merging and Transformation of Raster Images for Cartoon Animation," SIGGRAPH '81 proceedings, *Computer Graphics,* 15(3), 253–262.

WALLACE, V. L. (Spring 1976). "The Semantics of Graphics Input Devices," *Computer Graphics,* 10(1).

WARN, D. (July 1983). "Lighting Controls for Synthetic Images," SIGGRAPH '83 proceedings, *Computer Graphics,* 17(3), 13–21.

WARNER, J. R. (Oct. 1981). "Principles of Device-Independent Computer Graphics Software," *IEEE Computer Graphics and Applications,* 1(4), 85–100.

WEGHORST, H., G. HOOPER, AND D. P. GREENBERG (Jan. 1984). "Improved Computational Methods for Ray Tracing," *ACM Transactions on Graphics,* 3(1), 52–69.

WEILER, K., AND P. ATHERTON (Summer 1977). "Hidden Surface Removal Using Polygon Area Sorting," SIGGRAPH '77 proceedings, *Computer Graphics,* 11(2), 214–222.

WEILER, K. (July 1980). "Polygon Comparison Using a Graph Representation," SIGGRAPH '80 proceedings, *Computer Graphics,* 14(3), 10–18.

———— (Jan. 1985). "Edge-Based Data Structures for Solid Modeling in Curved-Surface Modeling Environments," *IEEE Computer Graphics and Applications,* 5(1), 21–40.

WEINBERG, R. (Aug. 1978). "Computer Graphics in Support of Space Shuttle Simulation," SIGGRAPH '78 proceedings, *Computer Graphics,* 12(3), 82–86.

WHITTED, T. (June 1980). "An Improved Illumination Model for Shaded Display," *Communications of the ACM,* 23(6), 343–349.

WOLFRAM, S. (Sept. 1984). "Computer Software in Science and Mathematics," *Scientific American,* 251(3), 188–203.

WOODSFORD, P. A. (July 1976). "The HRD-1 Laser Display System," SIGGRAPH '76 proceedings, *Computer Graphics,* 10(2), 68–73.

YAMAGUCHI, K., T. L. KUNII, AND K. FUJIMURA (Jan. 1984). "Octree-Related Data Structures and Algorithms," *IEEE Computer Graphics and Applications,* 4(1), 53–59.

YESSIOS, C. I. (Aug. 1979). "Computer Drafting of Stones, Wood, Plant, and Ground Materials," SIGGRAPH '79 proceedings, *Computer Graphics,* 13(2), 190–198.

SUBJECT INDEX

FUNCTION INDEX